Programming Informix SQL/4GL: A Step-by-Step Approach

Second Edition

ISBN 0-13-675919-X

9 780136 759195

90000

Programming Informix SQL/4GL: A Step-by-Step Approach

Second Edition

Cathy Kipp

To join a Prentice Hall PTR Internet mailing list, point to
http://www.prenhall.com/mail_lists/

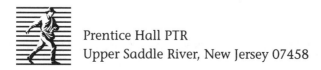

Prentice Hall PTR
Upper Saddle River, New Jersey 07458

Library of Congress Cataloging-in-Publication Data
Kipp, Cathy.
    Programming INFORMIX SQL/4GL : a step-by-step approach / Cathy
    Kipp. -- 2nd ed.
        p.   cm.
    Includes index.
    ISBN 0-13-675919-X
    1. Relational databases. 2. INFORMIX-SQL 3. INFORMIX-4GL
(Computer program language) I. Title.
QA76.9.D3K498   1997
005.75'65--dc21   97-34776
                                                               CIP

Editorial/Production Supervision: *Craig Little*
Acquisitions Editor: *Mark L. Taub*
Buyer: *Alexis R. Heydt*
Cover Design: *Anthony Gemmellaro*
Cover Design Direction: *Jerry Votta*
Art Director: *Gail Cocker-Bogusz*
Series Design: *Claudia Durrell Design*
Compositor: *East End Publishing Services*
Marketing Manager: *Dan Rush*
Manager, Informix Press: *Sandy Emerson*

© 1998 Prentice Hall PTR
Prentice-Hall, Inc.
A Simon & Schuster Company
Upper Saddle River, NJ 07458

Informix Press
Informix Software, Inc.
4100 Bohannon Drive
Menlo Park, CA 94025

The publisher offers discounts on this book when ordered in bulk quantities. For more
information, call the Corporate Sales Department at 800-382-3419; FAX: 201-236-714,
email corpsales@prenhall.com or write Corporate Sales Department, Prentice Hall PTR,
One Lake Street, Upper Saddle River, NJ 07458

Prentice Hall books are widely used by corporations and government agencies for training, marketing, and resale.

The following are worldwide trademarks of Informix Software, Inc., or its subsidiaries, registered in the
United States of America as indicated by ®, and in numerous other counties worldwide:
    INFORMIX®, Informix {___} DataBlade® Module, Informix Dynamic Scalable Architecture™,
Informix Illustra™ Server, InformixLink®, INFORMIX®-4GL, INFORMIX®-4GL Compiled,
INFORMIX®-CLI, INFORMIX®-Connect, INFORMIX®-ESQL/C, INFORMIX®-MetaCube™,
INFORMIX®-Mobile, INFORMIX®-NET, INFORMIX®-NewEra™ INFORMIX®-NewEra™ Viewpoint™,
INFORMIX®-NewEra™ Viewpoint™ Pro, INFORMIX®-OnLine, INFORMIX®-OnLine Dynamic Server™,
INFORMIX®-OnLine Workgroup Server, INFORMIX®-OnLine Workstation, INFORMIX®-SE,
INFORMIX®-SQL, INFORMIX-Superview™, INFORMIX®-Universal Server
    All other product names mentioned herein are the trademarks or registered trademarks of their respec-
tive owners.

Printed in the United States of America

10 9 8 7 6 5 4 3 2 1

ISBN 0-13-675919-X

Prentice-Hall International (UK) Limited, *London*
Prentice-Hall of Australia Pty. Limited, *Sydney*
Prentice-Hall Canada Inc., *Toronto*
Prentice-Hall Hispanoamericana, S.A., *Mexico*
Prentice-Hall of India Private Limited, *New Delhi*
Prentice-Hall of Japan, Inc., *Tokyo*
Simon & Schuster Asia Pte. Ltd., *Singapore*
Editora Prentice-Hall do Brasil, Ltda., *Rio de Janeiro*

Contents

Preface xv

Acknowledgments xix

Chapter 1 Relational Database Design 2
What is a Relational Database? 3
Elements of a Database: Tables, Columns, and Rows 4
   Tables 4
   Columns 4
   Rows 4
Primary Keys 5
Foreign Keys 6
Types of Relationships 7
   One-to-One or Zero 7
   One-to-Many (or Many-to-One) 8
   Many-to-Many 9
What Is Normalization? 10
Formal Normalization 10
   First Normal Form 11
   Second Normal Form 12
   Third Normal Form 13
Intuitive Normalization 15
Indexing Strategies 19
   Composite Indexes 20
   Unique Indexes 21
   Duplicate Indexes 21
   Shorter Is Better 21

Numeric versus Character Indexes   22
Clustered Indexes   22
Small Tables   22
Description of the Sample Database   23
Summary   23

Chapter 2   The SQL Working Environment   26
About Informix's Implementation of SQL   27
About DB-Access   27
Setting UNIX Environment Variables   28
Environment Variables Needed by Informix   30
Optional Environment Variables   32
Using DB-Access   39
DB-Acess Options with Ring Menus   41
Getting Around in Informix Ring Menus   42
Choosing Options from a List   43
Working From the Command Line   43
Viewing Error Messages   45
Summary   45

Chapter 3   Creating the Database   48
The Database Administrator   49
INFORMIX Database Engines   50
Database Statements   52
Data Types   54
Character and String Data Types   55
Numer Data Types   55
Date, Time, and Interval Data Types   57
Extra data types for INFORMIX-OnLine   59
Summary of Data Type Conversions   61
Tables   62
Creating a New Table   62
Changing an Existing Table   71
Deleting a Table   74
Renaming Tables and Columns   74
Privileges   75
Granting Database Privileges   75
Granting Table Privileges   77
Revoking Privileges   80
Roles   81
Creating Schema Authorization   82

Indexes 83
Creating the Sample Database 86
Viewing the Database 88
Summary 91

Chapter 4   Maintaining the Database 98
Update Statistics 99
Checking Database Integrity 102
   INFORMIX-SE Database Integrity 102
   INFORMIX-OnLine Database Integrity 105
Database Backups 107
   INFORMIX-SE Backups 108
   INFORMIX-OnLine Backups 108
Logging 111
   What Is a Transaction? 111
   Transaction Logging in INFORMIX-SE 114
   Transaction Logging in INFORMIX-OnLine 117
Audit Trails—INFORMIX-SE Only 121
Summary 123

Chapter 5   Data: Adding, Changing, and Deleting 126
Insert 127
Update 129
Delete 131
Locking 132
   Locking a Database 132
   Locking a Table 133
   Set Lock Mode 134
   INFORMIX-OnLine Table Option 135
Load and Unload 136
   Loading Data 136
   Unloading Data 138
dbload 139
   The Command File 140
   Examples 143
dbexport and dbimport 145
   dbexport 145
   dbimport 147
Tips for Faster Data Loads 148
Summary 149

Chapter 6   The Select Statement 152

Overview of the Select Statement 153
Select 154
From 156
Where 157
  Conditional Expressions 158
  Matches and Like 161
  Other Conditionals 163
Group By 163
Having 165
Order By 167
Into Temp 169
Union 170
Joins 171
Outer Joins 173
Output To 176
Summary 177

Chapter 7   The 4GL Programming Environment 180

INFORMIX-4GL Flavors: r4gl and c4gl 181
INFORMIX-4GL File Name Suffixes 182
Menu Driven Development 183
Command Line Development 184
  Compiling and Running 4GL Code
      in the Rapid Development System 184
  Compiling and Running Compiled 4GL Code 185
  Compiling Informix Screen Forms 187
Make Files 188
  Make Rules 188
  The Make File 189
Prototyping 193
Summary 193

Chapter 8   4GL Program Structure 196

Overview 197
Database 199
Globals 199
Main 200
Modules 201
Functions 201
Exit Program 203
Comments 203
Summary 204

Chapter 9   Data Types and Definitions 206

4GL Data Types 207
  Character and String Data Types 207
  Numeric Data Types 207
  Date, Time, and Interval Data Types 208
  BLOB Data Types 208
  INFORMIX-4GL Only Data Types and Indirect Typing 208
Defining Variables 209
Scope of Variables 211
Use of Nulls 211
Operators in 4GL 212
Converting between Data Types 213
  Character and String Data Types 213
  Numeric Data Types 214
  Date, Time, and Interval Data Types 215
Formatting Data with the using Clause 217
  Formatting Dates 217
  Formatting Numbers 218
Summary 320

Chapter 10   Menus 222

Overview of Menus 223
A Simple Ring Menu 225
Menu Simplicity and Consistency 226
Menu Features 226
  Command Keys 226
  Help 227
  Next Option 227
  Continue Menu 229
  Hidden Menu Options 229
  Hide Option 230
  Show Option 231
  Before Menu 232
Summary 233

**Chapter 11   Output and Standard
                    Program Statements 234**

Overview 235
Assignment 235
Output 235
  Display 236
  Error 237

Message 238
Prompt 239
Sleep 240
Conditionals 241
If-then-else 241
case 242
Looping 243
for 244
while 245
goto-label 246
Running UNIX Commands 247
Summary 248

Chapter 12 Screen Forms 250
What Is a Screen Form? 251
Screen Form Design 252
Screen Form Implementation 253
Database 254
Screen 254
Tables 255
Attributes 256
Instructions 256
Example of an INFORMIX-4GL-Generated Form 257
Example of a Modified Generated Form 258
Single Record Form 260
Multiple Record Form 261
Combination Form 262
Form Attributes 263
upscol 272
Summary 273

**Chapter 13 Adding Forms and Windows
            & Displaying Data 276**
Window Handling 277
Displaying Forms 280
Overview of Display 282
Display 282
Display Example 283
Sample Module 285
Display Array 295
Display Array Example 297

      Scroll 299
      Sample Module 300
   Display a One-to-Many Relationship 306
   Summary 319

Chapter 14   Setting Options 322

   Overview of Options 323
   Output Lines 324
   Keys 326
   Help File 327
   Attributes 328
   Input Wrap 329
   Field Order 329
   Sql Interrupt 330
   Line or Form Mode 330
   Example 331
   Summary 332

Chapter 15   Help! 334

   About Context-Sensitive Help 335
   Help Files 335
   mkmessage 337
   Using Help 337
   Summary 339

Chapter 16   Error Handling 340

   Defer Interrupt 341
   Defer Quit 341
   Whenever 342
   Error Log 344
   Sample Main Program and Error Function 346
   Summary 347

Chapter 17   Built-in Functions, Constants, and Variables 350

   INFORMIX-4GL Functions Called from 4GL 351
   INFORMIX-4GL Functions Called from C 374
   INFORMIX-4GL Constants 374
   INFORMIX-4GL Global Variables 375
   Summary 378

Chapter 18   The Input Statement 382

Input Overview 383
Editing the Input 386
Data Validation 387
Adding/Changing a Row 390
Summary 395

Chapter 19   Using SQL in 4GL 398

Using Direct SQL in 4GL 399
prepare 401
execute 402
declare 403
foreach 405
open 406
fetch 409
where current of 411
put 412
flush 413
close 413
free 414
Summary 415

Chapter 20   More Sophisticated SQL 518

Views 419
Synonyms 421
Expressions 423
    Operators 423
    Columns 425
    Literal Constants 425
Built-in Functions 426
Aggregates 436
    Using Aggregate Functions 438
Subqueries 439
    Subqueries with Relational Operators 439
    in and not in 440
    exists and not exists 441
    all, any, and some 442
    insert 442
    update 443
    delete 443
Self-Joins 443

Query Optimization 444
   Set explain on 444
   Temp Tables 444
   or versus union 445
   Indexes 445
   Forcing Use of Indexes 445
   Pattern Matching and Substrings 446
   Subqueries 447
INFORMIX-OnLine Topics 447
   Accessing Tables in Other Databases
       on the Same INFORMIX-OnLine System 448
   Isolation Levels 448
Summary 450

Chapter 21 Stored Procedures and Triggers 454
Stored Procedures 455
   dbinfo 471
   Sample Stored Procedures 472
   Privileges 474
   Changing and Deleting Existing Stored Procedures 474
   Update Statistics 475
Triggers 475
   Examples 478
   Looking at Existing Triggers 479
   Changing and Deleting Existing Stored Procedures 479
Summary 480

Chapter 22 User-Defined Searches 486
Overview 487
From the User's Perspective 487
Constructing a where Clause 490
Construct Features 493
Completing the select Statement 499
Sample Function 500
Summary 501

Chapter 23 The Input Array Statement 504
Input Array Overview 505
4GL Functions 506
Editing the Input 509
Data Validation 510

Sample Function 514
Summary 522

Chapter 24   Input of a One-to-Many Relationship 524

One-to-Many Input Overview 525
Sample Module 525
Summary 545

Chapter 25   Basic Report Writing 546

Report Overview 547
Getting the Report Data 548
Formatting the Report 553
Output 555
Order by 556
Control Blocks 557
On every row 562
Headers and Footers 562
Aggregates 565
Grouping 566
Final Totals 569
Sample Report 570
Summary 576

Chapter 26   Complex Reports 578

Using Temp Tables, Unions, and Other SQL Tricks 579
Matrix Reports 579
Multi-Part Reports 586
Summary 599

Chapter 27   The 4GL Debugger 600

Overview 601
Get Me Started, Quick! 601
Environment 603
   DBSRC 603
   Debugger Files (.4db) 604
   fgldb Command Line Options 604
   Creating a Custom Debugger Runner 605
Debugger Commands 606
Summary 623

Chapter 28 Mixing C and 4GL 628

Calling C Functions from 4GL 629
  Linking Compiled 4GL Code 632
  Linking Rapid Development System Code 632
Calling 4GL Functions from C 634
  Linking Compiled 4GL Code 637
  Linking Rapid Development System Code 638
Summary 639

Appendix A INFORMIX-4GL Functions
           Called from C 642

Appendix B CD Contents and Contributors 662

CD Contents 662
Software Contributors 665

Bibliography and Other Informix Books
           from Prentice Hall PTR 670

Books on Informix 670
Informix Manuals 671
General Database 671

Index 672

Preface

- *About this book*
- *Conventions used in this book*

About This Book

Are you tired of wading through all those Informix manuals?
This book will take you step-by-step from database design to working with Informix's implementation of SQL, and finally, to implementing programs in INFORMIX®-4GL.

- Topics are discussed in the order in which you will need to know the material.
- There are plenty of examples.
- The index is comprehensive.
- The chapter summaries provide a useful reference.
- The CD-ROM included with the book includes code examples from this book, and more.

The book has been revised and updated to cover the most recent Informix product features, plus a whole new chapter on the INFORMIX-4GL Interactive Debugger.
This book takes on the broad task of describing how to design and develop a database application using Informix's implementation of SQL and INFORMIX-4GL. The first chapter of the book contains an overview of relational database design. The next few chapters (2-6) show you how to create and maintain an Informix database, and explains the use of

all the basic commands in Informix's implementation of SQL. Chapters 9-19 cover basic INFORMIX-4GL in an order designed to get you up and working quickly. Chapter 19 explains how to use Informix's version of SQL in INFORMIX-4GL and is followed by two chapters of advanced SQL topics. The rest of the book includes more advanced INFORMIX-4GL topics, including user defined searches, more complex screen input/output, report writing, the debugger and using INFORMIX-4GL with C.

Going through this book chapter by chapter will allow you to design, create, maintain, and write applications for your own database system. The subjects are covered in the order in which you will typically need them when building a new system. A comprehensive table of contents and index allow quick reference to specific topics. A summary at the end of each chapter provides a quick reference for all the syntax and information covered in each chapter.

Please feel free to e-mail any comments about this book to the author, Cathy Kipp (ckipp@verinet.com).

Conventions Used in This Book

Sample code is displayed in the following font:

```
sample code font
```

Information enclosed between greater than and less than symbols is a description of the type of information that should be used in that location. The greater than and less than symbols when used in this context should not be typed in; only the item being described should be entered. For instance:

```
<select statement>
```

would be interpreted as an Informix's SQL select statement.

Syntax is displayed in the same font, but in bold typeface and boxed as shown below:

```
Informix's SQL and INFORMIX-4GL syntax
is shown boxed and bolded
```

Syntax is described using a regular expression-like syntax. The following table defines all of the typographical conventions used in this book.

Convention	Description
`text`	This font is used for all code examples.
`text`	Type all text in this font as shown in the syntax diagrams.
`<text>`	The italicized information enclosed between greater than and less than symbols indicates the type of information that will be used in that location. When used in this context, these symbols should not be entered as part of your code (unless otherwise indicated).

If the name of the database is `toymaker`, then:

`database <database name>`

would be typed by the user as:

`database toymaker`

[ ]	Information enclosed within square brackets is an optional part of the syntax. The brackets should not be typed as part of your code (unless otherwise indicated).
|	The pipe symbol means "or." Choose only one option in the list of options separated by pipes. The list of items will be enclosed by either the square brackets described above, or the curly braces described below. The pipe should not be typed as part of your code (unless otherwise indicated).

`[ unique | distinct ]`

This syntax would allow you to choose unique or distinct or neither, since the information inside the square brackets is optional.

{ }	Curly braces contain a list of options separated by pipes. The curly braces should not be typed as part of your code (unless otherwise indicated).

`{ all | unique | distinct }`

In this example, you would be required to choose either *all*, *unique* or *distinct* since this list is enclosed within curly braces.

text   Underlined text indicates that if no option is explicitly chosen, the default will be the option represented by the underscored text.

> [<u>all</u> | unique | distinct]

In this case, if none of these options was selected by the user, *all* would be used.

. . .   Three dots indicate optional repetition of what appeared previously.

> again [and ...]

would translate to any of the following:

> again

> again and again

> again and again and again and again

Explanation   This font is used only for explanations.

Acknowledgments

Many thanks to Jonathan Leffler of Informix Software, Inc., for taking the time to thoroughly review and make suggestions for the second edition of this book.

Many thanks also to my friend Jannine Mohr who spent a considerable number of hours slaving over the indexing and other administrative details of this second edition.

And special thanks to my wonderful husband, Don.

Programming Informix SQL/4GL: A Step-by-Step Approach

Chapter

1

Relational Database Design

- *What is a relational database?*
- *Elements of a database: tables, columns, and rows*
- *Primary keys*
- *Foreign keys*
- *Types of relationships*
- *What is normalization?*
- *Formal normalization*
- *Intuitive normalization*
- *Indexing strategies*
- *Description of the sample database*
- *Summary*

What is a Relational Database?

A database is a collection of data. A *relational* database is a collection of data stored in such a way that the elements within the set of data are related to one another.

For instance, if a toymaker makes toys and sells them to toy stores, a relationship exists between the toymaker and each toy store. A relationship would also exist between the toymaker and the vendors from whom it purchases the supplies used to make the toys. Yet another relationship would exist between the toymaker and its employees.

The diagram in Figure 1-1 illustrates the relationships of various entities with our toymaker. The lines in the diagram indicate direct relationships between the entities in the diagram.

Because the above information relates in one way or another to our toymaker, the example database we will create for use in this book will be called *toymaker*.

There are no set rules about how much information can be stored in a single database or at what point one database should be split into two or more databases. Informix products provide the capabilities of working among separate databases on the same machine or on different machines. The key is to do what makes sense for your organization and for your application.

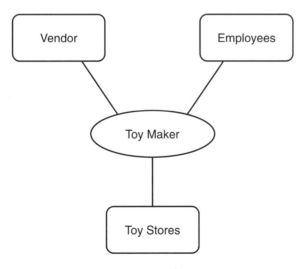

Figure 1-1   *Relationship of various entities with a toymaker.*

Elements of a Database: Tables, Columns, and Rows

Tables

A relational database is comprised of sets of information called *tables*. Each table is comprised of a single type of information. A database may have any number of tables.

For example, a table called "toy stores" might contain information about each of the stores to whom our toymaker sells toys. Any of the entities related to the toymaker in Figure 1-1 might be a table in the toymaker database.

Columns

Each table contains one or more *columns*. The terms *column* and *field* are often used interchangeably and have the same meaning.

A column is a piece of information that in some way describes the information stored in a table, or it may describe how one table is related to another table. In the latter case, the column would be called a key. Primary and foreign keys are discussed in detail later in the chapter. A table may have any number of columns.

Information in our toy store table might include the following: store number, store name, street address, city, state, zip code, telephone number, etc., as shown in Figure 1-2.

Store Number	Store Name	Street	City	State	Zip Code	Telephone Number

Figure 1-2   *Sample columns for a database table.*

Rows

A *row* is a single instance of information comprising all the columns in a table. A table may contain any number of rows. The terms *row* and *record* are often used interchangeably and have the same meaning.

In our toy store table example, a row would include the information used to describe one toy store. A matrix representation of the toy store table will help you to understand how the elements

Store Number	Store Name	Street	City	State	Zip Code	Telephone Number
1	Don's Toy Dungeon	615 Second St	Breckenridge	CO	80876	303-222-1111
2	Kever's Kiddie Korner	117 Main St	Vail	CO	80880	303-433-9482
3	Games for Grownups	90 Garrett St	Aspen	CO	80776	303-804-2345
4	Toy Town	768 Quent Dr	Estes Park	CO	80348	970-668-0988
5	Pete's Playhouse	888 Eightieth St	Denver	CO	80201	303-552-6953
6	Puzzles	7666 Taft Dr	Loveland	CO	80538	970-667-8844
7	Farley's Fun House	2011 Drake Ave	Fort Collins	CO	80525	970-229-3401
8	Tiny's Toy Terrace	322 Quincy Ave	Englewood	CO	80211	303-216-8471
...	...	...	...	...	...	...

Figure 1-3   *Rows of data in a database table.*

of a table fit together. In the two-dimensional matrix shown in Figure 1-3, the matrix is the table, the rows contain records of information, and the columns describe the information stored within each row.

A database may contain any number of tables, and tables may contain any number of columns and rows. A table will usually have more rows than columns. The number of columns in a table will usually remain fairly constant, while the number of rows and their contents may be subject to continual change.

Primary Keys

A *primary key* is a column or set of columns in a table that provides a way of uniquely identifying a specific row of data in a table.

A social security number could be a primary key used to look up an employee. You will typically want a unique way of identifying every row of data in a given table. This uniqueness gives you an easy way of distinguishing one row of data from another row when adding, changing, or deleting rows of data in a table.

A key may also be used to define relationships between tables. If a key in one table is also stored as a column in another table, the two tables are related by an equivalent key.

Now suppose we want to find out which stores ordered toys from our toymaker in the past six months? We would need to keep track of which store is associated with which order. When the store number is in the order table, it becomes a trivial matter of comparing the two columns for matching data. See Figure 1-4.

There are several reasons the store number was used as a key instead of, for instance, the store name.

First, shorter keys are more efficient. They are faster to search on, and they require less storage space—especially when references to the key are in more than one table.

Second, numeric keys tend to be more efficient for searching and storage than keys made up of character strings.

Third, although the chances of two stores having the same name might be very small, it could happen. When dealing with people this becomes a significant issue. For example, there may be several different people with the name Janet Jackson.

Toy Store Table

Toy Order Table

Store #	Store Name
1	DON'S TOY DUNGEON
2	KEVER'S KIDDIE KORNER
3	GAMES FOR GROWN-UPS
4	TOY TOWN
5	PETE'S PLAYHOUSE
...	...

Order #	Store #	Order Date	Shipping Date
1	1	7/11/97	7/13/97
2	2	7/11/97	7/14/97
3	3	7/12/97	7/15/97
4	4	7/13/97	7/15/97
5	5	7/14/97	7/19/97
...	...	...	...

Figure 1-4 *Compare the values in key columns to lookup desired information.*

Foreign Keys

When a key is the primary method of accessing information in a table, it is a primary key. When a key is referenced in another table, it is a *foreign key*.

In the above example, store number is a primary key in the toy store table, but it is a foreign key in the order table. The primary key in the order table would be the order number.

Foreign keys are necessary in a relational database to define the relationships that exist between tables.

Types of Relationships

There are several types of relationships that can exist between tables in a relational database. These are:

- One-to-one or zero
- One-to-many (or many-to-one)
- Many-to-many

Each of these relationships is discussed in detail here.

One-to-One or Zero

A *one-to-one relationship* between two tables means that for each row in Table A, there will be a corresponding single row in Table B. This relationship is actually rather rare in databases because if a database is properly *normalized* (normalization is described in the next section), these two tables will most likely be merged into a single table.

The *one-to-one or zero relationship* is more common, however. This relationship exists when for each row in Table A, there is either one or zero rows in Table B. If you have a situation where all customers have addresses, but very few customers have mailing addresses, you may want to have a customer table for all of your customers and a related table, say customer_mailing, to store mailing address information only for customers who have a mailing address. Figure 1-5 on page 8 shows an example of this situation.

While this will save you disk space when Table B has only a small percentage of the number of rows Table A has, you should understand that there is overhead in having an additional table. *Indexes* are described in detail later in this chapter. For now you should know that an index on a table allows for quick access to certain information in a table, like the index in this book allows you to easily locate information on topics in the book. The index to the first table will now need to be stored and indexed in two tables instead of one whenever there is information in Table B. The space for the data in Table B will need to be used only when data exists, as opposed to using space in every row in Table A, even when data does not exist. Make certain you will actually be

Customer Table

Customer Number	Customer Name	Address
1	Jannine Mohr	222 2nd St
2	Char McDaniel	87 Main St
3	Fred Johnson	33 Golf Dr
4	Philip Wilson	987 Adams Dr
5	Cynthia Crandall	888 Grey St
6	Cathy Kever	63 Mull Blvd
7	Tim Thorton	23 Guppy Rd
8	Susan Shroeder	387 Orbit Ln

Customer Mailing Table

Customer Number	Mailing Address
1	P.O. Box 7689
6	P.O. Box 37221

Figure 1-5 *Use a one-to-one or zero relationship to save disk space.*

saving space before you go to the trouble of implementing such a design. Also note that additional programming effort will be required to maintain an additional table.

One-to-Many (or Many-to-One)

The *one-to-many*, or reversed, the *many-to-one relationship*, is by far the most common type of database relationship. This is one of the reasons relational databases are so popular and powerful. It is the relationship defined when for every row in Table A, there may be any number of rows (i.e., zero, one, or many) in Table B that are related to it.

An example of this is that a person might own zero, one, or many cars. The person table then has a one-to-many relationship with the car table. An example of how this might work is shown in Figure 1-6.

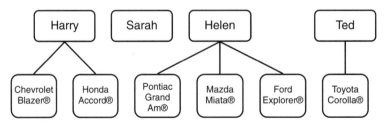

Figure 1-6 *Example of a one-to-many (or many to one) relationship.*

Many-to-Many

The *many-to-many relationship* exists when for every row in Table A, there may be many rows in Table B, and for every row in Table B, there may be many rows in Table A. Many is once again defined as zero, one, or many. This relationship can be rather complicated.

As an example (see Figure 1-7), we have a table of cars and a table of car parts. Any car might be able to use zero, one, or many of the parts in the parts table. Any part may fit in zero, one, or many of the cars in the car table.

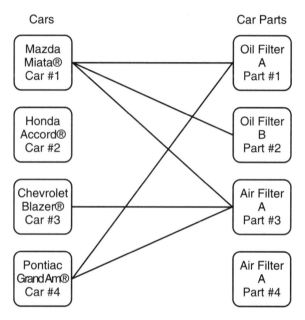

Figure 1-7 *Example of a many-to-many relationship.*

What you should probably do in this case is break this down into a more manageable relationship as shown in Figure 1-8.

Valid Cars Table

Car #	1	1	1	3	4	4
Part #	1	2	3	3	1	3

Figure 1-8 *Example of a table defining a many-to-many relationship.*

Now the valid cars table defines the relationship between the car and car parts tables.

What Is Normalization?

Normalization is the process of arranging your data into tables and columns to minimize the duplication of information in a database, to place columns in the appropriate tables, and to create efficient relationships between the tables in a database. Normalizing your database is the best defense against poorly organized and repetitious data infiltrating it. Database design is a crucial step that should be given as much attention as necessary up front. By doing a good job of normalizing your database at the start, you will save yourself much grief later on as you develop your application and even later when you have to maintain what you have written.

There are two ways to go about normalizing your data: (1) follow the formal rules of data normalization, and (2) use your intuition. I recommend a combination of these methods. Go through the formal normalization techniques (especially if you have not dealt much with relational databases), then review what you have done and make sure it makes sense.

note

Formal normalization is useful, but it can involve you so much in the detail that it can be difficult to pull back and review the overall results.

Both formal and intuitive normalization are described below.

Formal Normalization

There are three basic formal steps to follow to achieve database normalization. All of these steps have the same goal, however. This goal is to create a clean database structure that will result in storing the least amount of duplicate data.

A non-normalized toy order table appears as follows:

toy_order	order number	How to identify the order.
	store information	Who bought the toys?
	sales person info	Who sold the toys?
	toy information	What toys were ordered?
	quantity	How many of each toy?
	unit price	How much did each toy cost?
	order date	When were the toys ordered?
	shipping date & time	When were the toys shipped?
	primary key:	order number

First Normal Form

The *first rule of normalization* is to eliminate repeating groups. Review the non-normalized toy_order table. For each order, are there subgroups of information that will cause the order information to be stored multiple times?

Assuming orders may contain multiple items, any information relating to line items of the order should be stored separately:

toy_order	order number
	store information
	sales person info
	order date
	shipping date & time
	primary key: order number

toy_order_item	order number
	toy code
	toy description
	quantity of toy available
	manufacturing cost of toy
	normal sales price of toy
	quantity
	unit price
	primary key: order number + toy code

The order number becomes a key in the table toy_order_item so we will be able to tell which items in toy_order_item belong in which toy_order. For each row in toy_order_item to be unique, we have made a composite key (a key comprised of more than one column) from the columns order number and toy code.

Second Normal Form

The *second rule of normalization* is to eliminate from each table any information that does not rely fully on any composite primary keys.

Our only table with a composite primary key is toy_order_item. Let's have a look at this table.

Table	Column	Primary Key or Dependency
toy_order_item	order number	primary key
	toy code	primary key
	toy description	toy code
	quantity of toys available	toy code
	manufacturing cost of toy	toy code
	normal sales price of toy	toy code
	quantity	order number and toy code
	unit price	order number and toy code

In the toy_order_item table, much of the information relies upon only the toy code. The columns that comprise the composite primary key and the columns that rely on all columns of this key are appropriate items for the table. Therefore we will split the toy_order_item table:

toy_order_item	order number
	toy code
	quantity
	unit price
	primary key: order number + toy code

toy	toy code
	toy description
	quantity of toys available
	manufacturing cost of toy
	normal sales price of toy
	primary key: toy code

Third Normal Form

The *third rule of normalization* is to eliminate columns that are best described by a column other than the primary key. These are generally items that do not relate directly to the primary key.

Let's have a look at the tables we have so far—notice that we have fully expanded the elements of the toy_order table at this point.

Table	Column	Best Key for Column
toy_order	order number	primary key
	store number	order number
	store name	store number
	buyer last name	store number
	buyer first name	store number
	phone number	store number
	fax number	store number
	store street	store number
	store city	store number
	store state code	store number
	state name	state code
	store zip code	store number
	sales code	order number
	employee number	sales code
	last name	sales code
	first name	sales code
	order date	order number
	shipping date time	order number

Since several columns of the toy_order table have an ideal primary key other than order number, we will now split this table into four tables.

toy_order	order number
	store number
	order date
	shipping date time
	sales code
	primary key: order number

toy_store	store number
	store name
	buyer last name
	buyer first name
	phone number
	fax number
	store street
	store city
	store state
	store zip code
	primary key: store number

toy_sales_staff	sales code
	employee number
	last name
	first name
	primary key: sales code

state	state code
	state name
	primary key: state code

note

Note that each of our new tables has a primary key that relates it to another table. The state table exists as a lookup table so that the user can look up the name of the state if he doesn't know the state code.

Our other two tables are listed below, but notice that these are already in third normal form so no adjustments will be necessary.

Table	Column	Best Key for Column
toy_order_item	order number	primary key
	toy code	primary key
	quantity	order number + toy code
	unit price	order number + toy code
	primary key: order number + toy code	

Table	Column	Best Key for Column
toy	toy code	primary key
	description	toy code
	quantity	toy code
	cost	toy code
	sales price	toy code
	primary key:	toy code

Intuitive Normalization

While formal normalization is very useful, don't forget to use common sense when designing your database. The formal normalization process can become so detailed that it can be difficult to pull yourself back from the detail to see if what you have created makes sense.

What is the scope of your database?

Determine what you want the scope of your database to be. For our purposes, we have determined that the scope of the database is the ordering system for our toymaker. We can always decide to expand our definition if we later decide to expand the scope of the database, but you must determine the initial scope of your database in order to come up with any kind of reasonable design. If you don't know what you are designing, how can you design it?

Does each table in your database have a unique reason for existing?

Examine each table in your database and the columns within it. What is the main purpose of this table? Do all of the columns in the table relate directly to the purpose of this table? If a table has multiple purposes, examine it carefully to see if it should be divided into two or more tables. If any columns in the table don't relate directly to the purpose of the table, this is another reason to look closely at your table to see if it should be split into more than one table.

An example of this is when we split our toy_order table into the tables toy_order, toy_store, and toy_sales_staff. The purpose of the toy_order table should be to store information related to toy orders. But this table was also being used for the purposes of storing toy store and toy sales staff information. Looking at the columns in the toy_order table before it was divided into these three tables, it is possible to see that not all columns in the table were directly related to the purpose of the table.

If you delete a row from a table, does vital information disappear from your database?

Look at each table in your database and determine if a row is deleted from your database, will information be deleted that you would rather keep? In our example of the toy_order table before it was split into the toy_order, toy_store, and toy_sales_staff tables, if we deleted an order, the toy_store information would also disappear. If this was the first time the client ordered toys from our toymaker, we would lose all information for this store in our database.

With the exception of primary keys and foreign keys, are you storing each piece of information in only one place in your database?

Keep in mind that you only want to have to maintain each piece of information one time and in one place whenever possible. If a toy store were to get a new telephone number, you would not want to go through each order of toys the store placed and change the telephone number. Keeping this information in a single place (in this case, the toy_store table) makes the maintenance of accurate information in the database much easier. Additionally, we want to conserve disk space whenever possible. If there is no need to store something multiple times or to keep a history, don't.

You may also at some point want a list of all client toy stores. Rather than sorting through toy_orders, deleting duplicates, and trying to determine which information is the most recent, it is much easier to be able to get the most current information from a simple table.

Don't make the mistake of going overboard here. You will notice that in the toymaker database, the table toy has the column sales_price and the table toy_order item has the column unit_price. These should be stored in different places for several reasons. First, the sales_price of an item may change over time. We need to retrieve historical information of the prices of particular items. Or perhaps we're running a special or offering quantity discounts. Either of these situations could make the unit_price for an item different from the sales_price.

How are the tables in your database related to one another?

Draw a diagram of your database (see Figure 1-9). Place the names of each table in your database on a piece of paper. List the primary key of each table underneath the table name. Now draw

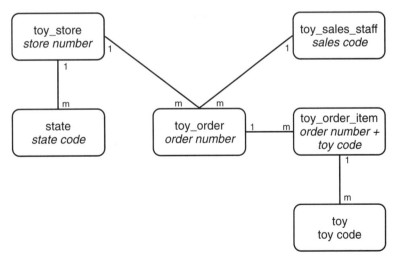

Figure 1-9 *Diagram of the toymaker database.*

lines between each of the tables that are directly connected to one another. That is, tables whose primary keys are stored as all or part of a primary key or a foreign key in another table. Now indicate the type of relationships that exist between the tables by placing a "1" or an "m" at either end of each line to represent one-to-one (or zero), one-to-many, and many-to-many relationships. Do the relationships you have diagrammed make sense? Are there relationships that should exist but don't? If you find problems at this point, take another look at the database structure.

Are you storing information in your database that could easily be derived from columns of information already stored in your database?

Derived data is what information is called that can be calculated based on information already stored in the database. For instance, in our toy_order_item table, we store the quantity and the unit_price, but not total_price. Since quantity multiplied by unit_price will always equal the total price, there is no need for us to store the total price and use extra space in the database.

Performance versus normalization?

Normalization reduces update anomalies, usually at the expense of performance. You may find a situation where the normalized solution doesn't yield adequate performance, and you opt for denormalization. As an example, if you have a column of information that can be derived from other information in the database, but the calculation to get this information is complex enough to slow your database performance (it must be recalculated each time it is accessed), you may just want to calculate it once and store it. If you choose to denormalize, you need to be aware that you have the responsibility of keeping any duplicated or derived data current. This is a space versus time decision you must make. What's the solution? You need to decide this for yourself—but for most applications, performance will win.

Indexing Strategies

An index in a database provides a quick way of looking up specific types of information. This can be compared to the entries in a telephone book. A telephone book is organized alphabetically by name. That means if you know a person's name it isn't too difficult to find that person's address and telephone number. But if all you have is a person's address, you could potentially look through every entry in the telephone book before you find the entry you are searching for.

An index is merely a way of organizing columns in a database to make information faster to access. For each row in a database, the index will contain the information specified for that index and a pointer to the location of that row in the database (see Figure 1-10). The index lists the information in a particular order so it is easy to find.

For instance, if you want a name search in your database to be fast, you will probably want to put an index on the name field(s) in your database.

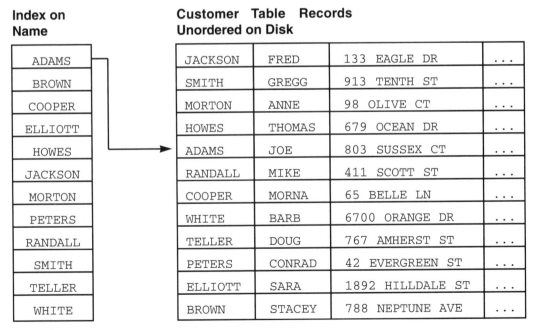

Index on Name

ADAMS
BROWN
COOPER
ELLIOTT
HOWES
JACKSON
MORTON
PETERS
RANDALL
SMITH
TELLER
WHITE

Customer Table Records Unordered on Disk

JACKSON	FRED	133 EAGLE DR	. . .
SMITH	GREGG	913 TENTH ST	. . .
MORTON	ANNE	98 OLIVE CT	. . .
HOWES	THOMAS	679 OCEAN DR	. . .
ADAMS	JOE	803 SUSSEX CT	. . .
RANDALL	MIKE	411 SCOTT ST	. . .
COOPER	MORNA	65 BELLE LN	. . .
WHITE	BARB	6700 ORANGE DR	. . .
TELLER	DOUG	767 AMHERST ST	. . .
PETERS	CONRAD	42 EVERGREEN ST	. . .
ELLIOTT	SARA	1892 HILLDALE ST	. . .
BROWN	STACEY	788 NEPTUNE AVE	. . .

Figure 1-10 *Indexes point to the records stored on disk.*

Keys in a database (both primary and foreign) are typically frequently accessed and therefore are usually indexed.

You can have multiple indexes on a given table, but for every index you add, your speed of accessing data increases, but you pay the penalties of using extra disk space and slower performance when adding, changing, and deleting information in your table.

Every index will use additional space in your database. As a table with indexes grows, all of the indexes grow. If you put an index on a column in a table, the column value will be stored once in the table, once in the index, and an additional amount of space will be needed to point from the index to the data record.

Every time you add, update, or delete information in a table with indexes, the indexes in the table need to be maintained. If you add a row, all indexes for the row must be updated at the same time. If you update a row, the indexes may need to be modified. If you delete a row, the index entry must be deleted. While these changes to the index may not take up a large amount of time individually, they may considerably slow the function of a table whose data changes frequently.

note

A general rule is to put indexes on information that needs to be accessed frequently or quickly. This will vary depending on the size of your tables and many other factors—such as what your database is used for and how it is used.

Several different indexing features and strategies are described below. This information can help you create more efficient indexes on your tables and improve database performance. There are trade-offs you will need to make as you create your indexes. These sections will point you in the right direction.

Composite Indexes

A *composite index* is an index which is comprised of more than one column or field.

We have discussed putting an index on a name. But it is likely that we will store a last name and first name in separate columns of a table. So rather than use just the last name, we can use a composite index that puts an index on the last name and then the first name. This is the equivalent of having a list sorted in order by "last name, first name." This means that finding the first name only would still require a sequential search through the table, but finding a last name only or a last name in combination with a first name would be much faster.

Unique Indexes

When creating an index for a table, one option is to force the values for that index to be unique. You will normally want to have one index in a table that can uniquely identify a row of information in a table, that is, the primary key. It is a good idea to create this index as a unique index. The database will then enforce the uniqueness of the index for every row of data entered.

Duplicate Indexes

When creating non-unique indexes, you need to minimize the number of duplicate values that will be stored in the index. Duplicate values in indexes make a database inefficient—the more duplicate values, the more inefficient it will be. While a small number of duplicate values in an index can be tolerated, many duplicates should not be tolerated, since the performance will plummet when data is added, changed, or deleted from a table with many duplicate index values.

An index for a column containing "A" for active and "I" for inactive is a really bad idea. If you have a need for such an index, turn it into a composite index with a unique column. Turn the index using the column "active" into a composite index containing "active + invoice number." The space used will be well worth the performance gained.

Shorter Is Better

It is a good idea to keep indexes as short as possible. Performance when creating and searching shorter indexes is better than when using longer indexes.

You will need to determine the best combination of indexes to serve your users. An index that searches for a customer by social security number is more efficient than one that searches by name. But if users frequently search for customers by name, a system that offers only a social security number search will cause your users great anxiety and grief. In this situation, an index on the name and another (unique) index on the social security number is an appropriate choice.

Numeric versus Character Indexes

Numeric indexes are faster to search on than character indexes and they generally require less storage space. When there is an opportunity to use a numeric index instead of a character index, use it. This will not make sense in every situation, but if it does, take advantage of it.

For instance, using the two-character state code as a key is certainly easier than creating a numeric code for each state and performing an additional translation. However, using a numeric order number for each toy_order makes sense. We could use a character code such as "A1234", but this is harder to assign and it produces a less efficient index. The choices will not always be this obvious, so just try to make the most reasonable decision.

Clustered Indexes

In addition to creating an index, a *cluster index* also physically places the data records on the disk in order by the cluster index. The effect of clustering information will, in many cases, enhance performance when retrieving information. Only one clustered index per table is allowed.

A cluster index is clustered only at the point at which it is created. Added, updated, and deleted records will not be placed physically in order. Clustered indexes should be reclustered periodically to physically reorder the index and data. The frequency of this operation will depend greatly on how quickly data is added, changed, and deleted.

Small Tables

Small tables containing fewer than 200 rows are not officially considered good candidates for indexing because the information in the table can usually be accessed more quickly by performing a sequential search.

From the unofficial view, there are several reasons you might want to consider indexing small tables. First, to ensure the uniqueness of a primary key is maintained, it is useful to index the table. Since the table is so small, the performance consequences of performing an indexed search on it should be negligible. Plus, if you keep your database statistics current, the optimizer should be able to choose a sequential scan even if the table is indexed.

Description of the Sample Database

This brings us to a description of the sample database we will use in this book. We will be using the database toymaker that we have been designing throughout this chapter. The purpose of this database is to track orders from toy stores for toys made by our toymaker.

The database toymaker contains the tables listed in figure 1-11 on page 24, along with their primary and foreign keys. Note that underscores ("_") have been added between the words that make up each column, since blank spaces are not allowed in database, table, or column names.

For a diagram of the database, see the section "Intuitive normalization" earlier in this chapter. The diagram presents a conceptual picture of the database and makes it easy to see how the tables within the database are related to one another.

In real life, we would probably add many more tables to this database to have a complete database system. These might include tables for purposes such as accounts receivable, accounts payable, tracking the vendors, inventory control, and employee payroll.

For our purposes, we will be using only a few tables to make the examples as clear and as easy to follow as possible. Complex examples can be illustrated even with these simple tables.

Summary

A *relational database* is a collection of data stored in such a way that the elements within the set of data are related to one another. Each *table* is comprised of a single type of information. A database may have any number of tables. Each table contains

Table	Column	Keys	Primary or Foreign Key
toy_order	order_number	order_number	primary key
	store_number	store_number	foreign key
	order_date		
	shipping_datetime		
	sales_code	sales_code	foreign key
toy_order_item	order_number	order_number +	primary key
	toy_code	toy_code	
	quantity		
	unit_price		
toy	toy_code	toy_code	primary key
	description		
	quantity		
	cost		
	sales_price		
toy_store	store_number	store_number	primary key
	store_name		
	buyer_last_name		
	buyer_first_name		
	phone_number		
	fax_number		
	store_street		
	store_city		
	store_state		
	store_zip_code		
toy_sales_staff	sales_code	sales_code	primary key
	employee_number		
	last_name		
	first_name		
state	state_code	state_code	primary key
	state_name		

Figure 1-11   *Description of the toymaker database.*

one or more columns. A *column* is a piece of information which in some way describes the information stored in a table, or it may describe how one table is related to another. A *row* is a single item of information in a table. A table may contain any number of rows.

A *primary key* is a column or set of columns in a table that provide a way of uniquely identifying a specific row of data in a table. A key may also be used to define relationships between tables. If a key in one table is also stored as a column in another table, the two tables are related by an equivalent key. When a primary key in one table is referenced in another table, it is a *foreign key*.

Types of relationships in a relational database are *one-to-one or zero, one-to-many* (or *many-to-one*), and *many-to-many*.

The *first rule of normalization* is to eliminate repeating groups.

The *second rule of normalization* is to eliminate from each table any information that does not rely fully on any composite primary keys.

The *third rule of normalization* is to eliminate columns that are best described by a column other than the primary key.

Also use *intuitive normalization*, or common sense, when designing your database.

An *index* is a way of organizing columns in a database to make information faster to access. The disadvantages of indexes include using extra disk space and a slower database performance when adding, changing, and deleting information.

Keys in a database (both primary and foreign) are normally indexed. A general rule is to put indexes on information that needs to be accessed frequently or quickly.

A *composite index* is one that is comprised of more than one column or field. A *unique index* in a table can identify a row of information in a table uniquely. Minimize the number of *duplicate index values* stored in an index. *Shorter indexes* improve database performance. *Numeric indexes* generally require less storage space and are faster to search on than character indexes. *Cluster indexes* improve performance by physically ordering data records on the disk. In SQL databases such as Informix, *small tables*, fewer than 200 rows, are generally not good candidates for indexing as the information in the table can most likely be accessed more quickly by performing a sequential search. If, however, you want to make certain that the uniqueness of a column in a small table is maintained, it may be indexed.

The SQL Working Environment

- *About Informix's implementation of SQL*
- *About DB-Access*
- *Setting UNIX environment variables*
- *Environment variables needed by Informix*
- *Optional environment variables*
- *Using DB-Access*
- *Working from the command line*
- *Viewing error messages*
- *Summary*

About Informix's Implementation of SQL

Informix's implementation of SQL (Structured Query Language), is used to communicate with the Informix database engine. Informix's implementation of SQL contains statements that allow you to create databases, load data, view data, change data, and generally maintain your database system.

Many database vendors including Informix have their own versions of SQL. The industry standards for SQL are defined by the American National Standards Institute (ANSI). Informix's implementation of SQL attempts to meet all SQL standards set by ANSI. Since ANSI standards for SQL are continually evolving, as are Informix database engines, check your Informix manuals to find out how compatible the version of Informix's SQL you are using is with the ANSI standards.

The book refers to Informix's implementation of SQL as *Informix's SQL*. This is definitely not to be confused with the Informix product called INFORMIX-SQL. The INFORMIX-SQL product contains utilities for creating and editing reports, forms, user menus, databases and tables. Additionally, INFORMIX-SQL allows you access to much of Informix's SQL language via an interactive editor and runtime facility as well as giving you an easy way to view information about your database tables.

Informix has made additions and extensions to Informix's SQL which give it more features and flexibility than ANSI-compliant SQL. If you are concerned about using only ANSI-compliant SQL statements within your database system, there are flags which are described later in this chapter that you can set to warn you if you use syntax that is not strictly ANSI-compliant. It can be difficult and very restrictive to maintain strict ANSI-compliance when using SQL.

About DB-Access

DB-Access is the program that comes with the Informix engine that allows you to run Informix's SQL statements and to easily create, change, and delete databases and tables. DB-Access can be accessed through the ring-menu interface or from the command line by using command files. Both of these options are described later in this chapter.

DB-Access is an invaluable tool for anyone developing a database system in Informix. Many People confuse DB-Access with the Informix product INFORMIX-SQL as both have some features which are quite similar, but in reality they are very different and distinct tools. DB-Access will allow you to run any of Informix's SQL language which is supported by the current engine and it also has features to help you manage more advanced database features such as referential integrity, stored procedures, triggers, and better control of the INFORMIX-OnLine database engine.

INFORMIX-SQL does not support the most recent versions of the database engine; however, it does have options for user screens, reports, and user menus. While INFORMIX-4GL gives you much more control over your application, the INFORMIX-SQL tools can be useful for people who want to create simple applications (or parts of applications) without having to do full-blown programming. For instance, the ACE report writer in INFORMIX-SQL is a very useful tool for creating ad hoc reports and the PER-FORM tool makes it easy to create simple data entry and lookup screens. Tools that are not part of DB-Access are not covered in this book, but depending on your application, they could prove useful to you. Jonathan Leffler's book *Using INFORMIX-SQL (2nd edition)* is the definitive resource guide for anyone wanting to learn more about INFORMIX-SQL.

Setting UNIX Environment Variables

Before you can start using Informix products, you will need to define your operating system environment. Your environment will define where your Informix products are installed and other items that Informix products need to run properly.

Informix products use operating system environment variables that allow you to set values for some environment variables and to change the defaults for others. This section on environment variables is split into two sections: (1) environment variables that must be set for Informix products to run properly, and (2) optional environment variables.

Setting and unsetting these environment variables in UNIX may vary slightly depending on the shell you are using. To set an environment variable:

Bourne shell: `FRUIT=grapes`
                             `export FRUIT`

C shell: `setenv FRUIT grapes`

The environment variable FRUIT will now be set to the value "grapes". Putting quotes around the value you are exporting will keep you from having problems if the environment variable's value contains any spaces or special UNIX characters. You can then refer to the value in the FRUIT environment variable (that is, "grapes") by specifying $FRUIT.

If the environment variable FRUIT did not exist in your environment before you set it, the above commands will add it to your environment and give it the initial value of "grapes". If the environment variable FRUIT did exist in your environment before the above commands were issued, the value of the variable is changed to "grapes" from whatever it was set to previously.

Type `env` at the prompt to see how your environment variables are set.

To unset an environment variable (this will delete the environment variable from your environment):

Bourne shell: `unset FRUIT`

C shell: `unsetenv FRUIT`

Now if you enter the `env` command, the environment variable FRUIT should no longer appear in your list of environment variables.

You will probably want to put commands in your `.profile` (Bourne shell), `.login`, or `.cshrc` (C shell) file to set the environment variables to their initial values each time you log in. If you want to define the environment for multiple users, you may wish to set the environment variables you want to use in the `/etc/profile` file, which is executed by all users at time of login.

Environment Variables Needed by Informix

This section describes operating system environment variables used by Informix products that should be set before using any Informix products.

INFORMIXDIR

Make sure that your INFORMIXDIR environment variable is set to the directory where your Informix products were loaded. If the directory informix has been loaded under the directory /usr/local, then INFORMIXDIR should be set to the value: /usr/local/informix. The length of the value in INFORMIXDIR may not exceed 64 characters.

PATH

The PATH environment variable specifies the search path UNIX uses to look for executable commands. The directories are searched through in the order in which they appear in the PATH variable. You will need to add the directory $INFORMIXDIR/bin to your path. You can do this without overwriting what is already specified in the path by using the following as the value for PATH:

```
$PATH:$INFORMIXDIR/bin
```

This uses the previous contents of PATH and adds a directory to the end of the PATH.

INFORMIXTERM

The INFORMIXTERM environment variable should be set to either termcap or terminfo depending on which of these files you use to define your terminal's capabilities. If INFORMIXTERM is not set, the default value is termcap. Not all platforms currently support terminfo.

TERMCAP or TERMINFO

Either the TERMCAP or TERMINFO environment variable will need to be set. If you are using a termcap file to define terminal capabilities, set the TERMCAP environment variable to your termcap file. If you are using a terminfo file to define terminal capabilities, set the TERMINFO environment variable to your terminfo file. Not all platforms currently support TERMINFO. You may wish to check out your $INFORMIXDIR/etc directory to see if the termcap or terminfo files provided by Informix would be useful to you.

TERM

TERM defines the type of terminal you are using. Whichever terminal type you specify, you will need to make certain an entry exists for it in your termcap or terminfo file.

ONCONFIG (INFORMIX-OnLine only) or TBCONFIG (prior to the 6.0 engine)

If you are running INFORMIX-OnLine, you will need to have prepared your INFORMIX-OnLine environment at this point, and your ONCONFIG or TBCONFIG environment variable should be set to the name of your INFORMIX-OnLine instance. A single INFORMIX-OnLine instance may contain several databases. Once you are working with more than one INFORMIX-OnLine instance at a time (on either the same machine or on separate machines), you will need to become familiar with Informix networking and the slightly different syntax needed for performing network operations.

INFORMIXSERVER (INFORMIX-OnLine 6.0 and above only)

If you are running INFORMIX-OnLine, you will need to set INFORMIXSERVER to the name of your default database server. This will be the same name assigned to the DBSERVERNAME variable in your ONCONFIG file (this file can be found in $INFORMIXDIR/etc/$ONCONFIG).

Optional Environment Variables

The following environment variables are used by Informix products to allow you to change various defaults it assumes. You may just want to skim this section now for general capabilities, then come back and refer to it in detail when you are ready to use one of these features.

DBANSIWARN

This environment variable is used to warn you when you use non-ANSI standard syntax. This environment variable does not need to be set to a value, it merely needs to exist in your environment for the Informix extension checking to be turned on.

DBCENTURY

This environment variable allows you to determine how years entered in a two digit format are interpreted by INFORMIX-4GL and engine products. This is a new feature available in version 7.2 and higher of the Informix engine and should be available in a newer release of INFORMIX-4GL products (the exact version was unavailable at the time of this writing).

Older versions of these products will automatically prepend a "19" to all two digit years, so the date entered as 3/5/02 (in mm/dd/yy format) would be interpreted as March 5, 1902. This behavior would occur regardless of which century you were in.

Versions of software which support DBCENTURY, also have a different default behavior if DBCENTURY is not set. In these versions the default behavior is to prepend a century based on the year in which the data entry occurs. So, if the year is 1999, all years would be prepended with "19" and if the year is 2000, all years would be prepended with a "20".

DBCENTURY may be set to any of the following values:

- C—Closest: Prepend a two-digit year which will leave the date closest to today's date. This is likely to be the behavior your users will expect.
- F—Future: All two digit years will result in the closest future date based on today's date. If today is December 5, 1998 and

the date entered is 1/1/99 (in mm/dd/yy format), the result will be 1/1/1999. The dates of 12/5/98 and 11/15/98 will respectively result as 12/5/2098 and 11/15/2098, since the dates are assigned the closest future date.

- **P**—Past: All two digit years will result in the closest date in the past based on today's date. If today is December 5, 1998 and the date entered is 11/15/98 (in mm/dd/yy format), the result will be 11/15/1998. The dates of 12/5/98 and 1/1/98 will respectively result as 12/5/1898 and 1/1/1898, since the dates are assigned the closest past date.
- **R**—Present century: This is the same as the default behavior of prepending a two digit year with the first two digits of the current year.

It is strongly recommended that you display four digit years on your data entry screens to make certain that the year has defaulted the way the user expected. There will be confusion and forgetfulness at the beginning of the year 2000 without adding to it unnecessarily. Your users will doubtless appreciate this later!

DBDATE

This environment variable allows you to specify the default date format you wish to use. You may adjust the order of the day, month, and year. You may use either a two-digit or a four-digit year. You may choose the separator used to separate parts of the date ("/", "-", ".", or none). The default format is "mm/dd/yyyy".

DBDATE values are specified by using an "M" to represent the month (1–12), a "D" to represent the day (1–31), "Y2" or "Y4" to represent a two-digit or a four-digit year, and any of the following as the last character in the string that will define the separator: "/", "-", ".", or "0" (zero) for no separator. Below are a few examples:

DBDATE *Value*	*Date Format*
MDY4/	mm/dd/yyyy
Y2MD0	yymmdd
DMY2-	dd-mm-yy
MDY4.	mm.dd.yyyy

DBDELIMITER

This environment variable specifies the character to be used as a column delimiter when loading and unloading data files using the `load` and `unload` statements. The default delimiter is "|" (a pipe).

DBEDIT

This environment variable specifies the default text editor used with Informix products. The default value (for most systems) is `vi`.

DBFORMAT

This environment variable allows you to specify the format of the following data types: *decimal, float, integer, money, smallfloat* and *smallint*. The format is specified as follows:

```
'<leading symbol>:<thousands separator>:
        <decimal separator>:<trailing symbol>'
```

The leading and trailing symbols represent currency symbols. The leading currency symbol default is "$". There is no default for the trailing currency symbol. These values are optional and can be from one to seven characters.

The default thousands separator is optional and may be set to anything except: digits, "<", ">", "|", ":", "?", "!", "=", "[", or "]". The thousands separator is not displayed unless specified by a format attribute or the `using` operator, but it can be entered into a screen by the user without causing problems. If the thousands separator is a "*" or no separator means no separators are used.

The decimal separator must be entered. The traditional value for this is a ".", but it may be set to any value except: digits, "<", ">", "|", ":", "?", "!", "=", "[", "]", or "*".

All three colons must be specified and the quotes are recommended to avoid misinterpretation of special characters. Some examples follow:

DBFORMAT *Value*	*Number*	*Result*
`'$:,:.:'`	`1000.00`	`$1,000.00`
`':,:.:AU'`	`1000.00`	`1,000.00AU`
`'CAN$:.:.:'`	`1000.00`	`CAN$1.000.00`
`'#:.:,:***'`	`1000.00`	`#1,000.00***`

Note that currency symbols are only printed for values defined as money data types.

If both `DBFORMAT` and `DBMONEY` are set, `DBFORMAT` will be used for money types (except for the string returned by the `construct` statement in 4GL where the decimal separator is specified by `DBMONEY`, and otherwise is defaulted to ".", and no other currency or separator symbols are used).

DBLANG

This environment variable allows you to specify a message directory other than `$INFORMIXDIR/msg` as the directory containing compiled message files. This is described for Informix engines prior to 7.2. For engines 7.2 and up, you should refer to to GLS (Global Language Support) documentation as this becomes more complicated.

For Informix engines prior to 7.2, if you need messages from your program to be printed in another language, say French, then you could do the following:

1. Create a new directory under `$INFORMIXDIR`, perhaps `msg.french`. The UNIX file permissions for this directory will need to be set to 755 with the user and group set to `informix`. The following is an example of the UNIX commands which can help you to do this:

```
cd $INFORMIXDIR
mkdir msg.french
chmod 755 msg.french
chown informix msg.french
chgrp informix msg.french
```

2. Copy the files ending in `.msg` and `.iem` from `$INFORMIXDIR/msg` to `$INFORMIXDIR/msg.french`. The permissions on the files should be 644 with the user and group set

to `informix`. The files ending in `.msg` are the files containing the original text of the messages and the `.iem` files are the compiled message files.

3. Edit the `.msg` file(s) you wish to change. You may change the text in the messages, but do not change the lines beginning with a "`.`" (period). A period at the beginning of a line followed by a number represents the message number Informix products will need to refer to, to read each message. As an example, here is part of an Informix message file:

```
.-1301
This value is not among the valid possibilities
.-1302
The two entries were not the same — please try
    again
.-1303
You cannot use this editing feature because a
    picture exists
```

4. When you have finished editing the `.msg` file, compile it from the command line as follows:

```
mkmessage <message file>.msg <message file>.iem
```

The `mkmessage` utility comes with INFORMIX-4GL.

5. Set `DBLANG` to the name of the new message directory which is under `$INFORMIXDIR` (do not include `$INFORMIXDIR` in the path). For example, the directory we created above would be assigned to `DBLANG` simply as `msg.french`.

Now, when you run your program with the `DBLANG` environment variable set, you will see the messages you edited instead of the original Informix versions.

DBMONEY

This environment variable allows you to specify the format values for the *money* data type. The format is specified as follows:

```
<leading symbol><decimal separator><trailing symbol>
```

The leading and trailing symbols represent currency symbols. The leading currency symbol default is "$". There is no default for the trailing currency symbol. These values are both optional and can be from one to seven characters in length, but may not include " . " (period) or " , " (comma).

The decimal separator is optional and may be either a " . " or a " , ".

The default value for DBMONEY is: $.

DBPATH

This environment variable specifies a database path (similar to the UNIX environment variable PATH) that contains directories to search for forms, executable programs and other files, that might be used by your database system running either INFORMIX-SE or INFORMIX-OnLine. For INFORMIX-SE, this would also include the directory where your databases are stored. The current directory will be searched for relevant files in addition to any directories in your DBPATH (these will be searched in order, from left to right). Use a " : " to separate directory names as done with the UNIX PATH environment variable.

DBPRINT

This environment variable specifies the default printer (or print command) that will be used by Informix products. The default will usually be the same as for the operating system, lp or lpr.

DBREMOTECMD (INFORMIX-OnLine Only)

You may need to override the default value of the remote shell for use with the remote tape facility for INFORMIX-OnLine. This value can be a full pathname or a command already found in your path.

DBTEMP

This environment variable specifies which directory you want temporary files written to. The default is /tmp.

NOSORTINDEX

Starting with version 5.0 of the Informix engine, when creating
an index for a table with more than 30 pages or more than 500
rows, the data for the indexes is read and sorted prior to its insertion into the index. This can greatly speed the process of creating
the index. If you don't wish to use this option, indexes can still be
created the same way as they were prior to 5.0 simply by setting
this environment variable. The variable does not need to be
assigned a value, it simply needs to exist in your environment.

OPTCOMPIND (INFORMIX-OnLine 6.0 and above only)

This environment variable helps the query optimizer to deter-
mine how joins should be performed. A value is set for the entire
INFORMIX-OnLine instance by the OPTCOMPIND variable in your
ONCONFIG file ($INFORMIXDIR/etc/$ONCONFIG). Setting the
OPTCOMPIND environment variable will override the value set for
the instance. This allows you to try out different values to see how
they will affect your applications.
  OPTCOMPIND may be set to the following values:

- **0**—Compatible with pre-6.0 Informix engines.
- **1**—Same as 0 if you are using an isolation mode of repeatable
  read, otherwise, same as 2. This setting is recommended in
  order to avoid creating excessive locks. Repeatable read can
  cause excessive locks with the sort-merge and hash joins used
  by the 6.0 and above Informix engines.
- **2**—Selects appropriate join method based on costs.

PDQPRIORITY (INFORMIX-OnLine 6.0 and above only)

This environment variable allows you to determine how much of
the INFORMIX-OnLine resources to use for Parallel Database
Queries (PDQ). It may be set to the following values:

- **0**—PDQ turned off.
- **1**—Parallel scans only.

- **2** through **100**—Percentage of resources the PDQ query can use (up to the limit set in the ONCONFIG file ($INFORMIXDIR/etc/$ONCONFIG) by the `MAX_PDQPRIORITY` variable.)

Note: This value may be overridden from within the application by using the `set pdqpriority` statement.

SQLEXEC

This environment variable needs to be set if you are running both INFORMIX-SE and INFORMIX-OnLine engines on your computer and you want to access INFORMIX-SE. To access INFORMIX-SE, `SQLEXEC` should be set to the value

    $INFORMIXDIR/lib/sqlexec.

To access INFORMIX-OnLine, either unset `SQLEXEC`, or set it to

    $INFORMIXDIR/lib/sqlturbo.

You will also need to use SQLEXEC if you are planning to use the relay module to use tools compatible with 5.x Informix engines with 7.x Informix engines. You should avoid using the relay module if at all possible as is quite slow. You will have much better success when converting to the 7.x Informix engine if you use tools designed specifically for that level of engine. If you must use the relay module, see your *INFORMIX-OnLine Dynamic Server Administrator's Guide* for more information.

Using DB-Access

To enter DB-Access, simply type `dbaccess` at the operating system prompt.

    -> dbaccess

This will bring up a ring menu with the main DB-Access menu items.

If you experience problems at this point, make sure you have the appropriate environment variables set. These were discussed in the previous section. If you are using INFORMIX-OnLine, make certain that your INFORMIX-OnLine system has been created and that it is online.

Figure 2-1 indicates the options available to you in DB-Access and their menu structure. As a general overview, Query-Language allows you to enter and run Informix's SQL statements. Database gives you an easy way of creating, selecting, and deleting databases. Table gives you an easy way of creating, viewing, and deleting tables. Exit from the main menu allows you to leave DB-Access. Exit from other levels takes you back to the previous menu level.

The SQL statements described in the following chapters can be entered and run under the Query-Language option. Options under Query-Language, such as Choose and Save, allow you to manipulate SQL command files. SQL command files are files that contain SQL statement(s). Multiple SQL statements need to be separated by semicolons (" ; ").

Be very careful about typing ahead and not paying attention when you are working in DB-Access. A slip of a finger and a couple of bad keystrokes and you could accidentally delete a table or an entire database. While all Drop options will give you a No or Yes option (not shown in Figure 2-1), this makes mistakes

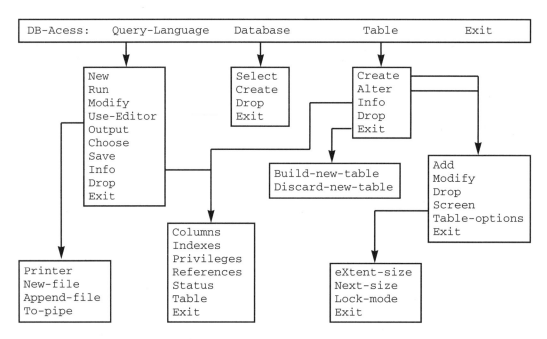

Figure 2-1 *Menu structure of DB-Access.*

unlikely, but not impossible. Likewise, be careful if you should dial into your system on a noisy phone line. Noise can be responsible for accidentally chosen options!

You may be asked to choose which database or table you want to work with before going to the next menu. These items can be chosen with arrow keys or typed from the keyboard.

The Table-options option and submenu exist for INFORMIX-OnLine only. If you are working with INFORMIX-OnLine, you will probably want to work under the Query-Language menu rather than directly under Database or Table—at least when you start working on your production system. Informix's SQL statements give you control over where in your INFORMIX-OnLine system databases and tables are stored, which will become very important to you later. Additionally, there is table information that you will want to keep track of that is not easily retrievable by INFORMIX-OnLine version 5.01 (and earlier).

DB-Access Options with Ring Menus

Several of the options listed below will take you to various menus within DB-Access. When you exit that menu level, you exit DB-Access.

dbaccess	calls DB-Access and invokes the main menu
dbaccess -ansi	calls DB-Access and invokes the main menu. Any non-ANSI-compliant syntax will produce warning messages for the user. This switch can be used in conjunction with any of the other DB-Access switches.
dbaccess **<database name>**	calls DB-Access with a specific database and invokes the main menu
dbaccess -d	calls DB-Access and goes directly to the database submenu
dbaccess **<database name> -q**	calls DB-Access with a specific database and goes directly to the Query-Language submenu

```
dbaccess
   <database name> -t    calls DB-Access with a specific data-
                         base and goes directly to the table
                         menu
```

In addition to these switches, you can also specify two flags
when calling DB-Access. The first flag would be either "d" for
database, "q" for query-language, or "t" for table as described
above. After selecting one of these, take the first initial of the
option on the submenu which you wish to use, and add it. The
only options that will not work for this are Run and Output under
Query-Language. For example:

```
dbaccess toymaker -qi
```

will choose the database toymaker, then place you into the Info
menu under the Query-Language option which allows you to
lookup information about the tables in the toymaker database.
When you exit the Info menu, you exit DB-Access.

Actually, some of these options are fairly useless since you exit
immediately after executing the indicated option. For instance:

```
dbaccess toymaker -qn
```

will allow you to type in a new statement, but it doesn't allow
you to run it or save it. You can, however, add a run option, -r,
that would allow you to type in an sql statement and then run it
before exiting:

```
dbaccess toymaker -qnr
```

Getting Around in Informix Ring Menus

Informix ring menus are fairly intuitive, but they are described
here for those unfamiliar with this type of environment.

The current option is always shown in reverse video.
Underneath the current option, a brief display gives a description
of what will happen if you choose the current option.

There are two ways of making a selection from an Informix
ring menu. You can use your arrow keys to move to an option
and display it in reverse video, then press *return*, or you can

simply type the first letter (or sometimes the capitalized letter) of the option you want.

If a menu is too wide to fit in the current window, three dots at the far right of the menu indicate that there are more options available in the menu. You can use your right arrow key to move past the dots and view the options. If the menu is really wide, you may see three dots at the left and right sides of the menu indicating there are more options in both directions. Your left and right arrow keys will allow you to view all options on the menu. If your cursor is on the first menu option and you press the left arrow key, the next menu option you will be on is the last menu option. This is how ring menus got their name, because of their circular structure.

Choosing Options from a List

A list is slightly different than a menu. A list is made up of items that you, the user, have defined, such as table names, database names, and command file names.

When selecting an option from a list, a list of options will be presented on the screen below the current menu line. Your arrow keys will move you from option to option (the current option will be displayed in reverse video), or you can just type the entry in from your keyboard (it will display at the top of the screen). After you have selected an option (by typing or by using your arrow keys), press *return* to enter your selection.

Working From the Command Line

DB-Access, when called with extra options from the command line, will allow you to work from the UNIX command line instead of from the ring menu.

Avoiding the menu driven structure of DB-Access by working from the command line can be very important for some applications. This section discusses the options available to you while working from the command line. When working with DB-Access in this mode, you will probably be running in background, so remember to specify standard output and error files just as you would with any other commands you run in background from UNIX.

```
dbaccess -{v|V}
```

Either of these options prints the version number of DB-Access and your serial number.

Example: dbaccess -v

```
dbaccess [-e] [-ansi] {<database name> | -}
                                    <command file>
```

This option allows you to run the specified command file from the command line.

-e	The -e switch echoes the output from the command file as the statements are being executed. Without using this switch, you could not easily tell how much of your command file has already executed.
-ansi	The -ansi switch gives the user warnings when extensions to ANSI SQL are used. If specifying standard output and standard error files, any warnings will print to the error file.
<database name>, -	If the name of the database is not specified on the command line, the "-" on the command line indicates that the database is specified in the command file.
<command file>	The command file contains Informix's SQL statement(s) that are to be run. All command file names end in .sql. The .sql extension does not need to be specified when running the command from the command line.

Some examples of this command are:

```
dbaccess -e toymaker toy_add.sql
dbaccess -e ansi - fix_db
dbaccess -e - toy_stores
```

Viewing Error Messages

If you get an error message while working with Informix products, note the error number of the message. Then, at the operating system prompt, type:

```
finderr <error number>
```

This command will display a detailed error message. Informix error numbers are negative numbers, but you may enter either a positive or negative error number and Informix will interpret it for you. If you should receive a positive error number, this is most likely an operating system error, in which case you will need to check your operating system manuals for the source of the error.

This feature can end up saving you quite a bit of time compared to looking up the error messages in manuals.

Summary

Informix's SQL is the language used to communicate with the Informix database engine. Informix has made additions and extensions to ANSI-compliant SQL to give Informix's SQL more features and flexibility than ANSI-compliant SQL.

DB-Access is a program that allows you to run SQL statements and to easily create, change, and delete databases and tables.

Before you can start using any Informix products, you will need to define your operating system environment. Environment variables you should look at before trying to run Informix products are:

```
INFORMIXDIR
PATH
INFORMIXTERM,
TERMCAP or TERMINFO,
TERM
INFORMIXSERVER (INFORMIX-OnLine only)
ONCONFIG or TBCONFIG (INFORMIX-OnLine only)
```

Many other environment variables exist that can be used optionally to change Informix defaults.

To enter the DB-Access ring menu, simply type dbaccess at the operating system prompt.

DB-Access options with ring menus are as follows:

dbaccess -ansi	warn user when using non-ANSI-compliant SQL
dbaccess *<database name>*	invoke DB-Access with specified database
dbaccess -d	invoke DB-Access in database submenu
dbaccess *<database name>* **-q**	invoke DB-Access with database in query submenu
dbaccess *<database name>* **-t**	invoke DB-Access with database in table submenu

You can also specify a second flag where the first flag is d, t, or q as described above. Use the first initial of the option on the submenu you wish to use for the second flag.

DB-Access options for working with the command line only are:

dbaccess -{v|V}	get DB-Access version number and serial number

Or to run SQL command files from the command line:

```
dbaccess [-e] [-ansi] {<database name> | - }
    <command file>
```

To display a detailed error message, type the following from the operating system command line:

```
finderr <error number>
```

Chapter

3

Creating the
Database

- *The database administrator*
- *Informix Database Engines*
- *Database statements*
- *Data types*
- *Summary of data type conversions*
- *Tables*
- *Privileges*
- *Indexes*
- *Creating the sample database*
- *Viewing the database*
- *Summary*

The Database Administrator

If you are working with an existing database system, you may already have a database administrator. If so, it is a good idea to know who this is. If you do not have a database administrator already, one of the first things you should do when creating a database system is to appoint a database administrator. Your database administrator may be one person or a group of people. The database administrator is generally responsible for making adjustments to the database: adding, changing, and deleting databases, tables, columns, and indexes, and for other issues involving maintenance of the database system.

tip

It is a good idea to create a separate login for the database administrator. Whenever you add, change, or delete databases, tables, columns, indexes, or privileges, you should do so as this user. If the account name you choose is dba, then dba will be the owner of the database and all of the structures that make up the database. This can prevent situations where your database administrator quits and you must keep his or her personal account online because he or she is the owner of all the databases and tables. You can always recreate your database under a different owner name, but that's not something you would want to do often.

A single database administration account can also be useful if there are several people who act as database administrators. The database may be owned by one person, and the tables in it may belong to any number of people who are acting as database administrators. Using a single account for these activities will keep all databases and tables under a single owner. Having a single account also makes future database changes easier and maintains a more consistent database system.

Using a single database administration account makes it more difficult to accidentally delete a database (or perform any of other countless disaster scenarios). If only one account is used for database administration, and it is used only for database administration, a user logged onto his or her own account would not be able to delete a table or a database. The user would need to be logged on as the database administrator to make this kind of mistake.

Another advantage of a separate database administration account is that when your personal account does not have special privileges by virtue of database or table ownership, you will quickly find out when you have failed to grant necessary database and table privileges to users.

Informix Database Engines

Informix has historically had two database engine technologies: INFORMIX-SE and INFORMIX-OnLine.

INFORMIX-SE is very useful for creating databases that require a minimum of administration, are not required to be available 100 percent of the time (eg. during database backups), and do not need the additional performance that INFORMIX-OnLine provides.

INFORMIX-OnLine does require more database administration than INFORMIX-SE, but it allows you more control over your database environment. INFORMIX-OnLine acts, in many ways, as the operating system, allowing more control of the database environment.

Some SQL statements contain slightly different syntax for INFORMIX-SE and for INFORMIX-OnLine. The syntax differences usually reflect INFORMIX-OnLine data storage options and data retrieval options. There are also some statements which can only be issued when using either INFORMIX-SE or INFORMIX-OnLine.

Today, the Informix database engine product line is continuing to expand at a rapid pace. INFORMIX-XPS and INFORMIX-US or Universal Server products are leading edge products built on top of the INFORMIX-OnLine DSA product. (DSA refers to versions 6.x and 7.x of INFORMIX-OnLine. DSA was a complete rewrite of the INFORMIX-OnLine 5.x engine and is quite different and much improved.) The INFORMIX-SE product looks like it is slated for eventual replacement by the new INFORMIX-WGS or Work Group Server product.

INFORMIX-XPS is generally used for data warehousing applications where it is necessary to work with very large amounts of data. INFORMIX-XPS leaves out some DSA features while adding in a new set of features and algorithms suitable for working on extremely large datasets.

INFORMIX-US or Universal Server allows you to use an infinite number of data types or objects by using data blades.

Database Administration Topic	Description
Performance	INFORMIX-OnLine can be much faster than the same database and application running on the same platform using INFORMIX-SE. How much faster will vary depending on the size of your database and on your application.
Backups	INFORMIX-OnLine allows backups to be performed while your database system is up and running. The database may not be used for the duration of the backup under INFORMIX-SE.
Recovery	Both INFORMIX-SE and INFORMIX-OnLine provide transaction logging facilities, which, along with the database backups, allow you to recover from a database problem. While both systems work, INFORMIX-OnLine implements the backup, logging, and recovery features differently, making INFORMIX-OnLine disaster recovery more reliable.
Maintenance	INFORMIX-OnLine has more capabilities than INFORMIX-SE, but the time required and the complexity involved in creating and maintaining a database system is greater with INFORMIX-OnLine. INFORMIX-OnLine has many parameters that allow you to tune the engine to optimize performance, but taking advantage of these features requires time. INFORMIX-SE is easy to set up and use and does not require an in-depth knowledge of the inner workings of the Informix database engines.
Features	INFORMIX-OnLine has several features that INFORMIX-SE does not. INFORMIX-OnLine allows you to store and manipulate BLOBs (Binary Large Objects), which can include long text documents, spreadsheets, word processing files, and images. INFORMIX-OnLine also allows you to use variable-length character strings (varchars). While there are trade-offs when using varchars, this technology can end up saving you disk space. Several other INFORMIX-OnLine features exist as well and are discussed throughout this book.

INFORMIX-Universal Server was written by incorporating the Informix DSA technology (for performance and connectivity) with what was the world's leading object database, Illustra. This object database technology promises to be the wave of the future and will eventually incorporate all of the best elements of the XPS product as well.

INFORMIX-WGS or Work Group Server is designed to be an easy to understand, use and maintain version of INFORMIX-OnLine. Once this product has matured, it will probably replace the INFORMIX-SE engine which will allow the two basic classes of database products to stay more closely aligned instead of diverging into completely separate products.

Database Statements

The database statements described in this section are generally only used by the database administrator.

To create a database, you must first decide on a database name. The database name is typically a description of the set of data that will be stored in the database.

The basic form of the statement used to create a database is:

```
create database <database name>
```

The database name must begin with a letter and may contain letters, numbers, and underscores. The database name may be up to ten characters long.

In our case, to create the toymaker database, we would simply type:

```
create database toymaker
```

There are additional optional extensions for this statement depending on whether you are using INFORMIX-SE or INFORMIX-OnLine.

The syntax for INFORMIX-SE is:

```
create database <database name>
  [ with log in "<pathname>"[ mode ansi ] ]
```

The syntax for INFORMIX-OnLine is:

```
create database <database name>
    [ in <dbspace> ]
    [ with { [ buffered ] log | log mode ansi } ]
```

The term `log` refers to transaction logging, which is discussed in Chapter 4. You will need to determine if you will be using an ANSI-compliant database or not. A mode ANSI database uses transaction logging with implicit transactions as opposed to the explicit transaction logging used in non-ANSI databases (see Chapter 4). Mode ANSI will also force you to specify the owner names of tables, indexes, views and other Informix objects whenever they are used. So if the user `dba` creates a table called `toys`, the table would need to be referred to as "dba".`toys` instead of simply as `toys`.

If you are using INFORMIX-OnLine, this is a good place to determine where you want your database to reside. If you don't specify a `dbspace`, *the database by default will reside in the root dbspace, and unless you're creating a temporary database, this is not a good idea. The root dbspace should be saved for INFORMIX-OnLine administrative information and for temporary space needed by the database system.*

Given that we can now create databases, the following statement will delete, destroy, and permanently remove databases:

```
drop database <database-name>
```

The `drop database` statement is not one you will want to execute on a regular basis. Do this only if you really want the entire database to disappear. Be very careful with this statement! Once this statement has been run, there is no way to undo it. Nobody can be using the database when it is dropped.

The `database` statement gives you a way of specifying that you want the indicated database to be opened as the current database. This is useful if you are working with several databases.

```
database <database-name> [ exclusive ]
```

The keyword `exclusive` will allow only the user process that issued the statement to access the database. The database may only be opened in `exclusive` mode when no other users are already accessing the database. When a database is opened in `exclusive` mode, it must be closed before it can be opened again.

To close a database, use the statement:

```
close database
```

The `close database` statement closes the current database. Once the database is closed, it cannot be accessed until it is reopened or started.

The `start database` statement is used only by INFORMIX-SE. It allows you to start a new transaction logging file or to start transaction logging on a database that previously did not have transaction logging. Transaction logging is discussed in Chapter 4.

```
start database <database name>
   [ with log in "<pathname>" | with no log ]
   [ mode ansi ]
```

Data Types

Now we are ready to create tables, but we can't create them until we know what data types are available for use in assigning data types to columns. Chapter 8 includes additional information about data types. There are data types that are available in INFORMIX-4GL (see Chapter 8) that are not available in Informix's SQL.

Take time to review these data types, then go through the columns in your tables and decide which data types (including the length and precision where applicable) should be assigned to each column.

Character and String Data Types

`char (<length of string>)`
A single character or a string of characters from one to more than 32,000 characters in length (32,511 for INFORMIX-SE and 32,767 for INFORMIX-OnLine). The default string length is one character.

`character (<length of string>)`
Same as `char`.

Numeric Data Types

`dec (<precision> [, <scale>] )`
Same as `decimal`.

`decimal (<precision> [, <scale>] )`
The `decimal` data type allows you to specify a *precision* of up to 32 digits. The *precision* is the total number of digits allotted for the decimal number. The number in *scale* is the number of digits that are to the right of the decimal point. The *scale* must be less than or equal to the *precision*. The default *precision* is 16. If no *scale* is entered, the number is treated as a floating decimal when performing arithmetic, as opposed to a fixed decimal.

`double precision (<precision>)`
Same as `float`.

`float (<float precision>)`
The `float` data type typically stores 14 to 15 significant digits of a double-precision floating-point number (the actual number is machine dependent). The double data type in C is equivalent to `float`, so the range of numbers valid for the `float` data type is the same as the range of numbers valid for the C double data type on your computer. The number retrieved from a `smallfloat` may vary slightly from the number inserted into a `smallfloat` column, since only the most significant digits are stored.

`int`
Same as `integer`.

integer

The integer data type can store whole numbers ranging from -2,147,483,647 to 2,147,483,647.

money (<precision> [, <scale>])

The money data type defines *precision* and *scale* in the same way as the decimal data type and allows the same range of values. There are two differences between the money and decimal data types. The default *precision* is 16 and the default *scale* is 2 (money (16,2)). Also, money data types print a leading "$" (or a user defined currency symbol) by default when displayed or printed. (You can specify the currency symbol you wish to use by using the DBMONEY environment variable found in Chapter 2.)

nchar (Informix engines 6.0 and above)

Same as char, except that it is sorted in NLS order instead of in ASCII sequence. It supports 8-bit ASCII character sets, but does not support multi-byte character sets such as those required by Chinese. (GLS [Global Language Support] is available starting in Informix 7.2 and up engines.)

numeric (<precision> [, <scale>])

Same as decimal.

real

Same as smallfloat.

serial (<starting number>)

A serial number may contain the same values as an integer. Serial numbers can be automatically inserted into the database as the largest number in the column plus one. If the current highest number in a serial column is 313, the next serial number assigned would be 314. You have the option of specifying the *starting number* for a serial column; if none is specified the default is 1. You can also explicitly insert specific numbers (including negative numbers) into a serial column. You may only have one column in a table with a serial data type. Serial numbers cannot be changed after they have been inserted into the database (except by deleting the row and reinserting it). You will probably want to assign a unique index to your serial column since using the serial data type does not insure uniqueness. You may alter the *starting number* at any time using the `alter table` statement, however this may or may not have an effect depending on whether the new value is greater than the maximum value already inserted.

smallfloat

The `smallfloat` data type typically stores 6 to 7 significant digits of a single-precision floating-point number (the actual number is machine dependent). The `float` data type in C is equivalent to `smallfloat`, so the range of numbers valid for the `smallfloat` data type is the same as the range of numbers valid for the C `float` data type on your computer. The number retrieved from a `smallfloat` may vary slightly from the number inserted into a `smallfloat` column, since only the most significant digits are stored.

smallint

The `smallint` data type can store whole numbers ranging from -32,767 to 32,767.

Date, Time, and Interval Data Types

date

A `date` is simply a calendar date with the default format of `mm/dd/yyyy`, where `mm` represents the month (1–12), `dd` represents the day of the month (1–31), and `yyyy` represents the four-digit year (0001–9999). If only two digits of the year are inserted, you need to refer to the documentation of the DBCENTURY environment variable in Chapter 2 to determine how the date will be interpreted (eg. 12/5/98 could end up being in 1898, 1998 or 2098). You can change the default date format by using the DBDATE environment variable also described in Chapter 2.

datetime *<largest datetime value>*
to *<smallest datetime value>* [(*<fraction precision>*)]

The `datetime` data type allows you to specify a date and time with as much or as little accuracy as you like. A list of `datetime` values appears on page 58, ordered from the largest value (year) to the smallest value (fractions of a second). The *smallest datetime value* must be equal to or less than the *largest datetime value*. The datetime variable will include the *largest* and *smallest datetime values* and all of the values in between.

Datetime Values

Datetime Value	Smallest Valid Number	Largest Valid Number	Description
year	1	9999	year, A.D.
month	1	12	month
day	1	31	day of month
hour	0	23	hour on a 24-hour clock
minute	0	59	minute in hour
second	0	59	second in minute
fraction	0	99999	fractions of a second

The format of the datetime data type must be exact:

```
yyyy-mm-dd hh:mm:ss.fff
```

It is important not to rearrange the hyphens, the space, colons, or the period when entering a datetime variable. If you are only using a part of the datetime field, you only need to specify the parts you are using. For instance, datetime month to second would be: mm-dd hh:mm:ss.

```
interval <largest datetime value> [ (<precision>) ]
      to <smallest datetime value> [ (<precision>) ]
```

An interval specifies a period of time. The periods of time that may be used as the datetime values in the definition of your interval time period are listed below in order of magnitude from the largest (year) to the smallest (fraction of a second).

There are two different classes of intervals: *Year-Month* which may include only year and month, and *Day-Time*, which may include day through fraction intervals. An interval cannot include items from both classes. The *smallest datetime value* specified must be the same or smaller than the *largest datetime value* specified. The interval will contain both the *largest* and the *smallest datetime values* and all of the datetime values in between.

The Intervals chart gives the interval class, the default number of digits of precision, and the maximum number of digits of precision allowed for each datetime value.

Intervals

Interval Class	Datetime Value	Default Precision	Maximum Precision
Year-Month	year	4	9
Year-Month	month	2	9
Day-Time	day	2	9
Day-Time	hour	2	9
Day-Time	minute	2	9
Day-Time	second	2	9
Day-Time	fraction	2	5

For example, if you want to specify a period of 2000 minutes, you would need to specify a precision of:

```
interval minute (4) to minute
```

If the *smallest datetime value* is not used to specify the `interval`, it is considered to be the same as the *largest datetime value*.

Extra Data Types for INFORMIX-OnLine

The following three data types are available in INFORMIX-OnLine only: `byte`, `text`, and `varchar`. These three data types are discussed individually below, but since both `byte` and `text` data types are stored as BLOBs, let's take a minute to discuss these.

BLOB is the acronym used for Binary Large Objects. Basically what BLOBs do is allow you to store large amounts of `text` or `byte` data associated with rows of data. For instance, if you were storing an image of a photograph on each row of your table, you would store it as a BLOB. The BLOB is actually stored separately from the other data stored in your row. Information about the BLOB and where to find it is stored in the row of data.

BLOBs are manipulated differently from other data types. Not all database functionality applies when working with BLOBs.

While the size of a text BLOB has a theoretical size limit of 2^{31} bytes, actually you are limited to the amount of disk space you have available.

Note that starting with the INFORMIX-Universal Server product, an infinite number of data types from simple to very complex are available. The conversion to data blades should be a simple process, and allow you infinitely more flexibility in dealing with these objects.

`byte [ in { table | <blobspace name> } ]`
The `byte` BLOB can be used for storing large strings of binary data that cannot be stored in a `text` BLOB.

`text [ in { table | <blobspace name> } ]`
The `text` BLOB can be used for storing large strings of printable ASCII characters (including tabs (Control-i), newlines (Control-j), and page breaks (Control-l)).

`varchar (<maximum length> [, <reserve length>] )`
A `varchar` data type is a variable length character string of up to 255 characters (or 254 if the column is indexed). You must specify the *maximum length* of the `varchar` column.

The *reserve length* specifies that each `varchar` in the column should have a minimum amount of space reserved for it. This will make it easier later if your rows grow in size. Without this reserve space, the rows would need to be physically moved to a new location on the disk. The *reserve length* must be equal to or less than *the maximum length* of the `varchar`. The *reserve length* does not need to be specified; its default is 0.

Don't decide to use a `varchar` just because you think you can save space. Consider the following information about `varchar` data types:

- If a `varchar` becomes longer than the reserve space, the row containing the `varchar` needs to be physically moved to a new location on the disk. The old location then contains a storage gap which may be used later by another row of data.
- If a `varchar` becomes shorter, the additional space it contained is wasted—unless another row can later be fit into the freed space.
- If a `varchar` doesn't have the reserve length number of characters in it, the additional reserve space is wasted.

note

If your space savings by using varchar data types looks to be significant, go ahead and use them. It is important, however, to understand how they work, so that you won't experience difficulties later on. One example of a good place to use a varchar data type is for a notes column where most notes are only a few characters in length, but a small number of the notes are much longer.

nvarchar (Informix engines 6.0 and above)
Same as `varchar`, except that it is sorted in an NLS order instead of in ASCII sequence. It supports 8-bit ASCII character sets, but does not support multi-byte character sets such as those required by Chinese. (GLS [Global Language Support] is available starting in Informix 7.2 and up engines.)

Summary of Data Type Conversions

This section contains a brief summary of data type conversions. For more details, including examples, see Chapter 8.

Informix's SQL will attempt to convert between data types as long as the conversion makes sense to Informix. We will have additional flexibility in data type conversions when we start using INFORMIX-4GL.

For the most part, numbers will convert to other numeric data types. There will be cases where you will lose information (for instance, in converting 67.89 to an integer, Informix will round the number to 68). You will get an error if you try to assign numbers with more significant digits to data types that can't handle them (for instance, 50,000 assigned to a `smallint` won't work).

Numbers can be assigned to character strings, and character strings containing valid numbers (numeric characters only) can be assigned to numeric data types.

`Date` and `datetime` data types can be converted into `character` strings, and `character` strings with precisely the right format can be converted to `date` or `datetime` data types.

Some SQL functions described later will make it possible to convert from `date` to `datetime` values and from `datetime` to `date` values. As always, when dealing with values of different precisions, there is a potential for losing information. Also, remember that while `date` and `datetime` may seem very similar to us, they are handled very differently by Informix products.

Tables

Now that we have a database and we know about data types, we need to learn how to create and manipulate tables within the database. This section is divided into the following topics:

- Creating a new table
- Changing an existing table
- Deleting a table
- Renaming tables and columns

Creating a New Table

The syntax for creating a table can may seem very complicated if we try to tackle the whole thing at once, so we are going to divide the `create table` statement into several parts:

- Basic `create table` statement—no frills
- Defaults
- Constraints and referential integrity
- INFORMIX-SE options
- INFORMIX-OnLine options
- Temporary tables

Basic `create table` statement—no frills

The syntax used to create a basic database table is listed below.

```
create table <table name>
  ( <column name> <data type> [ not null ] [, ...]
  )
```

The expression `not null` tells Informix's SQL not to admit any null (or empty) values into the indicated column. An example of the `create table` statement is:

```
create table toy_order
    ( order_number         serial              not null,
      store_number         integer             not null,
      order_date           date                not null,
      shipping_datetime    datetime year to minute,
      sales_code           smallint            not null
    )
```

As you can see, four of the five columns will not accept a null value. Order numbers will be assigned sequentially using the serial data type. We have limited our sales_code to 32,767 values (unless we use negative numbers). This means that we will encounter an error if we have more than this number of sales persons. And finally, order_date and shipping_datetime are defined so that we can experiment with date and datetime columns.

Defaults

You can assign a default value to any column when you create a table. If no other value is assigned, the default will then be assigned to the column when the row is inserted into the database. The default designation will go between the data type and the not null designations in the create table statement.

```
default { <data type value> |
          current <datetime qualifier> |
          dbservername |
          sitename |
          today |
          user
        }
```

The *data type value* is a numeric value, a quoted character string containing the proper format, or null. BLOBs may only be defaulted to null.

The rest of the values indicated in the syntax are functions that return values as shown in the following chart.

Function	Description
current	Returns the current `datetime` to the indicated precision (year, month, day, hour, minute, second, fraction); the default is `current year to fraction (3)`.
dbservername	Used in INFORMIX-OnLine only, returns the database server name to a `char` or `varchar` of at least 18 characters in length.
sitename	Same as `dbservername`.
today	Returns today's date.
user	Returns the user's login name to a char at least eight characters in length.

Functions returning system date and time get their values from your computer's internal date and time settings.

As an example, let's assign default values to the toy_order table from the previous example:

```
create table toy_order
    ( order_number       serial                 not null,
      store_number       integer default 1      not null,
      order_date         date default today     not null,
      shipping_datetime  datetime year to minute
                         default "1997-07-01 15:00",
      sales_code         smallint               not null
    )
```

In this example, the store_number is defaulted to one, the order_date to the current date, and the shipping_datetime to July 1, 1997 at 3:00 P.M.. Instead of an actual date for the shipping date and time, we could also have specified the default to be `current year to minute`.

Constraints and referential integrity

Constraints allow us to assign characterisics, value checking, and *referential integrity* to columns and tables. Referential integrity constraints allow you to define relationships between tables so that you cannot inappropriately add, change, or delete items in one table that are dependent on another table. There are five basic types of constraints: not null, unique, primary key, foreign key, and check. Each of these constraints is an optional part of the create table syntax. The create table syntax for each type of constraint is below. The syntax varies slightly for columns and for tables, so these are shown separately.

The constraint syntax for columns is:

```
not null [ constraint ( <constraint name> ) ]

unique [ constraint ( <constraint name> ) ]

primary key [ constraint ( <constraint name> ) ]

references <table name> [ ( <column name> ) ]
    [ on delete cascade ]
    [ constraint ( <constraint name> ) ]

check ( <condition> )
    [ constraint ( <constraint name> ) ]
```

A column constraint follows the optional not null portion of a column definition.

The constraint syntax for tables is:

```
not null ( <column name> [,...] )
    [ constraint ( <constraint name> ) ]

unique ( <column name> [, ...] )
    [ constraint ( <constraint name> ) ]

primary key ( <column name> [, ...] )
    [ constraint ( <constraint name> ) ]

foreign key ( <column name> [, ...] )
    references <table name>
    [ ( <column name> [, ...] ) ]
    [ on delete cascade ]
    [ constraint ( <constraint name> ) ]

check ( <condition> )
    [ constraint ( <constraint name> ) ]
```

A table constraint follows the column definitions but falls before the close parenthesis (") "), and is separated from the column names by a comma (" , ").

The not null constraint indicates that a column may not be null.

The unique constraint defines each value in a column or a set of columns as unique.

The primary key constraint implies the key is both not null and unique. The constraints primary key and unique cannot be used together when defining a column. A table can have only one primary key.

The foreign key or references constraint defines which table and column(s) contain the primary key constraint against which the foreign key is referenced. When inserting or updating values into a foreign key, the engine checks to make certain the indicated value(s) exist in the corresponding primary key. If the primary key does not contain the value in the foreign key, the foreign key insert or update statement will fail and return an error. Starting in version 7 of the Informix engine, you have the ability of performing cascading deletes as part of your referential integrity. This means that if a primary key is deleted, you can specify that the foreign key reference can cause the deletion of the foreign key rows as well.

The check constraint allows you to conditionally check the value in a column. A check on a column compares the value of that column to a constant expression. It can check a column against a constant expression or against values in other columns in the table. The conditional expression may not include functions, stored procedure calls, aggregates, or subqueries.

You can name any of your constraints, including not null *constraints starting in version 7 of the Informix engine. A user-defined constraint name may be useful at a later point when working with constraints. If you do not assign your constraint a name, the Informix engine will assign one for you.*

The constraints unique, primary key, *and* foreign key *all create indexes on the specified columns. If you are loading an initial set of data into your database, your data loads will be faster if the indexes for the table are created after the information has been loaded. You can then use the* alter table *statement to add constraints to the table.*

Note that while constraints can be very useful for helping to insure data integrity, they only produce an error after you have tried to insert or update a bad value into the database. You will very likely want to catch errors as users are entering the data onto the screen. You can always use validation at both the program level and at the database engine level to provide an additional level of protection.

Let's look at the toy_order and the toy_store tables, which now have some column constraints:

```
create table toy_order
  ( order_number        serial                  primary key,
    store_number        smallint                not null
                        references toy_store (store_number),
    order_date          date default today   not null,
    shipping_datetime   datetime year to minute,
    sales_code          smallint                not null
                        references toy_sales_staff (sales_code)
  )

create table toy_store
  ( store_number        integer
                        primary key constraint fred,
    store_name          char (30)
                        not null unique,
    buyer_last_name     char (25),
    buyer_first_name    char (15),
    phone_number        char (10)               not null,
    fax_number          char (10),
    store_street        char (25),
    store_city          char (25)
                        check (store_city <> "METROPOLIS")
                        constraint city,
    store_state         char (2) default "CO",
    store_zip_code      char (9)
  )
```

Order_number is now a primary key in the toy_order table, and store_number is a primary key in the toy_store table. Notice that we have named the primary key constraint in the toy_store table *fred,* and the `check` constraint for store_city was named *city.*

Store_number is a foreign key in the toy_order table and it references the primary key store_number in the toy_store table. Note that in the foreign key references in the toy_order table, we could have referred to the table name only and omitted the column name since the columns for the foreign keys have the same names as the primary key columns in the indicated tables. You may wish to to use the column name for the sake of clarity, but it is optional.

We have assigned the store_name column in the toy_store table a unique constraint to prevent any two stores from having the same name.

There is a check constraint on the store_city column in the toy_store table. An insertion or update to the database will produce an error if anyone attempts to add a store_city named METROPOLIS.

In the following code the same tables are created with table constraints instead of column constraints. Notice that the constraints have a slightly different format and that they are separated from the column definitions section by a comma (" , ").

```
create table toy_order
  ( order_number        serial,
    store_number        smallint              not null,
    order_date          date default today    not null,
    shipping_datetime   datetime year to minute,
    sales_code          smallint              not null,
    primary key (order_number),
    foreign key (store_number)
          references toy_order (order_number),
    foreign key (sales_code)
          references toy_sales_staff (sales_code)
  )

create table toy_store
  ( store_number        integer,
    store_name          char (30)             not null,
    buyer_last_name     char (25),
    buyer_first_name    char (15),
    phone_number        char (10)             not null,
    fax_number          char (10),
    store_street        char (25),
    store_city          char (25),
```

```
store_state          char (2) default "CO",
store_zip_code       char (9),
primary key (store_number) constraint fred,
unique (store_name),
check (store_city <> "METROPOLIS") constraint city
)
```

Using a table-level constraint, you can also define composite indexes, or indexes that have more than a single column. For example:

```
unique (buyer_last_name, buyer_first_name)

primary key (first_column, second_column)

foreign key (first_column, second_column) references primary_table
```

note *You may use both column and table constraints to define a table. They are shown separately here so you can easily distinguish the two ways of creating them. For consistency in your own database design, you may want to come up with standards for when you use column constraints and when you use table constraints.*

INFORMIX-SE options

The following option may appear at the end of the `create table` statement for INFORMIX-SE only.

```
[ in "<pathname>" ]
```

This statement allows you to specify a full operating system path-name (including the file name) where you want the table to be stored. This extension is optional and only necessary if you want to store a table somewhere other than with the rest of the database.

INFORMIX-OnLine options

The following options may appear at the end of the create table statement for INFORMIX-OnLine only.

```
[ in <dbspace> ]
[ extent size <kbytes in first extent> ]
[ next size <kbytes in next extents> ]
[ lock mode { page | row } ]
```

By this time you have probably already created the *dbspaces* you will be using for your INFORMIX-OnLine engine. A *dbspace* is an area of disk you have set aside for the operation of your INFORMIX-OnLine system. Your *root dbspace* is always the default *dbspace*, but it is best if you can keep your data, logical logs, and physical logs in different *dbspaces* on different disks when possible. You may also want to split your data into separate *dbspaces* on separate disks to help even out the disk accesses depending on the size of your database and the volume of transactions.

An extent size is the number of kilobytes you want reserved for the initial disk allocation of the table. Extents allow INFORMIX-OnLine to set aside contiguous blocks of disk space for a table, improving performance. You will generally want to allow an extent size large enough to hold your table along with its data and indexes and to allow for some growth.

The next size is the size of additional extents in your table after your initial extent fills up. You should keep the number of extents as small as possible, and definitely under eight. After you have used the first eight extents, INFORMIX-OnLine will start doubling the *next extent size* every time it allocates an additional extent. Multiple extents will cause your data to become noncontiguous, and your database performance may deteriorate significantly.

The INFORMIX-OnLine Administrator's Guide *contains guidelines for how to calculate the amount of space needed for your initial and next extents. Spending some time figuring this out in the beginning will help you to avoid having to recreate your tables later.*

The lock mode determines if your data is locked a page at a time or a row at a time. In the majority of circumstances, you will want to use *row-level locking*. Therefore the default is *page-level lock-*

ing. Huh? Nobody knows who decided this, but you will probably want to specify *row-level locking* on your tables. If *row-level locking* is causing you to run out of locks, you can always switch to *page-level locking* by using the `alter table` statement. *Page-level locking* is useful if you know that the rows you are locking are stored together in pages in the same order you are accessing them.

Temporary tables

A temporary table is just that, a temporary table. It exists for the duration of your application or until you explicitly drop it using the `drop table` statement. This temporary table exists only for the process that created it—no one else can see it or access it. The syntax for creating a temporary table is:

```
create temp table <table name>
  ( <column name> <data type> [ not null ] [, ...]
  )
  [ with no log ]
```

As with permanent tables, you may use `default`, `unique`, `primary key`, and `check` when creating a `temp table`. You may not use the words `foreign key`, `references`, or `constraint` when creating a `temp table`.

tip

You will nearly always want to use the `with no log` *option when using the* `create temp table` *statement. If you do not use this statement and you do use logging, the transactions involving your temporary table will be logged. In most cases, you won't want them logged because you won't want them to be run again should you have to recover your database. If you don't do logging, the* `with no log` *statement is ignored. Transaction logging is discussed in Chapter 4.*

Changing an existing table

This section describes how to change an existing table by using the `alter table` statement. Keep in mind that if you add a column to a table, its initial contents will be null (unless you specify a default for the column). If you delete a column, you delete the data in the column and anything else based on the column (e.g., constraints, indexes, and views). If you change a column, you may lose data if the precision of the data type changes.

```
alter table <table name>
  { add ( <new column name> <new column type>
          [ default <default column value> ]
          [ not null ]
          [ <constraint>
              [ constraint <constraint name> ]
          ]
          [ before <old column name> ]                |
          [, ...]
      )
    drop { <old column name> |
          (<old column name> [, ...])
        }                                              |
    modify ( <old column name> <new column type>
             [ default <default column value> ]
             [ not null ]
             [ <constraint>
                 [ constraint <constraint name> ]
             ]
             [, ...]
         )                                             |
    add constraint
        [ <constraint>
          [ constraint <constraint name> ]
        ]
    drop constraint
      { <constraint name> |
        ( <constraint name> [, ...] )
      }
  } [, ...]
```

note

Note that the modify *option will change the column definition for the column name you specify, therefore you may not rename a column using this statement.*

The following options are for INFORMIX-OnLine only. These may be appended at the end of the `alter table` statement.

```
[ modify next size <number of kbytes> ]
[ lock mode ( { page | row } ) ]
```

The following examples use all of the `alter table` options to alter the toy_order tables. The first example adds the field discount percent to the toy_order table.

```
alter table toy_order
    add discount_percent smallint default 0 not null
        before shipping_datetime
```

The next example deletes the column sales_code from the toy_order table.

```
alter table toy_order
    drop sales_code
```

The next example changes the order_date field in the toy_order table to a new data type and default.

```
alter table toy_order
    modify order_date  datetime year to minute
                       default current year to minute
```

The next example adds two constraints to the toy_order table.

```
alter table toy_order
    add constraint
        (check (quantity >= 1) constraint quan,
         check (unit_price > 0) constraint price)
```

The next example deletes the constraint *city* from the toy_order table.

```
alter table toy_order
    drop constraint city
```

The final two examples are for INFORMIX-OnLine only. The first statement changes the next extent size for the table to 64, and the second changes the `lock` mode to `row`.

```
alter table toy_order
    modify next size 64

alter table toy_order
    lock mode row
```

Deleting a Table

This section describes how to delete a table by using the `drop table` statement. Remember, once a table has been dropped, you cannot get it back. Use this statement with extreme caution.

```
drop table <table name>
```

Example: drop table toy_order

Renaming Tables and Columns

Since the `alter table` statement does not allow you to change the names of tables or columns, the `rename table` and `rename column` statements provide these options. The syntax is pretty straightforward.

```
rename table <table name> to <new table name>
```

Example: rename table toy_order to store_orders

```
rename column <table name>.<column name>
          to <new column name>
```

Example:
rename column toy_order.sales_code to sales_number

Privileges

Now that we have created a database and tables, we need to decide who should be able to access data, and what they should have the ability to access. There are different levels and types of database privileges. This section has the following subsections:

- Granting database privileges
- Granting table privileges
- Revoking privileges
- Roles
- Creating schema authorization

note

You may also use the `grant` *and* `revoke` *statements to grant and revoke privileges on views and synonyms (discussed in Chapter 20) and to grant and revoke execute privileges from stored procedures (Chapter 21).*

Granting Database Privileges

When you first create a database, you as the current user are the owner of the database or table and you are the only person who has access to it. The following syntax allows you to grant database-level access to other users for the current database.

```
grant { connect | resource | dba }
   to { public | <user name> [, ...] }
```

The terms `connect`, `resource`, and `dba` describe the *type* of access being granted as shown on page 76. The next part of the statement determines *who* is being granted the access. The word `public` specifies any user. A list of user login names specifies the users being granted access to the database.

Privilege	Description
connect	The connect privilege allows a user access to the database. A user must have at least the connect privilege to have any access to the database. Provided the user has the appropriate table-level privileges, he will be able to view and change information in tables. The connect privilege is adequate access for most users. The following statement will grant the connect privilege to all users. Example: `grant connect to public` Or you may wish to control privileges more closely by assigning them on a user by user basis, especially if not everyone who connects to your server should have access to your database. Example: `grant connect to harry` If you do this, you will need to remember to add (and revoke) connect permissions whenever users are added or removed from the system.
resource	The resource privilege grants all connect privileges, and it allows users the ability to create new tables, indexes, and procedures. Example: `grant resource to bill`
dba	The dba (or database administrator) privilege grants all resource privileges, and all other privileges needed to maintain the database system. This is the most privileged level of database access for Informix databases. Example: `grant dba to sue` The dba can also make another user the owner of a table (or other database object) by specifying an owner name (i.e., "owner_name".<object name>) as part of the name of the object at the time the object is created. Example: `create table "stacey".toy_order` . . .

As suggested at the beginning of this chapter, there are advantages to having a single database administration account as your only dba (and resource) user and having all other users assigned the connect privilege only.

Granting Table Privileges

There are several levels of table privileges. If your table-level privileges conflict with your database-level privileges, whichever privilege is more restrictive takes precedence. The syntax for granting table-level privileges is as follows:

```
grant { all [ privileges ] |
        { insert |
          delete |
          select [ (<column name> [, ...] ) ] |
          update [ (<column name> [, ...] ) ] |
          references
                   [ (<column name> [, ...] ) ] |
          index |
          alter
        } [, ...]
      }
    on <table name>
    to { public | <user name> [, ...] }
    [ with grant option ] [ as <granting user> ]
```

There are seven table-level privileges: insert, delete, select, update, references, index, and alter. All specifies all seven of these privileges. When a table is created, by default all of the table-level privileges except alter are granted to public (except for mode ANSI databases where public access is not automatically granted). Each of these privileges is described in the chart on page 78.

Table Level Privileges

Privilege	Description
insert	Grants privilege to insert rows into the table.
delete	Grants privilege to delete rows from the table.
select	Grants privilege to select columns from the table. You may specify columns you wish to grant access to.
update	Grants privilege to update rows in the table. You may specify columns you want the user to have the ability to change.
alter	Grants privilege to add and drop columns, to modify data types for columns, and to add and drop constraints.
index	In combination with resource privilege, index privilege allows the user to create permanent indexes on a table. The requirement to have resource privilege for index privilege is a bit odd since you can create unique, primary key, and foreign key constraints if you have the alter privilege (which only requires connect privilege)—and since each of these constraints creates an index.
references	In combination with resource privilege, references allows a user to create foreign key references on a table or for particular columns in a table. As in the index privilege, the requirement for resource privilege for this privilege is also a bit odd since you can create a foreign key constraint with references if you have the alter privilege, which only requires connect privilege.

The `with grant option` clause allows the user being granted a privilege to, in turn, grant that privilege to other users. Be careful how frequently you use this option and the `as` option. Permissions can get out of control quickly when these options are used.

The `as <granting user>` clause allows a person with DBA privilege to grant privileges to a user under another users name (that user must have the ability to grant the privilege). Note that in doing this, you will not be able to revoke the privilege you have granted as another user. Only the user who grants the privilege may revoke it (this includes users with `dba` privileges).

Since a table may, by default, have privileges assigned that you don't want, you may want to issue the following statement before assigning new privileges:

```
revoke all on mytable from public
```

This will revoke privileges from all users and allow you to start with no assigned privileges. (The revoke statement is discussed in the next section.)

Here are some examples of granting table-level privileges:

```
grant all privileges on toy to stacey

grant insert, delete,
      update (order_date, shipping_datetime)
   on toy_order to harold

grant select on toy_store to rani with grant option

grant alter on toy_order to barb as dba

grant index, references (order_number)
   on toy_order to anne
```

Revoking Privileges

You may use the `revoke` statement to revoke privileges you previously granted to users on the database or the table-level. The `revoke` statement can also be used to revoke execute privileges from a stored procedure. This is discussed under the topic of stored procedures in Chapter 21.

The syntax for revoking database-level privileges from users is:

```
revoke { connect | resource | dba }
  from { public | <user name> [, ...] }
```

Example: revoke connect from public

The syntax for revoking table-level privileges from users is:

```
revoke { all [ privileges ] |
        { insert      |
        delete        |
        select [ (<column name> [, ...] ) ] |
        update [ (<column name> [, ...] ) ] |
        references
                [ (<column name> [, ...] ) ] |
        index         |
        alter
        } [, ...]
        }
     on <table name>
     from { public | <user name> [, ...] }
```

Examples: revoke all from public
            revoke update, delete from jerry

If you revoke a table-level privilege created with grant option, you not only revoke the privilege from the user, but any privileges which were caused to be granted by that user having grant privilege are also revoked.

Roles

Roles were created to allow permissions to be granted and revoked easily from within applications and to help tighten your database security. Roles were introduced to Informix databases engines starting in version 7.1.

To use a role, you need to create, grant privileges to, and assign users to the role. To actually use the role, you must first set the role. The role may be unset after it is used to help prevent access to the role outside of the application. (Users actually could use the role outside of the application if they knew how to use roles, however, it is one more hurdle for a person with sabotage in mind to jump over.)

Here is the syntax for creating and maintaining a role

```
create role <role name>

<use grant statements to grant privileges to a
role as you would to a user>

grant <role name> to <user name> [, ...]
drop role <role name>
```

As an example, let's create two roles for the toy_order table. One role will only have the ability to look up information in this table, and the other will have look up and edit privileges.

```
create role toyo_sel;
create role toyo_all;

grant select on toy_order to toyo_sel;
grant select, insert, update, delete on toy_order
    to toyo_all;

grant toyo_sel to fred, barney;
grant toyo_all to wilma, betty;
```

Role names must be kept to eight characters since this is what login names are limited to. Also, role names cannot be any name that you would give to a user since they will be stored in the sys-tabauth table in the same column as the user names.

note

Note that before granting a privilege to a role, you will probably want to remove any public or other relevant permissions to the table first.

If you should later want to remove the roles, it is quite simple:

```
drop role toyo_sel;
drop role toyo_all;
```

To use the role, the relevant syntax is:

```
set role <role name>
set role [ none | null ]
```

In your application (or in dbaccess), in order to be able to use the privileges assigned to the role, you must set the role:

```
set role toyo_sel;
set role toyo_all;
```

If you do not set the role before using it, you will not be permitted to access the table.

When you have finished using a role, set role to none or null:

```
set role none;
```

This will prevent the role from being used until it is once again set.

Creating Schema Authorization

This statement allows you to issue a group of create and grant statements as a single unit. This statement exists for ANSI compatibility since ANSI SQL has no concept equivalent to create database other than create schema. The syntax for this statement follows the previous create table and grant syntax already discussed. Additionally, it will work for index, view, and synonym creations, which are discussed later (indexes in the next section, and views and synonyms in Chapter 20).

```
create schema authorization <user name>
      { <create table statement>    |
        <create index statement>    |
        <create view statement>     |
        <create synonym statement>  |
        <grant statement>
      } [, ...]
```

The *user name* specifies the user who will own the `schema authorization` and everything it creates.

Indexes

This section describes how to create indexes. Actually, we already know how to create some indexes by creating constraints in the `create table` and `alter table` statements. The constraints `unique`, `primary key`, and `foreign key` (or `references`) automatically create indexes.

An index equivalent to a `unique` constraint can be produced by using a `create index` statement.

Primary keys and foreign keys help to enforce *referential integrity* in a database, and this functionality cannot be reproduced by the `create index` statement. A primary key index is by definition not null and unique, and only one primary key is allowed per table. The foreign key (or references) indexes are produced as indexes that allow duplicates. The foreign key references a primary key and enforces the one-to-many relationship by not allowing any foreign key values to be entered into the foreign key that do not exist in the primary key.

The other way to create indexes on tables is to use the `create index` statement.

```
create [ unique | distinct ]
       [ cluster ]
       index <index name>
    on <table name>
      ( <column name> [ asc | desc ] [, ...] )
```

Unique and distinct have the same meaning in a create index statement. The effect is the same as the unique constraint. No duplicate values are allowed in the column or set of columns that comprise a unique index. If you do not choose the unique or distinct option, duplicate values will be permitted in your index.

A cluster index arranges the data rows on the disk in the same order as the index. In many cases, a cluster index will improve your performance. After your clustered index has been created, new rows added to the table will not be clustered, so if you use cluster indexes it is a good idea to drop your clustered indexes and recreate them periodically to maintain the clustered index effect. Only one clustered index per table is permitted. A cluster index is the only type of index that will physically reorder your data rows on disk. You can also use the cluster index to regain space in your table caused by deleted rows in INFORMIX-SE or in INFORMIX-OnLine where varchar data types cause row sizes to change.

The *index name* is simply the name of your index. You will use this later when you want to drop your index.

Table name specifies the name of the table for which the index is being created.

You may specify a single column or a list of column names for your index. When an index is made up of more than one column, it is called a *composite index*. You may specify whether each column of the index is sorted in ascending or descending order. The default option is ascending order.

Examples:

```
create index i_toy_desc on toy (description)

create unique index i_order_item
  on toy_order_item (order_number, toy_code)

create unique cluster i_order_number
  on toy_order (order_number asc)
```

If you will be using transaction logging (see Chapter 4), your index creations will be much faster if you are able to turn the logging off before you create your index. You will not be permitted to create a `cluster` index if you are using INFORMIX-SE and have an audit trail (see Chapter 4) on the table.

The performance of your data loads will be affected if you have an index on your table while your data is being loaded. When possible, drop your index, load your data, then recreate the index. This sequence of events can save you quite a bit of time.

Currently, the syntax of Informix's SQL does not permit you to create a clustered index with a primary key constraint. But you can get the same effect by:

- using the `alter table` statement to drop the primary key constraint
- creating a clustered index on the column(s) that used to be your primary key
- dropping the newly created index
- using the `alter table` statement to add your primary key constraint back to the table

tip

Since a clustered index is only clustered for records in a table up to the point in time when the index was clustered, it is a good idea to periodically recluster indexes in order not to lose the performance advantage of having clustered indexes

```
alter index <index name> to [ not ] cluster
```

Example: `alter index i_my_index to cluster`

note

When reclustering, make certain you have enough space on the disk for INFORMIX-SE or in the dbspace for INFORMIX-OnLine to hold another entire copy of the table or else the recluster of the index will fail.

To delete or drop an index, use the following syntax:

```
drop index <index name>
```

Example: `drop index i_toy_desc`

Creating the Sample Database

The statements listed below are used to create the sample database toymaker. But first, there are a few things you should know about the listing.

The semicolons (" ; ") at the end of each statement are needed to separate individual statements in an Informix SQL command file.

You can't create a foreign key that references columns in a table that do not yet exist. This is why the `create table` statements may seem to be ordered oddly.

The table toy_order_item has indexes on (order_number, toy_code), (order_number), and (toy_code). The database designer would need to decide whether all of these indexes are really necessary. In this case, it was decided to use all of these indexes to insure referential integrity.

Notice that we didn't bother creating a foreign index on state_code in the toy_store table. This was done for three reasons: (1) an index on state_code would produce a fairly large number of duplicate values thereby decreasing database performance, (2) we won't perform lookups by state_code very often, and (3) we can handle the state_code integrity at the program level instead of at the database engine level.

While you may choose any name as a constraint name, the following method makes the constraint names easy to remember. Each index starts with an "i_", this is followed by the initials of the table name, an underscore, and finally the initials of the column name(s) that makes up the index.

```
create database toymaker;

create table toy
( toy_code              smallint,
  description           char (50)       not null,
  quantity              integer         not null,
  cost                  money (16,2)    not null,
  sales_price           money (16,2)    not null,
  primary key (toy_code) constraint i_t_tc
);
```

```
create table toy_store
( store_number          integer,
  store_name            char (30)          not null,
  buyer_last_name       char (25),
  buyer_first_name      char (15),
  phone_number          char (10)          not null,
  fax_number            char (10),
  store_street          char (25),
  store_city            char (25),
  store_state           char (2),
  store_zip_code        char (9),
  primary key (store_number) constraint i_ts_sn
);

create index i_ts_sn on toy_store (store_name);
create index i_ts_bn
  on toy_store (buyer_last_name, buyer_first_name);

create table toy_sales_staff
( sales_code            smallint,
  employee_number       char (9)           not null,
  last_name             char (25)          not null,
  first_name            char (15)          not null,
  primary key (sales_code) constraint i_tss_sc,
  unique (employee_number) constraint i_tss_en
);

create table state
( state_code            char (2),
  state_name            char (25)          not null,
  primary key (state_code) constraint i_s_sc
);

create table toy_order
( order_number          serial,
  store_number          integer            not null,
  order_date            date default today not null,
  shipping_datetime     datetime year to minute,
  sales_code            smallint           not null,
  primary key (order_number)
    constraint i_to_on,
  foreign key (store_number)
```

Continued

```
         references toy_store (store_number)
         constraint i_to_sn,
       foreign key (sales_code)
         references toy_sales_staff (sales_code)
         constraint i_to_sc
);

create table toy_order_item
( order_number         integer,
  toy_code             smallint,
  quantity             integer        not null,
  unit_price           money (16,2)   not null,
  primary key (order_number, toy_code)
    constraint i_toi_ontc,
  foreign key (order_number)
    references toy_order (order_number)
    constraint i_toi_on,
  foreign key (toy_code)
    references toy (toy_code)
    constraint i_toi_tc
);
```

Viewing the Database

Now that you have created your database, the statements
described in this section will allow you to view what you have created.

info

Info allows you to view an assortment of information about your
database. There are two ways to use this statement. The first is an
option from the DB-Access ring menu, and the other is by using
an Informix's SQL statement.

To use Info from the DB-Access ring menu, either:

- select the Query-Language option, then choose the Info option
  (dbaccess -qi), or
- select the Table option, then take the Info option
  (dbaccess -ti)

From there you can view a list of tables and various information about each table.

The `info` statement allows you to view the same information as that from the DB-Access ring menu, but from an Informix's SQL statement instead.

To get a list of tables in the current database, the syntax is:

```
info tables
```

To get information about a specific table, the syntax is:

```
info { columns          |
       indexes          |
       privileges       |
       status
     }
   for <table name>
```

dbschema

The `dbschema` command is entered from the operating system command line to create a database schema that can be used to recreate your database, including tables, indexes, and privileges.

```
dbschema
       [ -t { all | <table name> } ]
       [ -s { all | <synonym user name> } ]
       [ -p { all | <privilege user name> } ]
       [ -f { all | <stored procedure name> } ]
       -d <database name>
       [ -ss ]
       [ -r ]
       [ -hd ]
       [ <output file name> ]
```

The basic command:

```
dbschema -d toymaker
```

will create a schema for your entire database. The default output is to the screen; to capture the output to a file, simply append a file name where you want to store the schema at the end of the command.

The -t switch will give a schema for the specified table or for all tables if the all keyword is used. The -s switch will give a schema for all synonyms available to the specified user, or for all users if the all keyword is used, or for a specific table when used in conjunction with the -t switch. The -p switch will give a schema for all privileges available to the specified user, for all users if the all keyword is used, or for a specific table when used in conjunction with the -t switch. The -f switch will list the stored procedures, for all stored procedures if the all keyword is used, or for a specific stored procedure when used in conjunction with the -t switch.

note

INFORMIX-OnLine users should note that in all version 5 engines (and earlier versions), the dbschema *command does not reproduce the INFORMIX-OnLine specific options of the* create table *statement: in <dbspace>,* extent size, next size, *and* lock *mode. You will probably want to keep the original command file you used to create your database. The* dbschema *command in versions 6 and up of the engine has the* -ss *option which preserves the above mentioned server specific information.*

The -r switch will print the create and grant statements for the role(s). The -hd switch will print histograms of the distributions created by update statistics (see Chapter 4).

Summary

The following syntax summarizes the information presented in this chapter. Statements are separated by semicolons ("; ").

Database statements are:

- To create a database in INFORMIX-SE:

```
create database <database name>
  [ with log in "<pathname>" [ mode ansi ] ]
```

- To create a database in INFORMIX-OnLine:

```
create database <database name>
  [ in <dbspace> ]
  [ with { [ buffered ] log | log mode ansi } ]
```

- Database statements available in both engines:

```
drop database <database-name>

database <database-name> [ exclusive ]

close database

start database <database name>
  with log in "<pathname>" [ mode ansi ]
```

Character and string data types are: char, character, varchar, nchar, and nvarchar.

Numeric data types are: dec, decimal, double precision, float, int, integer, money, nchar, numeric, real, serial, smallfloat, and smallint.

Date and time data types are: date, datetime, and interval.

Data types used only in INFORMIX-OnLine are: byte BLOB, text BLOB, nvarchar, and varchar.

Table statements are:

- To create a table:

```
create table <table name>
    ( <column name> <data type> [ not null ] [, ...] )
```

- Defaults follow the data type definition for the column:

```
default { <data type value> | current <datetime qualifier> |
        dbservername | sitename | today | user }
```

- Constraints for columns follow the optional not null portion of a column definition:

```
not null                 [ constraint ( <constraint name> ) ]

unique                   [ constraint ( <constraint name> ) ]

primary key              [ constraint ( <constraint name> ) ]

references <table name> [ ( <column name> ) ]
                         [ on delete cascade ]
                         [ constraint ( <constraint name> ) ]

check ( <condition> )    [ constraint ( <constraint name> ) ]
```

- Table-level constraints follow all column definitions (after a
  " , " and before the ") "):

```
not null ( <column name> [, ...] )
        [ constraint ( <constraint name> ) ]


unique ( <column name> [, ...] )
        [ constraint ( <constraint name> ) ]


primary key ( <column name> [, ...] )
        [ constraint ( <constraint name> ) ]


foreign key ( <column name> [, ...] )
        references <table name> [ ( <column name> [, ...] ) ]
        [ on delete cascade ]
        [ constraint ( <constraint name> ) ]


check  ( <condition> ) [ constraint ( <constraint name> ) ]
```

- INFORMIX-SE extension to create table:

```
[ in "<pathname>" ]
```

- INFORMIX-OnLine extensions to create table:

```
[ in <dbspace> ]

[ extent size <kbytes in first extent> ]

[ next size <kbytes in next extents> ]

[ lock mode { page | row } ]
```

- Temporary tables:

```
create temp table <table name>
    ( <column name> <data type> [ not null ] [, ...] )
    [ with no log ]
```

- `alter table` statement:

```
alter table <table name>
   { add ( <new column name> <new column type>
           [ default <default column value> ]
           [ not null ]
           [ <constraint>
             [ constraint <constraint name> ]
           ]
           [ before <old column name> ]
           [, ...]
         )
     drop { <old column name> |
           (<old column name> [, ...])
         }
     modify ( <old column name> <new column type>
             [ default <default column value> ]
             [ not null ]
             [ <constraint>
             [ constraint <constraint name> ]
             ]
             [, ...]
           )
     add constraint
         [ <constraint>
           [ constraint <constraint name> ]
         ]
     drop constraint
         { <constraint name> |
           ( <constraint name> [, ...] )
         }
   } [, ...]
```

- INFORMIX-OnLine extensions to `alter table`:

```
[ modify next size <number of kbytes> ]

[ lock mode ( { page | row } ) ]
```

- To delete a table:

```
drop table <table name>
```

- To rename a table:

```
rename table <table name> to <new table name>
```

- To rename a column:

```
rename column <table name>.<column name> to <new column name>
```

- To grant database-level privileges:

```
grant { connect | resource | dba }
    to { public | <user name> [, ...] }
```

- To grant table-level privileges:

```
grant { all [ privileges ] |
        { insert | delete | index | alter |
         select [ (<column name> [, ...] ) ] |
         update [ (<column name> [, ...] ) ] |
         references [ (<column name> [, ...] ) ] } [, ...]
        } on <table name> to { public | <user name> [, ...] }
    [ with grant option ] [ as <granting user> ]
```

- To revoke database-level privileges:

```
revoke { connect | resource | dba }
    from { public | <user name> [, ...] }
```

- To revoke table-level privileges:

```
revoke { all [ privileges ] |
        { insert | delete | index | alter |
         select [ (<column name> [, ...] ) ] |
         update [ (<column name> [, ...] ) ] |
         references [ (<column name> [, ...] ) ]
        } [, ...]
        } on <table name> from { public | <user name> [, ...] }
```

- Roles are a good way to create privileges for use within applications:

```
create role <role name>

<use grant statements to grant privileges to a role
 as you would to a user>

grant <role name> to <user name> [, ...]

role <role name>

set role <role name>

set role [ none | null ]
```

- To create a schema block for creating objects and granting privileges the syntax is:

```
create schema authorization <user name>
      { <create table statement>    |
        <create index statement>    |
        <create view statement>     |
        <create synonym statement>  |
        <grant statement>
      } [, ...]
```

- The syntax to create and drop indexes is:

```
create [ unique | distinct ] [ cluster ]
  index <index name> on <table name>
  ( <column name> [ asc | desc ] [, ...] )

alter index <index name> to [ not ] cluster

drop index <index name>
```

- To view information about your database, use DB-Access, or:

```
info tables

info { columns | indexes | access | privileges|
      references | status } for <table name>
```

- The dbschema command is used to reproduce the database schema. It is entered from the operating system command line:

```
dbschema
        [ -t { all | <table name> } ]
        [ -s { all | <synonym user name> } ]
        [ -p { all | <privilege user name> } ]
        [ -f { all | <stored procedure name> } ]
        -d <database name>
        [ -ss ]
        [ -r ]
        [ -hd ]
        [ <output file name> ]
```

Maintaining the Database

- update statistics
- *Checking database integrity*
- *Database backups*
- *Logging*
- *Audit trails—INFORMIX-SE only*
- *Summary*

Update Statistics

Run the `update statistics` statement regularly! This statement goes right up front so you won't miss it.

Database statistics are stored in Informix system tables. These statistics are used by the query optimizer, which attempts to find the fastest ways to retrieve the database information you request. These statistics are updated when you run the `update statistics` statement; they are not updated automatically. If you create a database and use it without ever running the `update statistics` statement, you will watch your performance degrade over time.

note

I recommend running `update statistics` *nightly if possible, through a UNIX cron job. If your data doesn't change often enough to run* `update statistics` *nightly or if it takes too long, do it weekly or monthly. Just don't forget to run it for long periods of time. Your data may at any time cross some magic number of rows in a table (or some other criterion) that will make for slow retrievals until you run* `update statistics`*. This is because the Informix engine is optimizing your query based on what it thinks the statistics are instead of what they actually are.*

Unfortunately, Informix's SQL doesn't supply a randomize statistics statement which would replace your valid statistics with random numbers. After trying to run with bad statistics, you will realize how important it is to remember to run `update statistics`.

The syntax is shown on page 100 (the high, medium and low are valid starting with the 6.0 Informix engine).

```
update statistics
    [ { high [ for table [ <table name>
               [ (<column name> [,...] ) ] ]
               [ resolution <resolution percentage>
               [ distributions only ] ] |
        medium [ for table [ <table name>
               [ (<column name> [,...] ) ] ]
               [ resolution <resolution percentage>
               [<confidence percentage>]
               [ distributions only ] ] |
        low    [ for table [ <table name>
               [ (<column name> [,...] ) ] ]
               [ drop distributions ]
      } |
      for table [ <table name> ] |
      for procedure [ <procedure name> ]
    ]
```

Update statistics by itself updates all statistics for the current database.

Update statistics for table, without specifying a table name, updates statistics for all tables in the current database. Specifying a table name will update statistics for only the indicated table.

Update statistics for procedure, without specifying a procedure name, updates statistics for all stored procedures (see Chapter 21) in the current database. Specifying a procedure name will update statistics for the indicated stored procedure only.

If you run update statistics high or medium, you will be sampling the distribution of the data in the table and/or columns. This takes both additional time and space, and high will take more time and space than medium. The space used will be in your root dbspace. If you use this feature, it is recommended you apply statistics as follows:

1. `update statistics medium` on all tables using distributions only without listing single columns and using the default resolution parameters.
2. `update statistics high` for all columns which are at the beginning of an index or for important columns which are used in queries. Execute a separate `update statistics` command for each column.
3. `update statistics low` for all other columns in composite indexes (one statement per table).

This is a good way to start, but no single solution will be perfect for all databases. You may need to try out several different scenarios before finding the best set of `update statistics` statements for your database.

The confidence percentage may have values from 0.80 through 0.99 with a default of 0.95. This percentage indicates the percentage of time update statistics medium is expected to give the same results as `update statistics high`.

The resolution percentage has a default value of 2.5 for update statistics medium and of 0.5 for `update statistics high`. The resolution percentage of data represents how much of the data is sampled for use in creating the distributions.

The distributions only keywords will perform distributions for your tables but not for the indexes. Getting distributions on index information can be very time consuming, so distributions only may give you the information you need much faster.

tip

`Update statistics` *takes longer to run in INFORMIX-OnLine than in INFORMIX-SE because INFORMIX-OnLine keeps track of more statistics. The larger your database, the longer* `update statistics` *will take to run. Try to have your* `update statistics` *run at time when database usage is low, perhaps 3:00 am, to reduce the affect of the statement overhead on your users. Also, if you have tables with static data (the data never changes), you only need to update the statistics one time, it does not need to be continually updated.*

Checking Database Integrity

Check your database integrity often. Your database may become corrupted without your being aware that there is a problem. There are statements and commands you can run to make certain your database is free of problems. These commands differ greatly between INFORMIX-SE and INFORMIX-OnLine because the internals of the two engines are so different. I recommend running these commands through a UNIX *cron* job on a weekly basis. If you think you might have experienced corruption, run them sooner.

INFORMIX-SE Database Integrity

When corruption appears in INFORMIX-SE, the problem is almost always index corruption. You may also experience corruption in the form of a hardware failure in which you lose part of your data. If this occurs, you will need to recover from backups, and then from your transaction logs or audit trails (discussed later in this chapter) if you have them.

check table

The `check table` statement checks the indexes of the specified table. The table being checked cannot be in use while this statement is being run. The person running the statement must have `dba` access or be the owner of the table.

```
check table <table name>
```

The amount of time this statement takes to run will depend on the size of the table and on the number and size of your indexes.

The `check table` statement checks to see if there are problems with an index, but does not attempt to fix them; it does, however, notify you of any problems. Running the `check table` statement is the equivalent of running the `bcheck` utility and answering no to the questions asking if you wish to repair the table.

The check table statement can only be used from within DB-Access INFORMIX-SQL, it cannot be used from INFORMIX-4GL. Also, it can only be run on local databases, not on remote ones.

bcheck

The bcheck utility is used to check and repair indexes. The bcheck utility is run from the UNIX command line.

You must be in the directory where the database and index files are stored when you run this command, and the specified table must not be in use. This will be under your database.dbs directory (unless you have specified an alternative storage location for your table).

The files in the database directory have extensions ending in .dat and .idx. Your data is stored in the .dat file, and your index is stored in the .idx file. The file name is a combination of part of your table name and its unique table number. You will need to find the file names used to store your table.

If you want to run the bcheck command on the toy_order table, you would look at all files starting with toy_o. This will bring back four file names in the toymaker database.

```
toy_ord108.dat        toy_ord108.idx
toy_ord110.dat        toy_ord110.idx
```

The names of the tables toy_order and toy_order_item are the same up to a certain point. This presents us with the problem of trying to figure out which file name to use when running the bcheck command. The numbers 108 and 110 are the unique table numbers assigned to these tables by the Informix engine at the time the tables were created. We are going to jump ahead and run a query to allow you to figure out which table number is associated with the toy_order table. Run DB-Access, then select Query-Language, then New. Now enter the following query:

```
select * from systables where tabname = "toy_order"
```

Press the *accept* key to go back to the main menu, and then choose Run to run the query. One of the pieces of information that will be returned is the tabid, that is, the unique number assigned to each table. In this case the tabid returned is 108, so we now know the file name we will specify with the bcheck command is toy_ord108 (with no extension).

Now that we have a file name, the syntax for the bcheck command is:

```
bcheck -[ i | l | y | n | q | s] <file name without extension>
```

The switches to the bcheck command have the following meanings:

- -i   Check the index file only. Normally the index file is compared with the data file.
- -l   List the entries in the B+ trees.
- -y   Answer yes to all questions. Actually, this is probably not a good idea. When repairs are needed, it is a good idea to run bcheck interactively.
- -n   Answer no to all questions. This is useful when running bcheck as a *cron* job. This will allow you to see any problems before attempting to fix them.
- -q   Don't print the program banner.
- -s   Resize the index file node size.

repair table

The repair table statement calls upon the bcheck utility to check the table and to make the repairs. The difference is that repair table is run from within Informix's SQL while bcheck is a utility run from the UNIX command line.

```
repair table <table name>
```

The repair table statement can only be used from within DB-Access INFORMIX-SQL, it cannot be used from INFORMIX-4GL. Also, it can only be run on local databases, not on remote ones.

When repairing the table doesn't work

After you have repaired a table, run an additional check to make certain the table was actually fixed. Sometimes you will be told the indexes have been repaired when they are still corrupted.

The other scenario you may come across is when `check table` and `bcheck` cannot run because there is some other problem with your data or index file.

In this case, you still have access to your database and the data, so you will need to recreate the table. This involves some things we haven't yet discussed yet, but the steps for recreating a table are as follows:

1. Make sure no users are accessing the table.
2. Unload all of the data from the table (see Chapter 5).
3. Make sure you can recreate your table, its indexes, and anything else you may have created for the table (i.e., privileges, views, synonyms, constraints). Running a `dbschema` for your table will give you this information.
4. Delete the table using the `drop table` statement.
5. Recreate the table (but not the indexes, etc.).
6. Load the data back into the table.
7. Recreate the indexes and any privileges, views, synonyms, and constraints that formerly existed.
8. You now have a new table but it wouldn't hurt to run a `bcheck` on it before allowing your users to use it.

INFORMIX-OnLine Database Integrity

There are several commands with a number of switches that allow you to discover many interesting things in your INFORMIX-OnLine system. The INFORMIX-OnLine log file also stores a record of general activity in the INFORMIX-OnLine system.

Review the INFORMIX-OnLine log file

The INFORMIX-OnLine log file is stored in the file specified by the `MSGLOG` variable in the `$INFORMIXDIR/etc/$ONCONFIG` (or the `$INFORMIXDIR/etc/$TBCONFIG` prior to the Informix 6.0

engine). You should review the contents of this file periodically to make certain errors are not occurring in the INFORMIX-OnLine system. If errors do occur, you will need to determine what the problem is, then solve it.

The `onstat -m` command (or `tbstat -m` prior to the Informix 6.0 engine) will display the last few lines of this file for you. This shortcut is useful when system problems are occurring and you want to know what has happened most recently in the log file.

Keep a paper copy of the INFORMIX-OnLine configuration

Run the `onstat -cd` command (or `tbstat -cd` prior to the Informix 6.0 engine) on a regular basis (for instance, before each database backup), and keep a paper copy of the output of this command. This command produces a copy of your INFORMIX-OnLine configuration—information that will be necessary for you to recover if your *root_dbspace* is destroyed.

Keep an on line copy of files you have modified in the `$INFORMIXDIR` directory

Keep a copy of any files in the $INFORMIXDIR directory which have been modified for your system configuration on line and in an area which is regularly backed up. This would include your `$INFORMIXDIR/etc/$ONCONFIG` file and your `$INFORMIXDIR/etc/sqlhosts` files. Often these files will not be backed up by your system backup since the system administrator will assume all products in the `$INFORMIXDIR` directory can simply be reinstalled.

Check your database regularly

Run the following commands on a regular basis to make sure your INFORMIX-OnLine system is as healthy as it appears. Some of these commands may briefly lock a table and they require some overhead, so run this command when your database system usage is lowest. Each command is described briefly below. See the *Informix OnLine Database Administrator's Guide* for more detail.

These commands are run from the operating system command line. The standard output and error from each of these commands should be stored in individual files and reviewed. If you run across any errors, you will need to consult the *Informix OnLine Database Administrator's Guide.* INFORMIX-OnLine is a complicated subject, and this book makes no pretense of covering all INFORMIX-OnLine topics.

- **oncheck -cr** (or **tbcheck -cr** prior to the Informix 6.0 engine)
  This command validates INFORMIX-OnLine reserved pages that reside at the beginning of the initial chunk of the *root_dbspace.*

- **oncheck -cc** (or **tbcheck -cc** prior to the Informix 6.0 engine)
  This command validates the system catalogs.

- **oncheck -ce** (or **tbcheck -ce** prior to the Informix 6.0 engine)
  This command validates that the extents don't overlap.

- **oncheck -cI** *<database name>* (or **tbcheck -cI** prior to the Informix 6.0 engine)
  This command validates indexes on each table in the specified database. You will need to drop the index and recreate it if there are errors within an index. This command should be run for each database in your INFORMIX-OnLine system.

- **oncheck -cD** *<database name>* (or **tbcheck -cD** prior to the Informix 6.0 engine)
  This command validates the pages for each table. This command should be run for each database in your INFORMIX-OnLine system.

Database Backups

This section covers database backups. Whether you are using INFORMIX-SE or INFORMIX-OnLine, it is important to backup your database system regularly. Backing up your database will allow you to recover to the point of your last backup if you should need to. The next section discusses transaction logging, which, when used in combination with backups, should allow you to recover completely.

In determining the frequency of your backup schedule, ask yourself the questions: how much data am I willing to lose? and how long do I want my recovery to take?

INFORMIX-SE Backups

You may use standard UNIX utilities to backup and to recover your Informix database files. The database files should not be accessed while the system is being backed up (or recovered).

Your database is comprised of a set of files that are related to each other at a certain point in time. If you back up files that are related to one another at different times (even just the amount of time it takes to back up one file, and move onto the next file), and you try to recover from this state, your data and indexes are likely to be out of sync.

This is also true for moving database files from one place to another place by copying to tape or with a move command. This is not recommended. If you need to move your database or any tables to another location, the supported procedure is to unload your data, recreate the database and tables elsewhere, then reload your table into the new location. The statements for performing these operations are described in Chapter 5.

INFORMIX-OnLine Backups

INFORMIX-OnLine has its own backup facilities which perform an archive of an INFORMIX-OnLine instance. This section covers the most basic utility, `intake` (or `tbtape`). If you need more sophistication in your backups, you might consider looking into the newest utility, OnBar. The OnArchive utility is available in the 6.x and 7.x INFORMIX-OnLine engines, but while some people have made a valiant effort to take advantage of its features, it is difficult to use and at least the early versions were somewhat buggy.

`Ontape` (or `tbtape` prior to the 6.0 Informix engine) is an easy to use backup and restore facility which has proven to be reliable

for many years. Ontape allows you to perform database backups
while your users are up and running. The syntax of the ontape
and tbtape commands are:

```
ontape
{ -a | -c | -l | -p |
  -r [ -D <dbspace list> |
  -s [ -L <archive level> ]
      [ -A <database list> ]
      [ -B <database list> ]
      [ -N <database list> ]
      [ -U <database list> ]
}

tbtape { -a | -c | -r |
         -s [ [ -B <database list> ]
              [ -N <database list> ]
              [ -U <database list> ]
```

-a   Automatic logical log backup
-c   Continuous logical log backup
-l   Logical restore
-p   Physical restore for HDR
-r   Full restore of the listed dbspaces/blobspaces (all if none
     are listed)
-s   Archive database
-A   Set the database(s) to ansi logging
-B   Set the database(s) to buffered logging
-N   Set the database(s) to unbuffered logging

There are three levels of archives:

Level 0 Archive   Creates a complete backup of an
                   INFORMIX-OnLine system.

Level 1 Archive   Archives everything since the last level 0
                   archive.

Level 2 Archive   Archives everything since the last level 1
                   archive (or the last level 0 archive if a level
                   0 was done more recently).

An archive allows recovery of your system to the point of the most recent archive.

A level 0 archive will take the most amount of time to perform because it archives the entire database system. The length of a level 1 archive will depend on how much information has changed since the most recent level 0 archive. The length of a level 2 archive will depend on how much information has changed since the most recent level 1 (or level 0) archive.

To recover, you should use the most recent level 0 archive, your most recent level 1 archive (if one was created since the most recent level 0 archive), and your most recent level 2 archive (if one was created since the most recent level 1 or level 0 archive).

You may use commands from the operating system command line or from the `tbmonitor` program to create archives and restore database information from archives.

From **tbmonitor** (available only prior to the 6.0 Informix engine)

To create archives and restore database information from archives, you must be logged on as user `informix`. From the operating system command line, type `tbmonitor`. This will put you into the `tbmonitor` ring menu. To create an archive, choose Archive, then Create from the ring menu, then follow the directions and answer the questions. To restore database information from an archive, choose Archive, then Restore from the ring menu, then follow the directions and answer the questions.

From the command line

To create archives and restore database information from archives from the operating system command line, use the `ontape` or `tbtape` command.

To create an archive, type `ontape -s` or `tbtape -s` at the operating system command line, then follow the directions and answer the questions.

```
ontape -s [ -L <archive level> ]
            (version 6.0 and up of INFORMIX-OnLine)

tbtape -s    (prior to version 6.0 of INFORMIX-OnLine)
```

To restore database information from an archive, type `ontape -r` or `tbtape -r` at the operating system command line, then follow the directions and answer the questions.

```
ontape -r [ -D <dbspace list> ]
              (version 6.0 and up of INFORMIX-OnLine)

tbtape -r     (prior to version 6.0 of INFORMIX-OnLine)
```

Starting with version 6.0 of INFORMIX-OnLine you have the option of performing a *warm restore*. You may selectively restore specific dbspaces while the database engine is up and running (so long as the dbspaces to restored do not include any *critical dbspaces*—that is your root dbspace or any dbspace containing logical or physical logs).

Logging

Both INFORMIX-SE and INFORMIX-OnLine offer transaction logging. Transaction logging allows you to recover the transactions that occurred since your last backup or archive. We're going to start by discussing the statements that INFORMIX-SE and INFORMIX-OnLine both use to create database transactions before we discuss each engine separately. While both engines support transaction logging, each engine implements it very differently.

The use of logging is optional. If recent data changes are important to you and not trivial to reconstruct, logging is probably worth your time and is highly recommended.

What Is a Transaction?

A *transaction* is either a single Informix's SQL statement, or a group of Informix's SQL statements executed as a single unit.

An example of a single statement transaction would be to add a new toy to the toy table.

An example of a group of statements that should be treated as a single transaction would be: Delete an order from the toy_order table, and delete any toy_order_items belonging to that toy order. In grouping these transactions, we tell the database engine that if either of these transactions is applied to the database, both must be applied. If one statement fails, the entire transaction fails.

The following statements may be used only in databases with transaction logging:

```
begin work

commit work

rollback work
```

If the above statements are not used, each Informix's SQL statement is treated as a single transaction. These statements are used primarily to group several Informix's SQL statements as a single transaction.

The begin work statement goes before the first Informix's SQL statement in a transaction. When you want the group of transactions applied to the database, use the commit work statement. If an error occurs, or for some other reason you don't want the statements applied to the database, use the rollback work statement instead of the commit work statement.

A begin work statement must always be matched by a commit work or a rollback work statement. These statements may not be nested, that is, you may not issue two begin work statements before entering a commit work or a rollback work statement. A transaction may not contain other transactions.

If you created an ANSI-compliant database, each statement following a commit work, rollback work, or opening a database is considered an implicit begin work statement. The begin work statement may not be used with ANSI-compliant databases. Example:

```
begin work;
rename toy.quantity to inventory_level;
alter table toy add (shipping_weight decimal (8,2));
commit work;
```

When using grouped transactions, keep the number of statements between your `begin work` and `commit work` statements as small as possible. Creating lengthy transactions increases the database overhead.

Additionally, each row of data affected when using the `insert`, `update`, and `delete` statements (see Chapter 5) during a transaction has a lock placed on it until the transaction is completed. This occurs whenever logging is used and whether or not the transaction is surrounded by `begin work` and `commit work` (or `rollback work`) statements. If you affect a large number of rows within a transaction, your operating system or INFORMIX-OnLine system may run out of locks. For these types of transactions, which are by nature large, you may want to consider removing the logging for the duration of the transaction.

If you do decide to turn off logging to make changes to your database and then turn it back on, the following steps are recommended (some are merely precautions):

1. Turn off your logging. Make sure no users are working on the system while the logging is turned off. This will give you control over any changes made to the system while transactions are not being logged, and you will be able to reproduce these changes in case of any problems. Also, any programs that contain `begin work`, `commit work`, or `rollback work` statements will produce errors if run while the logging is turned off.
2. Perform a full backup of your database before you start making changes to your system.
3. Make the changes.
4. Perform another full backup of your database.
5. If your are using INFORMIX-SE, start a new transaction log. If you are using INFORMIX-OnLine, restart your logging.
6. You may now allow users back into the database.

Transaction Logging in INFORMIX-SE

This section discusses maintaining your transaction logs, backups, and recovery when using transaction logging in INFORMIX-SE.

Turning on transaction logging

There are two ways to turn on transaction logging in your database. The first is to use the `create database` statement, the second is to use the `start database` statement. Both of these statements are described in Chapter 3, but the `start database` statement requires some extra discussion.

To start transaction logging in an existing database, use the following statements (you must be logged on as a user with `dba` privileges and no one else may be accessing the database):

```
close database;
start database <database name>
     with log in "<pathname>" [ mode ansi ];
close database;
database <database name>;
```

The first `close database` statement prevents a current database from being open before starting the database. The `start database` statement puts an exclusive lock on the database that will prevent anyone else from accessing it. The second `close database` statement closes the database so that it may be reopened in a nonexclusive mode using the database statement.

Turning off transaction logging

Version 6 of INFORMIX-SE will allow you to turn transaction logging off by using the new `with no log` option as part of the `start database` statement. But oddly enough, until version 6, this has never been officially supported. Prior to version 6, Informix manuals say that once transaction logging is turned on, it cannot be turned off.

For many reasons, the inability to turn transaction logging off when desired isn't very practical. If you call Informix Technical Support, however, they will to tell you how to do it. The instructions are as follows:

1. Log in as user `informix`.
2. Run `dbaccess` from the command line. Then choose the Query-Language menu option.
3. Issue the statement:

```
select * from systables where tabtype = "L"
```

4. Make sure only one row that contains information about your log file is returned. If more than one row is returned, make sure you typed the statement correctly.
5. Issue the statement:

```
delete from systables where tabtype = "L"
```

Creating backups

The process of creating backups for your database becomes a little more involved when you are using transaction logs. This is because your database backup and your log file must be properly synchronized for you to recover the transactions written to the log file.

These are the steps to follow when creating a backup for your database when using transaction logging:

1. Prevent users from accessing the database during this process.
2. Create a backup of your database directory and files.
3. Move your current transaction log file to an archive location. If you don't wish to archive old transactions logs, you can delete your old transaction log. (It's a good idea to save some old logs and database backups to be safe.)
4. Create a current transaction log of size 0. You can use the UNIX command: `touch <file name>` to create the file. Make certain that the permissions on this file are exactly the same as the original log file. If you have enough disk space, you can simply copy your transaction log file to another location instead of moving it, then use the following UNIX command to empty the current log file: `cat /dev/null > <file name>`. All permissions remain intact using this second method.
6. Permit users to reenter the database.

Recovery

The `rollforward` statement can help you recover your database. To use this statement, you must have a database backup and all transaction logs created since the database backup. The syntax for the `rollforward` database statement is:

```
rollforward database <database name>
```

The following steps describe how to recover your database using the most recent database backup and the current log file. The current log file should contain transactions beginning immediately after the completion of the most recent backup.

1. Users should not be accessing the database at this point since it is most likely corrupted.
2. It is a good idea to make a backup of the existing database before you attempt to perform a recovery. If you don't, you could be in for an unpleasant surprise if you find that the backup tapes are bad or have been corrupted.
3. Delete the existing database directory and database files from the system.
4. Recover the database directory and database files from the most recent database backup.
5. Run `dbaccess` and select the Query-Language menu option. You will need to be logged on as a user with `dba` privileges.
6. Issue the statement:

```
close database
```

7. Issue the statement:

```
rollforward database <database name>
```

8. When this statement finishes running, the database will be in exclusive mode to give you a chance to check for problems. When everything looks good to you, continue.

9. Issue the statement:

```
close database
```

10. Issue the statement:

```
database <database name>
```

11. Permit users to reenter the database.

Viewing the transaction logs

You may view the contents of a log file by using the dblog utility. The dblog utility is run from the operating system command line. The output from this command may be difficult to interpret. Refer to your *INFORMIX-SE Administrator's Guide* for more information about this command.

Transaction Logging in INFORMIX-OnLine

This section discusses maintaining your transaction logs, backups, and recovery when using transaction logging in INFORMIX-OnLine. It is worth repeating that this book is not intended as a full guide to INFORMIX-OnLine database administration. You will find additional information about the topics discussed in this section in the *Informix OnLine Administrator's Guide*.

Types of logging

For each database in your INFORMIX-OnLine engine, you may specify no logging, unbuffered logging, buffered logging, or unbuffered logging—mode ANSI. The exception to this is for ANSI-compliant databases. ANSI databases automatically use unbuffered logging. The types of logging are described in the chart on page 118.

Types of Transaction Logging

Type of Logging	Description
No Logging	Don't log transactions. This is actually a misnomer since in INFORMIX-OnLine, some logging is done even when no logging is specified.
Unbuffered Logging	Unbuffered logging gives you the most complete set of logical logs to recover from in case of disaster. This is because each transaction is immediately written to the logical log files on disk as soon as it is completed. The performance of unbuffered logging will be slightly less than if using buffered logging.
Buffered Logging	Buffered logging may store many transactions worth of data in the buffer before writing it to the logical log files on disk. Buffered logging is used instead of unbuffered logging when the performance of the database is more important than the most recent data that could be lost if there was a disaster.
Unbuffered Logging, Mode ANSI	This option will make your database ANSI-compliant, which will cause it to use unbuffered logging. Warning: Once a database is ANSI-compliant, there's no going back.

Changing the logging mode

There are three ways to change the logging mode of your database. The first is to use the onmonitor utility (or tbmonitor prior to version 6.0 of the engine), the second is to use the ontape utility (or tbtape prior to version 6.0 of the engine) from the operating system command line, and the third is to use an Informix's SQL statement. Changing the logging mode through Informix's SQL changes the mode only for the current session.

To change the logging mode of your database using onmonitor or tbmonitor, you must be logged on as user informix. From the operating system command line, type onmonitor or tbmonitor. This will take you to the onmonitor or tbmonitor ring menu. To change the logging mode, you will first need to bring the database into quiescent mode. Next, choose Logical-Logs from the main ring menu, then choose Databases. Now, just follow the directions.

The only way to change a database to mode ANSI prior to version 6.0 of the database engine is through ontape or the onmonitor or tbmonitor utilities.

To change the logging mode of a database from the command line, use the following syntax:

```
ontape -s { -A | -B | -N  | -U } <database list>

or

tbtape -s { -B | -N  | -U } <database list>
```

-s   Use this switch to start an archive of your INFORMIX-OnLine system. This switch must be used when changing from no logging to logging.

-A   Change to ANSI logging

-B   Change to buffered logging.

-N   Change to no logging.

-U   Change to unbuffered logging.

To change the logging mode for your database using Informix's SQL for the current session only, issue the following statement:

```
set [ buffered ] log
```

This statement will change the log mode for your current session from unbuffered logging to buffered logging, or from buffered logging to unbuffered logging. Unbuffered logging is the default option.

Backing up logical logs

There are two modes for backing up logical logs: *automatic backup* and *continuous backup*. Automatic backup of logical logs is performed at the request of the user. Continuous backup is run continuously as logical logs fill up.

Running continuous logs will tie up a terminal and a tape drive. Every backup of logical logs must be on a separate tape, so automatic backup may cause you to use additional tapes. If your logical logs fill up, the INFORMIX-OnLine system will stop and wait (yes, this does mean your users will be stopped too) until you start backing up logical logs and the logical logs begin to be freed. Continuous backups help to prevent this sort of problem from occurring.

You may use tbmonitor or a command line command to run logical log backups. To backup logical logs, you must be logged on as user informix.

To run logical log backups from onmonitor (or tbmonitor prior to INFORMIX-OnLine 6.0), type onmonitor or tbmonitor on the operating system command line. This will take you to the ring menu. Choose the Logical-Log option from the ring menu, then choose either Auto-Backup or Continuous-Backup. You will be prompted for tapes.

To run logical log backups from the operating system command line, use the ontape (or tbtape prior to INFORMIX-OnLine 6.0) command.

To run an automatic logical log backup, type `ontape -a` or `tbtape -a` at the operating system command line; you will be prompted for a tape.

ontape -a	(version 6.0 and up of INFORMIX-OnLine)
tbtape -a	(prior to version 6.0 of INFORMIX-OnLine)

To run a continuous logical log backup, type `ontape -c` or `tbtape -c` at the operating system command line; you will be prompted for a tape.

ontape -c	(version 6.0 and up of INFORMIX-OnLine)
tbtape -c	(prior to version 6.0 of INFORMIX-OnLine)

Recovery

The recovery works the same way as described in the section on backups earlier in this chapter. One of the questions you will be asked is if you have logical logs to recover from. If you answer yes, you will be told the number of the logical log you should start with and you will be prompted for tapes.

Audit Trails—INFORMIX-SE Only

Audit trails are similar to transaction logs, but where transaction logs work on an entire database, audit trails work only on specified tables in a database.

You must choose to use either audit trails or transaction logs. Transaction logs are more sophisticated than audit trails. Audit trails are unsynchronized. If you recover using audit trails, you could end up with tables recovered to different points in time. If you have a good reason to use audit trails, go ahead. If not, use transaction logs.

The commands for using audit trails are described below. The syntax to create an audit trail is:

```
create audit for <table name> in "<pathname>"
```

You must issue this statement for each table you wish to audit. Each audit trail must be stored in a separate file. You can't create a cluster index on a table with an audit trail.

The syntax to delete or drop an audit trail is:

```
drop audit for <table name>
```

The syntax for recovering from an audit trail combined with a database backup is:

```
recover table <table name>
```

The same rules apply to backing up your database, archiving your audit trails, and recovering as apply to transaction logging. See the section on transaction logging in this chapter for more information. Instead of deleting and recreating the files through UNIX, when archiving your audit trails, you should use the drop audit and create audit statements.

Summary

Run the `update statistics` statement regularly.

```
update statistics
    [ { high [ for table [ <table name>
                [ (<column name> [,...] ) ] ]
                [ resolution <resolution percentage>
                [ distributions only ] ] |
            medium [ for table [ <table name>
                [ (<column name> [,...] ) ] ]
                [ resolution <resolution percentage>
                [<confidence percentage>]
                [ distributions only ] ] |
            low  [ for table [ <table name>
                [ (<column name> [,...] ) ] ]
                [ drop distributions ]
        } |
        for table [ <table name> ] |
        for procedure [ <procedure name> ]
    ]
```

Check your database integrity often. For INFORMIX-SE use the Informix's SQL statements:

```
check table <table name>

repair table <table name>
```

and the command line utility:

```
bcheck -[ i | l | y | n | q | s]
    <file name without extension>
```

For INFORMIX-OnLine: Review the contents of the `$INFORMIXDIR/online.log` file periodically. Run:

`onstat -cd` (or **`tbstat -cd`** prior to INFORMIX-OnLine 6.0)

on a regular basis and keep a paper copy of the output of this command.

Run the following commands on a regular basis:

```
oncheck -cr
oncheck -cc
oncheck -ce
oncheck -cI <database name>
oncheck -cD <database name>
```

(use the **tbcheck** version of these commands prior to INFORMIX-OnLine 6.0).

Backup your database system regularly. Backing up your database will allow you to recover to the point of your last backup if you should need to recover.

For INFORMIX-SE backups you may use standard UNIX utilities to backup and to recover your Informix database files.

INFORMIX-OnLine uses three levels of archives to backup and restore database information. From tbmonitor use the Archive menu option, then Archive or Restore. From the operating system command line:

```
ontape
{ -a | -c | -1 | -p |
  -r [ -D <dbspace list> |
  -s [ -L <archive level> ]
      [ -A <database list> ]
      [ -B <database list> ]
      [ -N <database list> ]
      [ -U <database list> ]
}

tbtape { -a | -c | -r |
         -s [ [ -B <database list> ]
              [ -N <database list> ]
              [ -U <database list> ]
```

Transaction logging allows you to recover transactions that occurred since your last backup or archive. A *transaction* is either a single Informix's SQL statement, or a group of Informix's SQL statements executed as a single unit. The following statements may be used only in databases with transaction logging:

```
begin work
```

commit work

rollback work

To turn on transaction logging in INFORMIX-SE databases (1) use the `create database` statement, or (2) use the `start database` statement. Recover your INFORMIX-SE database using the most recent database backup and the current log file.

rollforward database **<database name>**

You may view the contents of a log file by using the `dblog` utility.

For each database in your INFORMIX-OnLine engine, you may specify no logging, unbuffered logging, buffered logging, or unbuffered logging—mode ANSI. To change the logging mode of the database, use the `onmonitor` (or `tbmonitor` prior to INFORMIX-OnLine 6.0) or use the `ontape` (or `tbtape` prior to INFORMIX-OnLine 6.0) command.

ontape [-s] { -B | -N | -U } <database name>

To change the logging mode of your database for the current session only, use:

set [buffered] log

There are two modes for backing up logical logs: *automatic backup* and *continuous backup*. You may use the `onmonitor` or `tbmonitor` utility or the `ontape` (or `tbtape` prior to INFORMIX-OnLine 6.0) command with a `-a` switch for automatic backups and a `-c` switch for continuous backups.

Audit trails are similar to transaction logging, but audit trails work only on specified tables in a database. The statements used with audit trails are:

create audit for <table name> in "<pathname>"

drop audit for <table name>

recover table <table name>

Data: Adding, Changing, and Deleting

- insert
- update
- delete
- *Locking*
- load *and* unload
- dbload
- dbexport *and* dbimport
- *Tips for faster data loads*
- *Summary*

Insert

Now that we have a database assembled, it's time we added some data. The statement used for adding a row of data to the database is the `insert` statement.

```
insert into <table name> [ ( <column name> [,
...] ) ]
    { values ( <values> [, ...] ) |
        <select statement (with limitations)> |
        execute procedure <stored procedure name>
                    ( <arguments>  [, ...] )
    }
```

Let's start with the simple case of inserting a single row of data values into a table.

```
insert into state values ("CA", "California")

insert into state (state_code, description)
            values ("WA",        "Washington")
```

The values inserted into the table must be listed in the same order as the columns into which they are being inserted. If no columns are specified, the columns are assumed to be in the same order as in the table. The values being inserted must be of the same data types as the columns. The number of values listed must be equal to the number of columns.

The following examples show more complex data types being inserted:

```
insert into toy_order
            (order_number,
            store_number,
            order_date,
            shipping_datetime,
            sales_code)
        values (0, 8, "7/8/1997", "1997-07-13 15:15", 2)
```

```
insert into toy_order_item
        (order_number, toy_code, quantity,
        unit_price)
    values (1, 3, 75, 1.50)
```

Notice that a zero is being entered into the order_number column of the toy_order table. Since order_number is a serial data type, inserting a zero will cause the largest number in the column plus one to be entered into the table.

```
insert into toy_store
    (store_number, store_name, phone_number)
    values (1, "DON'S TOY DUNGEON", null)
```

The insert into toy_store statement demonstrates that not all columns in a table must be inserted. Any uninserted columns will default to a null (or an undefined empty) value. You may also use the word *null* as a value to explicitly insert a null into a column.

Several built-in functions can also be used as literal values in the insert statement: user, today, current, sitename, and dbservername. These functions were discussed in Chapter 3, and are defined in Chapter 20. An example of an insert statement using built-in functions is:

```
insert into toy_order
    (order_number,
     store_number,
     order_date,
     shipping_datetime,
     sales_code)
    values (1, 8, today, current year to minute, 2)
```

Today's date will be inserted as the order_date, and the current date and time will be entered as the shipping_datetime.

If you use the select statement with the insert statement, you may add as many rows of data as the select statement returns. The select statement allows you to conditionally retrieve any columns of data from any table, or group of tables that are related to each other. The select statement is discussed in detail in Chapter 6. For example:

```
insert into mytable
    (client_name, client_phone, client_money)
      select
    (client_name, client_phone, account_balance)
      from   client
      where account_balance > 10000
```

This `insert` statement inserts client information into mytable for each person in the client table whose balance is more than $10,000.

note

The number of columns returned by the `select` statement must match the number and data types of the columns inserted into the table. The limitations on the `select` statement when used in an `insert` statement are (1) the table being inserted into cannot be used in the `select` statement, (2) the `order by` clause cannot be used, and (3) the `into temp` clause cannot be used.

You may use the values returned from a stored procedure to insert data into a row. The number and data types passed back from the stored procedure must match the columns into which the values are to be inserted. Stored procedures are discussed in Chapter 21.

Update

Now that we can insert data into tables, we need to know how to change the data once it's in a table. Data is changed in a table by using the `update` statement.

```
update <table name>
  set { <column name> =
        { <expression> | <select statement> }
        [, ...] |
        [ * | ( <column name> [, ..] ) ] =
          ( { <expression> |
              <select statement>
            } [, ...]
          )
      }
  [ where <where clause> ]
```

An *expression* can be a single value, a column, a mathematical expression, a function (such as, today or current), or a combination of these. Expressions are defined in detail in Chapter 20.

The select statement may be used to return values for the update as long as only one row of information is returned.

The symbol "*" specifies all of the columns in a table listed in the order in which they are stored in the table. You can see the order of the columns by listing the columns of the table using DB-Access or the info statement.

The where clause specifies which row(s) of the table are to be updated. If you leave out the where clause, every row in the table will be updated. The where clause is discussed further in Chapter 6.

The following are examples of update statements:

```
update toy_order
    set shipping_datetime = current year to minute
    where order_number = 4
```

The first example sets the column shipping_datetime to the current date and time for the toy_order whose order_number is four.

```
update toy set sales_price = (cost * 2)
```

The second example sets the sales_price of a toy equal to twice the cost of the toy. This statement will update every row in the toy table, since there is no where clause.

```
update state
    set (state_code, state_name) = ("VT, "VERMONT")
    where description = "VREMONT"
```

This example corrects the spelling of Vermont in the state table. The following syntax is also correct:

```
update toy_store set buyer_last_name = "MCKEAN",
                     buyer_first_name = "DON",
                     phone_number = "3039998888"
    where store_number = 1
```

This is an example of the format that sets each column to the indicated value. This format is an alternative to setting a list of columns equal to a list of values.

```
update mytable
    set (toy_code, sales_price, quantity_desired)
        = ((select toy_code, sales_price from toy
                where description = "YO-YO"),
            25)
    where my_toy = "YO-YO"
```

The final example is an `update` statement that uses a `select` statement to find values for the columns. The `select` statement may return only one row of data.

Delete

Now that we can add and change data in a table, the only thing we haven't yet learned is to remove it. Data is deleted from a table by using the `delete` statement:

```
delete from <table name>
    where <where clause>
```

The `where` clause specifies which row(s) of the table are to be deleted. If you omit the `where` clause, every row in the table will be deleted. The `where` clause is discussed further in Chapter 6. Some examples of the `delete` statement are:

```
delete from toy_order_item
    where order_number = 8

delete from toy
```

The second `delete` statement has no `where` clause, therefore all the rows in the toy table will be deleted.

Do not omit the where clause unless you want to delete your entire table!

Locking

Locks are applied to data by the engine when one process is accessing the data in such a way that a problem could occur if another user were to try and access the data. For instance, if one process is currently changing a row of data, that row will have a lock placed on it so another process can't update or possibly delete the information at the same time. The discussion of isolation levels in Chapter 20 also relates to the topic of locking.

Your computer system has a maximum number of locks available to it. If you are using INFORMIX-OnLine, your maximum number of locks is defined in your INFORMIX-OnLine configuration. When performing database changes that require a large number of locks, you may want to use some of the locking techniques described in this section.

Another reason to lock data is to prevent users from working with it while you are making extensive changes. You may want to prevent other users from updating data while you are changing a table, or you may want to keep users from being able to access a database or table completely.

Locking a Database

You may lock an entire database by closing the current database and then opening it in exclusive mode. You will not be able to open a database in exclusive mode if the database is being accessed by another user. Once the database is in exclusive mode, users will not be able to access it. To bring the database out of exclusive mode, you will need to close the database again, then reopen it without using the keyword `exclusive`.

```
database <database name> [ exclusive ]
```

Example: close database;
            database toymaker exclusive;
            <work in the database>
            close database;
            database toymaker;

Locking a Table

Use the `lock table` statement to lock a table in *shared* or *exclusive* mode. If you lock the table in shared mode, other users will be able to read the data, but they won't be able to insert, update, or delete rows in the table. If you lock the table in exclusive mode, no other user will be able to read, insert, update, or delete rows in the table.

The syntax of the `lock table` statement is:

```
lock table <table name>
    in { share | exclusive } mode
```

This statement must be used differently depending on whether or not you are using transaction logging.

Without transaction logging

If you are not using transaction logging, use the `lock table` statement in combination with the `unlock table` statement. A table lock must be unlocked before another lock can be applied. If you want to change a lock from shared mode to exclusive mode or from exclusive mode to shared mode, the table must be unlocked before changing to another type of lock.

```
unlock table <table name>
```

Example: lock table toy_order in share mode;
            <work with the table>
            unlock table toy_order;
            lock table toy_order in exclusive mode;
            <work with the table>
            unlock table toy_order;

With transaction logging

If you are using transaction logging, the `lock table` statement must be run within a transaction. Use the `begin work` statement before issuing the `lock table` statement, and the `commit work` statement will release the lock and end the transaction. The `unlock table` statement will not work within a transaction.

A table lock must be released before another lock can be applied. If you want to change a lock from shared mode to exclusive mode or from exclusive mode to shared mode, you must end the transaction and start a new transaction before changing to another type of lock.

Example:
```
begin work;
lock table toy_order in share mode;
<work with the table>
commit work;
begin work;
lock table toy_order in exclusive mode;
<more work with the table>
commit work;
```

If the `lock table` statement is issued within a transaction before any data rows are accessed, this will automatically cause your table to override row-level locking for the duration of the transaction.

Set Lock Mode

The set lock mode statement allows you to specify that you want the engine to wait for other locks on the data to be released instead of returning an error when a lock is encountered.

```
set lock mode to
  { wait [ <number of seconds OnLine only> ] |
    not wait
  }
```

You may specify a maximum number of seconds you want to wait if you are using INFORMIX-OnLine. This statement is not very useful when using INFORMIX-SE because you could end up waiting a very long time and there is no way to specify a time limit.

For example, in INFORMIX-OnLine:

```
set lock mode to wait 2 seconds;
<do work>
set lock mode to not wait;
```

In this case, if locked data is encountered and the lock is released before two seconds are up, the desired statements will be executed. Otherwise, an error will be returned.

If data is locked in exclusive mode, an error message will be returned immediately. This statement does not allow you to wait for exclusive locks to be released.

INFORMIX-OnLine Table Option

When you create a table in INFORMIX-OnLine, you have the choice of using page-level or row-level locking. Page-level locking is the default option, but row-level locking will work better for most applications.

Page-level locking means that whenever a row in a page needs to be locked, a lock is placed on the whole page instead. This ties up the entire physical page of data so it cannot be accessed by other users. The advantage to page-level locking is that when another lock needs to be placed on a row in a page that is already locked, another lock does not have to be used. This has the potential of lowering the total number of locks needed, and this, in turn, could keep you from running out of locks.

Most of the time you will probably want to use row-level locking so that less data is tied up by locks.

Load and Unload

The load statement allows you to insert data into a table from a flat file. The unload statement allows you to put information from your database into a flat file.

Loading Data

The syntax of the load statement is:

```
load from "<file name>"
  [ delimiter "<delimiter>" ]
  insert into <table name>
  [ ( <column name> [, ...] ) ]
```

To load data from a flat file, the flat file will need to contain delimited data fields that contain information, and can be read into the corresponding table columns. If the value cannot be translated into the data type it is being read into, the load statement will return an error.

The default delimiter is the pipe ("|"). The delimiter must go in between each field of information and at the end of the line. Each row of data must be on a separate line.

Each line of the data file to be loaded must contain the same number of fields. If the fields are in the same order and contain the same number of columns as the table they are being inserted into, the column names do not need to be specified. If the fields in the data file are in a different order, or if not all of the fields are being entered into the table, then you will need to specify the column names. The first field of data in the file should match the first column name and so on for each field of data.

The following *load* file and load statement can be used to load data into the toy_order table:

```
toy_order.data:
1|8|7/8/1997|1997-07-13 15:15|002|
2|2|7/11/1997|1997-07-14 9:30|002|
3|4|7/11/1997|1997-07-13 15:30|003|
4|1|7/12/1997|1997-07-15 11:00|001|
5|9|7/12/1997|1997-07-15 14:30|002|
6|5|7/12/1997|1997-07-14 14:40|001|
7|3|7/12/1997|1997-07-15 8:00|003|
8|7|7/14/1997|1997-07-18 10:00|001|

load from "toy_order.data" insert into toy_order;
```

If we had wanted the database engine to supply the serial numbers for this table, we could have specified a zero for each row in the order_number column.

The default delimiter in your flat data file is the pipe ("|"). If your data contains any pipes, you can put a backslash ("\") in front of each pipe to ignore its special meaning, or you can specify an alternate delimiter. The alternate delimiter can be specified as part of the load statement, or by using the DBDELIMITER environment variable described in Chapter 2. The following characters cannot be used as delimiters: \ , 0 though 9, a through f, A though F, space, and tab.

If we wanted to use a comma (",") for a delimiter, we could use the following data file and load statement:

```
toy_store.data:
1,DON'S TOY DUNGEON,MCKEAN,DON,3039998888,
2,KEVER'S KIDDIE KORNER,KEVER,CATHY,3037776666,
3,GAMES FOR GROWN-UPS,LESTER,GREGG,3035554444,
4,TOY TOWN,NEWTON,SUE,3034443333,
5,PETE'S PLAYHOUSE,PETERS,PETE,3033332222,
6,WAYNE'S WORLD OF TOYS,JOHNSON,WAYNE,5058889999,
7,BUCKLEY'S BOOKS AND TOYS,BUCKLEY,MIKE,6026667777,
8,DAISY'S DELIGHTFUL TOYS,DOOLITTLE,DAISY,3074445555,
9,COOL TOYS FOR GIRLS AND BOYS,CONNER,JOE,4062223333,
10,TOY PALACE,BACH,STACEY,5051110000,

load from "toy_store.data" delimiter ","
   insert into toy_store
      (store_number, store_name,
       buyer_last_name, buyer_first_name,
       phone_number)
```

Since we aren't inserting data into all columns of the toy_store table, we simply listed the columns we would be inserting in the order they are listed in the flat file.

note

Inserting a backslash ("\") before any delimiters or other back-slashes in your data will take away the special meaning of these characters and will allow the data to be inserted into the table normally. You will also need to put backslashes in front of any newline characters in a varchar column and in front of any newlines at the end of a text BLOB value. Byte data must be entered in ASCII hex-adecimal format and may not begin or end with blanks.

Unloading Data

The syntax of the unload statement is:

```
unload to "<file name>"
  [ delimiter "<delimiter>" ]
  <select statement>
```

The unload statement is very similar to the load statement. If you unload a table, the resulting file can be used with the load statement. The delimiter clause is the same as in the load statement.

The unload statement writes information from the database into the specified file.

The unload statement is used in conjunction with the select statement. The select statement is discussed in detail in Chapter 6. The select statement gives you a very versatile way of retrieving information from your database. You can unload all rows and columns from a table, or you can just choose some rows and some columns. You can also combine columns from multiple tables into a single *unload* file.

Example:

```
unload to "toy.data"
  select toy_number, description from toy where toy_number <= 5
```

```
toy.data:
1|PLAYING CARDS|
2|DOLL|
3|JACKS|
4|JUMP ROPE|
5|BOOMERANG|
```

dbload

The dbload utility allows additional options to the Informix's SQL load statement. The load statement is less complicated to use, but dbload will allow you to perform much more complex options when loading data. The dbload utility is run from the operating system command line. The syntax is:

```
dbload -d <database name>
       -c <dbload command file name>
       -l <error logging file name>
     [ -e <number of bad records> ]
     [ -n <message number> ]
     [ -i <ignore number> ]
     [ -p ]
     [ -r ]
     [ -k ]
     [ -X ]
     [ -s [ > <syntax check file> ] ]
```

If any of the mandatory switches are left off, dbload will go into an interactive mode and prompt you for the needed information.

-d   Specifies the name of the database.

-c   Specifies the name of the dbload command file. dbload command files are described below.

-l   Specifies the name of the file to write error records and messages to.

-e   If the -p switch is specified, this switch allows you to specify the *<number of bad records>* dbload will read before ending or prompting the user.

-n   A status message is displayed after each *<message number>* of records is inserted.

-i   Does not insert the first *<ignore number>* lines in the data file.

-p   Prompts the user for instructions after the -n *<number of bad records>* has been read.

-r   Instructs dbload not to lock the table while loading. The default option is table-level locking during loading.

-k   Instructs dbload to lock the table exclusively while loading.

-X   Recognize HEX escapes in character fields.

-s   Tells dbload to check the syntax of the command file, but don't run it. If you want the output of the syntax check to be saved to a file, redirect the output to a file name using the greater than symbol (">").

The Command File

A *command file* is needed by the dbload command in addition to the *data file*. The command file allows you to specify the name of the data file, the format of the data file, and the tables and columns in which the data should be inserted. A single command file can specify multiple load statements. The command file is structured as follows:

```
FILE "<data file name>"
  { DELIMITER "<delimiter>"
          <number of fields in data records> |
  ( <field name> <start position>
    [ - <end position> ]
    [: ...]
    [ NULL =
        "<data value to use instead of null>" ]
    [, ...]
  )
} ;

INSERT INTO <table name>
                    [ ( <column name list> ) ]
  [ VALUES
    ( <list of field names and/or literals> )
  ] ;
  [...]

[...]
```

A command file must have at least one FILE statement and at
least one INSERT statement. Every FILE statement will have one
or more corresponding INSERT statements. A command file may
have multiple FILE statements.

FILE statement

The FILE statement defines the name of the data file and its
structure. If your data file contains variable length records, you
will use the DELIMITER clause. If your data file contains fixed
length records, you will define the fields and their positions in the
data file.

With the DELIMITER clause, you need to specify the character
string used as the field delimiter in the data file. You must also
specify the number of fields in each input data record.

The clause that allows you to define fields for fixed length
records, also allows you to specify any characters in the input
data row to be part of any field.

Example:

Data File: - person.data:
```
999-56-2222(303) 555-9876Y
999-34-6577(303) 555-2763N
```

Field Definitions in File Section:
```
FILE "person.data"
    (ss_number        1-3:5-6:8-11,
     phone_number     13-15:18-20:22-25,
     home_owner       26                NULL = "N"
    );
```

These field definitions are selecting the important data and leaving behind the formatting characters in the data file. The dashes indicate a range of values, and the colons separate the ranges. The final field contains only a single character. If the home_owner field in the data file is blank, an "N" will be inserted in the table instead of a null.

INSERT statement

The INSERT statement allows you to specify which values are inserted into which table and column(s). Each FILE statement may have multiple INSERT statements associated with it. You may have data in a single file that should have various parts inserted into several different tables.

The INSERT statement is used like the insert into statement in Informix's SQL to specify which table and columns are inserted.

In the VALUES section, the default is to use the order of fields specified in the FILE statement. You may specify field names or literals in the VALUES section. The field names from the DELIMITER section are assigned the names f01 for the first field, f02 for the second field, and so on.

Examples

Let's look at some examples of how a data file, a command file, and a command line work together. The first example is for a variable length data file, and the second example is for a fixed length data file.

Variable length data file example

<u>Data File - `variable.data`:</u>
```
1|DON'S TOY DUNGEON|MCKEAN|DON|3039998888|
2|KEVER'S KIDDIE KORNER|KEVER|CATHY|3037776666|
3|GAMES FOR GROWN-UPS|LESTER|GREGG|3035554444|
4|TOY TOWN|NEWTON|SUE|3034443333|
5|PETE'S PLAYHOUSE|PETERS|PETE|3033332222|
6|WAYNE'S WORLD OF TOYS|JOHNSON|WAYNE|5058889999|
7|BUCKLEY'S BOOKS AND TOYS|BUCKLEY|MIKE|6026667777|
8|DAISY'S DELIGHTFUL TOYS|DOOLITTLE|DAISY|3074445555|
9|COOL TOYS FOR GIRLS AND BOYS|CONNER|JOE|4062223333|
10|TOY PALACE|BACH|STACEY|5051110000|
```

<u>Command File - `variable.com`:</u>
```
FILE "variable.data"
  DELIMITER "|" 5;
INSERT INTO toy_store
  (store_number, toy_store,
   buyer_last_name, buyer_first_name,
   phone_number)
  VALUES (f01, f02, f03, f04, f05);
```

<u>`dbload` Command Line:</u>
```
dbload -d toymaker -c variable.com -l toy_store.err -
    e 10 -p -n 100
```

Notice that the VALUES section in the INSERT section is actually not necessary since the fields are inserted into the columns in the same order as defined in the FILE section. The errors will be logged in the file toy_store.err. We will be prompted for instructions after more than 10 errors have been found, and we will be notified after each 100 records have been inserted.

Fixed length data file example

Data File - fixed.data:

```
1DON'S TOY DUNGEON          MCKEAN      DON       3039998888
2KEVER'S KIDDIE KORNER      KEVER       CATHY     3037776666
3GAMES FOR GROWN-UPS        LESTER      GREGG     3035554444
4TOY TOWN                   NEWTON      SUE       3034443333
5PETE'S PLAYHOUSE           PETERS      PETE      3033332222
6WAYNE'S WORLD OF TOYS      JOHNSON     WAYNE     5058889999
7BUCKLEY'S BOOKS AND TOYS   BUCKLEY     MIKE      6026667777
8DAISY'S DELIGHTFUL TOYS    DOOLITTLE   DAISY     3074445555
9COOL TOYS FOR GIRLS AND BOYS CONNER    JOE       4062223333
10TOY PALACE                BACH        STACEY    5051110000
```

Command File - fixed.com:

```
FILE "fixed.com"
   (store_number        1,
    store_name          2-30,
    buyer_last_name     41-50,
    buyer_first_name    51-58,
    phone_number        59-69
   );


INSERT INTO toy_store  (store_number, toy_store,
                        buyer_last_name, buyer_first_name,
                        phone_number)
         values        (store_number, store_name,
                        buyer_first_name, buyer_last_name,
                        phone_number);
```

Dbload Command Line:

```
dbload -d toymaker -c fixed.com -l toy_store.err -e 10 -n 100 -p
```

       This example is functionally equivalent to the variable length example, except that we are reading in fixed length records instead of variable length records.

dbexport and dbimport

The dbexport and dbimport utilities allow you to export an entire database to flat files, and then to create a new database from the flat files. The load and unload statements and the dbload command, work on individual tables within a database.

dbexport

The dbexport utility is used to export the definition of a database and the contents of its tables to flat files.

If you are using INFORMIX-OnLine you should be aware of the following problem when using dbexport. This program uses dbschema, and in all versions of the engine prior to 6.0, the INFORMIX-OnLine dbspace, extent, and lock mode options are not recreated in the dbschema file. If all you want is a quick way to unload all of your tables, dbexport will work just fine. You can also use your own command file for recreating the database in place of the one created by dbexport. The format requirements on the .sql file are quite strict. In general, you are best off editing the .sql file generated by dbexport.

The dbexport utility is run from the operating system command line. It has the following syntax.

```
dbexport [ -c ] [ -q ] <database name>
  [ -o <output directory path> |
    -t <tape device name>
    -b <block size> -s <tape size>
  ]
  [ -f <path name of command file> ]
  [ -d ] [ -X ] [ -ss]
```

The output of this command will create a directory called <database name>.exp where all unloaded data and the command file for recreating the database will go.

-c   Continue running when errors occur. The dbexport.out file will contain any error or warning messages.

-q   Suppress standard output. The standard output contains a listing of the dbschema which is displayed as the database is unloading. Any error or warning messages are also displayed. The dbexport.out file will also contain this information.

-o   Specifies the name of the directory the output directory will be written to. The default is the current directory.

-t   Specifies the name of a tape device for the output to be written to. When writing dbexport direct to tape under INFORMIX-OnLine, always use the -f option also. If you don't, you cannot fix lock mode, extent size, or dbspace before doing the dbimport.

-b   Specifies the tape block size in Kbytes.

-s   Specifies how much data a single tape can hold.

-f   When using the tape device to write the data, you may want the command file (used to recreate the database) to be written to disk. This switch allows you to specify a pathname for this file.

-d   Export BLOB descriptors only, not BLOB data.

-X   Recognize HEX escapes in character fields.

-ss Preserves server-specific syntax for export (version 6.0 and up of dbschema).

Example: dbexport -c -o /usr/data -ss

dbimport

The dbimport utility is used to import the definition of a database and the contents of its tables from flat files, created by the dbexport utility, into a new database.

The dbimport utility is run from the operating system command line. It has the following syntax:

```
dbimport [ -c ] [ -q ] <new database name>
   [ -i <input directory path> |
     -t <tape device name>
     -b <block size> -s <tape size>
        [ -f <path name of command file> ]
   ]
   [ -d <dbspace name> ]
   [ -l [ <SE log pathame> | buffered ] ]
   [ -ansi ] [ -X ]
```

-c   Continue running when nonfatal errors occur. The dbimport.out file will contain any error or warning messages.

-q   Suppress standard output. The standard output contains a listing of any messages, warnings, and errors. The dbimport.out file will also contain this information.

-I   Specifies the name of the input directory where the directory <database name>.exp was created when the database was exported. The default is the current directory.

-t   Specifies the name of a tape device from which the output is to be read.

-b   Specifies the tape block size in Kbytes.

-s   Specifies how much data a single tape can hold.

-f   When using the tape device to read the data, you may want the command file (used to create the database) to be read from disk. This switch allows you to specify a pathname for this file if you also specified this switch when using the dbexport utility.

-d   Specifies the *dbspace* the new database will be put into.

-l   Turns transaction logging on for the new database. If using INFORMIX-SE, *<SE log pathname>* specifies the path and name of the log file. If using INFORMIX-OnLine, buffered specifies the database will be using buffered logging, the default option is unbuffered.

-ansi   The new database will be created as mode ANSI.

-X   Recognize HEX escapes in character fields.

Example: dbimport -c -i /usr/data

Tips for Faster Data Loads

When loading data in bulk, there are several steps you can take that can drastically improve your performance.

First, turn off transaction logging. If you are using transaction logging while loading data, the data will be written to both the table and to the transaction log. The transaction logging creates a large amount of system overhead, which you should avoid if at all possible.

Also, drop all indexes on a table before loading data into it. If indexes exist, they will be updated for every single row inserted. It is better to create an index after the data is loaded than to continually update it. Multiple indexes compound the problem. Be aware of implicit indexes created to enforce referential constraints.

Summary

The syntax for the `insert`, `update`, and `delete` statements are:

```
insert into <table name> [ ( <column name> [, ...] ) ]
  { values ( <values> [, ...] ) |
    <select statement (with limitations)> |
    execute procedure <stored procedure name>
                                ( <arguments>   [, ...] )
  }
```

```
update <table name>
  set { <column name> =
          { <expression> | <select statement> } [, ...] |
          [ * | ( <column name> [, ..] ) ] =
              ( { <expression> | <select statement> } [, ...] )
      }
  [ where <where clause> ]
```

```
delete from <table name> where <where clause>
```

Statements that affect locking include `lock mode row` and `lock mode page` in the `create table` statement, and:

```
database <database name> [ exclusive ]
```

```
lock table <table name> in { share | exclusive } mode
```

```
unlock table <table name>
```

```
set lock mode to
  { wait [ <number of seconds OnLine only> ] | not wait }
```

Batch data loading and unloading statements include the `load` and `unload` statements and the `dbload` utility:

```
load from "<file name>" [ delimiter "<delimiter>" ]
  insert into <table name> [ ( <column name> [, ...] ) ]
```

```
unload to "<file name>" [ delimiter "<delimiter>" ]
        <select statement>
```

dbload is run from the command line:

```
dbload -d <database name>
        -c <dbload command file name>
        -l <error logging file name>
     [ -e <number of bad records> ]
     [ -n <message number> ]
     [ -i <ignore number> ]
     [ -p ] [ -r ] [ -k ] [-X ]
     [ -s [ > <syntax check file> ] ]
```

The dbload command file is structured as follows:

```
FILE "<data file name>"
  { DELIMITER "<delimiter>"
                    <number of fields in data records> |
    ( <field name> <start position>
      [ - <end position> ]
      [: ...]
      [ NULL = "<data value to use instead of null>" ]
      [, ...]
    )
  } ;


INSERT INTO <table name> [ ( <column name list> ) ]
  [ VALUES ( <list of field names and/or literals> ) ] ;
  [...]

  [...]
```

The dbexport and dbimport utilities allow you to export an entire database to flat files, and then to recreate the database and import the database from the flat files. These utilities are run from the operating system command line:

```
dbexport [ -c ] [ -q ] <database name>
  [ -o <output directory path> |
    -t <tape device name>
    -b <block size> -s <tape size>
  ]
  [ -f <path name of command file> ]
  [ -d ] [ -X ] [ -ss]

dbimport [ -c ] [ -q ] <new database name>
  [ -i <input directory path> |
    -t <tape device name> -b <block size> -s <tape size>
       [ -f <path name of command file> ]
  ]
  [ -d <dbspace name> ]
  [ -l [ <SE log pathame> | buffered ] ]
  [ -ansi ] [ -X ]
```

To speed batch data loads, when possible, turn off transaction logging and drop all indexes on tables being loaded.

Chapter 6

The Select Statement

- *Overview of the* `select` *statement*
- `select`
- `from`
- `where`
- `group by`
- `having`
- `order by`
- `into temp`
- `union`
- *Joins*
- `outer` *joins*
- `output to`
- *Summary*

Overview of the Select Statement

The select statement allows you to retrieve information from your database. The select statement is probably the most frequently used statement in SQL. There are many parts to the select statement. Many of the parts are optional, but they can cause your select statement to range from very simple to quite complex. This chapter covers the basic select statement, and Chapter 20 will explain more complex things to do with the select statement.

tip

While you are reading through this chapter, try experimenting with the various forms of the select statement in your own database. As with other SQL statements, the select statement is run from DB-Access.

The general format of the select statement is:

```
select <information to retrieve>
  from <table(s) to retrieve info from>
  [where <conditions to retrieve rows of info>]
  [group by <info to be reported in groups>]
  [having <conditions on aggregate data>]
  [order by <order in which to display info>]
  [into temp <temporary table name> [with no log]]
  [union [all] <select statement>]
```

Each part of the select statement is described in detail in this chapter.

Select

The `select` clause of the `select` statement has the following syntax:

```
select
  { [ all | distinct | unique ]
    { [<table name>.]<column name> |
      <expression>
    } [ [as] <display label> ] [, ...] |
  [<table name>.]*
  }
```

The `select` portion of the `select` statement allows you to specify which columns of information you wish to retrieve. The columns specified must exist in the table(s) specified in the `from` clause of the `select` statement, described below. Columns are normally specified as a list of column names separated by commas.

```
select toy_code, description, sales_price
```

If a column exists in more than one of the tables specified in the `from` clause, you must also specify the table from which the column is being retrieved. You may always specify which table a column is in, even if the column name by itself is unambiguous.

```
select toy.toy_code, toy.description,
       toy_order_item.unit_price
```

If you wish to specify all columns from the table(s), you may use the "*" notation. An asterisk indicates all columns from each table in the `from` clause. These are listed in the order in which the tables in the `from` clause are listed, then in the order in which the columns are stored in the tables. The notation `<table name>.*` specifies only the columns from the specified table.

```
select *
```

```
select toy.*, toy_order_item.unit_price
```

Expressions may also be used in the `select` clause. These may include built-in functions, aggregates, mathematical expressions, and constants, which are discussed in detail in Chapter 20.

```
select toy.toy_code, toy.description,
    toy_order_item.quantity * toy_order.unit_price
```

You may also rename columns for use in the `select` statement by listing a *display label* after a column name or expression, separated only by a space (no commas) or by using the as keyword. This is particularly useful when using expressions. In the examples below, the expression multiplying the quantity and the unit_price produces a column in the `select` statement output called total_price.

```
select toy.toy_code, toy.description,
    toy_order_item.quantity * toy_order.unit_price
    total_price
```

```
select toy.toy_code, toy.description,
    toy_order_item.quantity * toy_order.unit_price
    as total_price
```

Depending on how much information you specify in your `select` clause, your output will appear across the screen in columns or it will be listed down the screen with blank lines separating each row.

From

The `from` clause of the `select` statement has the following syntax:

```
from <table name> [ [as] <display label> ]
[,
   { [ [outer] <table name>
   [ [as] <label alias> ]
     ]
     [ outer ( <table name>
   [ [as] <label alias> ] [, ...]
     )
   } [...]
]
```

The `from` clause allows you to specify a table or list of tables that is used in the `select` statement (in the `select` clause and the `where` clause). The table names are expressed as a list separated by commas.

```
from toy
```

```
from toy, toy_order_item
```

You may also rename tables for use in the `select` statement by listing a *label alias* or *correlation name* after the table name separated only by a space (no commas), or by using the `as` keyword.

```
from toy a, toy_order_item b
```

```
from toy as a, toy_order_item b
```

The method used to *join* tables together when you specify more than one table in your `from` clause is described later in this chapter. Right now you can easily build queries using the `select` clause and the `from` clause with only one table.

The `outer` clause allows you an alternative method of joining tables that produces different results than a normal join. `Outer` is an optional part of the `from` clause and is discussed under *outer joins* later in this chapter.

A combination of the `select` and `from` clauses will produce the simplest form of a complete `select` statement:

```
select * from toy
```

Where

The `where` clause is used as part of the `select` statement to determine which rows of information should be returned from the `select` statement. If no `where` clause is used, all rows of information in the table(s) specified in the `from` clause are returned.

The `where` clause is also part of the `update` and `delete` statements discussed earlier. In the case of the `update` statement, the `where` clause determines which rows in a table will be updated. Using a `where` clause with a `delete` statement determines which rows in a table will be deleted. Neglecting to use a `where` clause with either of these statements will result in all rows in a table being updated or deleted.

It is frequently useful to run a `select` statement before running an `update` or `delete` statement, using the same `where` clause you plan to use in an `update` or `delete` statement. Running a `select` statement first helps to make certain your `where` clause returns the information you intended. You may spend a little extra time doing this, but it is worth the time if you save yourself from making a major (or even a minor) mistake.

The `where` clause has the following syntax:

```
where
  [ not ] { [<table name>.]<column name> |
             <expression>
         }
  { { = | <> | != | < | <= | > | >= | }
    { [<table name>.]<column name> |
      <expression>
    }                                                    |
    is [not]  null                                       |
    [not] in ( <value> [, ...] )                         |
    [not] between { [<table name>.]<column name> |
                    <expression>
                  } and
                  { [<table name>.]<column name> |
                    <expression>
                  }                                      |
  [not] { matches | like }
              <string> [escape "<character>"]    |
  <subqueries>
  }  [ { and | or } ... ]
```

The `where` clause specifies which rows of information will be retrieved from the indicated table(s). If no where clause is used, all rows from the indicated table(s) will be displayed.

Conditional Expressions

The condition(s) in a `where` clause are Boolean expressions that will evaluate to either true or false. If the Boolean expression in the `where` clause evaluates to true for a particular row of data, that row will be retrieved as part of the output of the `select` statement. Any rows that produce a result of false or *null* are not part of the output of the `select` statement.

Parentheses can be used to logically group parts of the `where` clause. The `and` keyword has a higher precedence than the `or` keyword, but is usually a good idea to use parentheses to allow for greater clarity when reading a `where` clause.

Let's look at some examples:

```
select *
  from toy
  where sales_price > 10
```

The above `select` statement will select all rows of information from the toy table where the sales_price is more than $10.

```
select *
  from toy
  where (sales_price < 10 or sales_price > 100)
    and
        toy_code < 100
```

The `where` clause in the above `select` statement contains the `and` keyword and the `or` keyword, so parentheses are used to indicate that the `or` conditional should be evaluated before the `and` conditional.

```
select order_number, order_date, shipping_datetime
  from toy_order
  where order_date between "7/1/1997" and
                           "7/31/1997"
```

The above `select` statement will retrieve the order_number, order_date, and shipping_datetime for every toy_order with an order_date in July of 1997. The `between` keyword is an inclusive between, the values at either end of the `between` are included in the result.

```
select store_name, fax_number
  from toy_store
  where fax_number is not null
```

The above `select` statement will retrieve a list of store names and their fax numbers for every store whose fax number `is not null`. The *null* value is an undefined, empty value that cannot be compared using standard operators such as "=" and "<>." *Null* values must always be compared using `is null` or `is not null`.

Mathematical expressions, constants, substrings, and functions can be used within the `where` clause. Expressions and functions that can be used with `select` statements are listed in Chapter 20. The following constant expression is a commonly used `where` clause:

```
where 1 = 1
```

This `where` clause will evaluate to true for every row. It is used in many cases to keep from not having a `where` clause. The effect of 1 = 1 is the same as if there was no `where` clause, except that explicitly stating every row evaluates to true prevents the ambiguity of omitting the `where` clause and having someone later wonder if that was intended. Another use of this `where` clause will be made clear when we start to work with `construct` statements in INFORMIX-4GL.

```
select *
  from toy_store
  where store_state in ("CA", "OR", "WA")
```

The above `select` statement will return a list of stores in California, Oregon, and Washington. We could very easily reverse this `select` statement and select all toy_stores that are not in those states:

```
select *
  from toy_store
  where store_state not in ("CA", "OR", "WA")
```

Matches and Like

The operators `matches` and `like` allow you to compare columns with patterns. Each of these operators has a set of special characters that are used for pattern recognition.

matches	like	Description
*	%	Matches any string of characters (including none).
?	–	Matches any single character.
\	\	Used to ignore the meaning of special characters: matches * and \?, like \% and \-. It is used to match these special characters as literal values within a pattern. You can change the character used to ignore the special meaning of characters by using the following syntax after your matches or like expression: escape "<character>".
[ ]	none	Used to match characters or ranges of characters within the brackets. A caret matches any characters not within the brackets. [aeiou] matches any vowels, and [^aeiou] matches consonants or other characters. A range is indicated by the use of a dash such as [a-z], [A-Z], and [0-9]. A combination of ranges and characters can also be used: [A-Z0-9$,.] matches a capital letter, a digit, a dollar sign, a comma, or a period.

Here are some examples:

```
select *
   from toy
   where description matches "*BALL*"
```

The `select` statement above returns any toy descriptions containing the character string BALL.

```
select *
   from toy_store
   where buyer_last_name matches
      "[Ss][Mm][Ii][Tt][Hh]"
```

The above `select` statement returns store information for any store where the buyer's name is SMITH, smith, Smith, sMiTh, etc.

```
select *
   from toy_store
   where store_name matches "?????"
```

The above `select` statement matches any store names that contain exactly five characters. While the store name is defined as 30 characters, trailing spaces are not counted as characters. Therefore, the following strings would be matched: "12345" and "a b c" and these strings would not be matched: "321" and "a b c d".

```
select *
   from toy_store
   where store_name like "%&%%" escape "&"
```

The above conditional is a bit confusing. We are using the ampersand character (`&`) to take away the special meaning of the percent character (`%`) following the ampersand, but the other instances of the percent character still have special meanings. This will match any store_name that has a percent character anywhere within the store_name. Using `matches` to achieve the same purpose, we could simply have written:

```
select *
   from toy_store
   where store_name matches "*%*"
```

Using `matches` and `like` require more system resources than using traditional operators because pattern matching is a more complex operation than a simple equivalency.

Other Conditionals

The method for joining tables when the `from` clause specifies more than one table is done with the `where` clause, but is described later in this chapter. *Outer joins* are also described later in this chapter.

A *subquery* is a `select` statement that appears in the `where` clause of another `select` statement or in the `where` clause of another SQL statement. Subqueries are discussed in Chapter 20.

Group By

The `group by` clause is used to group information selected in the `select` clause, either to produce a list of individual items, or for use with *aggregates*. The `group by` has the syntax:

```
group by {  [<table name>.]<column name>  |
            <column number>
        }
        [, ...]
```

When using a `group by` clause, you must include every column in the `group by` which is part of the `select` clause, except for *aggregates*.

```
select order_date
   from toy_order
   group by order_date
```

The above `select` statement will produce a list of unique order_dates. You can see that if instead you use the `select` statement:

```
select order_number, order_date
   from toy_order
   group by order_number, order_date
```

you would end up with a list of all order_numbers and order_dates. We cannot simply leave the order_number off of the `group by` clause since order_number is used in the `select` statement. If you were permitted simply to group by the order_date, then many of the order numbers would be lost.

You may also use the column number as ordered in the `select` clause, instead of a column name in the `group by` clause.

```
select order_number, order_date
   from toy_order
   group by 1, 2
```

Order_number is the first column in the `select` clause, and order_date is the second column. It is this order which is referred to in the `group by` clause. Pay attention when using numbers instead of column names. If the number of columns or the order of columns in your `select` clause changes, you may need to change the numbers in the `group by` clause. You may also use a combination of column names and column numbers in the `group by` clause.

The `group by` clause is most commonly used with *aggregates*. Aggregate functions available in Informix's SQL are: `count`, `avg`, `max`, `min`, `sum`. The aggregate function is listed in the `select` clause. An example is:

```
select order_number, sum (quantity * unit_price)
         total_price
   from toy_order_item
   group by order_number
```

The above select statement will produce a list of all order_numbers with the total_price charged for each order:

```
order_number        total_price

     3              $1105.00
     1               $682.50
     2              $2232.50
     4              $1850.00
     9               $500.00
     6               $850.00
     7              $1100.00
    10              $1850.00
     5              $1455.00
     8               $100.00
```

Aggregates are discussed in detail in Chapter 20. As you can see from the results of this `select` statement, the `group by` statement merely groups the data; if you wish to order it, this can be done using the `order by` clause described later in this chapter.

Having

The `having` clause allows you to place conditions on aggregate information. The syntax for the `having` clause is:

```
having <conditional expression>
```

For instance, if in the above `group by` query, we only wanted to return rows of information in which the total order price was at least $1000, we could do the following:

```
select order_number, sum (quantity * unit_price)
       total_price
  from toy_order_item
  group by order_number
  having sum (quantity * unit_price) >= 1000
```

Adding the `having` condition to this `select` statement will produce the following output:

order_number	total_price
3	$1105.00
2	$2232.50
4	$1850.00
7	$1100.00
10	$1850.00
5	$1455.00

Or suppose we just wanted to print this list for orders in which more than three types of toys had been purchased:

```
select order_number, sum (quantity * unit_price)
       total_price
  from toy_order_item
  group by order_number
  having count (*) > 3
```

The function `count (*)` simply counts the number of rows that make up each aggregate row (the rows we are outputting from the `select` statement). This list below prints totals of orders that contain more than three types of toys (that is, four or more rows per order in the toy_order_item table).

order_number	total_price
3	$1105.00
1	$682.50
2	$2232.50
10	$1850.00
5	$1455.00

Order By

The `order by` clause instructs the `select` statement to return the requested information in a particular order. The information may be ordered by any of the columns selected in the `select` clause.

If more than one `order by` column is selected, the information will be sorted first by the first column in the `order by` clause, then by the second column (when the first column values match), then by the third column (when the first and second column values match), and so on.

The syntax for the order by clause is:

```
order by { [<table name>.]<column name> |
          <column number> |
          <new column name>
       }
       [ asc | desc ]
       [, ...]
```

You may also specify the column number (as ordered in the `select` clause) instead of specifying column names. This can be useful when ordering by expressions. While using column numbers is sometimes useful, you must remember that if you add columns into the `select` clause, these numbers may change. Also, it is easier to review a list of names in an `order by` clause than a list of numbers if you are trying to figure out what someone else was trying to do.

A *display label* may be used to order columns if you have renamed a column (or an expression) or a table for use in the `select` statement.

You may specify that each column be sorted in either ascending or descending order. Ascending order is the default.

Let's look at some examples:

```
select store_name, buyer_last_name, buyer_first_name
   from toy_store
   order by store_name
```

This `select` statement orders the result by the store name:

store_name	buyer_last_name	buyer_first_name
BUCKLEY'S BOOKS AND TOYS	BUCKLEY	MIKE
COOL TOYS FOR GIRLS AND BOYS	CONNER	JOE
DAISY'S DELIGHTFUL TOYS	DOOLITTLE	DAISY
DON'S TOY DUNGEON	MCKEAN	DON
GAMES FOR GROWN-UPS	LESTER	GREGG
KEVER'S KIDDIE KORNER	KEVER	CATHY
PETE'S PLAYHOUSE	PETERS	PETE
TOY PALACE	BACH	STACEY
TOY TOWN	NEWTON	SUE
WAYNE'S WORLD OF TOYS	JOHNSON	WAYNE

Using the `select` statement from the discussion of the `having` clause, we can now sort it:

```
select order_number,
       sum (quantity * unit_price) total_price
   from toy_order_item
   group by order_number
   having sum (quantity * unit_price) >= 1000
   order by total_price desc, order_number
```

Adding this `order by` clause to this `select` statement will produce the following output:

order_number	total_price
2	$2232.50
4	$1850.00
10	$1850.00
5	$1455.00
3	$1105.00
7	$1100.00

If we didn't give the sum expression a name, we could phrase the above `select` statement as follows:

```
select order_number, sum (quantity * unit_price)
   from toy_order_item
   group by order_number
   having sum (quantity * unit_price) >= 1000
   order by 2 desc, order_number
```

Into Temp

The `into temp` clause allows you to save the result of a `select` statement to a *temporary table*. If you have a query with many tables listed in the `from` clause, it is usually best to run the query in parts and then to store intermediate query results in temporary tables. Splitting the query into parts will frequently make the query run faster.

The syntax for the `into temp` clause is:

```
into temp <temporary table name>  [with no log]
```

The `with no log` clause is optional, but recommended. It will prevent the temporary table from being logged and taking up space in your transaction logs. It will also run more quickly and reduce system overhead. Should you need to recover from your logs, using `with no log` will help you to recover faster. This clause will be ignored if you do not use logging, and it is generally a good idea to use it.

Let's look at a quick example:

```
select order_number, order_date, shipping_datetime
   from toy_order
   into temp a1 with no log
```

note

Temporary tables exist for only the current process or until you explicitly drop them using the `drop table` *statement. When naming temporary tables, you should give them names that are very different from your normal table names so you don't accidentally drop a permanent table. Names for temporary tables such as a1, a2, a3, and so on give you an easy and consistent way to remember what you've done.*

Union

The union clause allows the results of two select statements retrieving similar data to be merged together. The union clause has the format:

```
<select statement 1>
union
<select statement 2>
```

The select statements must retrieve the same data types in the same column positions and the same number of columns. If corresponding columns don't have the same name, the name of the column in the first select statement will be used.

You can only use an order by with the second select statement. This will order the entire result. You may also only use column numbers to order a select statement when using a union.

The union clause is frequently useful for ordering items as defined by a user. For example, if you want to display all toy_stores that have the pattern "TOY" somewhere in the store_name before the toy_stores that don't have the pattern "TOY" somewhere in the store_name you can do the following:

```
select "A", store_name,
       buyer_last_name[1,10], buyer_first_name[1,10]
   from toy_store
   where store_name matches "*TOY*"
union
select "B", store_name,
       buyer_last_name[1,10], buyer_first_name[1,10]
   from toy_store
   where store_name not matches "*TOY*"
   order by 1, 2
```

The square brackets containing [1,10] simply print the first ten characters of the indicated columns to allow us to print the columns across the page instead of down the page. This select statement will produce the output:

(con- stant)	store_name	buyer_last_name	buyer_first_name
A	BUCKLEY'S BOOKS AND TOYS	BUCKLEY	MIKE
A	COOL TOYS FOR GIRLS AND BOYS	CONNER	JOE
A	DAISY'S DELIGHTFUL TOYS	DOOLITTLE	DAISY
A	DON'S TOY DUNGEON	MCKEAN	DON
A	TOY PALACE	BACH	STACEY
A	TOY TOWN	NEWTON	SUE
A	WAYNE'S WORLD OF TOYS	JOHNSON	WAYNE
B	GAMES FOR GROWN-UPS	LESTER	GREGG
B	KEVER'S KIDDIE KORNER	KEVER	CATHY
B	PETE'S PLAYHOUSE	PETERS	PETE

You may find many other uses for the union clause as well. Merging tables is another common use for the union clause. For instance, if you have a charges table and a deposits table, you may wish to merge them with a union clause to produce output of information from both tables ordered by date.

Joins

Whenever you specify more than a single table in the from clause of a select statement, you will need to define how the tables are related to one another. This is done in the where clause.

Table relationships are defined by one or more columns in each table that contain the same information. All we need to do is to make certain the key fields are equal to one another.

```
select *
  from toy_order, toy_store
  where toy_order.store_number =
    toy_store.store_number
```

The foreign key store_number in the toy_order table has the same value as the store_number primary key in the toy_store table whenever rows in the two tables are connected.

If toy_order and toy_store were connected by a set of keys, say store_key1 and store_key2, then we would need to make certain both parts of the key are connected:

```
select *
   from toy_order, toy_store
   where toy_order.store_key1 = toy_order.store_key1 and
         toy_order.store_key2 = toy_store.store_key2
```

You should always check to make certain that every table in the `from` clause is joined directly or indirectly to every other table in the `from` clause.

You may join as many tables as you like, but the more tables you add, the slower your retrieval will become. This is where temporary tables come in handy. By splitting a query into parts and storing intermediate results in temporary tables, you can often drastically improve the performance of a query.

note

If you neglect to join two tables, every row of the first table will be joined to every row of the second table. This is called a Cartesian product (named after the famous French mathemetician and philosopher René Descartes). Unjoined queries can take a very long time to run, use up quite a lot of temporary space, and will not give you the results you were looking for (unless, of course, you intended to create a Cartesian product—which is very unusual, but not unheard of).

Let's look at an example that connects all of the tables in the toy_order database:

```
select *
   from toy_order, toy_order_item, toy, toy_store, sales_staff, state
   where toy_order.order_number  =  toy_order_item.order_number and
         toy_order_item.toy_code=  toy.toy_code                  and
         toy_order.store_number  =  toy_store.store_number       and
         toy_order.sales_code    =  sales_staff.sales_code       and
         toy_store.store_state   =  state.state_code
```

Notice that the tables are joined in the order in which they are listed in the `from` clause. This makes it easier to go back and check your work for errors or omissions.

Outer Joins

Outer joins are used to join tables when you want to retrieve all rows of information from table A and any information in table B that is related to table A.

There are two forms of the outer join: the *simple outer join* and the *nested outer join*.

Let's start with a *simple outer join*. First, we need to make the assumption that we may have a null state_code for any of the toy_stores in our examples.

```
select store_name, state_name
    from toy_store, outer state
    where toy_store.store_state = state.state_code
    order by store_name
```

This `select` statement will return a list of all toy_stores and the state information for any toy_store that has a state_code.

store_name	state_name
BUCKLEY'S BOOKS AND TOYS	ARIZONA
COOL TOYS FOR GIRLS AND BOYS	MONTANA
DAISY'S DELIGHTFUL TOYS	WYOMING
DON'S TOY DUNGEON	COLORADO
GAMES FOR GROWN-UPS	
KEVER'S KIDDIE KORNER	COLORADO
PETE'S PLAYHOUSE	COLORADO
TOY PALACE	NEW MEXICO
TOY TOWN	
WAYNE'S WORLD OF TOYS	NEW MEXICO

Notice that an outer join has some additional consequences. If I want a list of all states where the state description is "COLORADO", the following `select` statement will yield some interesting results:

```
select store_name, state_name
   from toy_store, outer state
   where state_name          = "COLORADO"          and
         toy_store.store_state = state.state_code
   order by store_name
```

The output of this statement follows. Notice that the state_name qualification doesn't limit the number of rows returned, it merely limits the information brought back from the outer table.

```
store_name                               state_name

BUCKLEY'S BOOKS AND TOYS
COOL TOYS FOR GIRLS AND BOYS
DAISY'S DELIGHTFUL TOYS
DON'S TOY DUNGEON                         COLORADO
GAMES FOR GROWN-UPS
KEVER'S KIDDIE KORNER                     COLORADO
PETE'S PLAYHOUSE                          COLORADO
TOY PALACE
TOY TOWN
WAYNE'S WORLD OF TOYS
```

Now let's have a look at *nested outer joins*. An outer join is nested when the `outer` keyword is followed by table names listed within parentheses. The joins within the parentheses are joined first, then the results of this join are joined with an `outer` to the other table(s) in the query.

```
select store_name, order_date, state_name
   from toy_order, outer (toy_store, outer state)
   where toy_order.store_number = toy_store.store_number and
         toy_store.store_state = state.state_code
   order by store_name
```

Actually, in this case there was no reason (except for the example) to perform an outer join on the toy_store table since every toy_order has an existing toy_store attached to it. The results of this query are as follows:

store_name	order_date	state_name
BUCKLEY'S BOOKS AND TOYS	07/20/1997	ARIZONA
BUCKLEY'S BOOKS AND TOYS	07/14/1997	ARIZONA
COOL TOYS FOR GIRLS AND BOYS	07/12/1997	MONTANA
COOL TOYS FOR GIRLS AND BOYS	07/22/1997	MONTANA
DAISY'S DELIGHTFUL TOYS	07/20/1997	WYOMING
DAISY'S DELIGHTFUL TOYS	07/08/1997	WYOMING
DON'S TOY DUNGEON	07/15/1997	COLORADO
DON'S TOY DUNGEON	07/21/1997	COLORADO
DON'S TOY DUNGEON	07/12/1997	COLORADO
GAMES FOR GROWN-UPS	07/19/1997	
GAMES FOR GROWN-UPS	07/12/1997	
KEVER'S KIDDIE KORNER	07/20/1997	COLORADO
KEVER'S KIDDIE KORNER	07/11/1997	COLORADO
PETE'S PLAYHOUSE	07/12/1997	COLORADO
PETE'S PLAYHOUSE	07/22/1997	COLORADO
TOY PALACE	07/19/1997	NEW MEXICO
TOY TOWN	07/20/1997	
TOY TOWN	07/11/1997	
TOY TOWN	07/18/1997	
WAYNE'S WORLD OF TOYS	07/15/1997	NEW MEXICO

A nested join is actually the only way to perform an outer join to a table that is itself an outer join using a single select statement.

Output To

By default, the output from the `select` statement will be written to your screen. You may also specify that the output be written elsewhere. The syntax for the output to statement is:

```
output to { <file name> | pipe <program name> }
   [ without headings ]
   <select statement>
```

The `without headings` option will print the results of the query without any column headings. Some examples are:

```
output to "toy.query" without headings
   select * from toy
```

This will store the results of the query in a file called `toy.query` in the current directory with no column headings. The file name may optionally be in quotes.

```
output to pipe "more"
   select * from toy
```

This statement will run the results of the query through the specified program, in this case `more`. If the program command line contains any spaces, it should be enclosed in quotes, otherwise the quotes are optional. Note that this statement can only be run from within DB-Access and INFORMIX-SQL, but not from within INFORMIX-4GL.

Summary

The general format of the `select` statement is:

```
select <information to retrieve>
  from <table(s) to retrieve info from>
  [where <conditions to retrieve rows of info>]
  [group by <info to be reported in groups>]
  [having <conditions on aggregate data>]
  [order by <order in which to retrieve info>]
  [into temp <temporary table name>
                              [with no log]]
  [union [all] <select statement>]
```

The complete syntax of the `select` statement is:

```
select
  { [ all | distinct | unique ]
    { [<table name>.]<column name> |
      <expression>
    } [ [as] <display label> ] [, ...] |
    [<table name>.]*
  }
from <table name> [ [as] <display label> ]
  [,
    { [[outer] <table name> [ [as] <display label> ] ]
      [ outer (<table name> [ [as] <display label> ] [, ...])
    } [...]
  ]
```

```
where
   [ not ] { [<table name>.]<column name>|
              <expression>
           }
   { { = | <> | != | < | <= | > | >= | }
     { [<table name>.]<column name>                              |
        <expression>
     }                                                           |
     is [not] null                                               |
     [not] in ( <value> [, ...] )                                |
     [not] between { [<table name>.]<column name>                |
                     <expression>
                   } and
                   { [<table name>.]<column name> |
                      <expression>
                   }                         |
     [not] { matches | like }
               <string> [escape "<character>"]   |
     <subqueries>
   }   [ { and | or } ... ]
group by { [<table name>.]<column name> | <column number> }
         [, ...]
having <conditional expression>
order by { [<table name>.]<column name> |
           <column number> |
           <new column name>
         } [ asc | desc ] [, ...]
into temp <temporary table name>   [with no log]
```

The union clause allows the results of two select statements
retrieving similar data to be merged together. The union clause
has the format:

```
<select statement 1>
union
<select statement 2>
```

Whenever you specify more than a single table in the `from` clause of a `select` statement, you will need to define how the tables are related to one another by *joining* the tables. *Outer joins* are used to join tables when you want to retrieve all rows of information from table A and any information in table B that is related to table A.

By default the output from the `select` statement will be written to your screen. You may also specify that the output be written to a file or be piped through a program.

```
output to { <file name> | pipe <program name> }
           [ without headings ]
           <select statement>
```

Chapter

7

The 4GL Programming Environment

- *INFORMIX-4GL flavors: r4gl and c4gl*
- *INFORMIX-4GL file name suffixes*
- *Menu driven development*
- *Command line development*
- *Make files*
- *Prototyping*
- *Summary*

INFORMIX-4GL Flavors: r4gl and c4gl

There are two basic INFORMIX-4GL flavors: r4gl and c4gl.

r4gl is the Informix *rapid development system* (or rds). When 4GL code is compiled under r4gl, it produces an interpreted code called *p-code*. This code is machine independent, so that you can develop the code and compile it on one machine, and the p-code will run on another machine using the same executable code as the system that compiled the original code. The part of r4gl that is machine dependent is the runner. The runner is an executable program that accepts the file containing the p-code as an argument, and runs the application. r4gl compiles very quickly. The compiled p-code files are simply appended to create the program file.

c4gl is Informix *compiled 4GL*. When c4gl code is compiled, it translates the 4GL code into INFORMIX-ESQL/C code, the INFORMIX-ESQL/C code into C code, and the C code is then compiled to create standard object files. These files are linked to create an executable program file. c4gl code takes longer to compile, but the startup time of a program under c4gl can be significantly faster than that of the r4gl program. Using c4gl makes it easier to link in external C functions than when using r4gl. i4gl is the name of the command used to start c4gl.

The 4GL code for both varieties of code is identical, except that you will have to initialize all your variables in c4gl, where r4gl takes care of this for you.

note

Many people use r4gl *for prototyping and development, and then use* c4gl *to compile production code. If you decide to do this, don't neglect testing of your production code.* r4gl *and* c4gl *are not guaranteed to be bug-for-bug compatible.*

INFORMIX-ESQL/C is basically a version of C which allows you to embed Informix's SQL commands within it. If you are going to link INFORMIX-ESQL/C with an c4gl program, the general rule is to compile with the c4gl script. This gets around all of the complex problems. This is more complicated for r4gl users. For r4gl users, compile any INFORMIX-ESQL/C code (or C code with INFORMIX-ESQL/C headers) with the INFORMIX-ESQL/C version corresponding to the one used with the version of r4gl you are using. If the version of INFORMIX-ESQL/C isn't available, you will need to use the c4gl compiler.

INFORMIX-4GL File Name Suffixes

This section discusses the file name suffixes used when developing applications in INFORMIX-4GL. You should be aware of these suffixes so that you can create appropriate file names and recognize the different files created by INFORMIX-4GL.

The following list contains the suffixes of file names used when writing and compiling 4GL code.

Suffix	Type of File
.4gl	4GL code
.4go	r4gl compiled module
.o	c4gl compiled module
.4gi	r4gl interpreted program. Created by appending .4go files together.
.4ge	c4gl executable program. Created using `make` files (see next section).
.per	screen form code
.frm	compiled screen form
.err	an error file is created when the compile of a 4GL module or a screen form fails.
.erc	created when an error occurs in trying to compile or link non-4gl code
.c	created by c4gl during compilation—file contains equivalent C code
.ec	created by c4gl during compilation—intermediate source code file

The Programmer's Environment creates backups of the original code whenever you edit or compile. These file names are:

Backup File Suffix	Type of File
.4bl	backup of a .4gl file
.4bo	backup of a .4go or .o file
.4be	backup of a .4gi or .4ge file
.pbr	backup of a .per file
.fbm	backup of a .frm file

Menu Driven Development

You may use the menu driven system for application development, or you may perform your development from the command line. This section discusses using the menu driven development system, also known as the Programmer's Environment.

To get into the INFORMIX-4GL Programmer's Environment, at the command line type:

```
i4gl        for compiled 4GL, or
r4gl        for the rapid development system
```

The following ring menu will appear at the top of your screen:

```
INFORMIX-4GL:   Module   Form   Program   Query-Language   Exit
```

Each of these options is covered briefly below:

Module
: Allows you to create, modify, compile and run 4GL modules and programs. Files containing 4GL code will have the suffix .4gl when viewed from the operating system. r4gl compiled modules have the suffix .4go, and c4gl compiled modules have the suffix .o. r4gl executable code has the suffix .4gi, and c4gl executable code has the suffix .4ge.

Form
: Allows you to create, modify, and compile 4GL screen forms. Files containing screen form code have the suffix .per. Compiled screen forms have the suffix .frm.

Program
: Allows you to define and compile 4GL programs. I do not recommend this option. Instead, I recommend the use of make files that are covered later in this chapter. If you are going to do anything large or extensive with 4GL, the INFORMIX-4GL menu options do not allow enough flexibility and will end up causing you extra work.

Query-Language	This is the same as the Query-Language option under DB-Access. (This is actually a call to run dbaccess -q.)
Exit	This menu option allows you to exit from the INFORMIX-4GL Programmer's Environment.

Command Line Development

This section describes how to compile and run 4GL code from the command line. The rapid development system commands (r4gl) are described first, followed by the compiled 4GL commands (c4gl), and then the screen form commands.

Compiling and Running 4GL Code in the Rapid Development System

To compile and run programs using the rapid development system, use the following sequence of commands from the UNIX command line:

```
fglpc <file name>[.4gl]

cat <file name(s)>.4go > <program name>.4gi

fglgo <program name>.4gi
```

The command fglpc compiles the 4GL code and creates the p-code file <file name>.4go. The cat command simply appends all .4go modules that are used in a program together, to create the p-code file <program name>.4gi. (The command cat is a UNIX command). The command fglgo is the name of the INFORMIX-4GL program runner that runs your <program name>.4gi application.

The syntax of the `fglpc` command is:

```
fglpc { -V |
          [-ansi] [-a]
          [-p <directory for compiled code>]
          <4GL source file>[.4gl] [, ...]
       }
```

The `fglpc` switches work as follows:

-V	Displays the 4GL version number.
-ansi	Checks code for ANSI compatibility.
-a	Adds code to check array bounds at runtime.
-p	Compiled code will be stored in the specified directory.

Compiling and Running Compiled 4GL Code

To compile and run programs using compiled 4GL code, the following sequence of commands can be issued from the UNIX command line:

```
c4gl -c <file name>.4gl

c4gl -o <program name>.4ge <file name(s)>.o

<program name>.4ge
```

The `c4gl` command creates the `<file name>.o` object files and then links the object modules to create the executable file `<program name>.4ge`.

The first command uses a C compiler switch to prevent the linking of the module into executable code. This command simply compiles the module `<file name>.4gl` and produces the object module, `<file name>.o`.

The second command links the various compiled modules (the `.o` files) to create `<program name>.4ge`.

The file `<program name>.4ge` is now an executable program like any other and it can be run as such.

Keep in mind that the `c4gl` command will leave the intermediate files *<file name>*.ec and *<file name>*.c. You may delete these if you wish.

The syntax of the `c4gl` command is:

```
c4gl {  -V |
        [-a] [-e] [-q] [-c] [-z]
        [ -ansi ] [ -anyerr ]
        [ -phase { 1 | 2 | 3 | 4 | 5 } [...] ]
        [ -globcurs | -localcurs ]
        [ -linenos  | -nolinenos ]
        [ -keep     | -nokeep ]
        [ -static   | -shared ]
        [<C compiler switches/arguments> [,
...]]

        [-o <output file name> ]
        <4GL source file>.4gl [, ...]
        [<esql/c source file>.ec [, ...]]
        [<C source file>.c [, ...]]
        [<object files to link>.o [, ...]]
        [<other function libraries>]
    }
```

The `c4gl` switches work as follows:

-V	Displays the 4GL version number.
-a	Adds Code to check array bounds at runtime.
-e	Preprocesses the command, does not compile or link.
-q	Quiet mode for phase 1 of compilation (i4glc1).
-c	Preprocess and compile only. Do not link.
-z	Allow functions to accept a variable number of arguments.
-ansi	Checks code for ANSI compatibility.
-anyerr	Set error status variable after expressions (otherwise only set after SQL statements).
-phase 1..5	Process only the specified phase. There are 5 phases. If you specify more than one phase, the phases must be in consecutive order and any previous phases must have already been run.

`-globcurs`	Make cursor definitions global to program.
`-localcurs`	Make cursor definitions local to program -default.
`-linenos`	Generate line numbers in .c file - default.
`-nolinenos`	Don't generate line number in .c file.
`-keep`	Keep intermediate files (.4ec, .ec and .c).
`-nokeep`	Delete intermediate files (.4ec, .ec and .c) -default.
`-static`	Use static libraries - default.
`-shared`	Use dynamic linking and shared libraries. Shared libraries can help reduce your executable size and improve performance.
`-otherargs`	Any other arguments you want passed to the C compiler (eg. optimization).
`-o`	The output file name is the name of the executable program, *<program name>*.4ge.

Compiling Informix Screen Forms

To compile an INFORMIX-4GL screen form, enter the following command from the UNIX command line:

```
form4gl <file name of form without .per suffix>
```

This is the basic form of the command that will compile your screen form in a `.per` file and create the compiled form *<file name>*.`frm`.

The full syntax of the `form4gl` command is:

```
form4gl
  { -d |
    [ -l <number of display lines on terminal>  ]
    [ -c <number of display columns on terminal> ]
    [ -v ]
   <file name of form without .per suffix>
  }
```

The switches for the `form4gl` command are defined as follows:

-d   Creates and compiles a default screen form file (you will be prompted for inputs).

-l   Indicates the number of display lines available on terminal.

-c   Indicates the number of display columns available on terminal.

-v   Verifies that the screen field width is large enough for specified character fields.

Make Files

Using the UNIX `make` file utility is the easiest way of compiling programs in 4GL. Make files allow you to define which modules are associated with which programs. You can also define dependencies so that modules that are dependent on other modules are compiled if the module has not been compiled since it was last changed, or if it has not been compiled since the module it is dependent upon was last compiled.

Make files are rather cryptic, but you will find it is worth the overhead of learning how to use them if you plan to do anything at all complex in 4GL.

Make Rules

The first thing you will need are *make rules*. Most versions of make allow you to insert the make rules into your make file. Some versions will require your make rules to be in a separate file. Make rules defines what commands are run on different types of files.

If you need a separate make rules, check your documentation to find out where your UNIX system stores its default make rules file. Make a copy of this file. Now we're going to modify the copy of the file. Do not delete anything from the file, we merely need to add information to the file to explain to make what it needs to do to compile Informix files. The best way to insert the code is to put it where it looks like it belongs and try it out.

The following are sections of make rules code. Comments are lines beginning with a pound (#) sign, and a backslash (\) before a newline ignores the special meaning of the newline character.

First, we're going to define some terms for the make rules. This is similar to setting environment variables in UNIX:

```
C4GL=$(INFORMIXDIR)/bin/c4gl
FGLPC=$(INFORMIXDIR)/bin/fglpc
FORM4GL=$(INFORMIXDIR)/bin/form4gl
```

Next, add the following suffix definitions:

```
.SUFFIXES:   .4gl  .4go  .o  .per  .frm
```

Last comes the definition of the rules. The indentations at the beginning of the lines are tabs.

```
# *** Informix compiled 4GL ***
.4gl.o:
    $(C4GL) -c -nokeep $<

# *** Informix rapid development system 4GL ***
.4gl.4go:
    $(FGLPC) -p $(<D) $<

# *** Informix screen forms ***
.per.frm:
    $(FORM4GL) -q $<
```

The Make File

The default name of a make file is (you guessed it) makefile. You may also use other names if you prefer. You may want to keep a make file in each source code directory. The sample make file on page 190-192 demonstrates how a make file can be set up.

```
#************************************************************
# Sample make file
#
# This sample make file includes both r4gl and c4gl compiles
#
# include the make rules or make rules file you created
include /my/make/rules/dir/make.rules

# Source Code Directories
GLOBAL=/my_source/global/
LIB=/my_source/lib/
PROJECT=/my_source/project/main/
REPORT=/my_source/project/report/

# Definitions
ALL_PROGRAMS=program1 program2 program3 program4 forms

COMMON_SOURCE=module1.4gl \
          module2.4go \
          $(LIB)module3.4go \
          $(GLOBAL)module4.4go

R_COMMON_OBJECTS=module1.4go \
          module2.4go \
          $(LIB)module3.4go \
          $(GLOBAL)module4.4go

C_COMMON_OBJECTS=module1.o \
          module2.o \
          $(LIB)module3.o \
          $(GLOBAL)module4.o

PROGRAM1_OBJECTS=program1.4go module6.4go $(R_COMMON_OBJECTS)

PROGRAM2_OBJECTS=program2.4go module7.4go $(R_COMMON_OBJECTS)

PROGRAM3_OBJECTS=program1.o module6.o $(C_COMMON_OBJECTS)

PROGRAM4_OBJECTS=program2.o module7.o $(C_COMMON_OBJECTS)

FORMS=form1.frm form2.frm form3.frm
```

```
# Create executable targets

# if you type: make all - everything in ALL_PROGRAMS will be
made
all: $(MAKEFILE) $(ALL_PROGRAMS)

# make program1
program1.4gi:
    cat $(PROGRAM1_OBJECTS) > program1.4gi

# make program2
program2.4gi:
    cat $(PROGRAM2_OBJECTS) > program2.4gi

# make program3
program3.4ge:
    c4gl -o program3.4ge $(PROGRAM3_OBJECTS)

# make program4
program4.4ge:
    c4gl -o program4.4ge $(PROGRAM4_OBJECTS)

# make forms
forms:  $(FORMS)

# Define Dependencies
module1.o: $(GLOBAL)module4.o module1.4gl

module1.4go: $(GLOBAL)module4.4go module1.4gl

module2.o: $(GLOBAL)module4.o module2.4gl

module2.4go: $(GLOBAL)module4.4go module2.4gl

module3.o: $(GLOBAL)module4.o module3.4gl

module3.4go: $(GLOBAL)module4.4go module3.4gl

module4.o: module4.4gl

module4.4go: module4.4gl
```

```
module5.o: $(GLOBAL)module4.o module5.4gl

module5.4go: $(GLOBAL)module4.4go module5.4gl

module6.o: $(GLOBAL)module4.o module6.4gl

module6.4go: $(GLOBAL)module4.4go module6.4gl

module7.o: $(GLOBAL)module4.o module7.4gl

module7.4go: $(GLOBAL)module4.4go module7.4gl

program1.4go: $(GLOBAL)module4.4go program1.4gl

program2.4go: $(GLOBAL)module4.4go program2.4gl

program3.o: $(GLOBAL)module4.o program3.4gl

program4.o: $(GLOBAL)module4.o program4.4gl

form1.frm: form1.per

form2.frm: form2.per

form3.frm: form3.per
#************************************************************
```

Notice that if the file in the globals directory (module4.4gl) is changed or recompiled, that many other programs will also be recompiled. This is because many of the 4GL source code files are dependent on changes in this module; in this case, the definition of global variables.

Please refer to the documentation on your system for more detail about the make utility.

Prototyping

Creating prototypes is relatively easy in 4GL. A prototype is a simple program which will give your users an idea of what the real application will look like and it will give your users an opportunity to provide you with feedback. Once you have determined your preference for how you want various screens and functions to work, it is largely a matter of copying 4GL files and adjusting them for the current applications.

If you ignore data checking and business rules, you can develop prototypes very quickly. This will help you develop a look and feel for your application as it is developed.

You will probably want to set up standards for your organization, for instance, standard menu options, types of screens, function keys, etc.

Summary

INFORMIX-4GL comes in two flavors: `r4gl` and `c4gl`. `r4gl` is the Informix *rapid development system* (or rds) and `c4gl` is *compiled 4GL*.

You may use the menu driven system for application development, or you may perform your development from the command line.

To get into the INFORMIX-4GL Programmer's Environment, at the command line type:

i4gl   for compiled 4GL, or

r4gl   for the rapid development system

The following list contains the suffixes for file names that are used when writing and compiling 4GL code and screens with INFORMIX-4GL: `.4gl`, `.4go`, `.o`, `.4gi`, `.4ge`, `.per`, `.frm`, `.err`, `.erc`, `.c`, `.ec`, `.4bl`, `.4bo`, `.4be`, `.pbr`, and `.fbm`.

To compile and run programs using the rapid development system:

```
fglpc <file name>[.4gl]

cat <file name(s)>.4go > <program name>.4gi

fglgo <program name>.4gi
```

The syntax of the `fglpc` command is:

```
fglpc { -V |
        [-ansi] [-a]
        [-p <directory for compiled code>]
        <4GL source file>[.4gl] [, ...]
      }
```

The syntax of the `c4gl` command is:

```
c4gl {    -V |
          [-a]  [-e]  [-q]  [-c]  [-z]
          [ -ansi ]  [ -anyerr ]
          [ -phase { 1 | 2 | 3 | 4 | 5 } [...] ]
          [ -globcurs  | -localcurs ]
          [ -linenos   | -nolinenos ]
          [ -keep      | -nokeep ]
          [ -static    | -shared ]
          [<C compiler switches/arguments> [, ...]]
          [-o <output file name> ]
          <4GL source file>.4gl [, ...]
          [<esql/c source file>.ec [, ...]]
          [<C source file>.c [, ...]]
          [<object files to link>.o [, ...]]
          [<other function libraries>]
     }
```

The full syntax of the `form4gl` command is:

```
form4gl {    -d |
             [ -l <number of display lines on terminal>  ]
             [ -c <number of display columns on terminal> ]
             [ -v ]
             <file name of form without .per suffix>
        }
```

The UNIX `make` file utility is the easiest way of compiling programs in 4GL. You will need a new *make rules* file and a *make file* to use this utility.

4GL Program Structure

- *Overview*
- *database*
- *globals*
- *main*
- *Modules*
- *functions*
- *exit program*
- *Comments*
- *Summary*

Overview

This section contains an overview of the major elements of an INFORMIX-4GL program. Let's start by looking at a very simple 4GL program.

```
main
   display "Hello World!"
end main
```

Type this in, compile it, and try it out.

This is about the shortest program you can write in INFORMIX-4GL. Every program is required to contain a main section, and that's about the only minimum restriction you will find.

INFORMIX-4GL is not case sensitive. Keywords and variables may be typed in uppercase, lowercase, or any combination of uppercase and lowercase. You will probably want to set up standards for how you plan to use uppercase and lowercase letters within your 4GL programs.

Notice that this program doesn't do anything at all with databases. INFORMIX-4GL allows you to write programs that don't use databases, like other languages you may have worked with.

The syntax on page 198 very generally shows you the major elements of an INFORMIX-4GL program.

```
[ database <database name> ]

[ globals
    <global variable definitions>
  end globals
]

main
  <local variable definitions>

  <4GL program statements>
end main

[ function <function name> (<function parameters>)
    <local variable definitions>

    <4GL program statements>

    [ return <return variables> ]
  end function
]

[ report <report name> (<report parameters>)
    <local variable definitions>

    <4GL program and report statements>
  end report
]
```

The parts of an INFORMIX-4GL program may be divided between several files or modules, or they may be contained completely within a single module. This is up to you.

Database

The database statement simply indicates which database you want to work with. You may write a program without using a database. If you wish to do this, simply omit the database statement. The database statement only affects programs containing a main section or using define statements with the like syntax.

The syntax for the database statement is the same as making a database the current database in INFORMIX-SQL:

```
database <database name>
```

The database name must appear at the beginning of each module or file that needs to know which database you are using in order to compile. For instance, if you use the like keyword to define variables, you will need to have a database defined at the top of the module so the compiler will know which database to use.

You may change the database you are working with within a program at runtime by using this syntax as a regular program statement instead of as a special section at the beginning of a module.

Globals

The globals statement allows you to define any variables which you wish to use globally throughout your application. In earlier versions of INFORMIX-4GL you were limited to a single globals section in any program. This restriction has been removed starting in revisions 4.16 and 6.04 of INFORMIX-4GL.

```
globals
   <global variable definitions>
end globals
```

If your `globals` will be used in modules outside the module containing the main section of the program, you should store and compile the global definitions in a separate module.

Next, at the beginning of each module that uses any of the global variables, put the statement:

```
globals "/your/globals/directory/my_globals.4gl"
```

You will still need to link the `globals` object module when you create your `.4gi` or `.4ge` executable program file.

You can also put the `database` statement within the module that contains the `globals` in addition to, or to avoid having to list the `database` name and the `globals` statement within each module.

Variable definitions are discussed in Chapter 9, but a sample `globals` module might contain the following:

```
database toymaker

globals
   define g_username      char (14)
   define g_printer       char (20)
end globals
```

You can also define variables which have a modular scope (see the section *Scope of Variables* in Chapter 9).

Main

Every program must have one and only one `main` section. The `main` section is what is executed when your program is run. Everything done in your program must be done directly or indirectly from the `main` section of the program.

The syntax of the `main` section is:

```
main
   <local variable definitions>

   <4GL program statements>
end main
```

The following is an example of the `main` section of a program:

```
main
   call Initialize_Globals ()
   call Main_Menu ()
end main
```

This `main` section simply contains calls to functions that may be contained in in the `main` module or in other program modules.

Modules

A module is a file that contains program code. A program may consist of a single module or of many modules. A module may be very long or very short. It is up to the programmer to determine how much code should go into a module. You may wish to have a separate module for your global declarations, for your main program code, and then as many modules as necessary each containing as many or as few functions as the programmer deems appropriate.

These modules are compiled and then linked together into a program.

Functions

A `function` may be called from wherever a 4GL program statement can be issued. The syntax for calling a `function` is:

```
call <function name> (<function parameters>)
   [ returning   <return variables> ]
```

Or, if the `function` returns a single value, you may use the `function` without preceding it with the keyword `call`. For example:

```
       let interest = Calculate_Interest (principal,
                                           interest_rate,
                                           num_days)
```

or: `if Balance_Due (order_number) > 1000 then`
      `...`
      `end if`

The syntax for the `function` itself is:

```
function <function name> (<function parameters>)
   <local variable and parameter definitions>

   <4GL program statements>

   [ return <return variables> ]
end function
```

`Function` statements in INFORMIX-4GL pass all variables by value (except for text and byte datatypes which are passed by reference), that is, if you change the value of a `function` parameter while it is in the `function`, the value of the variable passed into the `function` is not changed outside of the `function`. If you do wish to change the value of a variable, simply `return` the value from the `function` into a variable. For example:

```
call Calculate_Sales_Tax (price, sales_tax_rate)
    returning sales_tax

...

function Calculate_Sales_Tax (price,
    sales_tax_rate)
   define price            decimal (8,2)
   define sales_tax_rate   decimal (5,2)
   define sales_tax        decimal (8,2)

   let sales_tax = price * (sales_tax_rate / 100)

   return sales_tax
end function
```

Exit Program

The `exit program` statement allows you to exit from your program immediately, no matter where you are or what you are doing. The syntax for the `exit program` statement is.

```
exit program [ <exit status> ]
```

You may return an exit status with a value of 0 through 255 to the operating system if desired, 0 is returned otherwise.

Comments

As in other languages, INFORMIX-4GL comments are for the programmer's use only and are ignored by the compiler. Comments in INFORMIX-4GL may be any of the following:

{ }   Curly braces may surround comments. An open curly brace ({) indicates the beginning of a comment, while a closed curly brace (}) indicates the end of a comment. Curly braces may not be contained within other curly braces.

\#   A pound sign indicates that the rest of the line is a comment.

--   Two dashes indicate that the rest of the line is a comment.

Summary

The syntax below very generally shows the major elements of an INFORMIX-4GL program.

```
[ database <database name> ]

[ globals
    <global variable definitions>
  end globals
]

main
  <local variable definitions>

  <4GL program statements>
end main

[ function <function name> (<function parameters>)
    <local variable definitions>

    <4GL program statements>

    [ return <return variables> ]
  end function
]

[ report <report name> (<report parameters>)
    <local variable definitions>

    <4GL program and report statements>
  end report
]
```

The syntax for calling a `function` is:

```
call <function name> (<function parameters>)
    [ returning   <return variables> ]
```

Functions in INFORMIX-4GL pass all variables by value.

The `exit program` statement allows you to exit from your program immediately.

```
exit program [ <error number> ]
```

Comments in INFORMIX-4GL may be any of the following: {}, #, or --.

Chapter

9

Data Types
and Definitions

- *4GL data types*
- *Defining variables*
- *Scope of variables*
- *Use of nulls*
- *Operators in 4GL*
- *Converting between data types*
- *Formatting data with the* using *clause*
- *Summary*

4GL Data Types

The data types that are common to both INFORMIX-SQL and INFORMIX-4GL were described in detail in Chapter 3. By category these are:

Character and String Data Types

char (<length of string>)

character (<length of string>)

varchar (<maximum length> [, <reserve length>])

Numeric Data Types

dec (<precision> [, <scale>])

decimal (<precision> [, <scale>])

double precision (<float precision>)

float (<float precision>)

int

integer

money (<precision> [, <scale>])

numeric (<precision> [, <scale>])

real

smallfloat

smallint

Date, Time, and Interval Data Types

```
date

datetime <largest datetime value>
    to <smallest datetime value>
        [ (< fraction precision> ) ]

interval <largest datetime value>
        [ ( <precision> ) ]
    to <smallest datetime value>
        [ ( <precision> ) ]
```

BLOB Data Types

```
byte

text
```

In addition to the data types listed above, 4GL also gives you the following data types to work with.

INFORMIX-4GL Only Data Types and Indirect Typing

```
array "[" <integer value>
        [, <integer value>
        [, <integer value> ] ] "]"
    of <non-array data type>

like <table name>.<column name>

record { like <table name>.* |
        <variable name> <data type> [, ...]
        end record
        }
```

Each of the INFORMIX-4GL only data types or indirect typing is described here in detail:

```
array "[" <integer value>
        [, <integer value>
        [, <integer value> ] ] "]"
    of <non-array data type>
```

An `array` can have from one to three dimensions. Where the square brackets are surrounded by quotation marks, the square brackets are part of the syntax. Arrays in INFORMIX-4GL are like arrays in other programming languages.

```
like <table name>.<column name>
```

This syntax allows for indirect typing of variables. The variable will be defined as the same data type as the specified column in the table.

```
record { like <table name>.* |
        <variable name> <data type> [, ...]
        end record
    }
```

This syntax will allow you to define a `record` structure, or group of variables that can be treated as a whole or individually. A `record` can be defined to have the same elements (same names and data types) as a table, or you can define each variable that will be in the `record` separately. The INFORMIX-4GL `record` is similar to `record` structures in other programming languages. The `record` structure may be referred to as *<record name>.**, and individual components of the `record` may be referred to as *<record name>.<variable name>*. You can define nested records but they have very limited use.

Defining Variables

Variables may be defined within the `globals` statement, at the beginning of the `main` section of a program, at the beginning of a module, at the beginning of a `function`, or at the beginning of a report.

The syntax of variable definitions is shown on page 210.

```
define <variable name> <data type> [, ...]
```

The variable name may contain letters, digits, and underscores. The first character of the variable name may be a letter or
an underscore. Variable names may be up to 50 characters in
length.

In this book, the following conventions are observed when
naming variables:

- variables that are treated as constants are typed in capital letters
- global variable names begin with g_
- record structures declared like a table begin with t_
- record structures declared as an array like a table begin with
  ta_
- variables, not in records, that are defined as like column
  names usually begin with p_

Based on the data types defined in the previous section, any of
the following define statements would be valid:

```
define counter            smallint

define start_date         date

define p_order_number     like toy_order.order_number

define t_toy_order        record like toy_order.*

define ta_toy_order       array [100] of record like
                          toy_order.*

define toys_ordered       record
       order_number       like toy_order.order_number,
       toy_description    like toy.description,
       quantity           like toy_order_item.quantity,
       unit_price         like toy_order_item.unit_price,
       total_price        decimal (16,2)
     end record
```

Scope of Variables

Variables defined within the `globals` section of a program are global throughout the entire program. Each module which uses the global variables must include a `globals` section defining the globals which need to be defined for that module.

Variables may be defined at the beginning of a module (before any functions are defined). Variables defined at the beginning of a module are global to that module and all functions (and main sections of code) in that module.

Variables defined at the beginning of the `main` section of program code are valid only within that section. These variables are local to the `main` section of code and cannot be used by `functions` called from that section unless they are passed to the `function` as parameters.

Variables defined at the beginning of a `function`, `main`, or `report` are treated as local variables for that `function` and may not be accessed outside of that `function` unless specifically passed as a parameter to another `function`.

If two variables have the same name, first local variables will be used (`function`, `main`, or `report` variables), then module variables, then global variables.

Use of Nulls

A `null` is an undefined empty value. Because nulls are undefined, one `null` is never equivalent to another `null`. Any variable of any data type may have a `null` value.

To assign `null` values to a variable, use the syntax:

```
initialize <variable name> [, ...] to null

or

let <variable name> = null
```

Examples: `initialize counter, start_date to null`
            `let toys_ordered = null`

To check to see if a variable has a `null` value (or does not have a `null` value), use the operator:

```
is [ not ] null
```

note *Relational operators such as equal (=) and not equal (<>) will not work with nulls.*

Examples: `if start_date is null then ...`

   `while answer is not null do ...`

Operators in 4GL

The following operators are described in Chapter 20 and are used in both INFORMIX-SQL and INFORMIX-4GL:

Mathematical operators: unary +, unary −, +, −, *, and /

Relational operators: <, >, <=, >=, =, <>, and !=

Boolean operators: `not, and,` and `or`

String operators: `like` and `matches`

Null operators: `is null` and `is not null`

The following operators are used only in INFORMIX-4GL:

Mathematical operators:

`**`   Exponentiation (only whole numbers may be used as exponents).
   Example: $2**3 = 2^3 = 8$
`mod` Modulus, is the remainder from a division. Example: `14 mod 4 = 2`

String operators:

,	Concatenates strings
clipped	Clips trailing spaces from a string expression
using	Allows you to specify a format for displaying data (see *Formatting data with the* using *clause* section at the end of this chapter)

Converting between Data Types

This section explains how to convert values between various data types.

The first rule of converting between different data types in INFORMIX-4GL is that INFORMIX-4GL will try to figure out how to perform a given conversion. For each general category of data type that follows, we'll discuss data type conversions within that category and how to convert data types from other categories into it.

Character and String Data Types

The only concern when converting character strings to other character strings is the length (keep in mind that trailing blanks are not significant). If you assign a larger character string to a smaller character string, the result will be a truncated version of the larger character string.

The value of any data type can be assigned to a character string. Again, your main concern will be the length of the character string. Assigning one data type to a character string, and then assigning the character string to a different data type is a common way of getting around difficult type conversions. Once a value is stored in a character string, INFORMIX-4GL will try to interpret the character string into any type you specify.

Numeric Data Types

Converting between numeric data types is relatively easy. There are two things to watch for, however. First, your value may be rounded if you try to assign a number with more precision to a data type with less precision. Also, if you try to assign a large number to a data type the large number can't fit into, the resulting value will overflow and be displayed as asterisks ("*****").

A `character` value containing a valid number can easily be converted into a numeric value by the use of an assignment statement. For example:

```
define my_string          char (10)
define my_number          smallint

let my_string = "377"
let my_number = my_string
```

If you want to assign a `date` value to a number, INFORMIX-4GL will allow this since the internal representation of a `date` is an `integer` (the number of days since December 31, 1899). This number might not mean a whole lot to you, but the conversion is possible.

On the other hand, if you wanted to convert a `datetime` to a numeric value, you would need to choose some part of the `datetime` value, store it in a `character` string, then assign the `character` string containing the numeric value to a numeric data type.

If you are working with an `interval` data type or `units`, you can assign the number you want to a `character` string, and then assign the `character` string to the numeric data type. It is interesting to note that INFORMIX-4GL cannot do some conversions that seem easy to accomplish. For instance, if we are talking about a ten-day period, although it might appear that we should be able to make a simple conversion from ten days to the number ten, we must still tiptoe around the obvious:

```
define temp_string          char (10)
define number_of_days       smallint

let temp_string = 10 units day
let number_of_days = temp_string
```

Date, Time, and Interval Data Types

The most difficult data types to convert are `datetimes` and
`intervals`. Working with `dates` alone is fairly simple, but when
they are combined with `datetimes`, conversion becomes more
difficult. Remember that `date` and `datetime` variables are not
the same; INFORMIX-4GL handles them quite differently.

You can easily convert a `date` to a `character` string or a
numeric data type by using a single assignment statement. If you
wish to choose a particular portion of the `date`, you can use the
`day`, `month`, `year`, or `weekday` functions to retrieve part of the
`date` and assign it to a numeric data type.

You can also perform these `date` conversions in reverse. If a
`character` string contains a valid `date` format, simply use an
assignment statement to assign it to a `date` type. You can also
assign a numerical value to a `date` that will be interpreted as the
number of days since December 31, 1899. You can also use the
`mdy` function to assemble a `date` from numeric day, month, and
year values.

To convert a `date` to a `datetime` value, simply use the `extend`
function to convert your `date` value to the desired `datetime` precision.

```
define p_date              date
define p_datetime          datetime year to second


let p_date = today
let p_datetime = extend (p_date, year to second)
```

A character string must be assigned a `datetime` value in the
appropriate format—some portion of: yyyy-mm-dd
hh:mm:ss.fffff to be converted to a `datetime` value.

A `datetime` may be converted to a `date` value by use of the
`date` function.

```
define p_datetime          datetime year to second
define p_date              date


let p_datetime = current year to second
let p_date = date (p_datetime)
```

Converting to and from an `interval` is similar to converting to and from the `datetime` data type. Remember that an `interval` may range from *year* to *month* or from *day* through *fraction*. *Year to month* and *day to time* `interval`s may not be mixed.

You may use arithmetic expressions to add and subtract `date`, `datetime`, `interval`, and `unit` values to and from one another. You can also multiply and divide these values. The rules of what can and cannot be done and what the result of any particular operation will be are not always easy to understand. The best way to understand what you are doing is to write a short program that is quickly and easily compiled to run as a test. For example:

```
{ Date, datetime, interval, and unit tester }
main
    define p_date          date
    define p_datetime      datetime year to fraction
    { any other declarations you like }
    define temp_string     char (20)

    let p_date = today
    let p_datetime = current
    { any other assignments you like }

    let temp_string = { whatever you want to test out }
    display temp_string
end main
```

The `temp_string` variable will display the results of any mathematical expressions you try (unless they produce an error). This technique will help you develop a feel for working with `date`, `datetime`, and `interval` values.

warning

Warning: If you try to add one month to January 31, 1998, the result will be an error. This is because the ANSI standard and INFORMIX-4GL require users to decide whether the result should be February 28, 1998 or March 1, 2 or 3. If you add two months to January 31, 1998 your result will be March 31, 1998 since March also has 31 days. Writing code for this may be annoying, but it is not difficult. If you need to perform month addition, it is a good idea to write a function that will handle this situation.

Formatting Data with the using Clause

The using clause allows you to format the output for numeric and date values. The syntax for the using clause is:

```
<numeric or date value> using "<format string>"
```

The format string can be used when displaying characters on the screen, or for outputting values to a report.

There are several formatting characters available for use with the using clause. Some formatting characters are used with numeric values and some for date values. Any characters that are not defined as formatting characters may be included in the format string and will be treated simply as additional characters to print.

Formatting dates

The following format templates are used to format dates:

dd	Displays the day of the month ranging from 01 to 31.
ddd	Displays an abbreviation for the day of the week: Sun, Mon, Tue, Wed, Thu, Fri, Sat.
mm	Displays the number of the month ranging from 01 to 12.
mmm	Displays an abbreviation for the name of the month: Jan, Feb, Mar, Apr, May, Jun, Jul, Aug, Sep, Oct, Nov, Dec.
yy	Displays the last two digits of the year, e.g., 1997 displays as 97.
yyyy	Displays the year as a four-digit number.

Some examples of formatted dates are shown on page 218.

Date Format Examples

Format String	Value	Output
"mm/dd/yy"	9/28/1997	09/28/97
"mm/dd/yyyy"	9/28/1997	09/28/1997
"mm-dd-yyyy"	9/28/1997	09/28/1997
"ddd mmm dd, yyyy"	9/28/1997	Wed Sep 28, 1997
"ddd"	9/28/1997	Wed
"dd"	9/28/1997	28
"mmm"	9/28/1997	Sep
"mm"	9/28/1997	09
"yy"	9/28/1997	97
"yyyy"	9/28/1997	1997
"yyyymmdd"	9/28/1997	19970928

Formatting numbers

The characters listed below are used to format numbers. Some of these characters when used in groups, float to the right. That is, only a single character is printed in the rightmost position available before the number. These symbols may be mixed and matched in order to achieve the desired results.

#	Print a number or a blank.
&	Print a number or a leading 0.
*	Print a number or a leading asterisk.
<	Left justify the number and trailing characters are blank.
,	Display a comma in this position if there is a number to the left of this position.
.	Display a period in this position. Only one period per format string is permitted.
−	Display a minus sign in front of a negative number. Groups of minus signs float to the right. All numbers are printed without any sign unless the plus or minus sign is used.

+	Display a plus or minus sign in front of a number. Groups of plus signs float to the right. All numbers are printed without any sign unless the plus or minus sign is used.
( )	Parentheses are printed around a negative number. Groups of left parentheses float to the right.
$	Print a dollar sign character. Groups of dollar signs float to the right.
@	Trailing currency symbol in more recent versions of INFORMIX-4GL.

Some examples of formatting numbers are:

Numeric Format Examples

Format String	Value	Output
"##########"	-1234.567	1235
"&&&&&&&&&&"	-1234.567	0000001235
"**********"	-1234.567	******1235
"<<<<<<<<<<"	-1234.567	12345
"#######.##"	-1234.567	1234.57
"&&&&&&.&&"	-1234.567	0001234.57
"$$$$$$&.&&"	-1234.567	$1234.57
"———&.&&"	-1234.567	-1234.57
"+++,++&.&&"	-1234.567	-1,234.57
"$$$,$-&.&&"	-1234.567	$-1,234.57
"((((,$&.&&)"	-1234.567	($1,234.57)
"a#b#c#d#e#f"	-1234.567	a b1c2d3e5f
"#####.####"	-1234.567	1234.5670

Summary

In addition to INFORMIX-SQL data types (except for `serial`, `nchar`, and `nvarchar`), data types available for use in INFORMIX-4GL are:

```
array "[" <integer value>
        [, <integer value>
        [, <integer value> ] ] "]"
     of <non-array data type>

like <table name>.<column name>

record { like <table name>.* |
           <variable name> <data type> [, ...]
         end record
       }
```

Variables may be defined within the `globals` statement, at the beginning of the `main` section of a program, at the beginning of a module, or at the beginning of a `function`.

```
define <variable name> <data type> [, ...]
```

Variables defined within the `globals` section of a program are global throughout the entire program. Variables defined at the beginning of a module are global to that module. Variables defined in the `main` section of program code or in a `function` are local to those areas.

A `null` is an undefined empty value.

```
initialize <variable name> [, ...] to null
```

The following operators are used in INFORMIX-4GL:

Mathematical operators: unary +, unary −, +, −, *, /, **, and mod

Relational operators: <, >, <=, >=, =, <>, and !=

Boolean operators: `not`, `and`, and `or`

String operators: `like`, `matches`, `clipped`, `using`, and , (comma)

Null operators: is null and is not null

It is possible to convert between most data types, although it can be tricky.

The using clause allows you to format the output for numeric and date values.

<numeric or date value> using "*<format string>*"

The following strings can format a date value: dd, ddd, mm, mmm, yy, and yyyy.

The following characters can format numeric values: #, &, *, <, ,, ., -, +, (), and $.

Menus

- *Overview of menus*
- *A simple ring menu*
- *Menu simplicity and consistency*
- *Menu features*
- *Summary*

Overview of Menus

The INFORMIX-4GL user interface relies heavily upon ring menus. The ring menus used when working with DB-Access and in the INFORMIX-4GL Programmer's Environment are the same type of menus INFORMIX-4GL allows us to create for our users.

The ring menu is a horizontal menu that allows the user to choose from among available options. If you press down on the right arrow key several times, it will eventually come back to the option you were originally positioned on. This is why it is called a ring menu: the menu automatically wraps from the end, to the beginning (and vice versa) like a circle or a ring.

There are several ways to choose an option from a ring menu. One method that will always work is to use your arrow keys to position the cursor on the desired menu option, then press the *return* key. The other options involve typing a key. If the programmer has not specified an alternate key with which to choose an option, a menu is accessed by typing the first letter of the menu option. If more than one option begins with the same letter(s), you will be prompted to continue typing characters that make up the name of the menu option until a unique menu option is selected.

The programmer may also select alternate letters or keys with which to choose an option. If the programmer makes this selection, the first letter of the `menu` option will no longer automatically choose the menu option. The programmer sets the keys and is responsible for letting the user know which key will select which option. If more than one option begins with the same letter, you may wish to assign an alternate key to one of these options. You can let the user know which key to use to choose an option simply by capitalizing the letter in the menu option. This option will then be displayed for the user in the menu. You may also choose any other method you prefer to handle these situations.

Three dots on either side of the ring menu indicate that there are more menu options in that direction.

The syntax of the menu statement is shown on page 224.

```
menu <menu name>
   { { before menu |
       command { [ key ( <command key> [, ...] ) ]
                   <command name>
                   [ "<description>" ]
                   [ help <help number> ]                     |
                   key ( <command key> [, ...] ) ]
                 }
       { hide option
           { all | <command name> [, ...] }                   |
         show option
           { all | <command name> [, ...] }                   |
         <program statement>                                  |
         next option <command name>                           |
         continue menu                                        |
         exit menu
       } [...]
     }
   } [...]
end menu
```

Any INFORMIX-4GL program statements may be used within
the menu statement. You will often want to call another function
from within a menu option.

A Simple Ring Menu

Let's look at a simple ring menu:

```
menu "Sample Menu"
   command "A"   "This is a description of option A."
         error "Menu option A was chosen."
   command "B"   "This is a description of option B."
         error "Menu option B was chosen."
   command "C"   "This is a description of option C."
         error "Menu option C was chosen."
   command key ("E","X")
         "Exit" "This option will exit this menu."
         exit menu
end menu
```

If you put this inside a main section of code then compile and run it, the following will appear at the top of your screen:

```
Sample Menu:   A   B   C   Exit
This is a description of option A.
```

Option A will be displayed in reverse video since this is the first option listed for this menu. Refer to Chapter 11 for information on setting options to change the position of the menu in your form. By default, the menu is positioned at the top of the form.

You can see that the menu options display as defined in the form. A brief description of each option can be defined by the programmer. This description will be listed just below the menu line.

The first rule of menus is always give yourself a way out. The exit menu statement associated with the command Exit will exit the menu. Notice that we have given the menu option Exit two command keys, "E" and "X". This means that you may enter either letter to exit the menu.

The error statements in each menu option simply provide feedback about which option was chosen. These may be deleted and replaced with function calls or any other INFORMIX-4GL program statements.

Menu Simplicity and Consistency

It is important to keep your menus simple and consistent. Here are a few general tips to keep your user interface as easy to use and as standard as possible.

Simple means easy for users to understand. For instance, some users prefer the word Change to Update or Modify. Other users may prefer the word Modify. Whatever wording you use, it should be understood easily.

You should try to avoid huge menus with so many options that you must view several screens to see them all. It is better to have more menu levels with fewer options on each level.

It is important to be consistent with your menu wording and choices. Don't use Change in one part of your application and use Modify in another. Random changes in your user interface will confuse users.

For your more common options, always use the same letter to choose an option. If you have the option Change, don't use "C" part of the time and "N" the rest of the time. Pick a standard and stick with it as much as possible.

Before you start designing your application, it is a good idea to decide on a set of standards for your menus.

Menu Features

This section describes additional features available when using the menu statement.

Command Keys

Above we used "E" and "X" as command keys for the menu option Exit. We can use letters, function keys, control character letters, and special keys as command keys.

Any letter may be used. And any function key in the range from F1 through F64 may also be used.

Control-`<letter>` may be used, except for the following letters: a, d, h, i, j, l, m, r, and x. (Other letters may not be allowed if they have a special meaning to your operating system.)

The following words correspond to the keys on the keyboard and may also be used:

```
accept          help            prevpage
delete          insert          return
down            interrupt       right
esc             left            tab
escape          nextpage        up
```

Help

You have the option of listing a help number for each command in the menu statement. This allows you to provide context-sensitive help to your users whenever they press the *help* key. Defining help numbers and customizing your help screens are discussed in Chapter 14.

An example of a menu statement using help numbers is:

```
menu "Sample Menu"
   command "A"   "This is a description of option A."
         help 1
         error "Menu option A was chosen."
   command "B"   "This is a description of option B."
         help 2
         error "Menu option B was chosen."
   command "C"   "This is a description of option C."
         help 3
         error "Menu option C was chosen."
   command key ("E","X")
         "Exit" "This option will exit this menu."
         help 4
         exit menu
end menu
```

Next Option

You have the option of specifying which menu option will be displayed in reverse video after the completion of the current option. When an option is displayed in reverse video, if the user presses the *return* key, that option is the next option executed. This is a popular feature among many users who like to have their options as automated as possible. While the user always has the option of selecting the default menu choice by pressing the *return* key, the user can decide to do something else instead. An example of a menu statement using the next option is:

```
menu "Sample Menu"
   command "A"   "This is a description of option A."
         help 1
         error "Menu option A was chosen."
         next option "B"
   command "B"   "This is a description of option B."
         help 2
         error "Menu option B was chosen."
         next option "C"
   command "C"   "This is a description of option C."
         help 3
         error "Menu option C was chosen."
         next option "Exit"
   command key ("E","X")
         "Exit" "This option will exit this menu."
         help 4
         exit menu
end menu
```

This menu will start with "A" as the first default option. If the user chooses "A", the next default option is "B." If the user chooses "B", the next default option is "C." If the user chooses "C," the next default option is Exit. This means that the user can go from option "A" to "B" to "C" to Exit with only having to press the *return* key after each option. At any point the user may decide do something other than take the default option.

Continue Menu

The `continue menu` option stops executing the current menu option and returns to the list of menu options.

```
menu "Sample Menu"
   command "A"    "This is a description of option A."
         help 1
         error "Menu option A was chosen."
   command "B"    "This is a description of option B."
         help 2
         error "Menu option B was chosen."
   command "C"    "This is a description of option C."
         help 3
         error "Menu option C was chosen."
         if area <> "C" then
         continue menu
         end if
         call Option_D ()
         call Option_E ()
   command key ("E","X")
         "Exit" "This option will exit this menu."
         help 4
         exit menu
end menu
```

If menu option "C" is chosen, and the variable area does not have the value "C", the error message will be displayed and the rest of the statements in that menu option will be ignored. If the variable area equals "C", the functions Option_D and Option_E will be called.

Hidden Menu Options

If you are in a menu in DB-Access or the INFORMIX-4GL Programmer's Environment, and you type an exclamation point (!), an exclamation point is displayed at the bottom of the screen, and you may enter and run an operating system command at this point. This is an example of a hidden menu option.

Hidden menu options do not appear on the menu. They are available if the user knows they exist and wishes to run them. For example, suppose you want users to be able to perform a shell escape from your program, try the following code:

```
define unix_command   char (100)

menu "Sample Menu"
   command "A"   "This is a description of option A."
        help 1
        error "Menu option A was chosen."
   command "B"   "This is a description of option B."
        help 2
        error "Menu option B was chosen."
   command "C"   "This is a description of option C."
        help 3
        error "Menu option C was chosen."
   command key ("E","X")
        "Exit" "This option will exit this menu."
        help 4
        exit menu
   command key ("!")
        prompt "!" for unix_command
        run unix_command
end menu
```

The hidden menu option specifies the key that will cause the hidden option to be run without including a name for the menu option. The options statement is discussed in Chapter 14. The prompt and run statements are discussed in Chapter 11.

Now when users press an exclamation point from this menu, they will be prompted with an exclamation point to enter a UNIX command. Whatever the user enters will be run as an operating system command.

Hide Option

The hide option clause allows you to hide menu options and make them inaccessible to the user. The difference between the hide option and the hidden menu options discussed above is that the hide option prevents a user from accessing a particular option even if the option is chosen. It can be executed conditionally so that some users have a menu option that others don't.

For example, if you wanted your user to be able to choose either option "A", "B", or "C", but not to be able to choose all of them, you could use the following code:

```
menu "Sample Menu"
   command "A"    "This is a description of option A."
         help 1
         error "Menu option A was chosen."
         hide option "B", "C"
   command "B"    "This is a description of option B."
         help 2
         error "Menu option B was chosen."
         hide option "A", "C"
   command "C"    "This is a description of option C."
         help 3
         error "Menu option C was chosen."
         hide option "A", "B"
   command key ("E","X")
         "Exit" "This option will exit this menu."
         help 4
         exit menu
end menu
```

Any time one option is chosen, the other two options are hidden and made inaccessible to the user.

Show Option

The show option clause is typically used in conjunction with the hide option clause. You may decide to hide all menu options, then selectively decide who should be permitted to have certain options.

```
hide option all
if user_group <> 1 then
   show option "A", "Exit"
else
   show option all
end if
```

The show option clause can only be executed within a menu statement, so to give you more flexibility, it is frequently used inside of the before menu clause.

Before Menu

The before menu clause allows you to execute whichever statements you wish before the menu statement is executed. This allows you to select which options you want specific users to see before the user sees all the options listed. It also allows you to use the next option <command name> to set the first option the cursor will be positioned upon.

The example below allows some users to only see the options A and Exit, and other users to see all available menu options:

```
menu "Sample Menu"
   before menu
         hide option all
         if user_group <> 1 then
            show option "A","Exit"
         else
            show option all
         end if


   command "A"   "This is a description of option A."
         help 1
         error "Menu option A was chosen."
   command "B"   "This is a description of option B."
         help 2
         error "Menu option B was chosen."
   command "C"   "This is a description of option C."
         help 3
         error "Menu option C was chosen."
   command key ("E","X")
         "Exit" "This option will exit this menu."
         help 4
         exit menu
end menu
```

Summary

The syntax of the menu statement is:

```
menu <menu name>
  { { before menu |
      command { [ key ( <command letter> [, ...] )  ]
               <command name>
               [ "<description>" ]
               [ help <help number> ]                    |
               key ( <command letter> [, ...] ) ]
           }
    { hide option { all | <command name> [, ...] } |
      show option { all | <command name> [, ...] } |
      <program statement>
      next option <command name>                          |
      continue menu    |
      exit menu
    } [...]
  }
}
[...]
end menu
```

Output and Standard Program Statements

- *Overview*

- *Assignment*

- *Output*

- *Conditionals*

- *Looping*

- *Running UNIX commands*

- *Summary*

Overview

This chapter provides information on the types of statements available in INFORMIX-4GL that are also commonly available for use in other programming languages. The statements described in this chapter are the building blocks for most programs. Later chapters will discuss special INFORMIX-4GL statements, including how to get information in and out of databases.

Assignment

The assignment statement has the syntax:

```
let <variable name> = <expression>
```

Some examples of the assignment statement are:

```
let counter = 10
let lunch = "Turkey Sandwich"
let my_date = today
let my_record.balance =
  Calculate_Balance (order_record.order_number)
```

Output

There are several statements that exist to provide output in INFORMIX-4GL. These statements only display information to the screen; they do not provide the option of writing the information to a file. The only ways to output information to an operating system file are by using 4GL reports (see Chapters 25 and 26) or by using the `unload` statement (see Chapter 5). You will find that 4GL reports will allow you to do most of what you need to do when outputting to operating system files.

Remember that you can store most of the information you would want to store in a file in the database. Consider the option of using the database for data storage instead of operating system files.

The following statements provide output to the screen:

- `display`
- `error`
- `message`
- `prompt`
- `sleep`

The `prompt` statement is included here even though it is primarily used to read input from the user.

The `sleep` statement is included here because it is often used in conjunction with the other output statements.

All of these statements, except for `sleep`, may display to the screen using any of the following attributes supported by your terminal:

normal	yellow	white
bold	magenta	
reverse	red	
blink	cyan	
underline	green	
invisible	blue	
dim	black	

An *attribute* clause is available wherever these attributes may be used. Multiple attributes may be used for a single output statement, so you could specify `red`, `reverse`, and `blink`, if desired.

Any of these attributes will compile correctly whether or not your terminal will be able to display them. For instance, if you use the attribute magenta on a monochrome terminal, the output will still be displayed to your screen.

Display

The `display` statement allows you to display variables to the screen. The `display` statement is discussed in further detail in Chapter 13 because it is also used with screen forms. The syntax is:

```
display <variable name> [, ...]
    [ at <row number>, <column number>
      [attribute ( <attribute name>  [, ...] ) ]
    ]
```

The at clause specifies the screen or window row and column position at which to display the variable(s). If no row and column position are specified, the display switches to *line mode* from *form mode*, and the variable(s) are displayed on the next line. It is not a good idea to use line mode if you are not using menus or forms in your program. Line mode can cause problems with your form display. The display statement in line mode is very useful for short test programs that display before and after values when you want to determine how a feature works.

Examples:
```
let animal = "rabbit"
display animal
display animal at 4,40
display animal at 8,40 attribute (reverse)
```

Error

When the error statement displays to the screen, the terminal beeps and the text of the error message is by default displayed in reverse video. The error message will be displayed on the *error line* of the screen. The location of this line may be changed by using the options statement (see Chapter 14). The error statement is one of the more flexible output statements because it can take a combination of variables and literals as input. The error message will be cleared from the screen when any key is pressed or when another error message (or other display) writes over the displayed error message. The syntax for the error statement is:

```
error <variable name or string> [, ...]
    [ attribute ( <attribute name> [, ...] ) ]
```

Examples:
```
error "Please enter a valid value."
error "The value ", p_value,
  "is not valid here, press F3 for help!"
  attribute (normal, bold)
error "You've got to be kidding - you can't do that!"
error "Call for ""Help!"", you're really confused."
```

As you can see, you can use single quotes or two double quotes inside of a literal string.

The `error` statement, when used in combination with the `sleep` statement (described later in this section), can be a very valuable debugging tool.

```
error "counter = ", counter, "  p_date = ", p_date
sleep 3
```

Message

Like the `error` statement, the `message` statement also gives you flexibility in formatting your output message. The `message` statement will be displayed on the message line of the current screen or window. This location of this line may be adjusted by using the `options` statement (see Chapter 14). The syntax for the `message` statement is:

```
message <variable name or string> [, ...]
      [ attribute ( <attribute name> [, ...] ) ]
```

Examples:
```
message "This will take a few seconds.... please wait."
message "Enter your username ", p_username,
    "or press the F1 key for a list of valid users!"
    attribute (normal, bold)
message "You've got to be kidding - you can't do that!"
message "Call for ""Help!"", you're really confused."
```

As in the `error` statement, you can use single quotes or two double quotes inside of a literal string.

Unlike the output of `error`, the output of `message` always stays in place until overwritten or cleared.

Prompt

The `prompt` statement provides a quick method of prompting a user and getting a response. The syntax for the `prompt` statement is:

```
prompt <variable name or string> [, ...]
       [ attribute ( <attribute name> [, ...] ) ]
     for [ char ] <variable name>
       [ help <help number> ]
       [ attribute ( <attribute name> [, ...] ) ]
     [ on key ( <special key> [, ...] )
       <4GL program statement(s)> [, ...]
end prompt]
```

The variable name or string is a message that is printed to the screen to prompt the user for input. This message may be displayed with any desired attributes.

The `for` clause specifies the variable into which the user's input will be read. If the keyword `char` is used, the input may only be a single character, and the user will not have to press the *return* key after the character has been entered. The user input may be displayed with any desired attributes.

The `help` clause allows users to call up a customized, context-sensitive help screen. It is discussed in Chapter 15.

The `on key` clause allows the user to specify certain actions to be performed when the user presses a special key. Any number of `on key` clauses may be included within a `prompt` statement. When the `on key` clause is used, the `end prompt` clause must be used to complete the `prompt` statement. After an `on key` clause is selected and run, the `prompt` statement terminates and program control is passed to the statement following the `end prompt`.

Special keys that may be used with the `on key` clause are:

- Any function key from `F1` through `F64`,
- `Control-<character>` except for A, D, H, L, R, X and any other control characters that have special meaning in your operating system,
- `Escape` may be used if it is not defined as the *accept* key (see Chapter 14), and

- *Interrupt* may be used if the `defer interrupt` statement is in effect (see Chapter 16) - but the Informix global variable `int_flag` will be set to true (see Chapter 17).

note

Be aware when you are using the `prompt` *statement that unless you are prompting for a single character, user entry is terminated by use of the* return key *instead of by the* accept key. *The accept key is used in most other places to terminate user input. This inconsistency in the user interface has been known to confuse users.*

Examples:

```
prompt "Do you wish to continue? (Y/N) "
    attribute (reverse)        for char answer

prompt "Enter your secret password: "
    attribute (reverse) for password  help 123
    attribute (invisible)

    on key (F10)
       call Change_User_Password ()
end prompt
```

Sleep

The `sleep` statement simply puts the program to sleep for a specified number of seconds. This statement is often used in conjunction with output statements to force the program to pause long enough for the output statement to be read. This statement can come in handy when debugging programs.

```
sleep <number of seconds>
```

Example:

```
error "Debug value of p_account = ", p_account
sleep 3
```

Conditionals

INFORMIX-4GL allows you access to two types of conditional statements:

- if-then-else
- case

These statements have similar formats to their counterparts in other programming languages. They are described below in detail.

if-then-else

The if-then-else statement has the syntax:

```
if <Boolean expression> then
   <4GL statement(s)>
[ else
   <4GL statement(s)> ]
end if
```

A Boolean expression evaluates to true or false. True and false are recognized constants in INFORMIX-4GL. They are represented as smallint or integer values. Zero represents a false value and a non-zero number represents a true value.

Examples:

```
if balance_due > 100 then
   call Print_Current_Invoice (p_order_number)
end if

if p_username = "dba" then
   call Privileged_User ()
else
   call Non_Privileged_User ()
end if
```

Note that if a value is null, any comparison with that value besides is null or is not null will evaluate to false.

```
Examples:   initialize p_value to null
            if p_value       = null then ...  { false }
            if p_value      <> null then ...  { false }
            if p_value is      null then ...  { true  }
            if p_value is not null then ...   { false }
```

case

The case statement has the syntax:

```
case [ ( <expression> ) ]
  when <expression>
      { <4GL statement(s)> | exit case } [...]
  [...]
  [ otherwise
      { <4GL statement(s)> | exit case } [...]
  ]
end case
```

The exit case statement will immediately exit the case statement.

There are several different forms of the case statement. The first form of the case statement is probably more standard:

```
case p_letter
  when "A" let p_word = "Apple"
  when "B" let p_word = "Blueberry"
  when "C" let p_word = "Cherry"
  otherwise
    error "Not a valid letter."
end case
```

This checks the values in each when clause against the variable being cased.

The second form of the case statement allows each Boolean expression to be completely defined in each when clause:

```
case
   when p_letter = "A" let p_word = "Apple"
   when p_letter = "B" let p_word = "Blueberry"
   when p_letter = "C" let p_word = "Cherry"
   otherwise
      error "Not a valid letter."
end case
```

Note that the tested condition need not be the same in each when clause. This is the normal way to implement a sequence of if-then-else-if-else-if... statements.

```
case
   when p_letter = "J"
        let p_answer = "by Jannine R. Mohr"
   when p_number = 3
        let p_answer = "3 Little Pigs"
   when p_letter = "Z" and p_number = 99
        let p_answer = "THE END"
   otherwise
      error "Not a valid letter."
end case
```

Looping

Three standard looping statements are also provided in INFORMIX-4GL. These statements are similar to their counterparts in other programming languages.

- for
- while
- goto-label

note   *The* goto *statement is included here merely for completeness. To maintain good programming style, you should avoid using it.*

for

The for statement has the syntax:

```
for <integer variable name> =
    <integer expression> to <integer expression>
                    [ step <integer expression> ]
  { <4GL statement(s)> |
    continue for |
    exit for
  } [...]
end for
```

The for statement goes through the loop by initially setting the variable equal to the first *integer expression* and incrementing the variable each time until it reaches the second *integer expression*. The step *integer expression* indicates how much the variable is incremented (or decremented) at each iteration.

The continue for statement returns control to the top of the loop. Any statements remaining to be executed for that iteration of the for loop are not executed.

The exit for immediately exits the for loop.

Examples:
```
for counter = 1 to p_max_counter
  if account[counter].balance_due > 0 then
    call Bill_Client (account[counter].account_number)
  end if
end for


for counter = p_max_counter to 1 step - 2
  if client[counter].first_name is null then
    exit for
  end if

  case p_client[counter].first_name
    when "SUE"      let sue_count    = sue_count    + 1
    when "MIKE"     let mike_count   = mike_count   + 1
    when "STACEY"   let stacey_count = stacey_count + 1
    when "GREGG"    let gregg_count  = gregg_count  + 1
    otherwise continue for
  end for
end for
```

while

The while statement has the syntax:

```
while <Boolean expression>
  { <4GL statement(s)> |
    continue while |
    exit while
  } [...]
end while
```

The while loop is executed so long as the Boolean expression evaluates to true. If the Boolean expression always evaluates to true, the while loop will continue to execute forever (unless it reaches an exit while statement or until the program is stopped). Conversely, if the Boolean expression never evaluates to true, the statements inside the while loop will never be executed.

The continue while statement returns control to the top of the loop. Any statements remaining to be executed for that iteration of the while loop are not executed.

The exit while immediately exits the while loop.

Examples:
```
while true do
  let p_max_value = p_max_value * 2
  if p_max_value > 100000 then
    exit while
  end if
end while

while answer <> "Y" and answer <> "N"
  prompt "Would you like to continue? " attribute
                                         (reverse)
    for char answer
end while
```

goto-label

Inclusion of the `goto-label` statement in this book is not an endorsement to use it. But, in case you have to fix someone else's code that contains a `goto-label` statement, the syntax is:

```
goto [:] <label name>
```

The `goto` statement will transfer program control to the appropriate `label` statement. The `goto` and the `label` statement must be local to the same `main`, `function`, or `report`. The colon (:) in the `goto` statement is ANSI standard.

```
label <label name>:
```

Example:
```
function Why_Me (p_username)
    define p_username char (14)

    if p_username = Get_Username () then
        goto my_label
    end if

    <4GL statements>

    label my_label:
    <4GL statements>

end function  { Why_Me }
```

Running UNIX Commands

The `run` statement will run an operating system command or program from an INFORMIX-4GL program. This means that you can also run other Informix processes by using this command. The syntax of the `run` statement is:

```
run <operating system command>
[ in { line | form } mode ]
    [ returning <integer variable name> |
  without waiting ]
```

The operating system command must be a single quoted string or a single variable.

If you specify `form mode` the screen is not cleared and redrawn when the `run` statement is executed. The default is `line mode` (the screen is cleared and redrawn). This option is available in more recent versions of INFORMIX-4GL.

The `without waiting` clause starts running the command and immediately returns control to the 4GL program regardless of whether the operating system command has completed or not. If this option is not specified, the `run` statement will wait for the completion of the operating system command.

The `returning` clause option allows the numeric exit status of the program or shell script to be returned. In order to retrieve the actual value returned, you must divide the returned value by 256.

Examples:
```
let unix_command = "more ", report_name
run unix_command

let unix_command = "print.sh ", printer_name,
    " ", report_name
run unix_command in form mode without waiting

let unix_command = "my_shell.sh ", p_num
run unix_command returning exit_status
let exit_status = exit_status / 256
```

Summary

The assignment statement has the syntax:

```
let <variable name> = <expression>
```

Several statements exist to provide output to the screen in INFORMIX-4GL. The attributes available for use in these statements are:

```
normal          yellow          white
bold            magenta
reverse         red
blink           cyan
underline       green
invisible       blue
dim black
```

```
display <variable name> [, ...]
        [ at <row number>, <column number>
        [attribute ( <attribute name>  [, ...] ) ]
        ]

error <variable name or string> [, ...]
        [ attribute ( <attribute name> [, ...] ) ]

message <variable name or string> [, ...]
        [ attribute ( <attribute name> [, ...] ) ]

prompt <variable name or string> [, ...]
        [ attribute ( <attribute name> [, ...] ) ]
      for [ char ] <variable name>
        [ help <help number> ]
        [ attribute ( <attribute name> [, ...] ) ]
    [ on key ( <special key> [, ...] )
        <4GL program statement(s)> [, ...]
end prompt]

sleep <number of seconds>
```

INFORMIX-4GL allows you access to two standard types of conditional statements:

```
if <Boolean expression> then
  <4GL statement(s)>
[ else
  <4GL statement(s)> ]
end if

case [ ( <expression> ) ]
  when <expression>
      { <4GL statement(s)> | exit case } [...]
  [...]
  [ otherwise
      { <4GL statement(s)> | exit case } [...]
  ]
end case
```

Three standard looping statements are also provided in INFORMIX-4GL:

```
for <integer variable name> = <integer expression> to
                         <integer expression>
              [ step <integer expression> ]
  { <4GL statement(s)> | continue for | exit for } [...]
end for

while <Boolean expression>
  {<4GL statement(s)> | continue while | exit while } [...]
end while

goto [:]<label name>
label <label name>:
```

The run statement will run an operating system command from INFORMIX-4GL.

```
run <operating system command>
    [ in { line | form } mode ]
    [ returning <integer variable name> | without waiting ]
```

Screen Forms

- *What is a screen form?*
- *Screen form design*
- *Screen form implementation*
- *Single record form*
- *Multiple record form*
- *Combination form*
- *Form attributes*
- `upscol`
- *Summary*

What Is a Screen Form?

Screen forms are similar to paper forms that you fill out except that they are displayed on your screen. Screen forms are generally made up of fields and field labels that briefly indicate the type of information that should be entered into each field. You may enter information onto a form, change existing information on a form, delete information from a form, and search for information in a form.

Forms are the primary method used in most interactive database applications for collecting and maintaining database information.

Your screens may take on a windows-like appearance. You may have many forms of different sizes on a screen and the forms may overlap.

Figure 18-1 is a sample screen form.

A form is displayed on the screen or in a window on the screen. The border surrounding the screen is an attribute related to the window (as opposed to the form). Working with windows is discussed in Chapter 13.

The first two lines of the form are reserved for a menu. In this case, our menu will let us search for rows in the toy_store table,

```
Toy Store Menu:    Find   Add   Change   Next   Previous   Delete   Exit
Find a toy store.
-------------------------------------------------Press F1 for Help----
  Toy Store Number [             ]

  Store Name       [                                    ]

  Buyer name: Last [                      ] First [                    ]

  Phone number     [              ]       Fax number [                 ]

  Address:
    Street [                    ]
    City   [              ] State [  ] Zip Code [              ]
```

Figure 18-1   *A sample of a screen form.*

and add, change, and delete rows in that table. Creating menus was discussed in Chapter 10. We will learn how to perform the functions defined in this menu as we progress through these chapters.

Information below the dashed line is defined as part of the form. The text is ASCII text, and the square brackets ([ ]) define where each data field is located and its length.

Screen Form Design

This section discusses a few basic concepts to keep in mind when designing screens.

Your forms should be laid out clearly and they should be easy to use. This is the first and most important rule when designing screens. All other rules support this rule.

The text labels for each field should be clear and easy to understand. Use terminology your users are familiar with.

Use the form comment facility (described later in this chapter) to provide context-sensitive help for each field. The form comment is a single line of information for each field that can be displayed on the last line of your window.

Visually align the fields and field labels and any other text wherever possible in your form. This will help to make your screen form appear less cluttered. If you have room in your screen or window, use blank lines to make your screen form appear less crowded.

The fields should normally be ordered from left to right and then from top to bottom and should be in the order that is most convenient for the users of your application. You can always display the fields in one order and have the user enter them in another order, but in most cases this will tend to confuse users. There are exceptions to this, so do what makes sense for your application.

Screen Form Implementation

The source for each screen form is stored in separate files ending in `.per`. When a form is compiled, it is stored in a file with the same name as the `.per` file, except ending in `.frm`. A screen form is compiled either through the Form menu in the INFORMIX-4GL Programmer's Environment, or from the command line as described in Chapter 7. These `.frm` files are interpreted at program runtime when they are called by a 4GL program.

This means that your program may fail at runtime if (1) you are working with different versions of 4GL code and screen code, (2) you call the name of a form whose `.frm` file does not exist or cannot be found, (3) the form name specified in 4GL does not match the `.frm` file name, or (4) fields and/or records within the form are referred to by different names in your 4GL code.

A form file does not need to exist in order for a 4GL program which uses the form to compile. The compiled form file is read at runtime by your 4GL program, so it does need to exist before your program is run. Usually you will design a screen form, then write the 4GL code that will display and use that form.

A form source file contains several parts:

- database
- screen
- tables
- attributes
- instructions

Use the same syntax for comments in form files as you use for comments in your 4GL code.

Each of these form sections is discussed in detail below.

Database

Each screen file must contain a database section. This section defines which database you want to work with, or you may decide not to work with a database at all.

```
database { <database name> | formonly }
```

If you specify a database name, the screen form will assume that any tables and columns you refer to later in the form exist in the specified database.

If you specify formonly as the database name, you may not refer to any databases or tables later in the form file. Any fields you use will be defined within the form.

Screen

The screen section defines the size and the layout of your screen.

```
screen
[ size <lines on screen>
          [ by <columns on screen> ] ]
"{"
  [ <text> |
    \g <graphics character(s)> \g |
    "[" <field tag name>
          [ "|"  <field tag name> [...] ]
    "]"
  ]
  [ ... ]
"}"
[ end ]
```

Where the curly braces, the square brackets and the pipes appear inside double quotes, enter these characters as literals instead of using them as part of the syntax denoting options. Note that there are no comments in the screen section of a form.

The size clause allows you to specify the default size of your screen. If no size is specified, the default screen length is 24 lines, and the default screen width is defined by the number of columns in the widest row of your screen layout.

Everything in between the curly braces { } defines your screen layout. You may lay out your screens any way you wish. The fields of the screen are where data will later be entered and displayed. These fields are surrounded by square brackets ([ ]) and are associated with a particular database column or `formonly` column by a *field tag*. If you specify custom delimiters that have the same beginning and end characters, you can save screen space by using only a single delimiter bewteen fields eg. [a|b|c].

The *field tag* you specify here will also be used in the `attributes` section to relate the screen field to the data. Field tags are similar to variable names, but you will probably want to keep them short—because they must fit within the square brackets.

You may also use the following graphics characters if your termcap or terminfo definition supports them. A \g must be at the beginning and end of a graphics character string.

–	dashes for a horizontal line
|	vertical bars for a vertical line
p	upper left corner of box
q	upper right corner of box
b	lower left corner of box
d	lower right corner of box

Tables

If you specified a database name (not `formonly`) in the `database` section of the form, you will need to specify which tables are used in this screen.

```
tables
  { <table name> |
      <table alias> = <table name>
  } [...]
[ end ]
```

If the database is MODE ANSI, and you wish for users other than the table owner to execute the form, your table name must include the owner name, e.g., *<owner name>.<table name>*.

You must include an alias for the owner name and table name combination if you wish to refer to the table anywhere else in the form specification file.

Attributes

The `attributes` section relates the fields defined in the screen layout section to column names by the field tag names.

```
attributes
  <field tag name> =
    { <table name>.<column name> |
      formonly.<field name>
    }
  [ <field attributes> [, ...] ] ;
  [ ... ]
[ end ]
```

Field attributes may be defined for each field to assist in handling the data input. These attributes are discussed later in this chapter in the section *Form Features*.

Instructions

The `instructions` section allows you to specify characters other than square brackets [] to be printed as field delimiters and to define any screen records or arrays for the form. This section is optional.

```
instructions
  [ delimiters
          ""<start character><end character>" ]
  [ screen record <record name>
          [ "[" <array size> "]" ]
  ( { <table name>.* |
      <table name>.<column name> thru
      <table name>.<column name>          |
      <table name>.<column name>
    }
  )
[ end ]
```

The `delimiters` statement allows you to specify alternate field delimiters to display instead of square brackets (`[]`). The square brackets must still be entered as the field delimiters in the screen layout section, but they will be displayed for the user as whatever character(s) you like, including blanks.

If space is at a premium on your screen, you may wish to specify only a single delimiter between fields. To do this, your start delimiter character must be defined to be the same as your end delimiter character, and the fields must be separated by a pipe, |, in the screen layout section.

Example:
```
[f1                    ][f2           ][f3           ]
```

To make only one delimiter character appear between fields use:

```
[f1                    |f2          |f3          ]
```

If you specify the name of a screen record, you can refer to that screen record within your 4GL code. You can also specify an array of your screen record if you have several rows of data appearing on a single screen. The uses for this will become clear when we start using the `display`, `display array`, `input`, and `input array` statements.

Example of an INFORMIX-4GL-Generated Form

You can generate a form automatically by using the Generate option in the INFORMIX-4GL Forms menu or by entering the command: `form4gl -d` at the operating system command line. The `form4gl -d` command prompts for form name, database name and a list of tables or you can specify these on the command line:

```
form4gl -d <form name> <database name> <table name>
[ <table name> [...] ]
```

While you won't want to use the form as it is generated (it is exceptionally ugly), it can give you a good starting point to work from.

An example of a screen automatically generated from the toy_store table in the toymaker database follows:

```
database toymaker
screen size 24 by 80
{
store_number        [f000        ]
store_name          [f001                            ]
buyer_last_name     [f002                        ]
buyer_first_name    [f003              ]
phone_number        [f004    ]
fax_number          [f005    ]
store_street        [f006                        ]
store_city          [f007                        ]
store_state         [a0]
store_zip_code  .   [f008      ]
}
end
tables
toy_store
attributes
f000 = toy_store.store_number;
f001 = toy_store.store_name;
f002 = toy_store.buyer_last_name;
f003 = toy_store.buyer_first_name;
f004 = toy_store.phone_number;
f005 = toy_store.fax_number;
f006 = toy_store.store_street;
f007 = toy_store.store_city;
a0 = toy_store.store_state;
f008 = toy_store.store_zip_code;
end
```

Example of a Modified Generated Form

As you can see, the automatically generated form is not visually appealing, but now that it exists, we can easily modify it to produce a better looking form.

Notice that this form was used in combination with 4GL code to produce the sample form we displayed in the first section of this chapter.

Two lines are reserved by default above the first line of the screen layout when the form is displayed to allow for a menu to be displayed. This can be changed by specifying different options as discussed in Chapter 14.

```
{ * * * * * * * * * * * * * * * * * * * * * * * * * * * * * * * * * * * * * * * * * * * * * * * * * * * * * * * * * * * * * * * *
   toy_store
   This screen allows the user to maintain the toy_store table.
* * * * * * * * * * * * * * * * * * * * * * * * * * * * * * * * * * * * * * * * * * * * * * * * * * * * * * * * * * * * * * }

database toymaker
screen size 24 by 80

{
----------------------------------------------Press F1 for Help----
Toy Store Number   [f000        ]

Store Name         [f001                                      ]

Buyer name: Last [f002                    ] First [f003        ]

Phone number       [f004          ]      Fax number [f005       ]

Address:
   Street [f006                    ]
   City   [f007                ] State [a0] Zip Code [f008       ]
}
end

tables toy_store

attributes
   f000 = toy_store.store_number;
   f001 = toy_store.store_name;
   f002 = toy_store.buyer_last_name;
   f003 = toy_store.buyer_first_name;
   f004 = toy_store.phone_number;
   f005 = toy_store.fax_number;
   f006 = toy_store.store_street;
   f007 = toy_store.store_city;
   a0   = toy_store.store_state;
   f008 = toy_store.store_zip_code;
end
```

Single Record Form

A single record form contains only a single record or row of information. The toy store screen shown in the previous section is a single record form. Only a single toy store is displayed or entered at one time on the form.

For instance, if we wanted a form to allow us to enter toy order information, we might design the following form:

```
{ * * * * * * * * * * * * * * * * * * * * * * * * * * * * * * * * * * * * * * * * * * * * * * * * * * * * * * * * *
   toy_order
   This screen allows you to display and maintain toy_order
   information.
   * * * * * * * * * * * * * * * * * * * * * * * * * * * * * * * * * * * * * * * * * * * * * * * * * * * * * * * * *}
database toymaker
screen size 24 by 80

{
------------------------------------------------Press F1 for Help----
   Order number: [f000          ]

   Store:        [f001        ]    [f005                               ]

   Date Ordered: [f002        ]    Date Shipped:  [f003                ]

   Sales Code:   [f004   ]
}
end

tables toy_order toy_store

attributes
   f000 = toy_order.order_number;
   f001 = toy_order.store_number;
   f005 = toy_store.store_name;
   f002 = toy_order.order_date;
   f003 = toy_order.shipping_datetime;
   f004 = toy_order.sales_code;

instructions
   screen record s_toy_order
      (order_number,  store_number,        store_name,
       order_date,    shipping_datetime,  sales_code)
end
```

Multiple Record Form

A multiple record form contains more than one record or row of information.

As you can see in the single record form example, we now have a form that will allow us to enter toy_order information. But we also need a form that will allow us to enter toy_order_item information.

The screen below is a multi-line form that allows us to easily enter and view each line item of the order. Notice the screen record definition defined as an array at the end of the screen file.

```
{*************************************************************
   toy_item
   This screen allows you to display and maintain the toy_order_item
   table.
*************************************************************}
database toymaker
screen size 24 by 80

{
-----------------------------------------Press F1 for Help----
  Toy Code/Description                  Quantity Unit Price Total Price
[f001    |f004                         |f002      |f003      |f005       ]
[f001    |f004                         |f002      |f003      |f005       ]
[f001    |f004                         |f002      |f003      |f005       ]
[f001    |f004                         |f002      |f003      |f005       ]
[f001    |f004                         |f002      |f003      |f005       ]
[f001    |f004                         |f002      |f003      |f005       ]
[f001    |f004                         |f002      |f003      |f005       ]
[f001    |f004                         |f002      |f003      |f005       ]
}
end

tables toy_order_item toy

attributes
   f001 = toy_order_item.toy_code;
   f004 = toy.description;
   f002 = toy_order_item.quantity;
   f003 = toy_order_item.unit_price;
   f005 = formonly.total_price;
```

continued

```
instructions
   delimiters "   "
   screen record sa_toy_item [8]
      (toy_code, description, quantity, unit_price, total_price)
end
```

Combination Form

A combination form allows you to put a single record and a multiple line record together on the same screen form. This gives you additional flexibility when designing your applications.

The form below combines the single row and multi-row forms defined in the previous sections into a single form. Notice there are now two screen record definitions at the end of the form. These will allow us to easily work from the 4GL program with the different part of this screen.

```
{ * * * * * * * * * * * * * * * * * * * * * * * * * * * * * * * * * * * * * * * * * * * * * * * * * * * * * * * * * * * * *
   toy_order
   This screen allows you to display and maintain toy_order and
   toy_order_item information.
   * * * * * * * * * * * * * * * * * * * * * * * * * * * * * * * * * * * * * * * * * * * * * * * * * * * * * * * * * * * * *}
database toymaker
screen size 24 by 80

{

---------------------------------------------Press F1 for Help----
   Order number: [f000          ]

   Store:          [f001        ]      [f005                          ]

   Date Ordered: [f002          ]    Date Shipped:   [f003            ]

   Sales Code:   [f004   ]

  Toy Code/Description                Quantity Unit Price Total Price
[f011   |f014                      |f012      |f013      |f015        ]
[f011   |f014                      |f012      |f013      |f015        ]
[f011   |f014                      |f012      |f013      |f015        ]
[f011   |f014                      |f012      |f013      |f015        ]
[f011   |f014                      |f012      |f013      |f015        ]
```

```
[f011    |f014                    |f012     |f013       |f015       ]
[f011    |f014                    |f012     |f013       |f015       ]
[f011    |f014                    |f012     |f013       |f015       ]
}
end

tables toy_order toy_store toy_order_item toy

attributes
   f000 = toy_order.order_number;
   f001 = toy_order.store_number;
   f005 = toy_store.store_name;
   f002 = toy_order.order_date;
   f003 = toy_order.shipping_datetime;
   f004 = toy_order.sales_code;

   f011 = toy_order_item.toy_code;
   f014 = toy.description;
   f012 = toy_order_item.quantity;
   f013 = toy_order_item.unit_price;
   f015 = formonly.total_price;

instructions
   delimiters "   "

   screen record s_toy_order
      (order_number, store_number,        store_name,
       order_date,    shipping_datetime, sales_code)

   screen record sa_toy_item [8]
      (toy_code, description, quantity, unit_price, total_price)
end
```

Form Attributes

The form features discussed in this section are used in the attributes section of the screen. These screen features allow you to specify attributes and data validation, that are useful when defining what should happen when working with specific fields of the screen.

The following attributes may be used in any combination.

```
autonext       downshift     required     verify
color          format        reverse      wordwrap
comments       include       type
default        noentry       upshift
display like   picture       validate like
```

These attributes are described in detail in this section.

autonext

The `autonext` attribute causes the cursor to automatically move to the next field when the current field is filled.

```
autonext
```

Example: `attributes`
```
        f011 = toy_order_item.toy_code,  autonext;
        f014 = toy_store.state,          autonext;
```

color

The `color` attribute allows the user to specify how the text in a field will be displayed and the conditions under which it will be displayed.

```
color = <display attribute> [ ... ]
     [ where <conditional expression> ]
```

The display attribute may be any of the following:

```
blink        white         cyan
underline    yellow        green
reverse      magenta       blue
left         red           black
```

The attribute `left` causes the `date` in the field to be left justified. Text is normally left justified and numbers are right justified.
All display attributes are not supported by all terminal types.

The field tag names may be used like variables when using a `where` condition.

Keep in mind that the `blink` attribute can be extremely annoying!

Example:
```
attributes
    f012 = toy_order_item.quantity, color = reverse blue
                                    where f012 >= 100;
    f015 = formonly.total_price, color = red where f015 < 0;
```

comments

The `comments` attribute allows you to allow a line of context-sensitive help whenever the user enters a field that has a comment associated with it.

```
comments = "<field comment>"
```

The comment will be printed on the last line of the window or on line 23 of the screen unless otherwise specified by the `options` statement.

Example:
```
attributes
    f000 = toy_order.order_number,
            comment="Enter order number.";
    f001 = toy_order.store_number,
            comment="Enter store number or F3 for help.";
```

default

The `default` attribute allows you to specify a default value for a field when new data is being inserted into the form. You may not find much use for this feature since defaults are normally handled from within the INFORMIX-4GL code.

```
default = <default value>
```

Example:
```
f002 = toy_order.order_date, default = today;
f004 = toy_order.sales_code, default = 1;
```

display like

The `display like` attribute allows you to use the attributes assigned as defaults to the specified table and column. These are any attributes that have been assigned by the `upscol` utility in the `syscolatt` table, which is described in the next section. Also see the `validate like` attribute.

```
display like <table name>.<column name>
```

Example:
```
f000 = formonly.order_number,
    display like toy_order.order_number;
f001 = formonly.store_number,
    display like toy_store.store_number;
```

downshift

The `downshift` attribute allows you to automatically convert the entered letters in a string to lowercase.

```
downshift
```

Example:
```
f005 = toy_store.store_name,     downshift;
f014 = toy.description,          downshift;
```

format

The format string allows you to specify the format of a decimal, float, smallfloat, or date when it is printed to the screen. Format uses a different format string than the 4GL `using` function to specify numeric data types. Format does not constrain the user when they are typing, but when the cursor exits the field, the value will be redisplayed using the format.

```
format = "<format string>"
```

For numeric data types, you can specify the number of digits to be printed by using pound signs, "#" and a period ".". A number will be rounded to make it fit into the number of characters specified in the format string if necessary.

For date data types, the same formatting can be used as in the 4GL function `using`:

dd	Prints the number of the day of the month, i.e., 01–31.
ddd	Prints the first three letters of the weekday, i.e., Sun through Sat.
mm	Prints the number of the month, i.e., 01–12.
mmm	Prints the first three letters of the month, i.e., Jan through Dec.
yy	Prints the last two numbers of the year, i.e., 1998 prints as 98. Note that it is much better to use 4-digit years to avoid ambiguous dates - especially at any time close to a turn of the century.
yyyy	Prints the four digit number of the year, i.e., 1998 prints as 1998.

Example:

```
attributes
    f000 = toy_order.order_number,     format = "######";
    f002 = toy_order.order_date,       format = "mm/dd/yyyy";
    f012 = toy_order_item.quantity,    format = "######";
    f013 = toy_order_item.unit_price,  format = "######.##";
    f015 = formonly.total_price,       format = "######.##";
```

For formatting dates you are usually better off setting the DBDATE environment variable in order to allow different international formats to be easily accommodated, such as "dd/mm/yyyy" versus "mm/dd/yyyy"

include

The `include` attribute allows you to specify a list of valid values that may be entered in a field. A user will no be able to to enter a value that is not in the include list when the `include` attribute is used.

```
include = ( { <valid value> |
              <valid value> to <valid value>
            } [, ...]
          )
```

Example:
```
attributes
  f004 = toy_order.sales_code,      include = (1, 2, 4);
  f012 = toy_order_item.quantity,  include = (1 to 1000);
```

noentry

The noentry attribute prevents the cursor from entering a field when data is being added or changed. Serial fields are automatically noentry.

```
noentry
```

Example:
```
attributes
        f000 = toy_order.order_number;
        f001 = toy_order.store_number;
        f005 = toy_store.store_name,     noentry;
        f011 = toy_order_item.toy_code;
        f014 = toy.description,          noentry;
```

picture

The picture attribute allows you to specify the characters that should be entered as part of a string. The entire contents of the string including any literal format characters are passed back to your program variable. The picture attribute will not format your data during a construct statement, nor does it alter strings displayed to the field which do not match the picture format.

```
picture = "<format string>"
```

The formatting characters are:

A	For a letter.
#	For a digit.
X	For any printable character.
`<other characters>`	To specify any literal characters which should be included in the string.

If the user enters only part of the field, but in the correct format, this input will be accepted.

The user does not enter any of the literal characters specified as part of the string. These are entered automatically. The formatting characters will be stored in your database along with the actual data unless you modify the contents of your program variable before saving it to the database.

To make data entry easier for users, it may be better to write a routine that will allow a more flexible input format than the `picture` attribute. For instance, users may want to enter any of the following strings for a phone number: 555-1212, 3035551212, 303 555 1212, 303-555-1212, etc. The `picture` attribute is not flexible enough to accept any of these formats. Also, if you write your own functions, it is easier to avoid having to store the formatting characters in your database.

Example:
```
attributes
   f000 = toy_store.phone_number,
           picture = "(###) ###-####";
```

required

The `required` attribute will force the user to enter a printable character in a data field. Two things to keep in mind are: (1) if the user enters a character and then deletes it, this will be accepted, and (2) if the field has a default attribute, the user is not required to enter a value.

```
required
```

Example:
```
attributes
   f000 = toy_order.order_number,          required;
```

```
f001 = toy_order.store_number,        required;
f005 = toy_store.store_name,          noentry;
f002 = toy_order.order_date,          default=today;
f003 = toy_order.shipping_datetime;
f004 = toy_order.sales_code,          required;
```

reverse

The `reverse` attribute causes the specified fields to be displayed in reverse video.

```
reverse
```

Example:
```
attributes
    f003 = toy_order.shipping_datetime, reverse;
```

type

The `type` attribute allows you to assign an INFORMIX-4GL data type to a `formonly` field. Note that there is no comma separating the name of the field and the type definition in this case.

```
type { <4GL data type> [ not null ] |
       like [ <table name>.]<column name>
     }
```

If you are defining a `char`, `decimal`, or `money` type, do not specify a length or precision since this will be determined by the length of the field on the form.

The type does not need to be defined. If no type is assigned, a type of `char` is assumed.

Example: `formonly.p_date type date`

upshift

The `upshift` attribute allows you to automatically convert the letters entered in a string to uppercase.

```
upshift
```

Example: f005 = toy_store.store_name,   upshift;
          f014 = toy.description,   upshift;

validate like

The validate like attribute allows you to use the attributes assigned as defaults to the specified table and column. These are any attributes that have been assigned by the upscol utility in the syscolval table that is described in the next section. Also see the display like attribute.

```
validate like <table name>.<column name>
```

Example:
f000 = formonly.order_number,
                validate like toy_order.order_number;
f001 = formonly.store_number,
                validate like toy_store.store_number;

verify

The verify attribute requires users to enter information into a field twice in order to reduce the possibility of incorrect data being entered.

```
verify
```

Example: f000 = toy_order.order_number, verify;

wordwrap

The wordwrap attribute provides an easy way to allow users to enter long strings of data on multiple input lines. The wordwrap function automatically moves a word that will not fit on the current line to the next line. Compress prevents any spaces not entered by the user from being considered part of the data.

```
wordwrap [ compress ]
```

The keys listed below have the following meanings when data is entered into a field using the wordwrap attribute. Some of these keys will perform differently depending on how the input wrap option is set:

backspace   Go to the previous field if at the beginning of the field, or go back a space.
Control-a   Toggle between typeover and insert mode.
Control-d   Delete any characters from the cursor position to the end of the field.
Control-n   Go to the next line of the multi-line field.
Control-x   Delete the character under the cursor.
down arrow   Go to the next field if on the bottom line, or go to next line of the field.
left arrow   Go to the previous field if at the beginning of the field, or go back a space.
return   Go to the next field.
right arrow   Go to the next field if at the end of the field, or move to the right.
tab   Add a tab to the field. Action depends on insert or typeover mode.
up arrow   Go to the previous field if on the top line, or go to the previous line of the field.

Example: f000 = formonly.very_long_comment, wordwrap;

Upscol

Run the upscol utility from the command line to apply attributes and data validations to the columns in tables. If your form refers to a column in the database, and you have defined attributes to validate data for that column, these will be used as default attributes when the form is compiled. Any definitions made explicitly within the form will override any of the definitions made by using the upscol utility.

The syntax for `upscol` is simply:

```
upscol
```

This command will take you to a menu driven system where you can specify default attributes and data validation for columns.

Any attributes saved will be stored in the `syscolatt` table and any data validation will be saved in the `syscolval` table. These may be referenced by the `display like` and `validate like` attributes described in the previous section.

Summary

Forms are the primary method used in most interactive database applications for collecting and maintaining database information. Forms should be designed so they are easy to use.

The form source code file suffix is `.per`. The compiled form suffix is `.frm`. The `.frm` files are run at program runtime when they are called by a 4GL program. The general form file syntax is:

```
database { <database name> | formonly }
        [ without null input ]

screen
[ size <lines on screen> [ by <columns on screen> ] ]
"{"
   [ <text> |
     \g <graphics character(s)> \g |
     "[" <field tag name>
         [ "|"  <field tag name> [...] ]
     "]"
   ]
   [ ... ]
"}"
[ end ]


tables
   { <table name> | <table alias> = <table name> } [...]
[ end ]
```

```
attributes
   <field tag name> = {  <table name>.<column name> |
                         formonly.<field name>
                      }
                      [ <field attributes> [, ...] ] ;
   [ ... ]
[ end ]


instructions
   [ delimiters "<start character><end character>" ]
   [ screen record <record name> [ "[" <array size> "]" ]
      ( { <table name>.* |
           <table name>.<column name> thru
           <table name>.<column name>           |
           <table name>.<column name>
         }
      )
[ end ]
```

Where the curly braces and the square brackets appear inside double quotes, enter these characters as literals instead of using them as part of the syntax denoting options.

To specify only a single delimiter between fields, both field delimiter characters must be the same, and the fields must be separated by a pipe (|) in the screen layout section.

You can generate a form automatically by using the Generate option in the INFORMIX-4GL Forms menu or by entering form4gl -d at the command line.

A single record form contains only a single record or row of information. A multiple record form contains more than one record or row of information. A combination form allows you to combine a single record and a multiple line record on the same screen form.

Fields may have any combination of the following attributes:

```
autonext

color = <display attribute> [ ... ]
                 [ where <conditional expression> ]

comments = "<field comment>"
```

```
default = <default value>

display like <table name>.<column name>

downshift

format = "<format string>"

include = ( { <valid value> |
                <valid value> to <valid value>
          } [, ...]
      )

noentry

picture = "<format string>"

required

reverse

type { <4GL data type> [ not null ] |
      like [ <table name>.]<column name>
    }

upshift

validate like <table name>.<column name>

verify

wordwrap [ compress ]
```

Run the upscol utility from the command line to apply attributes and data validations to the columns in tables.

```
upscol
```

Adding Forms
and Windows
& Displaying Data

- *Window handling*

- *Displaying forms*

- *Overview of display*

- `display`

- `display array`

- *Display a one-to-many relationship*

- *Summary*

Window Handling

INFORMIX-4GL allows you to create windows within the INFORMIX-4GL screen. A window is a named, rectangular area on the screen. The default window is named `screen`. You may open windows, clear windows, make a window current, and close windows.

The syntax for opening a window on a screen is:

```
open window <window name>
            at <row number>, <column number>
  with
    { <number of rows> rows,
      <number of columns> columns |
      form "<form file name (no .per or .frm
            extension)>"
    }
  [ attribute ( <window attribute> [, ...] ) ]
```

You must give each of your windows a name. This name is used later to refer to a specific window when making it the current window and when closing a window. You may wish to use a naming convention to distinguish the names of your windows from other names you may have defined in 4GL. For instance, all window names in this book begin with: `w_`.

You will need to specify the top left corner of the screen location where you wish your window to be opened.

The `with` clause allows you to specify the size of the window, or to open a window that displays a form. To specify the size of the window, just specify the number of rows and columns that should be in your window. Keep in mind that if the window will not fit on the screen based on the combination of its size and starting location, you will get a runtime error. Opening a window using the `with` form clause is discussed in the next section.

You may use any of the following attributes when opening your window:

```
border                            normal      white      blue
reverse                           bold        yellow     black
prompt line <line number>         dim         magenta
message line <line number>        invisible   red
form line <line number>           cyan
comment line <line number>        green
```

Examples of opening a window are:

```
open window w_menu1 at 3,3 with 3 rows, 70 columns

open window w_box1 at 3,6 with 4 rows, 30 columns
    attribute (border)
```

The `border` attribute is very useful when using windows. It puts a border around your window that makes it stand out from other information on the screen.

If you open a new window without closing windows that are already open, the new window becomes the current window and the original window remains displayed on the screen. If the screens overlap one another, the current window will be fully displayed and any other windows will appear as though they are "behind" the current window.

Another useful trick, sometimes, is a blank window with no border which is the size of the screen. This allows you to display your blank window in the background and the screen you care about in the foreground.

If you have several open windows on a screen, you may switch between them using the `current window` statement.

```
current window is { <window name> | screen }
```

When you make a window current, it is displayed at the "front" of your screen and it is where any output statements you make will be written (unless they are written to the screen itself).

Examples: `current window is w_box1`
`current window is screen`

You can clear the current window at any time. Clearing a window removes any previously displayed text from the window. Variations on this statement will also clear a screen, a form, or specific fields within a form. To clear a window, use the `clear window` statement.

```
clear { screen |
        window <window name> |
        form [ <form field name> [, ...] ]
      }
```

Examples:
```
clear screen
clear window w_toy_order1
clear form
clear form last_name, first_name, street_address
```

When you close a window, the window is removed from the screen and the screen may not be referenced again until it is reopened.

```
close window <window name>
```

Example: `close window w_box1`

Displaying Forms

The forms you designed in Chapter 12 may be displayed to the screen in one of two ways. You may display the form within the current window (or the screen if there are no current windows), or you may display a form in a window at the time you are opening the window.

First, you need to open the form to declare the name of the form:

```
open form <form name>
from "<filename without .per or .frm extension>"
```

Once you have opened the form, if you have already opened a window in which you wish to display your form, or if you wish to display your form to the current screen, use the display statement:

```
display form <form name>
   [ attribute ( <window list> [, ...] ) ]
```

Note that your form must be able to fit within the screen or window in which you are displaying the form. If the form is too large to fit in the available space, you will receive a runtime error.

You must assign your form a name so that you can later close it.

You may use any of the following attributes when opening your form:

reverse	normal	white	cyan
blink	bold	yellow	green
underline	dim	magenta	blue
invisible	red	black	

Examples: display form f_myform
           display form f_myform attribute (reverse)

You may also display the form at the same time you are opening a window. The syntax is described in the previous section.

Example: `open window w_toy at 3, 5 with form "toy"`
           `attribute (border)`

When you open a window with a form, the size of the window is determined based on the width and length of the form. You must specify the position of the upper left corner of your window. Your form must fit within the amount of space available, or you will receive a runtime error.

One way of making sure your window will be of an appropriate width is to include a line similar to the following at the beginning of each of your forms.

`---------------------------Press F1 for Help-----`

This allows you to determine the width of your window in cases where your form by itself is narrower than you would like. This line also provides a border between the menu and the form and tells the user how to access help.

Also note that the following window attributes can have an impact on the display of the form within the window:

prompt line *<line number>*
message line *<line number>*
form line *<line number>*
comment line *<line number>*

These can also be set with the `options` *statement, but if you are adjusting a value for a single form, using these attributes is easier.*

If you open a form with the display form statement, you will need to close it with the close form statement. If you open a form with the open window statement, it will be closed when you close the window.

```
close form <form name>
```

Example: `close form f_myform`

Overview of Display

Now that we can retrieve data from a database, this chapter describes the display statements that allow you to display the data in a screen form.

Sample modules in this chapter will show you how to display data on a form in three ways: one record at a time in a single record form, several records at a time in a multiple line form, and a combination of a single record form and a multiple line form.

Display

The `display` statement was also discussed in Chapter 11 as one of the output statements available in INFORMIX-4GL. Here we discuss the `display` statement when it is used to display data on the screen. The syntax for the `display` statement is:

```
display
  { by name <variable name> [, ...]
     [ attribute ( <attribute name> [, ...] ) ] |
     <variable name or constant> [, ...]
     [ { to { <form field name> [, ...] |
            screen record name>
                          ["["<row number>"]"].*
          } [, ...]                              |
        at <row number>, <column number>
      }
      [ attribute ( <attribute name> [, ...] ) ]
    ]
  }
```

Where the square brackets are shown inside of double quotes, they are part of the syntax of the statement; they do not indicate an option.

There are two basic forms of the display statement that allow you to display data to a form.

First, the `display by name` statement allows you to display the contents of program variables to fields on the form if the program variables and the screen form use the same names for the fields. If the program variable is a record, only the portion of the variable name following *<record name>.* needs to match.

Display Example

Let's look at a form we can use as an example:

```
{*******************************************************************
    toy_order1
    This screen allows you to display and maintain toy_order
    information.
 ******************************************************************}
database toymaker
screen size 24 by 80

{
-----------------------------------------------Press F1 for Help-----
   Order number: [f000          ]

   Store:        [f001          ]    [f005                         ]

   Date Ordered: [f002          ]  Date Shipped:  [f003            ]

   Sales Code:   [f004   ]
}
end

tables toy_order toy_store

attributes
    f000 = toy_order.order_number;
    f001 = toy_order.store_number;
    f005 = toy_store.store_name;
    f002 = toy_order.order_date;
    f003 = toy_order.shipping_datetime;
    f004 = toy_order.sales_code;

instructions
    screen record s_toy_order
       (order_number,  store_number,       store_name,
        order_date,    shipping_datetime, sales_code)
end
```

Now let's look at an example of a display by name statement using this screen:

```
define p_toy_order record
      order_number like toy_order.order_number,
      store_number like toy_order.store_number,
      store_name   like toy_store.store_name,
      order_date   like toy_order.order_date,
      shipping_datetime              like
      toy_order.shipping_datetime,
      sales_code   like toy_order.sales_code
   end record

{ The record needs to be assigned values and
   the form needs to be displayed to the screen
   somewhere in here }

display by name p_toy_order.*
```

or:

```
display by name p_toy_order.order_number, p_toy_order.order_date
```

The second way of displaying information to a form is when the form fields and the program variables have different names. If this is the case, you merely need to specify both:

```
define p_order_number       like toy_order.order_number
define p_store_number       like toy_order.store_number
define p_store_name         like toy_store.store_name
define p_order_date         like toy_order.order_date
define p_ship_datetime      like toy_order.shipping_datetime
define p_sales_code         like toy_order.sales_code

{ The program variables need to be assigned values and the
   form needs to be displayed to the screen somewhere in here }

display p_order_number
     to   order_number
```

or:

```
display p_order_number,   p_store_number,      p_store_name,
p_order_date,             p_ship_datetime,     p_sales_code
to order_number,          store_number,        store_name,
order_date,               shipping_datetime,   sales_code
```

The `display` statement using the `at` clause discussed in Chapter 11 allows you to display data at specific window coordinates rather than to fields on the form.

Any of the following attributes may be used with the `display` statement:

```
normal      reverse     white       cyan
bold        blink       yellow      green
dim         underline   magenta     blue
invisible   red         black
```

Sample Module

Below is a sample module that will display the following form on the screen (Figure 13-1):

```
┌─────────────────────────────────────────────────────────────┐
│ Toy Order Menu:   Find  Next  Previous  Delete  Exit         │
│ Find toy orders.                                             │
│ ------------------------------------------Press F1 for Help------│
│   Order number: [            ]                                │
│                                                              │
│   Store:          [          ]     [                      ]  │
│                                                              │
│   Date Ordered: [          ]      Date Shipped:  [        ]  │
│                                                              │
│   Sales Code:    [        ]                                   │
└─────────────────────────────────────────────────────────────┘
```

Figure 13-1 *Sample menu and screen form as displayed for the user.*

Each of the menu options is associated with one of the functions in the module. The effects of each option are described briefly in the table on page 286.

Menu Option	Description
Find	This function uses a `construct` statement to allow the user to define a search. The search is performed and the first record returned from the search is displayed on the screen.
Next	This function fetches the next record available from the user's search. Keep in mind that if the user has previously fetched this record, any changes (including deletions) that have been made to the data since the record was originally fetched will not be reflected in the information displayed.
Previous	This function fetches the previous record available from the user's search. Keep in mind that any changes (including deletions) that have been made to the data since the record was originally fetched will not be reflected in the information displayed.
Delete	This function allows the user to delete the displayed record. A menu is used with a default of No to make certain the user intends to delete the record. Also note that to maintain referential integrity, whenever an entry in the toy_order table is deleted, any related records in the toy_order_item table will also be deleted.
Exit	This menu option simply exits the menu, which in this case, exits the program.

We will write the Add and Change options for this menu in Chapter 18.

The code for the sample module follows. A short `main` program is included to allow the module to run for testing purposes. The only thing missing is the function `Error_Recovery`, which you should define based on the information on *Error Handling* in Chapter 16, or use the `Error_Recovery` function defined in that chapter. The form used by this module is the same form defined earlier in this section, but it is also included in the following module for easy reference.

```
{ *****************************************************************
   display example
   This module allows you to display information in and delete
   information from the toy_order table.

   The following functions are in this module:
                        Toy_Order_Menu
                        Find_Toy_Order
                        Close_Toy_Order_Cursor
                        Next_Toy_Order
                        Previous_Toy_Order
                        Delete_Toy_Order
 ***************************************************************** }


database toymaker

{ Define variables global to this module }
define p_toy_order record
      order_number              like toy_order.order_number,
      store_number              like toy_order.store_number,
      store_name                like toy_store.store_name,
      order_date                like toy_order.order_date,
      shipping_datetime         like toy_order.shipping_datetime,
      sales_code                like toy_order.sales_code
   end record

define cursor_open             smallint

main
  defer interrupt
  options message line last
  call Toy_Order_Menu ()
end main



{ *****************************************************************
   Toy_Order_Menu
 ***************************************************************** }
function Toy_Order_Menu ()

   whenever error stop
```

```
let cursor_open = false

open window w_toy_order1 at 2,2 with form "toy_order1"
  attribute (border)

initialize p_toy_order.* to null

menu "Toy Order Menu"

   command "Find"                "Find toy orders."
          help 1
          call Find_Toy_Order ()

   command "Next"                "View the next toy order."
          help 2
          call Next_Toy_Order ()

   command "Previous"            "View the previous toy order."
          help 3
          call Previous_Toy_Order ()

   command "Delete"              "Delete this toy order."
          help 6
          call Delete_Toy_Order ()
          next option "Find"

   command key ("E","X") "Exit" "Exit from this menu."
          help 9
          exit menu
  end menu

  call Close_Toy_Order_Cursor ()

  close window w_toy_order1

end function  { Toy_Order_Menu }
```

```
{**********************************************************************
   Find_Toy_Order
   Find the toy order for the user and display the first order.
 *********************************************************************}
function Find_Toy_Order ()
   define where_clause           char(300)
   define sql_statement          char(600)
   define error_status           smallint

   clear form
   let int_flag = false
   call Close_Toy_Order_Cursor ()
   initialize p_toy_order.* to null

   display "" at 1,1
   display "" at 2,1
   display "Please enter your search criteria." at 1, 1

   construct by name where_clause on
        toy_order.order_number,      toy_order.store_number,
        toy_store.store_name,        toy_order.order_date,
        toy_order.shipping_datetime, toy_order.sales_code
      help 1

   { Allow user to press break during construct to cancel search }
   if int_flag then
      message "Toy order search cancelled."
      let int_flag = false
      return
   end if

   display "" at 1,1
   display "" at 2,1
   display "Searching..." at 1, 1

   let sql_statement =
     "select toy_order.order_number,      toy_order.store_number, ",
          "toy_store.store_name,          toy_order.order_date, ",
          "toy_order.shipping_datetime,toy_order.sales_code ",
       "from toy_order, toy_store ",
       "where ", where_clause clipped, " and ",
          "toy_order.store_number = toy_store.store_number ",
       "order by order_number"
```

```
whenever error continue
prepare statement1 from sql_statement
if sqlca.sqlcode < 0 then
  call Error_Recovery ()
  return
end if
declare toy_order1_cursor scroll cursor with hold for statement1
if sqlca.sqlcode < 0 then
  call Error_Recovery ()
  return
end if
open toy_order1_cursor
if sqlca.sqlcode < 0 then
  call Error_Recovery ()
  return
end if
let cursor_open = true

fetch first toy_order1_cursor into p_toy_order.*
if sqlca.sqlcode < 0 then
  call Error_Recovery ()
  return
end if
if sqlca.sqlcode = notfound then
  error "No toy orders meet your search criteria."
  return
end if

whenever error stop

display p_toy_order.* to s_toy_order.*

end function    { Find_Toy_Order }
```

```
{*********************************************************************
    Close_Toy_Order_Cursor
    Close and free the cursor.
 ********************************************************************}
function Close_Toy_Order_Cursor ()

    whenever error continue

    if cursor_open then
      close toy_order1_cursor
      if sqlca.sqlcode < 0 then
        call Error_Recovery ()
      end if
      free  toy_order1_cursor
      if sqlca.sqlcode < 0 then
        call Error_Recovery ()
      end if
      let cursor_open = false
    end if

    whenever error stop

end function  { Close_Toy_Order_Cursor }


{*********************************************************************
    Next_Toy_Order
    This function fetches the next row of information.
 ********************************************************************}
function Next_Toy_Order ()

    if p_toy_order.order_number is null then
      error "You must Find a toy order before you can see ",
            "the next toy order."
      return
    end if

    whenever error continue
    fetch next toy_order1_cursor into p_toy_order.*
    if sqlca.sqlcode <> 0 then
      if sqlca.sqlcode = notfound then
        message "You are at the end of the list."
          attribute (reverse)
```

```
      else
        call Error_Recovery ()
        return
      end if
    end if
    whenever error stop

    message ""
    display p_toy_order.* to s_toy_order.*

end function   { Next_Toy_Order }



{******************************************************************
  Previous_Toy_Order
  This function fetches the previous row of information.
 ******************************************************************}
function Previous_Toy_Order ()

    if p_toy_order.order_number is null then
      error "You must Find a toy order before you can see ",
            "the previous toy order."
      return
    end if

    whenever error continue
    fetch previous toy_order1_cursor into p_toy_order.*
    if sqlca.sqlcode <> 0 then
      if sqlca.sqlcode = notfound then
        message "You are at the beginning of the list."
                attribute (reverse)
    else
      call Error_Recovery ()
       return
      end if
    end if
    whenever error stop

    message ""
    display p_toy_order.* to s_toy_order.*

end function   { Previous_Toy_Order }
```

```
{*********************************************************************
   Delete_Toy_Order
   Delete the toy order currently being displayed.
*********************************************************************}
function Delete_Toy_Order ()

   if p_toy_order.order_number is null then
      error "You must Find a toy order before you can delete it."
      return
   end if

   menu "Delete?"
      command "No" "Do not delete this toy order."
            help 20
            message "Deletion of toy order cancelled."
                    attribute (reverse)
            exit menu

      command "Yes " "Delete this toy order item."
            help 21

            { First delete any related toy_order_items }
            whenever error continue
            delete from toy_order_item
               where order_number = toy_order.order_number

            if sqlca.sqlcode = 0 or
               sqlca.sqlcode = notfound then
               delete from toy_order
                  where order_number = toy_order.order_number
            else
               call Error_Recovery ()
               exit menu
            end if

            { If you are using transactions, you would put a
              begin work in front of the first delete, then you
              could do either a commit work or rollback work
              after the second delete, depending on the error
              status }
```

```
            if sqlca.sqlcode = 0 then
              message "Toy order deleted."
                     attribute (reverse)
            else
              call Error_Recovery ()
              exit menu
            end if

            clear form
            exit menu
    end menu   { Delete? menu }

end function   { Delete_Toy_Order }
```

The sample module uses the following screen form.

```
{ * * * * * * * * * * * * * * * * * * * * * * * * * * * * * * * * * * * * * * * * * * * * * * * * * * * * * * * * * * * * *
   toy_order
   This screen allows you to display and maintain toy_order
   information.
 * * * * * * * * * * * * * * * * * * * * * * * * * * * * * * * * * * * * * * * * * * * * * * * * * * * * * * * * * * * * * }

database toymaker
screen size 24 by 80

{
-----------------------------------------Press F1 for Help-----
   Order number: [f000          ]

   Store:         [f001         ]   [f005                        ]

   Date Ordered: [f002          ]  Date Shipped:   [f003         ]

   Sales Code:    [f004  ]
}
end

tables toy_order toy_store

attributes
   f000 = toy_order.order_number;
   f001 = toy_order.store_number;
   f005 = toy_store.store_name;
   f002 = toy_order.order_date;
```

```
      f003 = toy_order.shipping_datetime;
      f004 = toy_order.sales_code;
instructions
   screen record s_toy_order
      (order_number,  store_number,         store_name,
        order_date,     shipping_datetime,  sales_code)
end
```

Display Array

The display array statement allows you to display data to a multiple-line form. The syntax for the display array statement is:

```
display array <program array name>
  to <screen array name>.*
  [ attribute ( <attribute name> [, ...] ) ]
  { [ on key ( <special key> [, ...] )
    { <any 4GL statement> |
      exit display
    }
      end display
    ]                                       |
    [ end display ]
  }
```

Note that the display array statement is a specialized input statement. Unlike the display statement, the display array statement will not terminate unless the user hits the accept key.

Any of the following attributes may be used with the display array statement:

normal	reverse	white	cyan
bold	blink	yellow	green
dim	underline	magenta	blue
invisible	red	black	

The on key clause allows you to specify actions to be taken when the user presses a special key. Any of the following special keys may be used:

```
F1 through F64      Control-<letter -except a, d, h, l, r, or x>
accept              help                    prevpage
delete              insert                  return
down                interrupt               right
esc                 left                    tab
escape              nextpage                up
```

There are several functions that can be used in conjunction with the `display array` statement; these functions are also discussed in Chapter 17. They are:

arr_curr

The function `arr_curr` returns the record number within the `input array` or `display array` statement of the current cursor position.

```
arr_curr ()
```

scr_line

The function `scr_line` returns the current row of the screen array the cursor is positioned on in an `input array` or `display array` statement.

```
scr_line ()
```

set_count

The function `set_count` initializes the number of rows for an `input array` or `display array`. This function should be called before an `input array` or `display array` statement.

```
set_count ( <integer expression> )
```

For the `display array` statement, `set_count` indicates how many rows in the array contain data. For the `input array` without `defaults` statement, `set_count` indicates how many rows have been pre-initialized. For a plain `input array` statement (with defaults), `set_count` does nothing. Note that any given use of `set_count` applies only to the next `input array` or `display array` statement.

Display Array Example

Let's use the following multiple-line form as an example:

```
{**********************************************************************
    toy_order_item
    This screen allows you to display and maintain toy_order_item
    information.
**********************************************************************}

database toymaker
screen size 24 by 80

{
-----------------------------------------Press F1 for Help-----

  Toy Code/Description              Quantity Unit Price Total Price
[f011   |f014             |f012    |f013    |f015        ]
[f011   |f014             |f012    |f013    |f015        ]
[f011   |f014             |f012    |f013    |f015        ]
[f011   |f014             |f012    |f013    |f015        ]
[f011   |f014             |f012    |f013    |f015        ]
[f011   |f014             |f012    |f013    |f015        ]
[f011   |f014             |f012    |f013    |f015        ]
[f011   |f014             |f012    |f013    |f015        ]
}
end

tables toy_order_item toy

attributes
    f011 = toy_order_item.toy_code;
    f014 = toy.description;
    f012 = toy_order_item.quantity;
    f013 = toy_order_item.unit_price;
    f015 = formonly.total_price;
```

```
instructions
  delimiters "   "

  screen record sa_order_item [8]
     (toy_code, description, quantity, unit_price, total_price)
end
```

The following INFORMIX-4GL code will display the first records
of the search on the screen. The cursor remains in the screen and
the user is allowed to scroll through and view any of the records
he or she is interested in by using the arrow keys and the *page up*
and *page down* keys.

note

Do not forget to call the set_count *function with the number of
rows of data you have before running the* display *array statement.*

```
define pa_order_item array [100] of record
        toy_code      like toy_order_item.toy_code,
        description   like toy.description,
        quantity      like toy_order_item.quantity,
        unit_price    like toy_order_item.unit_price,
        total_price   decimal (8,2)
      end record

define number_rows    smallint

{ Initialize array and number of rows in array here }
if number_rows = 0 then
   error "No data to display."
   return
end if

call set_count (number_rows)

display array pa_order_item to sa_order_item.*
   on key (F1)
      call showhelp (13)
end display
```

Scroll

The scroll statement provides an alternative method of scrolling through a screen array. The scroll statement allows the programmer to position the rows of data from a certain starting location on the screen.

```
scroll { <screen record name>.* |
         <form field name> } [, ...]
       { up | down } [ by <number of rows> ]
```

Figure 13-2 is the starting position of a multiple-line form displayed on the screen:

Line Number	Description
1	JACKS
2	JUMP ROPE
3	DOLL
4	COLORING BOOK

Figure 13-2 *Starting position of multiple-line screen.*

The statement:

```
scroll sa_toy_screen.* down by 2
```

would move the lines down two rows as shown in Figure 13-3:

Line Number	Description
1	JACKS
2	JUMP ROPE
3	DOLL
4	COLORING BOOK

Figure 13-3 *Multiple-line screen after scrolled down two rows.*

From this position, the statement:

```
scroll sa_toy_screen.* up by 4
```

would move the lines up four rows as shown in Figure 13-4:

Line Number	Description
3	DOLL
4	COLORING BOOK

Figure 13-4   Multiple-line screen after scrolled up four rows.

It is the programmer's responsibility to keep track of what data is where on the screen.

Sample Module

The following sample module displays this sample form and menu on the screen (Figure 13-5):

```
Toy Order Menu:  Find   Next   Previous   Delete   Exit
 Find toy orders.
--------------------------------------Press F1 for Help------

 Toy Code/Description           Quantity Unit Price Total Price
[      |                        |        |          |         ]
[      |                        |        |          |         ]
[      |                        |        |          |         ]
[      |                        |        |          |         ]
[      |                        |        |          |         ]
[      |                        |        |          |         ]
[      |                        |        |          |         ]
[      |                        |        |          |         ]
```

Figure 13-5   Sample menu and screen form for a multiple-line screen.

The Find option finds the items to be displayed, and places the first items on the screen. The user remains in the screen and may scroll through the items in the array using the arrow keys and the *page up* and *page down* keys. The screen form used by this module is displayed at the end of this module. This module calls the `Error_Recovery` function defined in Chapter 16.

```
{ * * * * * * * * * * * * * * * * * * * * * * * * * * * * * * * * * * * * * * * * * * * * * * * * * * * * * * * * * * * * * * * *
   display array example
   This module allows the user to display toy items which have
   been ordered.

   The following functions are in this module:
                 Order_Item_Menu
                 Find_Order_Item
                 Display_Order_Item
* * * * * * * * * * * * * * * * * * * * * * * * * * * * * * * * * * * * * * * * * * * * * * * * * * * * * * * * * * * * * * * * }

database toymaker

define pa_order_item            array [100] of record
        toy_code                like toy_order_item.toy_code,
        description             like toy.description,
        quantity                like toy_order_item.quantity,
        unit_price              like toy_order_item.unit_price,
        total_price             decimal (8,2)
      end record

main
   defer interrupt
   options message line last
   call Order_Item_Menu (1)
end main


{ * * * * * * * * * * * * * * * * * * * * * * * * * * * * * * * * * * * * * * * * * * * * * * * * * * * * * * * * * * * * * * * *
   Order_Item_Menu
* * * * * * * * * * * * * * * * * * * * * * * * * * * * * * * * * * * * * * * * * * * * * * * * * * * * * * * * * * * * * * * * }
function Order_Item_Menu (p_order_number)
   define p_order_number        like toy_order.order_number
```

```
whenever error stop

open window w_toy_order2 at 2,2 with form "toy_order2"
   attribute (border)

menu "Order Item Menu"
   command "Find"       "Find the toys ordered for this order."
         help 1
         call Find_Order_Item (p_order_number)

   command key ("E","X") "Exit" "Exit this menu."
         help 9
         exit menu
   end menu

close window w_toy_order2

end function   { Order_Item_Menu }


{ ******************************************************************
   Find_Order_Item
   Find order items for this order.
 ***************************************************************** }
function Find_Order_Item (p_order_number)
   define p_order_number        like toy_order.order_number
   define sql_stmt              char (400)
   define counter               smallint

   clear form
   let int_flag = false

   let sql_stmt =
     "select toy_order_item.toy_code, toy.description, ",
           "toy_order_item.quantity, toy_order_item.unit_price, ",
           "(toy_order_item.quantity * ",
                   "toy_order_item.unit_price) total_price ",
       "from toy_order_item, toy ",
       "where toy_order_item.order_number = ? and ",
             "toy_order_item.toy_code = toy.toy_code ",
       "order by toy.description"
```

```
whenever error continue
prepare statement2 from sql_stmt
if sqlca.sqlcode < 0 then
   call Error_Recovery ()
   return
end if
declare ord_item_cursor scroll cursor for statement2
if sqlca.sqlcode < 0 then
   call Error_Recovery ()
   return
end if
open ord_item_cursor using p_order_number
if sqlca.sqlcode < 0 then
   call Error_Recovery ()
   return
end if

let counter = 0
while counter < 100  { Maximum number of records to display }
  let counter = counter + 1
  initialize pa_order_item[counter].* to null
  fetch ord_item_cursor into pa_order_item[counter].*
  if sqlca.sqlcode <> 0 then
    if sqlca.sqlcode = notfound then
      let counter = counter - 1
      exit while
    else
      call Error_Recovery ()
      return
    end if
  end if
end while

if counter = 0 then
  message "There are no items matching your search criteria."
          attribute (reverse)
else
  call Display_Order_Item (counter)
end if

close ord_item_cursor
if sqlca.sqlcode < 0 then
```

```
      call Error_Recovery ()
    end if
    free   ord_item_cursor
    if sqlca.sqlcode < 0 then
      call Error_Recovery ()
    end if
    whenever error stop


end function   { Find_Order_Item }



{ ***********************************************************
    Display_Order_Item
    This function displays the rows of data and allows the user to
    look through them
  *********************************************************** }
function Display_Order_Item (counter)
    define counter                 smallint

    { Display }
    display "" at 1,1
    display "" at 2,1
    display "Use the arrow keys and the Page Up and Page Down keys"
                                                    at 1,1
    display "to look through the items." at 2,1

    call set_count (counter)

    display array pa_order_item to sa_order_item.*
      on key (F1)
        call showhelp (13)
    end display

    let int_flag = false

end function   { Display_Order_Item }
```

The sample module uses the following screen form.

```
{*********************************************************************
    toy_order_item
    This screen allows you to display and maintain toy_order_item
    information.
 *********************************************************************}

database toymaker
screen size 24 by 80

{
------------------------------------------Press F1 for Help-----

   Toy Code/Description          Quantity Unit Price Total Price
[f011    |f014               |f012      |f013      |f015         ]
[f011    |f014               |f012      |f013      |f015         ]
[f011    |f014               |f012      |f013      |f015         ]
[f011    |f014               |f012      |f013      |f015         ]
[f011    |f014               |f012      |f013      |f015         ]
[f011    |f014               |f012      |f013      |f015         ]
[f011    |f014               |f012      |f013      |f015         ]
[f011    |f014               |f012      |f013      |f015         ]
}
end

tables toy_order_item toy

attributes
   f011 = toy_order_item.toy_code;
   f014 = toy.description;
   f012 = toy_order_item.quantity;
   f013 = toy_order_item.unit_price;
   f015 = formonly.total_price;

instructions
   delimiters "||"

   screen record sa_order_item [8]
      (toy_code, description, quantity, unit_price, total_price)
end
```

Display a One-to-Many Relationship

Displaying data to a form containing a one-to-many relationship is relatively simple. To do so, all you need is two separate statements: a display statement for the *one* part of the form, and a display array statement for the *many* part of the form.

When retrieving the information from the database, it is easiest to retrieve the *one* part of the relationship, then open a new cursor to retrieve the records which comprise the *many* part of the relationship.

The following module displays this sample form and menu on the screen (Figure 13-6):

```
Toy Order Menu:   Find   Next   Previous   Delete   Exit
Find toy orders.
----------------------------------------Press F1 for Help------
   Order number: [              ]

   Store:          [             ]     [                          ]

   Date Ordered: [            ]      Date Shipped:  [            ]

   Sales Code:    [        ]

 Toy Code/Description                 Quantity Unit Price Total Price
[         |                          |         |           |              ]
[         |                          |         |           |              ]
[         |                          |         |           |              ]
[         |                          |         |           |              ]
[         |                          |         |           |              ]
[         |                          |         |           |              ]
[         |                          |         |           |              ]
[         |                          |         |           |              ]
```

Figure 13-6 *Sample menu and screen form for a one-to-many relationship.*

The following descriptions define how each menu option operates:

Menu Option	Description
Find	The Find menu option allows the user to define a search based on the toy order information (the top part of the screen). The search will then be run and the first order will be displayed along with up to the first eight order items.
Next	The next option displays the next order and its first eight items.
Previous	The previous option displays the previous order and its first eight items.
Delete	The delete option deletes the displayed toy order and all related order items.
Items	The Items option puts the user into a display array and allows the user to scroll through all items associated with an order.

```
{ * * * * * * * * * * * * * * * * * * * * * * * * * * * * * * * * * * * * * * * * * * * * * * * * * * * * * * * * * * * * * * * * * * * * * * * * *
   display one-to-many relationship example
   This module allows you to display information in and delete
   information from the toy_order table.

   The following functions are in this module:
                    Toy_Order_Menu
                    Find_Toy_Order
                    Close_Toy_Order_Cursor
                    Next_Toy_Order
                    Previous_Toy_Order
                    Delete_Toy_Order
                    Find_Order_Item
                    Display_Order_Item
                    Scroll_Order_Item
 * * * * * * * * * * * * * * * * * * * * * * * * * * * * * * * * * * * * * * * * * * * * * * * * * * * * * * * * * * * * * * * * * * * * * }
```

```
database toymaker

{ Define variables global to this module }
define p_toy_order record
        order_number             like toy_order.order_number,
        store_number             like toy_order.store_number,
        store_name               like toy_store.store_name,
        order_date               like toy_order.order_date,
        shipping_datetime        like toy_order.shipping_datetime,
        sales_code               like toy_order.sales_code
    end record

define pa_order_item             array [100] of record
        toy_code                 like toy_order_item.toy_code,
        description              like toy.description,
        quantity                 like toy_order_item.quantity,
        unit_price               like toy_order_item.unit_price,
        total_price              decimal (8,2)
    end record

define cursor_open               smallint

main
  defer interrupt
  options message line last
  call Toy_Order_Menu ()
end main


{********************************************************************
   Toy_Order_Menu
 *******************************************************************}
function Toy_Order_Menu ()

  whenever error stop

  let cursor_open = false
  initialize p_toy_order.* to null

  open window w_toy_order3 at 2,2 with form "toy_order3"
    attribute (border)
```

```
menu "Toy Order Menu"

    command "Find"              "Find toy orders."
          help 1
          call Find_Toy_Order ()

    command "Next"              "View the next toy order."
          help 2
          call Next_Toy_Order ()

    command "Previous"          "View the previous toy order."
          help 3
          call Previous_Toy_Order ()

    command "Delete"            "Delete this toy order."
          help 6
          call Delete_Toy_Order ()
          next option "Find"

    command "Items"             "View all toy order items."
          help 60
          call Find_Order_Item (p_toy_order.order_number, "S")
          next option "Find"

    command key ("E","X") "Exit"       "Exit from this menu."
          help 9
          exit menu
  end menu

  call Close_Toy_Order_Cursor ()

  close window w_toy_order3

end function  { Toy_Order_Menu }


{***************************************************************
  Find_Toy_Order
  Find the toy order for the user and display the first order.
  **************************************************************}
function Find_Toy_Order ()
  define where_clause          char(250)
```

```
define sql_statement              char(300)

clear form
let int_flag = false
call Close_Toy_Order_Cursor ()
initialize p_toy_order.* to null

display "" at 1,1
display "" at 2,1
display "Please enter your search criteria." at 1, 1

construct by name where_clause on
    toy_order.order_number,          toy_order.store_number,
    toy_store.store_name,            toy_order.order_date,
    toy_order.shipping_datetime,     toy_order.sales_code
  help 1

{ Allow user to press break during construct to cancel search }
if int_flag then
   message "Toy order search cancelled."
   let int_flag = false
   return
end if

display "" at 1,1
display "" at 2,1
display "Searching..." at 1, 1

let sql_statement =
  "select toy_order.order_number,       toy_order.store_number, ",
        "toy_store.store_name,          toy_order.order_date,  ",
        "toy_order.shipping_datetime,   toy_order.sales_code ",
    "from toy_order, toy_store ",
    "where ", where_clause clipped, " and ",
          "toy_order.store_number = toy_store.store_number ",
    "order by order_number"

whenever error continue
prepare statement1 from sql_statement
if sqlca.sqlcode < 0 then
   call Error_Recovery ()
   return
```

```
      end if
      declare toy_order1_cursor scroll cursor with hold
              for statement1
      if sqlca.sqlcode < 0 then
        call Error_Recovery ()
        return
      end if
      open toy_order1_cursor
      if sqlca.sqlcode < 0 then
        call Error_Recovery ()
        return
      end if
      let cursor_open = true

      fetch first toy_order1_cursor into p_toy_order.*
      if sqlca.sqlcode <> 0 then
        if sqlca.sqlcode = notfound then
          message "No toy orders meet this criteria."
        else
          call Error_Recovery ()
          return
        end if
      end if
      whenever error stop

      display p_toy_order.* to s_toy_order.*
      call Find_Order_Item (p_toy_order.order_number, "D")

end function   { Find_Toy_Order }




{***************************************************************
   Close_Toy_Order_Cursor
   Close and free the cursor.
 ***************************************************************}
function Close_Toy_Order_Cursor ()

   whenever error continue

   if cursor_open then
     close toy_order1_cursor
```

```
      if sqlca.sqlcode < 0 then
        call Error_Recovery ()
      end if
      free  toy_order1_cursor
      if sqlca.sqlcode < 0 then
        call Error_Recovery ()
      end if
      let cursor_open = false
    end if

  whenever error stop

end function  { Close_Toy_Order_Cursor }


{******************************************************************
  Next_Toy_Order
  This function fetches the previous row of information.
******************************************************************}
function Next_Toy_Order ()

  if p_toy_order.order_number is null then
    error "You must Find a toy order before you can see ",
          "the next toy order."
    return
  end if

  whenever error continue
  fetch next toy_order1_cursor into p_toy_order.*
  if sqlca.sqlcode <> 0 then
    if sqlca.sqlcode = notfound then
      message "You are at the end of the list."
            attribute (reverse)
    else
      call Error_Recovery ()
      return
    end if
  end if
  whenever error stop

  message ""
  display p_toy_order.* to s_toy_order.*
```

```
      call Find_Order_Item (p_toy_order.order_number, "D")

end function   { Next_Toy_Order }


{**************************************************************
   Previous_Toy_Order
   This function fetches the previous row of information.
   ************************************************************}
function Previous_Toy_Order ()

   if p_toy_order.order_number is null then
      error "You must Find a toy order before you can see ",
            "the previous toy order."
      return
   end if

   whenever error continue
   fetch previous toy_order1_cursor into p_toy_order.*
   if sqlca.sqlcode <> 0 then
      if sqlca.sqlcode = notfound then
         message "You are at the beginning of the list."
               attribute (reverse)
      else
         call Error_Recovery ()
         return
      end if
   end if
   whenever error stop

   message ""
   display p_toy_order.* to s_toy_order.*
   call Find_Order_Item (p_toy_order.order_number, "D")

end function   { Previous_Toy_Order }


{**************************************************************
   Delete_Toy_Order
   Delete the toy_order and any related toy_order_items.
   ************************************************************}
function Delete_Toy_Order ()
```

```
if p_toy_order.order_number is null then
   error "You must Find a toy order before you can delete it."
   return
end if

menu "Delete?"
   command "No" "Do not delete this toy order."
      help 20
      message "Deletion of toy order cancelled."
               attribute (reverse)
      exit menu

   command "Yes " "Delete this toy order item."
      help 21

      { First delete any related toy_order_items }
      whenever error continue
      delete from toy_order_item
         where order_number = toy_order.order_number

      if sqlca.sqlcode = 0 or sqlca.sqlcode = notfound then
         delete from toy_order
            where order_number = toy_order.order_number
      else
         call Error_Recovery ()
         exit menu
      end if
      whenever error stop

      { If you are using transactions, you would put a begin
        work in front of the first delete, then you could do
        either a commit work or rollback work after the second
        delete, depending on the error status }

      if sqlca.sqlcode = 0 then
         message "Toy order deleted."
                  attribute (reverse)
      else
         call Error_Recovery ()
         exit menu
      end if
```

```
        clear form
        exit menu
    end menu   { Delete? menu }

end function   { Delete_Toy_Order }


{*************************************************************
    Find_Order_Item
    Find order items for this order.
    *********************************************************}
function Find_Order_Item (p_order_number, display_or_scroll)
    define p_order_number        like toy_order.order_number
    define display_or_scroll     char (1)
    define sql_stmt              char (400)
    define counter               smallint

    if p_order_number is null then
        error "You must Find an order before you can view ",
              "its items."
        return
    end if

    let int_flag = false

    let sql_stmt =
      "select toy_order_item.toy_code, toy.description, ",
            "toy_order_item.quantity, toy_order_item.unit_price, ",
            "(toy_order_item.quantity * ",
                     "toy_order_item.unit_price) total_price ",
        "from toy_order_item, toy ",
        "where toy_order_item.order_number = ? and ",
                     "toy_order_item.toy_code = toy.toy_code ",
        "order by toy.description"

    whenever error continue
    prepare statement2 from sql_stmt
    if sqlca.sqlcode < 0 then
        call Error_Recovery ()
        return
    end if
    declare ord_item_cursor scroll cursor for statement2
```

```
if sqlca.sqlcode < 0 then
  call Error_Recovery ()
  return
end if
open ord_item_cursor using p_order_number
if sqlca.sqlcode < 0 then
  call Error_Recovery ()
  return
end if

let counter = 0
while counter < 100   { Maximum number of records to display }
  let counter = counter + 1
  initialize pa_order_item[counter].* to null
  fetch ord_item_cursor into pa_order_item[counter].*
  if sqlca.sqlcode <> 0 then
    if sqlca.sqlcode = notfound then
      let counter = counter - 1
      exit while
    else
      call Error_Recovery ()
      return
    end if
  end if
end while
whenever error stop

if counter = 0 then
  message "There are no items matching your search criteria."
      attribute (reverse)
else
  display "" at 1,1
  display "" at 2,1
  display "Use the arrow keys and Page Up and Page Down keys"
          at 1,1
  display "to look through the items. Press ESC to exit."
          at 2,1
  if display_or_scroll = "D" then
    call Display_Order_Item ()
  else
    call Scroll_Order_Item (counter)
  end if
end if
```

```
whenever error continue
close ord_item_cursor
if sqlca.sqlcode < 0 then
  call Error_Recovery ()
end if
free  ord_item_cursor
if sqlca.sqlcode < 0 then
  call Error_Recovery ()
end if
whenever error stop

end function  { Find_Order_Item }



{*************************************************************
  Display_Order_Item
  This function displays the rows first eight rows of order
  items.
  ***********************************************************}
function Display_Order_Item ()
  define counter             smallint

  for counter = 1 to 8
    display pa_order_item[counter].* to sa_order_item[counter].*
  end for

end function  { Display_Order_Item }



{*************************************************************
  Scroll_Order_Item
  This function displays the rows of data and allows the user to
  look through them.
  ***********************************************************}
function Scroll_Order_Item (counter)
  define counter             smallint

  { Display }
  display "" at 1,1
  display "" at 2,1
  display "Use the arrow keys and the Page Up and Page Down keys"
                                                     at 1,1
```

```
      display "to look through the items." at 2,1

      call set_count (counter)

      display array pa_order_item to sa_order_item.*
        on key (F1)
           call showhelp (13)
      end display

end function  { Scroll_Order_Item }
```

This module uses the following screen form.

```
{****************************************************************
   toy_order
   This screen allows you to display and maintain toy_order and
   toy_order_item information.
   ****************************************************************}

database toymaker
screen size 24 by 80

{

-------------------------------------------Press F1 for Help-----
   Order number: [f000          ]

   Store:        [f001        ]   [f005                        ]

   Date Ordered: [f002       ]  Date Shipped:  [f003            ]

   Sales Code:   [f004   ]

  Toy Code/Description            Quantity Unit Price Total Price
[f011   |f014                     |f012      |f013      |f015       ]
[f011   |f014                     |f012      |f013      |f015       ]
[f011   |f014                     |f012      |f013      |f015       ]
[f011   |f014                     |f012      |f013      |f015       ]
[f011   |f014                     |f012      |f013      |f015       ]
[f011   |f014                     |f012      |f013      |f015       ]
[f011   |f014                     |f012      |f013      |f015       ]
[f011   |f014                     |f012      |f013      |f015       ]
}
end
```

```
tables toy_order toy_store toy_order_item toy

attributes
  f000 = toy_order.order_number;
  f001 = toy_order.store_number;
  f005 = toy_store.store_name;
  f002 = toy_order.order_date;
  f003 = toy_order.shipping_datetime;
  f004 = toy_order.sales_code;

  f011 = toy_order_item.toy_code;
  f014 = toy.description;
  f012 = toy_order_item.quantity;
  f013 = toy_order_item.unit_price;
  f015 = formonly.total_price;

instructions
  delimiters "   "

  screen record s_toy_order
     (order_number, store_number,      store_name,
      order_date,    shipping_datetime, sales_code)

  screen record sa_order_item [8]
     (toy_code, description, quantity, unit_price, total_price)
end
```

Summary

INFORMIX-4GL windows allow you to create windows within the INFORMIX-4GL screen. You may open windows, clear windows, make a window current, and close windows.

open window *<window name>* **at** *<row number>*, *<column number>*
  with { *<number of rows>* **rows**, *<number of columns>* **columns** |
      form "*<form file name without .per extension>*"
    }
  [**attribute** (*<window attribute>* [, ...])]

current window is *<window name>*

```
clear { screen |
      window <window name> |
      form [ <form field name> [, ...] ]
   }


close window <window name>
```

You may use any of the following attributes when opening a window:

border	normal	white	blue
reverse	bold	yellow	black
prompt line <line number>	dim	magenta	
message line <line number>	invisible	red	
form line <line number>	cyan		
comment line <line number>	green		

The forms designed in Chapter 12 may be displayed by using the open form and display form statements or as part of the open window statement. The open form and display form statements should have a corresponding close form statement.

```
open form <form name>
      from "<filename without .per or .frm extension>"

display form <form name>
   [ attribute ( <window list> [, ...] ) ]

close form <form name>
```

You may use any of the following attributes when opening your form:

reverse	normal	white	cyan
blink	bold	yellow	green
underline	dim	magenta	blue
invisible	red	black	

The display statement allows you to display data on the screen.

```
display
   { by name <variable name> [, ...]
```

```
      [ attribute ( <attribute name> [, ...] ) ]          |
      <variable name or constant> [, ...]
      [ { to { <form field name> [, ...] |
               <screen record name>["["<row number>"]"].*
             } [, ...]          |
          at <row number>, <column number>
        }
        [ attribute ( <attribute name> [, ...] ) ]
    ]
  }
```

Where the square brackets are shown inside of double quotes, they are part of the syntax of the statement—they do not indicate an option.

The display array statement allows you to display data to a multiple-line form.

```
display array <program array name> to <screen array name>.*
  [ attribute ( <attribute name> [, ...] ) ]
  { [ on key ( <special key> [, ...] )
       { <any 4GL statement> |
         exit display
       }
     end display
  ]                            |
  [ end display ]
  }
```

Functions that can be used in conjunction with the display array statement are:

arr_curr ()

scr_line ()

set_count (<integer expression>)

To display data to a form containing a one-to-many relationship use separate statements: a display statement for the *one* part of the form, and a display array statement for the *many* part of the form.

Chapter

14

Setting Options

- *Overview of* `options`
- *Output lines*
- *Keys*
- *Help file*
- *Attributes*
- `input wrap`
- `field order`
- `sql interrupt`
- *Line or form mode*
- *Example*
- *Summary*

Overview of Options

The `options` statement allows you to define default options for your INFORMIX-4GL program. The definable options include positioning of output lines on the screen, defining special keys, defining help information, defining input and display defaults, and permitting users to interrupt INFORMIX-SQL statements.

The `options` statement is normally executed at the beginning of a program to determine default settings for the program. You may, however, run the `options` statement at any time and as many times as you like. This allows you the flexibility of changing the settings for different types of display and entry screens within an application.

The syntax for the `options` statement is:

```
options
{   comment   line  <window line number>        |
    error     line  <screen line number>        |
    form      line  <window line number>        |
    message   line  <window line number>        |
    menu      line  <window line number>        |
    prompt    line  <window line number>        |
    accept    key   <key name>                  |
    delete    key   <key name>                  |
    help      key   <key name>                  |
    insert    key   <key name>                  |
    next      key   <key name>                  |
    previous  key   <key name>                  |
    help file <help file name>                  |
    display   attribute (<attribute name> [, ...]) |
    input     attribute (<attribute name> [, ...]) |
    input     { wrap | no wrap }                 |
    field order     constrained | unconstrained } |
    sql interrupt { on | off }                   |
    run in { line | form } mode                  |
    pipe in { line | form } mode
} [, ...]
```

You may specify as few or as many options you like. These options are discussed in detail throughout the remainder of this chapter.

Output Lines

The `options` in this section allow you to specify where in a screen or a window various types of output will be displayed.

Windows are discussed in Chapter 13, but in essence, windows are opened up within a screen. A window usually contains a menu or a form. When the options specify a window line number, this is relative to the first line in the window. When the options specify a screen line number, this is relative to the first line in the screen. If no window is opened, the screen is your current window.

There are two variables set by INFORMIX-4GL that you can use when specifying line numbers in the `options` statement: first and last. First and last are the first and last lines of the current window or screen. The line numbers you specify may have any of the following values:

```
{ <integer value or variable> |
   first + <integer value>      |
   last  - <integer value>
}
```

comment line *<window line number>*

The `comment line` is the line of the window on which screen comments are displayed. Screen comments are defined either in the screen definition itself or by using the Informix `upscol` utility (also see Chapter 12). The default is last for windows and last − 1 for the screen.

error line *<screen line number>*

The `error line` is the line of the screen on which the error messages written by the `error` statement are displayed. The default is the `last` line of the screen. Note that this is different from the other lines, which are relative to the window, not the screen!

form line *<window line number>*

The `form line` is the line of the window on which the form will start when a screen form is displayed in a window. Two lines at the top of the screen form are reserved by default for the menu to display above the form, so the default is `first + 2`.

message line *<window line number>*

The `message line` is the line of the window where messages displayed by the message statement are displayed. The default is `first + 1`.

menu line *<window line number>*

The `menu line` is the line of the window at which the menu will start. The menu will start on the first line of the window unless otherwise specified. A menu at the bottom of the window would be positioned at `last - 1` or `last - 2`, depending on where you wish screen comments, messages, and prompts to be displayed.

prompt line *<window line number>*

The `prompt line` is the line of the window that prompts the user for input when using the `prompt` statement. The default is `first`.

Keys

Several keys used in your INFORMIX-4GL programs have default values that may be changed.

The values that may be assigned to these keys are defined as follows:

- Any function key from F1 through F64,
- Control-<*letter*> except for a, d, h, i, j, l, m, q, r, x and any other control characters which have special meaning in your operating system, and
- Escape may be used for another key if it is not defined as the *accept* key.

accept key <*key name*>

The accept key is used to accept input to a screen or to allow the user to leave a display only screen. It is important that this key be easily identified by your users. The default key is escape.

delete key <*key name*>

The delete key is used to delete rows of information in input array statements. Input array statements are discussed in Chapter 23. The default key is F2.

help key <*key name*>

The help key will pull up context-sensitive, customized help screens wherever you have defined help within your application. Help is discussed in Chapter 15. The default key is Control-w.

insert key <*key name*>

The insert key is used to add new rows to an input array statement. Input array statements are discussed in Chapter 24. The default key is F1.

next key <key name>

The `next key` is used to scroll down through the data in `display array` or in `input array` statements one page at a time. This is much easier for users then using the arrow keys to look through the data one record at a time, particularly when dealing with large quantities of data. `Display array` statements are discussed in Chapter 13 and `input array` statements are discussed in Chapter 23. The default key is F3.

previous key <key name>

The `previous key` is used to scroll up through the data in `display array` or in `input array` statements one page at a time. This is much easier for users then using the arrow keys to look through the data one record at a time, particularly when dealing with large quantities of data. `Display array` statements are discussed in Chapter 13 and `input array` statements are discussed in Chapter 23. The default key is F4.

Help File

The `help key` will pull up context-sensitive, customized help screens wherever you have defined help within your application. Help is discussed in detail in Chapter 15.

help file <help file name>

The `help file` is the compiled file containing the help messages you have defined for your users. Chapter 15 describes how to create this file.

Attributes

Attributes allow you to define default display characteristics when data is being displayed or entered. You can display any of the following attributes that are supported by your terminal:

invisible	blink	yellow	blue
dim	underline	magenta	black
normal	red	white	
bold	cyan		
reverse	green		

Multiple attributes may be used for a single output statement, so you could specify `red`, `reverse`, and `blink`, if desired.

Any of these attributes will compile correctly whether or not your terminal will be able to display them. For instance, if you use the attribute `magenta` on a monochrome terminal, the output will still be displayed to your screen.

display attribute
(<attribute name> [, ...])

The `display attribute` specifies which attributes are the default attributes when data is displayed on a screen form. The default `display attribute` is `normal`.

input attribute
(<attribute name> [, ...])

The `input attribute` specifies which attributes are the default attributes when data is input to a screen form. The default `input attribute` is `normal`.

Input Wrap

The `input wrap` option specifies that when the user has reached the last field on a screen form, he will automatically be taken back to the first field of the screen form instead of exiting the screen form.

input { wrap | <u>no wrap</u> }

The `input wrap` and `no wrap` options work with the `construct` statement (see Chapter 22) and the `input` statement (see Chapter 18). The default option is `no wrap`.

Field Order

The `field order` allows you to specify one of two options about how up arrow and down arrow keys are treated when moving between fields in screen forms.

field order
{ <u>constrained</u> | unconstrained }

This option works with the `input` and `construct` statements. The default field order is constrained. `Constrained` specifies that the up arrow and down arrow keys will take you to the previous and next fields on the screen form, respectively. The `unconstrained` option allows you to specify that the up arrow key will take you to the field on the form that is above the current field, and the down arrow key will take you to the field on the form that is below the current field. Screens are discussed in Chapter 12.

Sql Interrupt

Sql interrupt is very useful if you want your users to be able to interrupt queries. I had some very unhappy users before this option was available. If you want to give your users flexibility in searching for information this option will be useful.

sql interrupt { on | <u>off</u> }

If sql interrupt is turned on and you are using defer interrupt (see Chapter 16), users have the ability to interrupt SQL statements. The default for this option is off. This means that by default, if a user accidentally starts a long query, they must wait for the query to complete because they will not be able to cancel it.

Line or Form Mode

You can set the run statement default and the report to pipe statement defaults by using the options statement. These options are available in more recent versions of INFORMIX-4GL.

run in { <u>line</u> | form } mode

By default, the run statement runs commands in line mode. You can change this to form mode so that the screen is not cleared and then redrawn when a run statement is executed.

pipe in { line | <u>form</u> } mode

The report to pipe command has a default of form mode, but can be changed to line mode with the options statement if desired.

Example

An example of the `options` statement using all available options is:

```
options  comment    line last,
         error      line last,
         form       line first + 2,
         message    line last,
         menu       line first,
         prompt     line last,
         accept     key  escape,
         delete     key  F12,
         help       key  F1,
         insert     key  F11,
         next       key  control-f,
         previous   key  control-b,
         help file  "help.ex",
         display    attribute (normal),
         input      attribute (normal),
         input      no wrap,
         field order    constrained,
         sql interrupt on,
         run in form mode,
         pipe in form mode
```

You do not need to specify every option, only those you wish to change. You will probably want to have a set of default options that is executed at the beginning of your application. If you want to have more than one standard set of options, you may wish to have a single function called with an argument, which will run the specified set of options to make them current.

Summary

The `options` statement allows you to define default options for your INFORMIX-4GL program.

```
options
    {    comment   line  <window line number>        |
         error     line  <screen line number>        |
         form      line  <window line number>        |
         message   line  <window line number>        |
         menu      line  <window line number>        |
         prompt    line  <window line number>        |
         accept    key   <key name>                  |
         delete    key   <key name>                  |
         help      key   <key name>                  |
         insert    key   <key name>                  |
         next      key   <key name>                  |
         previous key    <key name>                  |
         help file <help file name>                  |
         display   attribute (<attribute name> [, ...]) |
         input     attribute (<attribute name> [, ...]) |
         input     { wrap | no wrap }                |
         field order   { constrained | unconstrained } |
         sql interrupt { on | off }                  |
         run in { line | form } mode                 |
         pipe in { line | form } mode
    }    [, ...]
```

First and last are the first and last lines of the current window or screen. The line numbers you specify may have any of the following values:

```
    { <integer value or variable> |
      first + <integer value>     |
      last  - <integer value>
    }
```

You can display any of the following attributes that are supported by your terminal:

invisible	blink	yellow	blue
dim	underline	magenta	black
normal	red	white	
bold	cyan		
reverse	green		

Chapter

15

Help!

- *About context-sensitive help*
- *Help files*
- mkmessage
- *Using help*
- *Summary*

About Context-Sensitive Help

INFORMIX-4GL gives you several ways to easily provide your users with context-sensitive help, these are:

- customized help files (discussed in this chapter),
- menu descriptions (see Chapter 10), and
- screen comments (see Chapter 12).

The most comprehensive help is provided by the use of customized help files. These files contain customized help messages that you design. You assign a number to each of these help messages. Then, wherever you specify help within your application, the user can press the help key and display the appropriate help screens. The screens can also be displayed as specified by the programmer without the user pressing the help key.

Whenever you define a ring menu in INFORMIX-4GL, you may provide a description to accompany each menu option. This description will be displayed on the line underneath the menu whenever the cursor is positioned on a menu item containing a description. The menu statement is discussed in detail in Chapter 10.

Screen comments allow you to define a single line of help for each data entry or display field on a screen. Whenever the user is positioned on one of these fields for which a comment has been defined, the comment will be displayed at the bottom of the current window. This help allows you to describe what type of input is valid, what options are available, how to get further help, or anything else you like. Screen comments may be part of the screen definition itself, or may be entered using the Informix upscol utility. Both of these options are described in Chapter 12.

Help Files

A help file consists of help numbers and help messages. Each help message must be associated with a help number. You are responsible for assigning help numbers and for designing each help message.

The basic syntax of the help file is:

```
[ # <comment line> ]
.<help number>
<help message>
[ ... ]
```

Lines beginning with a period should be followed by a help number. You may want to decide on some general numbering scheme for your help numbers.

The help message may be as long or as short as you like. INFORMIX-4GL will display multiple pages of help text for the user. The message may contain only printable ASCII characters and blanks. Do not include tabs anywhere in your help file; you will get very strange results if you do.

Lines beginning with a pound sign (#) are help file comments. The following is a sample help file:

```
# 1 - Exit
.1
This menu option will exit you from the current menu.

Either "E" or "X" may be used to exit.

# 2 - Printer
.2
This menu option will allow you to change your
default printer.

The printers available for general use are:
      Main Office LaserJet
      Reception Area DeskJet
      Back Office Line Printer

Please see a computer staff member if you need to
print labels.

# 3 - Editing Commands
.3
The following commands are available for editing
input in a form:
   Control-A: Toggle between typeover and insert modes
   Control-D: Delete from current position to the end
             of the field
   ...
```

The blank lines within the message and at the end of the message are part of the help message that will be displayed to the user.

mkmessage

The Informix `mkmessage` utility allows you to compile a help file. The syntax for this command is very simple:

```
mkmessage <ASCII help file name>
   <executable help file name>
```

The ASCII help file name is the name of the help file you typed in the previous section. The executable help file name is the name of the compiled help file.

For example: `mkmessage help.iem help.ex`

If you use standard suffixes in your make file, you will find it easier to keep track of these files. Informix uses the extension `.iem` for its error message files.

Using Help

In order for your application to use a help file, you must specify the name of the executable help file in the options statement. You may specify the executable help file pathname in the `options` statement. If you specify the file name only (no path), the help file executable must be in the current directory or the directory must be contained in your `DBPATH` environment variable.

You may use more than one help file in a single program. The help file most recently specified in an `options` statement will be the help file used.

There are two ways of displaying a help message in 4GL. If the syntax for a statement permits, all you need to do is enter:

```
help <help number>
```

Example:

```
menu "Jannine's Menu"
     command "Find"            "Find an item."
            help 3
            call Find_Item ()
     command "Exit"            "Exit this menu."
            help 4
            exit menu
end menu
```

The help message will be displayed when the user presses the help key. The default help key is `Control-w`. You may change this by specifying your preference in the `options` statement (see Chapter 14).

You may also use the built-in function `showhelp` to display a help message at any time:

```
showhelp ( <help number> )
```

Example: call showhelp (22)

When help is displayed, the screen is cleared, and the following INFORMIX-4GL menu is brought up along with your help message:

```
HELP:   Screen   Resume
Displays the next page of Help text.


-------------------------------------------------
Your help message starts here.
```

If the help message is longer than a page, the Screen option is the default. The Screen option will display the next screen of your help message. If the help message is one page or less, the Resume option is the default. The Resume option will resume running your application from the point where the help message was called.

It is usually easier to add help messages to your code as you are writing it. The help messages can always be revised at a later point. When writing code, if you get to a point where you need a new help message, or if you need to look up the number of a particular help message, an easy way to do this is to issue an operating system command from within your text editor and call a shell script. For instance, this shell script is called `help`:

```
# This shell script edits and compiles the help file
cd <directory where my help file is stored>
vi help.msg
mkmessage help.msg help.ex
```

This procedure is very simple and it helps to keep your help file and programs current.

Summary

INFORMIX-4GL gives you several ways to easily provide users with context-sensitive help:

- customized help files (discussed in this chapter),
- menu descriptions (see Chapter 10), and
- screen comments (see Chapter 12).

The basic syntax of the help file is:

```
[ # <comment line> ]
.<help number>
<help message>
[ ... ]
```

The Informix mkmessage utility allows you to compile a help file.

```
mkmessage <ASCII help file name>
        <executable help file name>
```

In order for your application to use a help file, you must specify the name of the executable help file in the options statement.
To display a help message in your 4GL program, use:

```
help <help number>
```
or
```
showhelp ( <help number> )
```

Error Handling

- `defer interrupt`

- `defer quit`

- `whenever`

- *Error log*

- *Sample main program and error function*

- *Summary*

Defer Interrupt

The *interrupt* key in INFORMIX-4GL will interrupt your program and cause it to be immediately halted. This action is usually not desirable. To avoid this problem, the following statement must appear in the `main` section of your program code.

```
defer interrupt
```

This statement may appear only once in a program. Once `defer interrupt` has been set, there is no way to unset it.

The *interrupt* key can serve a useful purpose in INFORMIX-4GL programs if it doesn't immediately exit you from programs whenever it is pressed. If you use `defer interrupt`, you will be able to use the *interrupt* key as a *cancel* key to cancel out of screens without making changes. The *interrupt* key will cause the global INFORMIX-4GL variable `int_flag` to be set to true. You are responsible for checking the status of this variable and resetting it to false.

The *interrupt* keys used in INFORMIX-SQL and INFORMIX-4GL are the same. Depending on your operating system, this key will usually be the Control-c or Del.

Defer Quit

The *quit* key in INFORMIX-4GL will interrupt your program and cause it to be immediately halted. If you wish to disable the *quit* key, the following statement must appear in the `main` section of your program code.

```
defer quit
```

This statement may appear only once in a program. Once `defer quit` has been set, there is no way to unset it.

If `defer quit` is set, pressing the *quit* key will cause the global INFORMIX-4GL variable `quit_flag` to be set to true. You are responsible for checking the status of this variable and resetting it to false.

The *quit* key will usually be the Control-\ but depends on your operating system.

Whenever

The whenever statement is a compile-time directive which will cause whichever action you specify to be taken whenever certain conditions occur.

```
whenever { [ any ] error    |
           sqlerror          |
           warning           |
           sqlwarning        |
           not found
         }
         { call <function name> |
           continue             |
           stop                 |
           { goto | go to } [:] label
         }
```

The first and foremost thing to remember about the whenever statement is that it is a compile-time directive. This means that if you want a whenever statement to be in effect for an entire module, it should be the first statement in the first function of that module. If you wish to switch between different whenever actions, remember that the statement follows the physical sequence of the code, not the order in which the code is executed.

Therefore, the following code will not work as expected:

```
if x = y then
   whenever error continue
else
   whenever error stop
end if
```

In this example, since whenever error stop is the last whenever error statement executed, it will be in effect until the next whenever error statement in the module is executed. This is regardless of whether the if or the else portion of the statement is executed at runtime.

The whenever statement performs the specified action if an error occurs (whenever error), a warning occurs (whenever warning), or if no data is found (whenever not found). Sqlerror has the same meaning as error, and sqlwarning has the same meaning as warning.

Error and any error have different meanings. Error by itself will trap SQL, validate, and screen errors. Any error will trap these errors and also errors in evaluating INFORMIX-4GL expressions.

The actions that may be taken when using a whenever statement are: call a function, continue running the program, stop the program, or perform a goto-label. If you call a function, you must omit the parentheses that are part of the function call. You may not pass any arguments into the function.

Example: whenever error call For_Help

The default for whenever error is continue.

The goto documentation exists for completeness only. Try to avoid using it.

Examples: whenever error call Error_Recovery
            whenever any error call Error_Recovery
            whenever error continue
            whenever error stop
            whenever warning call Log_Warning
            whenever not found call No_Such_Data

When an error occurs, if you are using the continue or call function actions with the whenever error statement, the global INFORMIX-4GL variable status is set to contain an error number. A status of zero indicates no errors occurred.

You may also use the switch -anyerr with either the c4gl command or with the fglpc or fglgo commands. This switch causes the status variable to be set to the error value when an error occurs and the program continues. This switch has precedence over any whenever error statements that exist in the program.

In all cases where the program continues after an error, the programmer is responsible for checking the error status and resolving any problems that may have occurred.

Error Log

You may wish to keep a log of all errors that occur while your program is being run. You may do this by using the error log facility.

The function `startlog` may be used to create or append to an existing error log file.

```
call startlog ( <error log name> )
```

The error log name may either be a file name or a pathname.

The `startlog` function only needs to be executed once in any program. Once an error log has been started (typically at the beginning of your program), if `whenever error continue` is not in effect, an error message will be written to the error log file every time an error occurs. The error message will consist of the error date, time, location, error number, and a short description of the error.

Note that the `startlog` function does not indicate whether the log was started successfully or not. The `fgl_startlog` function will return a value indicating whether or not the error log was started:

```
let <numeric variable> =
fgl_startlog ( <error log name> )
```

A value of 0 will be returned if the error log is successfully started, otherwise a non-zero value will be returned.

The following functions may also be used when dealing with errors.

The errorlog function appends the specified error message to the error log. This may be used with whenever error call <function name> to print additional information whenever an error is written to the error log.

```
call errorlog ( <error message> )
```

The advantage of the fgl_errorlog function over the error-log function is that you can tell whether write to the error log was successful.

```
let <numeric variable> =
fgl_errorlog ( <character string or variable> )
```

A value of 0 is returned if the write to the error log is successful, a non-zero value is returned otherwise.

The err_get function accepts an error number as an argument and returns the error message associated with the number.

```
let <string variable> =
err_get ( <error number> )
```

The err_print function accepts an error number as an argument and prints the error message associated with the number on the error line.

```
call err_print ( <error number> )
```

The err_quit function accepts an error number as an argument and prints the error message associated with the number on the error line, then exits the program.

```
call err_quit ( <error number> )
```

Sample Main Program and Error Function

The following function is a sample of a main program and an error routine.

```
{ * * * * * * * * * * * * * * * * * * * * * * * * * * * * * * * * * * * * * * * * * * * * * * * * * * * * * * * * * * * * * * * * *
    The main section of code starts the error log, defers the
    interrupt and quit keys, and sets the Error_Recovery
    routine to be called when an error occurs in this module.
  * * * * * * * * * * * * * * * * * * * * * * * * * * * * * * * * * * * * * * * * * * * * * * * * * * * * * * * * * * * * * * }
main
    define err                             smallint

    let err = fgl_startlog ("/my/directory/error.log")
    if err then
        error "Error log start unsuccessful, error ", err
        exit program
    end if

    whenever error call Error_Recovery    { This should begin each
                                            module where you wish
                                            to use it }
    defer interrupt
    defer quit

    options help file "/my/directory/help.iem",
          help key F12,
          sql interrupt on

    <other 4GL statements>

end main
```

```
{**********************************************************
  Error_Recovery
  This function handles is called when errors occur in the
  program.  The errors are automatically written to the
  error.log file.
***********************************************************}
function Error_Recovery ()
  define p_status                        integer

  let p_status = status   { set local variable to global status
                            before status is reset to 0 }


  case (p_status)
   when 0           exit case
   when notfound  error "Information not found."
   when -213       error "Search interrupted at user request."
   when -239       error "Entry of duplicate value not permitted."
   otherwise       error "Error ", p_status
  end case

  { Reset interrupt and quit flags }
  let int_flag = false
  let quit_flag = false

end function   { Error_Recovery }
```

Summary

Defer interrupt will prevent the *interrupt* key in INFORMIX-4GL from interrupting program execution. The variable int_flag will be set to true when the *interrupt* key is pressed.

defer interrupt

Defer quit will prevent the *quit* key in INFORMIX-4GL from immediately halting your program. The variable quit_flag will be set to true when the *quit* key is pressed.

defer quit

The whenever error statement is a compile-time directive which will cause whichever action you specify to be taken whenever certain conditions occur.

```
whenever { [ any ] error              |
            sqlerror                   |
            warning                    |
            sqlwarning                 |
            not found
          }
          { call <function name>      |
            continue                   |
            stop                       |
            { goto | go to } [:] label
          }
```

When an error occurs, the global INFORMIX-4GL variable status is set to contain an error number.

The switch -anyerr may be used with the c4gl command or with the fglpc or fglgo commands.

The functions startlog and fgl_startlog will create a new error log file or append to an existing error log file. fgl_startlog has the advantage of returning a value to indicate whether or not the function was successful.

```
call startlog ( <error log name> )

let <numeric variable> =
        fgl_startlog ( <error log name> )
```

The errorlog and fgl_errorlog functions append the specified error message to the error log. fgl_errorlog has the advantage of returning a value to indicate whether or not the function was successful.

```
call errorlog ( <error message> )

let <numeric variable> =
        fgl_errorlog ( <error message> )
```

The `err_get` function returns the error message associated with the error number.

```
let <string variable> = err_get ( <error number> )
```

The `err_print` function prints the error message associated with the error number on the error line.

```
call err_print ( <error number> )
```

The `err_quit` function prints the error message associated with the error number on the error line, then exits the program.

```
call err_quit ( <error number> )
```

Built-in Functions, Constants, and Variables

- *INFORMIX-4GL functions called from 4GL*
- *INFORMIX-4GL functions called from C (see Appendix A for details)*
- *INFORMIX-4GL constants*
- *INFORMIX-4GL global variables*
- *Summary*

INFORMIX-4GL Functions Called from 4GL

The functions described in this section have been predefined for use in INFORMIX-4GL. Some of the places where these functions are used are not discussed until later chapters. Putting all of these built-in functions, operators, and keywords together in the same chapter will make them easier to find later. For now, you may just want to review the types of functions that are available, then come back and use them when you need them.

The following functions, operators, and keywords are available to be called from INFORMIX-4GL. Some of these functions may only be used in a limited context, but most of them can be called from anywhere within your 4GL program.

arg_val	extend	pageno
arr_count	fgl_drawbox	scr_line
arr_curr	fgl_errorlog	set_count
ascii	fgl_getenv	showhelp
clipped	fgl_keyval	space
column	fgl_lastkey	sqlexit
current	fgl_startlog	startlog
cursor_name	field_touched	time
date (no argument)	get_fldbuf	today
date (with argument)	infield	units
day	length	upshift
downshift	lineno	using
err_get	mdy	weekday
err_print	month	wordwrap
err_quit	num_args	year
errorlog		

arg_val

The function `arg_val` returns the value of the command line argument you specify. When you call a program from the command line you may specify arguments.

```
arg_val ( <integer expression> )
```

The first argument after the program name is `arg_val (1)`, the second is `arg_val (2)`, and so on. `Arg_val (0)` is the name of your program.

Example:

```
program_name.4ge 43 9/1/1998 "hello world"   { compiled 4GL }
```

            or

```
fglgo program_name.4gi 43 9/1/1998 "hello world"   { rds }
```

```
. . .

main
   define age_in_years          smallint
   define employment_date       date
   define program_comment       char (25)

   let age_in_years     = arg_val (1)
   let employment_date = arg_val (2)
   let program_comment = arg_val (3)
end main
```

Arguments are translated into character data types. Informix will attempt to perform the conversion if you assign the argument to a non-character data type.

arr_count

The function `arr_count` returns the number of rows stored in the current `input array`, or of the most recent `input array` if there is no current `input array`.

```
arr_count ()
```

Example: define max_rows   smallint
          let max_rows = arr_count ()

arr_curr

The function `arr_curr` returns the record number within the current `input array` or `display array` statement of the current cursor position, or of the last cursor position in the most recent `input array` or `display array` if there is no current `input array` or `display array`.

```
arr_curr ()
```

Example: define array_position   smallint
          let array_position = arr_curr ()

ascii

The function `ascii` converts the given decimal number to the ASCII character represented by that number. A decimal number is specified to indicate that we are working with base 10 numbers and not octal or hexadecimal numbers.

```
ascii ( <decimal number> )
```

Example:
let newline = ascii (10)   { put a newline character in the
                             variable named newline }

clipped

The operator `clipped` drops any trailing spaces from a character string.

```
<character string or variable>       clipped
```

Example:
```
define customer_name                       char (40)
define first_name, last_name               char (30)

let first_name  = "Dean"
let last_name   = "Flint"
let customer_name = first_name clipped, " ", last_name

{ customer_name = Dean Flint
  instead of
  customer_name =
    Dean                                               Flint }
```

column

The column function is for use within a report to specify the starting horizontal position of an item to be printed.

```
column <column number>
```

Example:
```
print column 10, date using "mm/dd/yyyy",
      column 65, "Page ", pageno using "<<<<<"
```

current

The function current returns the current system date and time to the specified precision.

```
current [ <larger datetime value> to
          <smaller datetime value> ]
```

The datetime values may be any of the following: year, month, day, hour, minute, second, or fraction. If no date-time values are specified, the precision is year to fraction (3).

The format of datetime values is very specific, all or part of the following format is used depending on the precision: "yyyy-mm-dd hh:mm:ss.fffff".

Examples:
```
define p_year_to_fraction    datetime year to fraction (3)
define p_day_to_minute       datetime day to minute

let p_year_to_fraction = current
let p_day_to_minute    = current day to minute

{ If the current system date and time is:
September 28, 1998 at 7:54:32.876 am
    p_year_to_fraction = "1998-09-28 07:54:32.876"
    p_day_to_minute    = "28 07:54"                         }
```

cursor_name

The function cursor_name is available in more recent versions of INFORMIX-4GL to help resolve cursor name "mangling" and is defined as follows:

```
cursor_name ( "  <cursor name>  " )
```

The function cursor_name is used to help resolve cursor name mangling in the following situation:

```
declare sel_cursor cursor for
    select * from toy_order for update
prepare upd_cursor from
    "update toy_order set shipping_datetime = ? ",
      "where current of sel_cursor"
```

This cannot work properly since sel_cursor is embedded in a string in the update statement and cannot be translated in the same way as the sel_cursor in the declare statement will be in order for it to be used. To resolve this problem, you need to use the cursor_name() function to make the translation as follows:

```
declare sel_cursor cursor for
    select * from toy_order for update
let upd_string =
    "update toy_order set shipping_datetime = ? ",
      "where current of ", cursor_name ("sel_cursor")
prepare upd_cursor from upd_string
```

date (with no argument)

The function date, called with no argument, returns the current system date in the format: `"www mmm dd yyyy"` or `"Wed Sep 28 1998"`.

```
date
```

Example:
```
define date_string    char (15)
        let date_string = date
```

date (with an argument)

The function date, when called with an argument, translates the argument, if possible, into a value of type date.

```
date ( <expression to be converted to type date> )
```

Example:
```
define p_date        date

let p_date = date ("9/28/1998")
let p_date = date ("1998-09-28 16:45:23.562")
let p_date = date (36065)

{ For each of these expressions, p_date = 09/28/1998 }
```

day

The function day returns the numeric value equal to the day of the month of the date argument.

```
day ( <date expression> )
```

Example:
```
define p_num        smallint
let p_num = day ( date ("9/28/1998") )   { p_num = 28 }
```

downshift

The function downshift converts any uppercase letters in the character string into lowercase letters.

```
downshift ( <character string or variable> )
```

Example:
```
define p_comment          char (40)

let p_comment = downshift
                ("Please press RETURN to continue: ")
{ p_comment is now: "please press return to continue: " }
```

err_get

The function err_get is passed an error number, and it returns the text of the associated error message.

```
err_get ( <integer expression> )
```

Example:
```
define error_message      char (80)
let error_message = err_get (status)
{ status is a global error variable defined and assigned
  a value by INFORMIX-4GL }
```

err_print

The function err_print is passed an error number, then displays the text of the associated error message on the error line of the screen.

```
err_print ( <integer expression> )
```

Example:
```
call err_print (status)
{ status is a global error variable defined and assigned
  a value by INFORMIX-4GL }
```

err_quit

The function `err_quit` is passed an error number, it displays the text of the associated error message on the error line of the screen, then terminates the program.

```
err_quit ( <integer expression> )
```

Example:
```
call err_quit (status)
{ status is a global error variable defined and assigned
  a value by INFORMIX-4GL }
```

errorlog

The function `errorlog` appends the specified character string to the error log file. The `startlog` function must be run to create and/or specify the error log file to write to. The advantage of the `fgl_errorlog` function over the `errorlog` function is that you can tell whether write to the error log was successful.

```
errorlog ( <character string or variable> )
```

Example:
```
call errorlog ("Add this line to the error log.")
```

extend

The function `extend` allows you to convert a `date` or `datetime` expression from one `datetime` precision to another `datetime` precision.

```
extend ( <date or datetime expression>
         [ , <larger datetime value> to
             <smaller datetime value> ] )
```

The datetime values may be any of the following: `year`, `month`, `day`, `hour`, `minute`, `second`, or `fraction`. If no datetime values are specified, the precision is `year to fraction (3)`.

Example:

```
define p_datetime          datetime year to fraction (3)
define p_day_minute datetime day to minute

let p_datetime = extend ( date ("9/28/1998") )
{ p_datetime = "1998-09-28 00:00:00.000" }

let p_datetime = "1998-09-28 15:30:41.833"
let p_day_minute = extend (p_datetime, hour to minute)
{ p_day_minute = "28 15:30" }

let p_datetime = extend (p_day_minute)
{ Fills undefined date digits with current system date,
  so if system date = 8/15/1998, then
  p_datetime = "1998-08-28 15:30:00.000" }
```

fgl_drawbox

The fgl_drawbox function will draw a rectangle of the specified size at the specified position in the window.

```
call fgl_drawbox (   <height>, <width>,
                     <vertical position of top of box>,
                     <horizontal position of left of box>
                     [ , <color number> ] )
```

The color numbers are:

Number	Color
0	White
1	Yellow
2	Magenta
3	Red
4	Cyan
5	Green
6	Blue
7	Black

fgl_errorlog

The function fgl_errorlog appends the specified character string to the error log file. The fgl_startlog or startlog function must be run to create and/or specify the error log file to write to. The advantage of the fgl_errorlog function over the errorlog function is that you can tell whether write to the error log was successful.

```
let <numeric variable> =
    fgl_errorlog ( <character string or variable> )
```

Example:
```
define result        smallint

let result =
    fgl_errorlog ("Add this line to the error log.")
```

A value of 0 is returned if the write to the error log is successful, a non-zero value is returned otherwise.

fgl_getenv

The function fgl_getenv allows you to retrieve the value of an operating system environment variable.

```
fgl_getenv ( <character string or variable> )
```

Example:
```
define p_string        char (100)

let p_string = fgl_getenv ("PATH")
{ p_string now contains the value of the user path
  environment variable (up to 100 characters) }
```

fgl_keyval

The function fgl_keyval returns the integer value of the specified special key. This function is designed for use with the fgl_lastkey function.

```
fgl_keyval ( <special key character string> )
```

The special key character string may be any of the following:

```
single printable characters F1 to F64  Control-a to Control-z
accept            help            prevpage
delete            insert          return
down              interrupt       right
esc               left            tab
escape            nextpage        up
```

Example:
```
define p_string      char (30)

prompt "Enter any string: " for p_string

if fgl_lastkey () = fgl_keyval ("return") then
   display "The return key was pressed last."
else
   display "The return key was not pressed last."
end if
```

fgl_lastkey

The function fgl_lastkey returns the integer value of the last key pressed. This function is designed for use with the fgl_keyval function.

```
fgl_lastkey ()
```

Example:
```
define p_string      char (30)

prompt "Enter any string: " for p_string

if fgl_lastkey () = fgl_keyval ("return") then
   display "The return key was pressed last."
else
   display "The return key was not pressed last."
end if
```

fgl_startlog

The function `fgl_startlog` creates the specified error log file if it does not already exist and then specifies that error messages are logged to this file (as long as `whenever error continue` is not in effect). If an existing file is used, it will be added to, not overwritten. The advantage of using `fgl_startlog` over `start-log` is that a value is returned to indicate whether or not the start of the error log was successful.

```
let <numeric variable> =
    startlog ( <error log file name or pathname> )
```

Example:
```
define result      smallint

let result = fgl_startlog ("/usr/local/error.log")
```

A value of 0 is returned if the start of the log is successful, otherwise a non-zero value is returned.

field_touched

The function `field_touched` will return a true or false value depending on whether the user pressed any keystrokes in the field(s) passed to the function that could potentially change the value of the field. `Field_touched` acts like an `or` condition: if any of the fields passed are touched, the function returns true. `Field_touched` can be used within the `construct`, `input`, and `input array` statements.

```
field_touched ( { <name of screen form field> |
                  <name of screen record>.*
                } [, ...]
              )
```

Example:
```
let search_flag = true
construct by name last_name on customer.last_name
   after construct
      if not field_touched (last_name) then
         error "Search field not changed, ",
               "no search will be performed."
         let search_flag = false
      end if
end construct
```

get_fldbuf

The function get_fldbuf will return the contents of the specified field(s) to a string. Get_fldbuf can be used within the construct, input, and input array statements.

```
get_fldbuf ( { <name of screen form field> |
              <name of screen record>.*
            } [, ...]
          )
```

Example:
```
let search_flag = true
construct by name last_name on customer.last_name
   after construct
      if length (get_fldbuf (last_name)) < 3 then
      error "Search must be on at least three characters ",
            "of name."
        let search_flag = false
   end if
end construct.
```

infield

The function `infield` is passed the name of a screen form field, returns true if the cursor is currently positioned in that field, and returns false otherwise. `Infield` may be used in conjunction with `input` and `input array` statements.

```
infield ( <screen form field name> )
```

Example:
```
define p_last_namechar (30)

input p_last_name from last_name
  on key (F1)
    if infield (last_name) then
      call Lookup_Clients ()
      returning p_last_name
    end if
end input
```

length

The function `length` returns the number of bytes of data in a character string excluding trailing spaces.

```
length ( <character string or variable> )
```

Example:
```
define toy_description        char (50)
define toy_length             smallint

let toy_description = "DOLL         "
let toy_length = length (toy_description)
{ toy_length = 4 }
```

lineno

The `lineno` function is used within a report to give the current line number of the report within a page. If the page length is 66 lines and the top margin is 2 and the bottom margin is 2, the `lineno` may have any value from 3 to 64.

```
lineno
```

Example:
```
if lineno > 60 then
    skip to top of page
end if
```

mdy

The function `mdy` allows you to create a `date` value from three numeric expressions representing the month, the day, and the year.

```
mdy ( <month number>, <day number>, <year number> )
```

The combination of these numbers must evaluate to a valid date or the function will produce an error.

Example:
```
define p_date      date
let p_date = mdy (9, 28, 1998) { p_date = 9/28/1998 }
```

month

The function `month` returns the numeric value of the month of the `date` argument.

```
month ( <date expression> )
```

Example:
```
define p_num       smallint
let p_num = month ( date ("9/28/1998") )
{ p_num = 9 }
```

num_args

The function num_args returns the number of arguments passed to a 4GL program from the command line.

```
num_args ()
```

Example:
```
program_name.4ge 43 9/1/1998 "hello world"  { compiled 4GL }
```

or

```
fglgo program_name.4gi 43 9/1/1998 "hello world"  { rds }
...

main
   define num_arguments      smallint

   let num_arguments = num_args ()  { num_arguments = 3 }
end main
```

pageno

The pageno function is used within a report to give the current page number of the report within a page.

```
pageno
```

Example:
```
print column 10, date using "mm/dd/yyyy",
      column 65, "Page ", pageno using "<<<<<"
```

scr_line

The function scr_line returns the current row of the screen the cursor is positioned on in an input array or display array statement.

```
scr_line ()
```

Example:
```
define num_records  smallint
define my_record record
          account_number                  char (9),
          last_name                        char (30),
          first_name                       char (15)
       end record
define record_number                       smallint
...
call set_count (num_records)
display array my_record to my_screen.*
  on key (F1)
    let record_number = scr_line ()
    call Bold_Screen_Line (record_number)
end display
```

set_count

The function set_count initializes the number of rows for an input array or display array. This function should be called before each input array and display array statement to let INFORMIX-4GL know how many rows of the array are initially filled.

```
set_count ( <integer expression> )
```

An implicit set_count function call is made at the end of an input array statement. The function arr_count will return the number of elements stored in the input array. Since the number of rows in a display array does not change during the display array, the value of arr_count after a display array is unchanged.

Example:
```
define num_records smallint
define my_record record
          account_number     char (9),
          last_name           char (30),
          first_name          char (15)
       end record
...
call set_count (num_records)
display array my_record to my_screen.*
```

showhelp

The function `showhelp` will display the help message associated with the specified help number.

```
showhelp ( <help number> )
```

Example: `call showhelp (12)`

space

The `space` function will print the specified number of spaces.

```
<integer> space

            or

<integer> spaces
```

Example: `print 25 spaces`

sqlexit

The `sqlexit` function is actually an ESQL/C function, but you may wish to write a C function to call from 4GL to allow its use. `Sqlexit` rolls back any open transaction, closes the current database, and disconnects the INFORMIX-4GL program from the database server. The `sqlexit` function returns a value of 0 after it is complete. (Note that currently the Informix manuals say that this function can be called directly from INFORMIX-4GL. Do NOT do this; this can cause you problems.)

```
let <numeric variable> = sqlexit ()
```

An example of the C function you might write to be called from INFORMIX-4GL is:

```
int i4gl_sqlexit(int nargs)
{
    if (nargs != 0)
    fgl_fatal("i4gl_sqlexit", 1, -1318);
    sqlexit();
    return(0);
}
```

Example:
```
database my_database
...
call i4gl_sqlexit ()
...
```

startlog

The function `startlog` creates the specified error log file if it does not already exist and then specifies that error messages are logged to this file (as long as `whenever error continue` is not in effect). If an existing file is used, it will be added to, not over-written. The advantage of using `fgl_startlog` over `startlog` is that a value is returned to indicate whether or not the start of the error log was successful.

> **startlog (<error log file name or pathname>)**

Example: `call startlog ("/usr/local/error.log")`

time

The function `time` returns the current system time (local time, not GMT) as a character string in the format `"hh:mm:ss"`.

> **time**

Example: `define p_timechar (8)`
           `let p_time = time`
           `{ If the current time is 6:30:44 pm,`
           `   then p_time = "18:30:44" }`

today

The function `today` returns the current system date as a `date` value.

```
today
```

Example:
```
define p_date   date
let p_date = today
{ If the current date is August 15, 1998,
  the p_date = 8/15/1998 }
```

units

The keyword `units` allows you to convert a numeric expression into an `interval` value containing the specified units. The unit values may be any of the following: `year`, `month`, `day`, `hour`, `minute`, `second`, or `fraction`.

```
<numeric expression> units <datetime unit value>
```

Example:
```
define p_day    interval day to day
define p_hour   interval hour to hour

let p_day  = 90 units day
let p_hour = interval (36) hour to hour
```

Note that when you are working with month `units`, if you add or subtract months to or from a date, if the day of the month is greater than 28, you may get an error. If the result month does not have as many days as the original month, and the result would be a day in the month that does not exist, the date will not be adjusted for you; you will get an error instead. You can write a function in 4GL to handle this problem for you.

Examples:

```
define p_month    interval month to month
define p_date     date

let p_date = date ("8/31/1998") + 1 units month
{ error - 9/31/1998 does not exist }
let p_date = date ("8/31/1998") + 2 units month
{ p_date = 10/31/1998 }
```

upshift

The function upshift converts any lowercase letters in the character string to uppercase letters.

```
upshift ( <character string or variable> )
```

Example:

```
define p_comment    char (40)

let p_comment =
    upshift ("Please press RETURN to continue: ")
    { p_comment is now:
        "PLEASE PRESS RETURN TO CONTINUE: "   }
```

using

The operator using allows you to define a format string for displaying numeric and date values.

```
<numeric or date expression>
using "<format string>"
```

The format string for a date value may consist of the special characters: dd, ddd, mm, mmm, yy, and yyyy.
The format string for a numeric value may consist of the special characters: *, &, #, <, -, +, (,), $, @, . and ,.
Any other characters used in the string are printed as literals.
The using function is discussed in detail in Chapter 9.

Example:
```
define p_string      char (25)

let p_string = today using "dd ddd mm mmm yy yyyy"
                                {today=9-28-1998}
{ p_string = "28 Wed 09 Sep 1998 }

let p_string = -15788 using "$$$$,$-&.&&"
{ p_string = "$-15,788.00" }
```

weekday

The function weekday returns a numeric value for the day of the week of the date or datetime argument.

```
weekday ( <date or datetime expression> )
```

The day of the week is returned as follows: Sunday = 0, Monday = 1, Tuesday = 2, Wednesday = 3, Thursday = 4, Friday = 5, Saturday = 6.

Example:
```
define p_weekday          smallint
let p_weekday = weekday (date ("9/28/1998"))
{ p_weekday=3 }
```

wordwrap

The wordwrap function is used within a report to print out long strings of characters.

```
<character value> wordwrap
  [ right margin <temporary right margin> ]
```

Example:
```
define long_string                    char (350)

let long_string = "Once upon a time, in a land ",
                  "far, far, away, there lived a frog. Now this",
                  "frog, you understand, was no ordinary frog, ",
                  "he was in fact a prince who had long ago ",
                  "been enchanted by an evil sorceress.  Many ",
                  "years before the prince had angered this ",
                  "sorceress by failing to give proper respect ",
                  "to her pet platypus."

print column 10, long_string wordwrap right margin 60
```

The output from this statement would look like:

```
Once upon a time, in a land far, far, away, there
lived a frog.  Now this frog, you understand, was
no ordinary frog, he was in fact a prince who had
long ago been enchanted by an evil sorceress.
Many years before the prince had angered this
sorceress by failing to give proper respect to her
pet platypus.
```

year

The function year returns the numeric value of the year of the date argument.

```
year ( <date expression> )
```

Example:
```
define p_num smallint
let p_num = year ( date ("9/28/1998") )
{ p_num = 1998 }
```

INFORMIX-4GL Functions Called from C

The use of C with INFORMIX-4GL is discussed in detail in Chapter 28. The functions that are defined in INFORMIX-4GL for use in C are described in the following list and discussed in detail in Appendix A. They are listed in alphabetical order:

decadd	decsub	popdate	pushdate	retdate
deccmp	dectoasc	popdec	pushdec	retdec
deccopy	dectodbl	popdtime	pushdtime	retdtime
deccvasc	dectoflt	popdub	pushdub	retdub
deccvdbl	dectoint	popflo	pushflo	retflo
deccvflt	dectolong	popint	pushint	retint
deccvint		popinv	pushinv	retinv
deccvlong		poplocator	pushlocator	
decdiv	fgl_call	poplong	pushlong	retlong
dececvt	fgl_end	popquote	pushquote	retquote
decfcvt	fgl_exitfm	popshort	pushshort	retshort
decmul	fgl_start	popvchar	pushvchar	retvchar

The functions beginning with dec allow you to perform type conversions and arithmetic with decimal numbers from within C. If you do not use these functions to manipulate decimal data types from within C, your results may vary.

The functions beginning with fgl_ allow you to call 4gl functions from C. These functions are demonstrated in Chapter 28.

The functions beginning with pop pop parameters off of the argument stack when they are passed from INFORMIX-4GL into C.

The functions beginning with push push parameters onto the argument stack for use in passing parameters into an INFORMIX-4GL function when called from C.

The functions beginning with ret are used when returning values to an INFORMIX-4GL function.

For details on how to use these functions, see Appendix A.

INFORMIX-4GL Constants

Three constants are used in INFORMIX-4GL. Like all INFORMIX-4GL keywords, these constants are not case sensitive.

false	False has the value of 0.
notfound	Notfound has the value of 100. This value may be returned from an SQL statement.
true	True has the value of 1.

INFORMIX-4GL Global Variables

Several variables are maintained by Informix throughout program execution. You may access these variables for information about errors, warnings, and program interrupts.

These variables are:

```
int_flag            integer
quit_flag           integer
status              integer

sqlca record
      sqlcode       integer,
      sqlerrm       char (71),
      sqlerrp       char (8),
      sqlerrd       array [6] of integer,
      sqlawarn      char (8)
   end record
```

Each variable is described here in detail.

int_flag

The variable int_flag is set to true whenever the *interrupt* key is pressed. It is the programmer's responsibility to check the status of this variable, take any necessary corrective action, and reset the int_flag to false. See Chapter 16 for further information on *interrupt* handling.

quit_flag

The variable quit_flag is set to true whenever the *quit* key is pressed. It is the programmer's responsibility to check the status of this variable, take any necessary corrective action, and reset the `quit_flag` to false. See Chapter 16 for further information on the `quit_flag`.

status

The variable `status` normally has the value 0. If an error occurs in an SQL statement, a screen input or output statement, or a validate statement, the value of status will be set to a negative error number. If no rows are retrieved from an SQL statement, the status variable will be set to the constant `notfound` or 100.

If you are using the `whenever any error` compile-time directive, or if you have compiled or are running with the `-anyerr` switch, the variable status will additionally be set with a zero (everything's okay) or a negative error message number whenever an expression is evaluated.

It is the programmer's responsibility to check the status of the status variable and take any necessary corrective action. Status will automatically be reset, so any error checking should be done immediately. See Chapter 16 for further information on error handling.

sqlca

The `sqlca` record contains information about the most recently executed SQL statement. Each element in the sqlca structure contains information as described below.

`sqlca.sqlcode`	Set to 0 if no errors occurred, set to a negative error number if an error occurred, or set to `notfound` (100) if no rows were returned.
`sqlca.sqlerrm`	Contains the variable which goes into the error message. Could be a table name, or for networking the error message from the networking software.
`sqlca.sqlerrp`	Internal use only.
`sqlca.sqlerrd [1]`	Contains the number of rows affected after a `select` cursor is opened or after a `prepare` of one of the following

statements: select, update, insert or delete.

sqlca.sqlerrd [2]	The value of the serial number or an ISAM error code.
sqlca.sqlerrd [3]	The number of rows processed.
sqlca.sqlerrd [4]	The estimated cost in CPU time for the query.
sqlca.sqlerrd [5]	The offset of the error into the SQL statement.
sqlca.sqlerrd [6]	The rowid of the last row processed.
sqlca.sqlawarn [1]	The first character of this string is blank if no warnings occurred, it is set to W if any warnings occurred. If this character is blank the rest of the sqlca.sqlawarn string will also be blank.
sqlca.sqlawarn [2]	The second character of this string is set to W if (1) any data was truncated to make it fit into a character string program variable, or (2) if a database statement selected a database with transactions.
sqlca.sqlawarn [3]	The third character of this string is set to W if (1) an aggregate function (see Chapter 20) found any null values, or (2) if a database statement selected a mode ANSI database.
sqlca.sqlawarn [4]	The fourth character of this string is set to W if (1) the number of items in the select list is different from the number of program variables in the into list of a select statement, or (2) if a database statement selected an INFORMIX-OnLine database.

`sqlca.sqlawarn [5]`	The fifth character of this string is set to W if (1) a float is stored as a decimal (when platform doesn't support float types), or (2) a prepared statement contains a `delete` or `update` statement without a `where` clause.
`sqlca.sqlawarn [6]`	The sixth character of this string is set to W if the `DBANSIWARN` environment variable is set and a non-ANSI-compliant statement is executed.
`sqlca.sqlawarn [7]`	The seventh character of this string is set to W if (1) `DATASKIP` is turned on and the query skips a fragment, or (2) the application is connected to the secondary server (read only) in a data replication pair.
`sqlca.sqlawarn [8]`	Not currently used.

Summary

The following functions have been predefined for use in INFORMIX-4GL.

`arg_val ( <integer expression> )`

`arr_count ()`

`arr_curr ()`

`ascii ( <decimal number> )`

`<character string or variable>     clipped`

`column <column number>`

`current [ <larger datetime value> to`
`        <smaller datetime value> ]`

```
date

date ( <expression to be converted to type date> )

day ( <date expression> )

downshift ( <character string or variable> )

err_get ( <integer expression> )

err_print ( <integer expression> )

err_quit ( <integer expression> )

errorlog ( <character string or variable> )

extend ( <date or datetime expression>
        [ , <larger datetime value> to
            <smaller datetime value> ] )

let <numeric variable> =
    fgl_errorlog ( <character string or variable> )

call fgl_drawbox ( <height>, <width>,
                   <vertical position of top of box>,
                   <horizontal position of left of box>
                   [ , <color number> ] )

fgl_getenv ( <character string or variable> )

fgl_keyval ( <special key character string> )

fgl_lastkey ()

let <numeric variable> =
    fgl_startlog ( <error log file name or pathname> )

field_touched ( { <name of screen form field> |
                  <name of screen record>.*
                } [, ...]
              )
```

```
get_fldbuf ( { <name of screen form field> |
                <name of screen record>.*
            } [, ...]
          )

infield ( <screen form field name> )

length ( <character string or variable> )

lineno

mdy ( <month number>, <day number>, <year number> )

month ( <date expression> )

num_args ()

pageno

scr_line ()

set_count ( <integer expression> )

showhelp ( <help number> )

<integer> space or <integer> spaces

let <numeric variable> = sqlexit ()

startlog ( <error log file name or pathname> )

time

today

<numeric expression> units <datetime unit value>

upshift ( <character string or variable> )

<numeric or date expression> using "<format string>"

weekday ( <date or datetime expression> )
```

```
<character value> wordwrap
    [ right margin <temporary right margin> ]


year ( <date expression> )
```

The functions listed below are defined by INFORMIX-4GL for
use with C and are discussed in detail in Appendix A.

decadd	decsub	popdate	pushdate	retdate
deccmp	dectoasc	popdec	pushdec	retdec
deccopy	dectodbl	popdtime	pushdtime	retdtime
deccvasc	dectoflt	popdub	pushdub	retdub
deccvdbl	dectoint	popflo	pushflo	retflo
deccvflt	dectolong	popint	pushint	retint
deccvint	popinv	pushinv	retinv
deccvlong	poplocator	pushlocator
decdiv	fgl_call	poplong	pushlong	retlong
dececvt	fgl_end	popquote	pushquote	retquote
decfcvt	fgl_exitfm	popshort	pushshort	retshort
decmul	fgl_start	popvchar	pushvchar	retvchar

Three constants are used in INFORMIX-4GL: false = 0,
notfound = 100, and true = 1.

Global variables used by INFORMIX-4GL may be accessed for
information about errors, warnings, and program interrupts:

```
int_flag          integer
quit_flag         integer
status            integer

sqlca record
    sqlcode       integer,
    sqlerrm       char (71),
    sqlerrp       char (8),
    sqlerrd       array [6] of integer,
    sqlawarn      char (8)
end record
```

Chapter

18

The Input Statement

- input *overview*
- *Editing the input*
- *Data validation*
- *Adding/Changing a row*
- *Summary*

Input Overview

The `input` statement allows you to add or change a row of information in a screen form. In Chapter 13, we created a module containing the menu options: Find, Next, Previous, Delete, and Exit. The sections in this chapter will give you two more menu options to add to the menu: Add and Change.

Since the syntax for both Add and Change are a part of the `input` statement, the syntax of the `input` statement and some general information about it is discussed here in the overview section.

The `input` statement is actually very similar in form to the `display` statement we discussed in Chapter 13. The main difference is that with the `display` statement we were limited to displaying information. With the `input` statement we will actually be able to enter and change values in the form and check each value to make certain it is valid.

```
input { by name <program variable> [, ...]
        [ without defaults ]                        |
        <program variable>  [, ...]
                              [ without defaults ]
        from { <form field name>        |
               <screen record name>.*
             } [, ...]
      }
 [ attribute ( <input attribute> [, ...] ) ]
 [ help <help number> ]
 [ { before input                                   |
     before field <form field name> [, ...]         |
     after   field <form field name> [, ...]        |
     after   input                                  |
     on key ( <special key> [, ...] )
   }
   { <any 4GL statement>}                            |
     next field { <form field name>                 |
                      previous | next }              |
     continue input                                  |
     exit input
   }
   end input
 ]
```

If the program variable names are the same as the form field
names, you can use the input by name form of the input statement. This works the same way as with the display by name
statement. If your program variable is a record, the *<record
name>* portion of the record name does not need to match the
form field name.

If the program variable names are not the same as the form
field names, you will need to use the input ... from form of
the input statement. This works the same way as in the display
statement. The program variable names should correspond in
type and order with the form field names.

The without defaults clause displays the information in your program variables to the screen form before your input statement.

Any of the following attributes may be used with the input statement:

normal	reverse	white	cyan
bold	blink	yellow	green
dim	underline	magenta	blue
invisible	left	red	black

The information following the help clause in the syntax description is discussed in the section on data validation later in this chapter.

The 4GL function infield can be used to check which form field a user is currently in. Infield is passed the name of a screen form field, and returns true if the cursor is currently positioned in that field, and returns false otherwise. Infield may be used within input and input array statements.

```
infield ( <screen form field name> )
```

Example:
```
define p_last_name                      char (30)

input p_last_name from last_name
 , on key (F1)
     if infield (last_name) then
        call Lookup_Clients () returning p_last_name
     end if
end input
```

Editing the Input

While adding and changing data in a form, you can use any of the following keys:

Key	Description
Control-a	Toggles between insert and typeover mode. Default is typeover mode.
Control-d	Deletes everything from the current position to the end of the field.
Control-h	Moves the cursor to the left.
Control-l	Moves the cursor to the right.
Control-r	Redraws the screen.
Control-x	Deletes the current character.
down arrow	Moves to the next field on the form or to the same field below the current row if you are in an input array statement. The action of the down arrow key may vary depending on whether the options statement has the field order set to constrained or unconstrained.
left arrow	If you are at the beginning of the field, moves to the previous field; otherwise, moves one space to the left.
right arrow	Moves one space to the right; if you are at the end of the field, moves to the next field.
up arrow	Moves to the previous field on the form or to the same field above the current row if you are in an input array statement. The action of the up arrow key may vary depending on whether the options statement has the field order set to constrained or unconstrained.

Unfortunately, short of remapping your keyboard, these keys cannot be redefined.

Data Validation

If you use any of the following statements in your `input` statement, you must end the `input` statement with an `end input`. Keep in mind that `before field`, `after field`, `after input`, `on key`, `next field`, and `exit input` must be physically located within the `input` statement. You can make calls to other functions, but the functions cannot contain any of these statements (unless they are contained within an `input` statement located in that function).

before input

The `before input` clause allows you to execute statements before the user enters the `input` statement. This allows you to initialize values for your form or issue other 4GL statements.

```
Example:    before input
                let my_record.username = p_username
                display by name my_record.username
```

before field <form field name> [, ...]

The `before field` clause allows you to execute statements just before a user enters the specified field. For instance, you could assign a default value to a field and display it to the form before the user enters a field or keep a particular user from editing a field.

```
Example:    before field department
                if p_my_record.department is null and
                    p_my_record.toy_code < 10 then
                    let p_my_record.department = 1
                else
                    let p_my_record.department = 2
                end if

                display by name p_my_record.department
```

after field <form field name> [, ...]

The after field clause allows you to execute statements immediately after the user exits the specified field. After field clauses are a great place for performing data validation.

```
Example:   after field account_number
             if p_my_record.account_name is null then
               next field account_number
             end if
```

after input

The after input clause allows you to execute statements after the input statements have been executed, but before the input statement has been exited. This allows you to check the information on the form and put the user back into the screen at a specific location if the data is invalid or incomplete.

```
Example:   after input
             if p_my_record.last_name is null and
               p_my_record.business_name is null then
               next field last_name
             end if
```

on key (<special key> [, ...])

The on key clause allows you to specify actions to be taken when the user presses a special key. Any of the following special keys may be used:

F1 through F64	Control-<letter -except a, d, h, l, r, or x>	
accept	help	prevpage
delete	insert	return
down	interrupt	right
esc	left	tab
escape	nextpage	up

Example: on key (F1)
              if infield (toy_code) then
                call Lookup_Toys (toy_code)
                  returning p_toy_item.toy_code,
                           p_toy_item.description

              display by name p_toy_item.toy_code,
                           p_toy_item.description
              end if

<any 4GL statement>

Any 4GL statement can go inside of a before field, after
field, after input, or on key clause.

next field { *<form field name>* |
previous | next }

The next field statement positions the cursor in the specified
field. The keyword previous specifies that the cursor is to be
positioned on the previous field of the form. The keyword next
specifies that the cursor is to be positioned on the next field of the
form. Make sure you give users a way out of the form or they
may get stuck in an infinite loop.

Example: next field last_name

The 4GL functions fgl_lastkey and fgl_keyval can be useful in determining which key was last pressed. This information
may be useful when determining the next field you want to be
positioned in.

continue input

Continue input returns the program control to the top of the
input statement. The cursor is returned to its most recent field
position in the form.

exit input

Exit input exits the input statement. The after input clause, if one exists, will be executed before the input statement is executed.

Adding/Changing a Row

The function below can be added to the display module we wrote in Chapter 13. This function can be called from the menu options Add and Change as demonstrated below and added to the menu in that module. This function uses the input statement to allow the user to add or change a record.

This function covers the basic elements of an add and change routine. The functions called to validate data and to lookup values of data are not shown.

It is easier to write and maintain a single function to handle both the add and change functionality since the code is very similar.

```
{ Global definition for module }
define p_toy_order record
        order_number            like toy_order.order_number,
        store_number            like toy_order.store_number,
        store_name              like toy_store.store_name,
        order_date              like toy_order.order_date,
        shipping_datetime       like toy_order.shipping_datetime,
        sales_code              like toy_order.sales_code
        end record

{*******************************************************************
  Toy_Order_Menu
*******************************************************************}
function Toy_Order_Menu ()

  whenever error stop

  let cursor_open = false
  initialize p_toy_order.* to null
```

```
open window w_toy_order3 at 2,2 with form "toy_order3"
    attribute (border)

menu "Toy Order Menu"

    command "Find"                  "Find toy orders."
          help 1
          call Find_Toy_Order ()

    command "Next"                  "View the next toy order."
          help 2
          call Next_Toy_Order ()

    command "Previous"              "View the previous toy order."
          help 3
          call Previous_Toy_Order ()

    command "Add"                   "Add this toy order."
          help 6
          call Add_Change_Toy_Order ("A")
          next option "Find"

    command "Change"                "Change this toy order."
          help 6
          call Add_Change_Toy_Order ("C")
          next option "Find"

    command "Delete"                "Delete this toy order."
          help 6
          call Delete_Toy_Order ()
          next option "Find"

    command "Items"                 "View all toy order items."
          help 60
          call Find_Order_Item (p_toy_order.order_number, "S")
          next option "Find"

    command key ("E","X") "Exit"  "Exit from this menu."
          help 9
          exit menu
end menu
```

```
   call Close_Toy_Order_Cursor ()

   close window w_toy_order3

end function  { Toy_Order_Menu }


{*************************************************************
   Add_Change_Toy_Order
   This function allows the user to add or change a row in the
   toy_order table.
 *************************************************************}
function Add_Change_Toy_Order (add_change)
  define add_change              char (1)
  define is_valid                smallint
  define orig_toy_order record
            order_number         like toy_order.order_number,
            store_number         like toy_order.store_number,
            store_name           like toy_store.store_name,
            order_date           like toy_order.order_date,
            shipping_datetime    like toy_order.shipping_datetime,
            sales_code           like toy_order.sales_code
         end record


  if add_change = "C" and p_toy_order.order_number is null then
     error "You must Find a toy_order before you can change one."
     return
  end if

  clear form

  display "" at 1,1
  display "" at 2,1
  display "Press Accept when finished or Interrupt to cancel."
                                                    at 2,1

  if add_change = "A" then
     display "ADD a new toy order." at 1,1
     initialize orig_toy_order.* to null
  else
     display "CHANGE a toy order." at 1,1
```

```
      let orig_toy_order.* = p_toy_order.*
end if

input by name p_toy_order.store_number thru
            p_toy_order.sales_code    without defaults
   help 14

   before input
      if p_toy_order.order_date is null then
         let p_toy_order.order_date = today
         display by name p_toy_order.order_date
      end if

   after field order_date
      if p_toy_order.order_date > (today + 91) then
         error "Order date cannot be over 90 days from now."
         next field order_date
      end if

   after field store_number, store_name
      if not Valid_Store (p_toy_order.store_number,
                          p_toy_order.store_name) then
        error "Not a valid toy store.  Press F3 for choices."
        next field store_number
      end if

   after field sales_code
      call Valid_Sales_Code (p_toy_order.sales_code)
               returning  is_valid

      if not is_valid then
         error "Not a valid sales_code.  Press F3 for choices."
         next field sales_code
      end if

   on key (F3)
      case
         when infield (store_number) or infield (store_name)
            call Lookup_Toy_Store (p_toy_order.store_number)
                     returning  p_toy_order.store_number,
                                p_toy_order.store_name
```

```
                display by name  p_toy_order.store_number,
                                p_toy_order.store_name

            when infield (sales_code) then
               call Lookup_Sales_Code (p_toy_order.sales_code)
                            returning  p_toy_order.sales_code

               display by name p_toy_order.sales_code

            otherwise
               error "Sorry, pop-up help is not available in ",
                     "this field."
        end case

after input
   if int_flag = false then
      if date (p_toy_order.shipping_datetime) <
                                p_toy_order.order_date then
         error "The shipping date cannot be before the ",
               "order date."
         next field order_date
      end if
   end if
end input

if not int_flag then
   if add_change = "A" then
      insert into toy_order
            (toy_order.order_number,
             toy_order.store_number,
             toy_order.order_date,
             toy_order.shipping_datetime,
             toy_order.sales_code)
         values
            (0,
             p_toy_order.store_number,
             p_toy_order.order_date,
             p_toy_order.shipping_datetime,
             p_toy_order.sales_code)

      if sqlca.sqlcode <> 0 then
         error "Error ", sqlca.sqlcode, " inserting toy_order."
```

```
            end if
      else   { add_change = "C" }
         update toy_order set
            (toy_order.store_number,            toy_order.order_date,
             toy_order.shipping_datetime,    toy_order.sales_code)
         = (p_toy_order.store_number,         p_toy_order.order_date,
             p_toy_order.shipping_datetime,    p_toy_order.sales_code)
         where order_number = p_toy_order.order_number

         if sqlca.sqlcode <> 0 then
            error "Error ", sqlca.sqlcode, " changing toy_order."
         end if
      end if   { add_change = "A" }
   else
      clear form
      let p_toy_order.* = orig_toy_order.*
      display by name p_toy_order.*
      let int_flag = false
      if add_change = "A" then
         message "User interrupt - row not added."
      else
         message "User interrupt - row not changed."
      end if
   end if
end function   { Add_Change_Toy_Order }
```

Summary

The input statement allows you to add or change a row of information in a screen form.

```
input { by name <program variable> [, ...]
        [ without defaults ]                        |
        <program variable>  [, ...]
                           [ without defaults ]
        from {  <form field name>        |
              <screen record name>.*
            } [, ...]
      }
      [ attribute ( <input attribute> [, ...] ) ]
```

```
[ help <help number> ]
[ { before input                                    |
    before field <form field name> [, ...]          |
    after  field <form field name> [, ...]          |
    after  input                                    |
    on key ( <special key> [, ...] )                |
  }
  { <any 4GL statement>}                            |
    next field { <form field name>                  |
                    previous | next }               |
    continue input                                  |
    exit input                                      |
  }
  end input
]
```

Any of the following attributes may be used with the `input` statement:

normal	reverse	white	cyan
bold	blink	yellow	green
dim	underline	magenta	blue
invisible	left	red	black

The 4GL function `infield` can be used to check which form field a user is currently in.

infield (<screen form field name>)

While adding and changing data in a form, the following keys may be used:

Key	*Description*
Control-a	Toggles between insert and typeover mode. Default is typeover mode.
Control-d	Deletes everything from the current position to the end of the field.
Control-h	Moves the cursor to the left.
Control-l	Moves the cursor to the right.
Control-r	Redraws the screen.
Control-x	Deletes the current character.

down arrow	Moves to the next field on the form or to the same field below the current row if you are in an `input array` statement. The action of the down arrow key may vary depending on whether the `options` statement has the field order set to `constrained` or `unconstrained`.
left arrow	If you are at the beginning of the field, moves to the previous field; otherwise, moves one space to the left.
right arrow	Moves one space to the right; if you are at the end of the field, moves to the next field.
up arrow	Moves to the previous field on the form or to the same field above the current row if you are in an `input array` statement. The action of the up arrow key may vary depending on whether the `options` statement has the field order set to `constrained` or `unconstrained`.

The `on key` clause allows you to specify actions to be taken when the user presses one of the following special keys:

F1 through F64	Control-<letter -except a, d, h, l, r, or x>	
accept	help	prevpage
delete	insert	return
down	interrupt	right
esc	left	tab
escape	nextpage	up

Chapter

19

Using SQL in 4GL

- *Using Direct SQL in 4GL*

- prepare

- execute

- declare

- foreach

- open

- fetch

- where current of

- put

- flush

- close

- free

- *Summary*

Using Direct SQL in 4GL

When using direct SQL in 4GL, the syntax is very simple. The SQL statement is entered into your program just as you would enter it into DB-Access, but with a few exceptions. Most SQL statements will be understood except for features that were introduced in or after version 5.0 of the engine (such as stored procedures and triggers). Using direct SQL you will be able to select, insert, update and delete data as well as execute a variety of other SQL statements. See chapters 3, 4, 5, 6 and 20 for Informix's SQL statement syntax for use with 4GL.

If you are running a `select` statement, the `select` clause will be followed by an `into` clause. The `into` clause specifies the names of the program variables the information from the `select` statement will be read into. The items in the `into` clause should correspond in order and type to the items listed in the `select` clause. When using direct SQL, your select statement may only return a single row of data. If you need to return more than a single row of data, you will need to see the other sections in this chapter which will teach you how to use SQL in 4GL using cursors.

You may use program variables as values in an SQL statement. If you wish to use a program variable as anything other than a value, for instance, a column name, a table name, or an SQL keyword, you will need to use a cursor with your SQL statement (see the rest of this chapter). This means that you can use program variables as values to be compared within your `where` clause, or as values with which to insert data into a table or to update it.

If you have a column name and a program variable with the same name, you should indicate that you are using the column name and not the program variable by putting an at sign (@) immediately in front of the column name: `@my_column`.

Examples:

```
define p_order_number    like toy_order.order_number
define p_order_date      like toy_order.order_date
define p_shipping_date   date

initialize p_order_date, p_shipping_date to null
```

```
select order_date, date (shipping_datetime)
  into p_order_date, p_shipping_date
  from toy_order
  where order_number = p_order_number

if p_shipping_date is null then
  call Print_Order (p_order_number)

  update toy_order
    set shipping_datetime = current year to minute
    where order_number = p_order_number
end if

update statistics

...

define r_toy              record
        toy_code          like toy.toy_code,
        description       like toy.description,
        quantity          like toy.quantity,
        cost              like toy.cost,
        sales_price       like toy.sales_price
  end record

<r_toy definitions>

insert into toy
 (toy_code, desription, quantity, cost, sales_price)
   values
 (r_toy.toy_code,
  r_toy.description,
  r_toy.quantity,
  r_toy.cost,
  r_toy.sales_price)

...

delete from toy
  where toy_code = r_toy.toy_code
```

As shown in the above examples, you will want to initialize your program variables before selecting information into them. If you don't initialize your program variables and no information is retrieved by your `select` statement, the values will contain garbage.

Also, note that in the insert example, we could easily have entered:

```
define r_toy      record like toy.*

insert into toy values r_toy.*
```

The problem with this syntax is that it is very likely to cause problems later if you should add a column to a table.

tip

In general, try to avoid using the `like` syntax for entire record structures, and limit its use to individual columns, where it is very useful.

prepare

The `prepare` statement will preprocess your SQL statement before you run it. The `prepare` statement is optional when using `select` and `insert` cursors. When using `select` and `insert` cursors, if you don't explicitly prepare your SQL statement, it will be prepared for you implicitly at the time you open your cursor. The `prepare` statement will preprocess your SQL statement at this point instead of when the statement is opened. This will make your code more efficient if you are able to perform a single prepare for more than one `open` statement. The `prepare` statement also allows you to use the question mark syntax described below.

```
prepare <statement identifier>
   from <character variable or string>
```

The *statement identifier* must be unique within a module. The *statement identifier* can only be used within the module in which it is prepared.

Example:
```
define sql_stmt1  char (100)

let sql_stmt1 = "select * from toy_store ",
                 "order by store_name"

prepare statement1 from sql_stmt1
```

You may use a question mark (?) in place of a value that will be supplied at the time the SQL statement is executed. Program variable names may not be included within the character variable or string that contains the SQL statement. You may include the value of the variable in the string when you create it, or use a question mark in place of the value.

Example:
```
define sql_stmt2  char (100)

let sql_stmt2 = "select * from toy_order ",
                "where order_date >= ? and ",
                  "shipping_datetime is null ",
                "order by order_number"

prepare statement2 from sql_stmt2
```

execute

The execute statement runs a previously prepared SQL statement.

```
execute
  <statement identifier from a prepare statement>
  [ using <program variable> [, ...]   ]
```

This statement is primarily used to execute SQL statements more efficiently than direct SQL and for SQL statements that are supported by the database engine, but not by your current version of INFORMIX-4GL. For instance, stored procedures and triggers are supported by the Informix 5.01 engines, but the 4.1 and earlier versions of INFORMIX-4GL do not support these features. Therefore, if you wish to run a stored procedure using INFORMIX-4GL version 4.1, you would need to use the `execute` statement.

If you prepare your SQL statement using question marks (?) as place holders for program variable values, you must use the `using` clause to specify with which values to replace the question marks. The program variables should be specified in the order of the question marks they are replacing in the prepared statement.

Example:
```
define p_order_number     like toy_order.order_number

let p_order_number = 12

prepare statement1 from
   "execute procedure Delete_Order (?)"
execute statement1 using p_order_number
```

declare

The `declare` statement allows you to define a cursor for a `select` statement or an `insert` statement.

The syntax of the `declare` statement is:

```
declare <cursor name> [ scroll ] cursor
                              [ with hold ] for
   {<select statement>
       [ for update
             [ of <column name> [, ...] ] ]      |
    <insert statement>                           |
    <statement identifier from prepare statement>
   }
```

The cursor name you choose must be unique within the module.

When you execute an SQL statement that may return many rows of data such as a `select`, the information returned is called a *list*. You may access each item in the list sequentially by using a cursor that points to a row of data. If you wish to fetch information from the list in any other order (including backwards), you need to declare your cursor to be a scroll cursor.

The with hold statement will keep the cursor open until it is closed or until a close database statement is issued. If you do not use the with hold statement, the cursor is closed at the end of each transaction.

The for update clause causes each fetched row to be locked in exclusive mode. If you are not using transaction logging, the lock is released when the next row is fetched or when you close the cursor. If you are using transaction logging, the lock is released when you issue a commit work or a rollback work at the end of a transaction.

There are several restrictions on the use of update cursors. The for update clause may not be used with a select statement that selects from more than one table, that uses an order by clause, or is declared as a scroll cursor. In a non-mode ANSI database with transaction logging, you are required to issue a begin work statement before opening a cursor for update and without hold. If you use the with hold clause with your for update cursor, you may open the cursor outside of a transaction, but you will not be able to roll back any of the updates. If your for update clause specifies column names, only these column names may be updated later if you update using the where current of clause (discussed later in this chapter).

The insert statement allows you to insert multiple rows into a table efficiently. Insert cursors can be quite dangerous in terms of actually inserting all of your data, and for this reason they are seldom used and I do not recommend them. The insert statement may not contain a subquery. The cursor for an insert statement may not be a scroll cursor.

Examples:

```
define start_date, end_date     date
define sqlstmt1                 char (200)
...
declare toy_ord1_cursor cursor for
   select * from toy_order
      where date (shipping_datetime) between start_date and
                                             end_date
   ...
```

```
let sqlstmt1 =    "select order_number, store_number ",
                  "from toy_order ",
                  "where order_date >= ? and ",
                  "sales_code = ? "

prepare statement2 from sqlstmt1
declare toy_ord2_cursor scroll cursor with hold
  for statement2
...
prepare statement3 from sqlstmt1
declare toy_ord3_cursor cursor for statement3 for update
...
let insert_stmt =
  "insert into state (state_code, state_name) ",
    "values (?, ?)"
prepare statement from insert_stmt
declare insert_cursor cursor for statement4
```

foreach

The foreach statement allows you to perform a set of 4GL statements for each row returned from a select cursor. The foreach
opens the cursor then performs fetch operations for each row.

```
foreach <cursor name>
  [ using <program variable> [, ...] ]
  [ into <program variable> [, ...] ]
  { <any 4GL statement> |
    continue foreach   |
    exit foreach
  } [, ...]
end foreach
```

If you prepared a select statement and you used question
marks (?) as place holders for program variable values, you must
use the using clause to specify which values to use to replace the
question marks. The program variables should be specified in the
order of the question marks they are replacing in the prepared
statement. Note that older versions of foreach do not support
the using syntax. Since the using syntax has been introduced for

use with the `foreach` statement, the `open/fetch` syntax is no longer necessary.

The `into` clause specifies the program variable(s) the items in the `select` clause will be read into. The program variables should be listed in the same order as the items in the `select` clause. You do not need to use an `into` clause if the `into` clause was included as part of your `select` statement (in which case it could only return a maximum of one row).

Unlike the `open` statement, the `foreach` statement does not give you a way of substituting program variables for question marks (?) that were part of a prepared SQL statement. This means that you may not use question marks as value placeholders in your `select` statement if you plan to use the `foreach` statement.

The `foreach` loop may contain any 4GL statements, plus the `continue foreach` and `exit foreach` statements. `Continue foreach` returns program control to the top of the `foreach` statement. The `exit foreach` statement exits the `foreach` statement and continues the program with the statement following `end foreach`.

Example:

```
define p_toy_store record            like toy_store.*

declare toy_store_cursor cursor for
   select *
      from toy_store
      order by store_name

foreach toy_store_cursor into p_toy_store.*
   call Process_Store_Orders (p_toy_store.*)
end foreach
```

open

The `open` statement opens a `select` or `insert` cursor, prepares the `select` statement for fetches, and prepares the `insert` statement for puts.

```
open <cursorname>
   [ using <program variable> [, ...] ]
```

If you prepared a `select` statement and you used question marks (?) as place holders for program variable values, you must use the `using` clause to specify which values to use to replace the question marks. The program variables should be specified in the order of the question marks they are replacing in the prepared statement. If you are using an `insert` cursor, you cannot use the `using` statement in the `open` statement, instead you must use the `from` clause in the `put` statement. (The `put` statement is described later in this chapter.)

The next section describes the `fetch` statement, that actually fetches the data from an opened `select` cursor. The relationship between the `open` and `fetch` statements is rather complex and deserves a few words of explanation at this point. When the `open` statement is run, it prepares the `select` statement (if it was not already explicitly prepared) and determines the search criteria to be used when the `select` statement is run. This means that any program variables in the `using` clause are evaluated at this time.

However, this is a little confusing because the `fetch` statement actually goes out and fetches the information one record at a time. If a change to the data is made before the data is fetched, including the addition or deletion of rows, the changes in the data will be fetched. The isolation mode you are using will affect whether another user could be making changes to your data set (see Chapter 20 for a discussion of isolation levels). If a change to the data is made after a row has been fetched, this information will not be reflected in the `fetch` statement. This is based on the first time a row is fetched. If you do a `fetch next` followed by a `fetch previous`, you will always see the information that was originally fetched — even if you or someone else has changed or deleted it or added a new record.

This means that once the data has been fetched, the list of information returned by any successive `fetch` statements will not change (unless you re-select the data). By the same token, if you assume that the list is static at the time you open the cursor, and in the process of fetching new rows you also happen to add new rows that meet the conditions of your `where` clause, there is a good chance that these new rows will also be fetched and you could end up in an infinite loop!

If the cursor is already open when you try to open it, the open statement will close the cursor and reopen it for you (except in mode ANSI where you would get an error).

Refer to the previous section on declaring a cursor for additional information on opening cursors declared for update. Also refer to the "where current of" section for information on use of the cursor_name() function in resolving cursor name mangling.

Examples:

```
define start_date, end_date    date
define p_order_date            like toy_order.order_date
define p_sales_code            like toy_order.sales_code
define sqlstmt1                char (200)
...
declare toy_ord1_cursor cursor for
  select * from toy_order
       where date (shipping_datetime)
                              between start_date and end_date
open toy_ord1_cursor
   ...
let sqlstmt1 =  "select order_number, store_number ",
                  "from toy_order ",
                   "where order_date >= ? and ",
                        "sales_code = ? "

prepare statement2 from sqlstmt1
declare toy_ord2_cursor scroll cursor with hold
  for statement2
open toy_ord2_cursor using p_order_date, p_sales_code
...
prepare statement3 from sqlstmt1
declare toy_ord3_cursor cursor for statement3 for update
begin work {only if non-mode ANSI using transaction logging}
open toy_ord3_cursor using p_order_date, p_sales_code
...
commit work  { only if using transaction logging }
...
let insert_stmt =
  "insert into state (state_code, state_name) ",
    "values (?, ?)"
```

```
prepare statement for from insert_stmt
declare insert_cursor cursor for statement4
open state1_cursor
```

fetch

The `fetch` statement allows you to fetch information from a `select` cursor and store the fetched data for the row in program variables.

```
fetch [ next | previous | prior |
        first | last | current |
        relative <relative row number> |
        absolute <absolute row number>
      ]
      <cursor name>
      [ into <program variable> [, ...] ]
```

If you do not specify a cursor position to fetch, the `fetch` statement will always retrieve the next item in the list.

If you are using a `scroll` cursor, you may use any of the positioning statements described here to fetch desired information. If you are not using a `scroll` cursor, you may only fetch the next row.

next	Position the cursor on the next row of the active list.
previous	Position the cursor on the previous row of the active list.
prior	Same as `previous`.
first	Position the cursor on the first row of the active list.
last	Position the cursor on the last row of the active list.
current	Position the cursor on the current row of the active list.
relative <x>	Position the cursor on current position + x rows of the active list. x may be a negative number.
absolute <x>	Position the cursor on row x of the active list.

The into clause specifies the program variable(s) the items in the select clause of the select statement will be read into. The program variables should be listed in the same order as the items in the select clause. You do not need to use an into clause if the into clause was included as part of your select statement (in which case it could only return a maximum of one row).

Examples:

```
define p_toy_store record            like toy_store.*

declare toy_store_cursor cursor for
    select *
      from toy_store
      order by store_name

open toy_store_cursor
fetch toy_store_cursor into p_toy_store.*

declare toy_store2_cursor scroll cursor for
    select *
      from toy_store
      order by store_name

open toy_store_cursor
fetch first      toy_store_cursor into p_toy_store.*
...
fetch next       toy_store_cursor into p_toy_store.*
...
fetch last       toy_store_cursor into p_toy_store.*
...
fetch previous toy_store_cursor into p_toy_store.*
```

where current of

If you are using an `update` cursor, you may perform updates and deletes based upon the current row that is being processed. The `where` clause in an `update` or `delete` statement may be substituted for:

```
where current of <cursor name>
```

Examples:

```
update toy_order
    set shipping_datetime = p_new_datetime
    where current of toy_ord1_cursor

delete from toy_order
    where current of toy_ord1_cursor
```

The function `cursor_name()` is available in more recent versions of INFORMIX-4GL to help resolve cursor name mangling in the following situation:

```
declare sel_cursor cursor for
    select * from toy_order for update
prepare upd_cursor from
    "update toy_order set shipping_datetime = ? ",
        "where current of sel_cursor"
```

This cannot work properly since `sel_cursor` is embedded in a string in the `update` statement and cannot be translated in the same way as the `sel_cursor` in the `declare` statement will be in order for it to be used. To resolve this problem, you need to use the `cursor_name()` function to make the translation as follows:

```
declare sel_cursor cursor for
    select * from toy_order for update
let upd_string =
    "update toy_order set shipping_datetime = ? ",
    "where current of ", cursor_name ("sel_cursor")
prepare upd_cursor from upd_string
```

The where current of clause is generally referred to as having a performance advantage over a regular where clause. However, in addition to the numerous rules and restrictions involved when using the where current of clause, this clause is also susceptible to the type of problem described above. Also, keep in mind that if another user updates the row since you fetched the row, your where current of clause will re-update the row based on the data you originally fetched. Refer to the the declare section earlier in this chapter for information on restrictions when using update cursors. It is usually not worth the problems and bother to use the where current of clause.

put

The put statement is used with an insert cursor to put information into an insert buffer that will later be inserted into the database.

```
put <cursor name>
   [ from <program variable> [, ...] ]
```

If you prepared the insert statement and you used question marks (?) as place holders for program variable values, you must use the from clause to specify which values to insert. The program variables should be specified in the order of the question marks they are replacing in the prepared statement.

See the next section on flushing the insert buffer for details on how the buffering works.

Examples:

```
put toy_insert_cursor
put toy_insert_cursor
    from p_toy.toy_code, p_toy.description
```

flush

You may explicitly flush the buffer used for an insert cursor by using the flush statement.

```
flush <cursor name>
```

If the values being inserted into an insert statement are constants, no buffering occurs and all rows are immediately inserted into the database.

If you use program variables to insert information into the database, the rows to be inserted are stored in a buffer until the buffer is full. When the buffer is full, the rows are automatically flushed, that is, inserted into the database. If you wish to make certain that rows are written to the database immediately whether or not the buffer is full, use the flush statement.

Keep in mind that the close statement will flush any remaining records in the buffer into the database. The flush must be successful or the records may not get written to the database. Remember to check your error flag (status or sqlca.sqlcode) for a negative status.

Example:

```
flush toy_insert_cursor
if sqlca.sqlcode < 0   then
   error "Flush of insert buffer failed."
   { Take some corrective action }
end if
```

close

When you are finished with a cursor for a select or insert statement, you should close it. The syntax for this is very simple:

```
close <cursor name>
```

If the cursor is an `insert` cursor, the buffer will be flushed and any rows will be written to the database before the cursor is closed. If an error occurs when flushing the information before the close, global error variables will be set (`status` and `sqlca.sqlcode`) and the cursor will not be closed. If the cursor is not closed or flushed, any remaining rows in the buffer will be lost.

You cannot use the cursor again after a `close` cursor statement until you reopen the cursor.

Example: `close toy_ord1_cursor`

free

The `free` statement will free the system resources that were allocated for an SQL statement that was either prepared or declared and then closed.

```
free   { <statement identifier from the prepare statement> |
         <cursor name>
       }
```

If you used a `prepare` statement for this cursor, use the statement identifier associated with the `prepare` statement with the `free` statement. Note that in INFORMIX-4GL version 6 and up, you need to free both the statement and the cursor. Prior to this you only need to free one, which automatically frees the other.

If you did not use a `prepare` statement, use the cursor name you used when you declared the cursor.

You cannot use the cursor again after a `free` cursor statement until you `prepare` and reopen the cursor.

Examples:

```
free statement1
free toy_ord1_cursor
```

Summary

When using direct SQL in 4GL, the syntax is very simple. The SQL statement is entered into your program, just as you would enter it into DB-Access, but with a few exceptions.

If you are running a `select` statement, the `select` clause needs to be followed by an `into` clause. You may use program variables as values in an SQL statement. If you have a column name and a program variable with the same name, put an at sign (@) immediately in front of the column name.

To execute an SQL statement not recognized by 4GL, use the following statements:

```
prepare <statement identifier>
  from <character variable or string>


execute <statement identifier from a prepare statement>
  [ using <program variable> [, ...] ]
```

To execute an SQL `select` statement use the following sequence of statements:

```
prepare <statement identifier>  { optional }
  from <character variable or string>

declare <cursor name> [ scroll ] cursor [ with hold ] for
  { <select statement>
[ for update [ of <column name> [, ...] ] ]            |
      <insert statement>                               |
      <statement identifier from a prepare statement>
  }
```

Then use either `foreach` or `open` and `fetch`:

```
foreach <cursor name>
  [ using <program variable> [, ...] ]
  [ into <program variable> [, ...] ]
  { <any 4GL statement> |
    continue foreach   |
    exit foreach
  } [, ...]
```

```
end foreach

open <cursor name> [ using <program variable> [, ...] ]

fetch [ next | previous | prior | first | last | current |
        relative <relative row number> |
        absolute <absolute row number>
      ]
  <cursor name>
  [ into <program variable> [, ...] ]
```

If you are using a for update cursor, you may update or delete the current row by substituting the following where clause for the where clause in your update or delete statement:

```
where current of <cursor name>
```

The function cursor_name() is used to help resolve cursor name mangling

To execute an insert statement with a cursor, use the following sequence of statements:

```
prepare <statement identifier>  { optional }
  from <character variable or string>

declare <cursor name> [ scroll ] cursor [ with hold ] for
  { <select statement>
        [ for update [ of <column name> [, ...] ] ]   |
      <insert statement>            |
      <statement identifier from a prepare statement>
  }

open <cursor name> [ using <program variable> [, ...] ]

put <cursor name> [ from <program variable> [, ...] ]

flush <cursor name>
```

When you are done with a prepared statement or a cursor, remember to close it and to free the system resources:

```
close <cursor name>

free { <statement identifier from the prepare statement> |
    <cursor name>
  }
```

Chapter

20

More Sophisticated SQL

- *Views*
- *Synonyms*
- *Expressions*
- *Built-in functions*
- *Aggregates*
- *Subqueries*
- *Self-Joins*
- *Query optimization*
- *INFORMIX-OnLine topics*
- *Summary*

Views

A *view* is a way of looking at all or part of the data in a single table or in a set of tables. A view is treated like a table in many of Informix's SQL statements.

The syntax for creating a view is:

```
create view <view name>
[ ( <new column name> [, ...] ) ]
as <select statement>
[ with check option ]
```

The `select` statement used to define a view has some limitations; it cannot contain: a `union`, an `order by` clause, an `into temp` clause, or *display labels* in the `select` clause. A `select` statement may select information from a view in the same way information is selected from a table. A view may be defined on top of another view, that is, one view may rely on the existence of another view. An example of a simple view is:

```
create view undelivered as
   select order_number, store_number, order_date,
          shipping_datetime, sales_code
      from toy_order
      where shipping_datetime is null
```

This view will create a pseudo table called undelivered that will include any toy orders that have not yet been shipped.

When a view is accessed by a statement (after it has been created), it is treated as a table. The `select` statement which defines the view is run to retrieve the most current information for the view. The only discrepancy is when an asterisk "*" is used in the `select` statement that defines the view—the "*" is interpreted as column names at the time the view is created. If the structure of an underlying table is altered to add or delete columns after the view has been created, any added columns will not be in the view and any deleted columns will cause an error to be returned.

You must explicitly grant privileges to users to allow them to access a view. No default privileges are given to a view, even if the user already has privileges on the underlying tables of the view. This allows you to have different privileges on views than on tables and it resolves any discrepancies that could otherwise occur when tables with different privileges are contained within the same view.

Be careful when defining views on top of other views: You may find this has serious performance implications depending on the complexity of the underlying view(s).

Since you cannot use display labels in the `select` clause, you may rename columns for the view by listing the name of each column in parentheses and separated by commas after the view name has been specified.

```
create view undelivered_toys
    order_number, order_date, toy_code, quantity, total_price)
  as select toy_order.order_number, order_date, toy_code,
          quantity, (quantity * unit_price)
      from toy_order, toy_order_item
      where shipping_datetime is null and
            toy_order.order_number = toy_order_item.order_number
```

Using multiple tables to define a view is a way of giving users access to specific information in prejoined tables without them having to connect the tables.

The `with check option` forces any updates made through the view to meet the definition of the view. In the example that follows, we could not insert or update information into the view unless the shipping_datetime is null.

```
create view undelivered as
  select order_number, store_number, order_date,
        shipping_datetime, sales_code
    from toy_order
    where shipping_datetime is null
  with check option
```

When information is added, changed, or deleted through a view, it is the information in the underlying table that comprises the view that is changed. There are several restrictions on being allowed to update a table through a view. The view must be based on only one table, the `select` statement may not contain aggregate functions or a `group by`, the `select` clause cannot contain the keywords `unique` or `distinct`, and the `select` clause cannot contain columns that contain functions or expressions. Additionally, the person creating the view must have update privileges on the underlying table and must have granted update privileges (`insert`, `delete`, and/or `update`) to those trying to use the view.

The following syntax will drop a view:

```
drop view <view name>
```

Example: `drop view undelivered`

Views may be used in place of table or synonym names in the following statements:

```
create schema          grant            revoke
create synonym         insert into      select
delete from            load             update
```

Synonyms

A synonym is simply a way of giving a table another name that may be used in place of the table name in many statements. This is particularly useful when using INFORMIX-OnLine and referring to tables in other databases in the same INFORMIX-OnLine system, or when using networking and referring to tables on other machines or in different INFORMIX-OnLine systems.

The syntax for creating a synonym is:

```
create [ public | private ]
    synonym [<owner name>.]<synonym name>
    for <table name>
```

A `public` `synonym` is one that can be accessed by all users who have the privileges necessary to access the underlying table. If a synonym is `private`, you must also use the *owner name* of the synonym to refer to the synonym: *<owner name>.<synonym name>*. Any combination of owner name and synonym name is considered to be a unique synonym. If you own a `private` synonym that has the same name as a public synonym, the private synonym is referred to if you do not include the synonym *owner name*.

All synonyms are public by default unless you are using an ANSI standard database in which all synonyms are private.

For example, suppose you want to give the toy table the synonym play_things:

```
create synonym play_things for toy
```

If you are using INFORMIX-OnLine, you may use the syntax *<database name>*:*<table name>* to refer to a table in another database in the same INFORMIX-OnLine system. A synonym is useful if you do not want to be required to specify the database name each time. For example:

```
create synonym toy_store for toymaker:toy_store
```

The following syntax describes how to drop a synonym:

```
drop synonym [<owner name>.<synonym name>]
```

Example: drop synonym toy_store

Synonyms may be used in place of table names or view names in the following statements:

alter table	drop table	revoke
create audit	drop view	select
create index	grant	unload table
create schema	insert into	update
delete from	load	update statistics
drop audit	lock table	

Expressions

Expressions include functions and mathematical expressions that may be used in Informix's SQL. This section includes information on these expressions, the next section discusses all of Informix's

SQL built-in functions, and the following section discusses Informix's SQL aggregate functions.

Chapter 9 contains detailed information about the results of operations using various data types and operators.

Operators

Mathematical operators:

+	unary plus, e.g., +4
–	unary minus, e.g., –4
+	addition, e.g., 3 + 4
–	subtraction, e.g., 6 – 2
*	multiplication, e.g., 5 * 3
/	division, e.g., 9 / 3

Relational operators:

<	less than
>	greater than
<=	less than or equal to
>=	greater than or equal to
=	equal
<>	not equal
!=	not equal
between	true if value is equal to or between the two values which define the range, e.g., value between low_value and high_value
not between	true if value is not equal to and not between the two values which define the range, e.g., value not between low_value and high_value

Boolean operators:

not	unary, e.g., not true
and	conditional and, e.g., true and true
or	conditional or, e.g., true or false

String operators:

||	concatenation, e.g., "egg" || "head"
like	pattern matching in where clause (see Chapter 6)
matches	pattern matching in where clause (see Chapter 6)

Set operators:

in	true if a value is contained in a set
not in	true if a value is not contained in a set
exists	true if a subquery returns a value (see section on subqueries later in this chapter)
not exists	true if a subquery does not return a value (see section on subqueries later in this chapter)
all	use with a relational operator to check if all values returned by a subquery are true (see section on subqueries later in this chapter)
any	use with a relational operator to check if any values returned by a subquery are true (see section on subqueries later in this chapter)
some	use with a relational operator to see if some (or any) values returned by a subquery are true (see section on subqueries later in this chapter)

Null operators:

is null	check for a null value
is not null	check for a non-null value

Parentheses may be used within an expression to indicate an order of operator precedence or to clarify an expression or to make it easier to read.

General rules of operator precedence apply when using these operators.

For mathematical operators, unary operators have the highest precedence. The binary operators "*" and "/" have the next highest precedence, followed by "+" and "-". Beyond this, the expression is evaluated from left to right.

For Boolean operators, not is evaluated first as a unary operator, then and, and finally or. After this, the expression is evaluated from left to right.

String operators are evaluated from left to right.

Note that the concatenation operator ("||") is not directly available in INFORMIX-4GL.

Columns

When referring to columns in tables, unique column names may be referred to simply by the column name. If the name is not unique, or if desired, the column may be referred to as: *<table name>*.*<column name>* or "*<owner name>*".*<table name>*.*<column name>*. In some cases, a synonym or view name may be substituted for the table name.

The column may be subscripted to access particular characters in the column.

```
<column name> [ <first character position> ,
                <last character position> ]
```

Therefore, if you have a column called candy with the value "chocolate," candy [6,9] is "late."

Literal Constants

Literal values have different formats depending on the type of data with which you are working.

Numeric values are simply numbers. You may specify a decimal point (.).

Character strings are enclosed in either single or double quotes (' or ").

Dates have the format "mm/dd/yy". This value should be in quotes when it is used in this context.

Datetime literals have the format of any or part of the following quoted string:

"yyyy-mm-dd hh:mm:ss.fff".

Year to month literal intervals have the format: interval (*<number>*) year to month or year to year or month to month.

Day to time literal intervals have the format: interval (*<number>*) day to fraction or a format that is structured from any larger unit to any smaller unit in the set day, hour, minute, second, or fraction.

To specify a number of units of time, the format is: *<number>* units *<datetime unit>* where the datetime unit is one of: year, month, day, hour, minute, second, or fraction.

Built-in Functions

In addition to the expressions discussed in the previous section, there are several functions that can be used in Informix's SQL. These are:

abs	dbservername	mod	tan
acos	dbinfo	month	today
asin	exp	pow	trunc
atan	extend	root	units
atan2	hex	round	user
cos	length	rowid	weekday
current	log10	sin	year
date	logn	sitename	
day	mdy	sqrt	

Each of these functions is discussed below. For each function which accepts an argument, if Informix's SQL can convert the argument into the data type needed by the function, that argument can be used. For instance, if a number is required and "3" is passed as a string, Informix's SQL would be able to convert this to a numeric value for use in the function.

Also note that in the examples below, a date format of "mm/dd/yyyy" is assumed.

The cos, sin, tan, acos, asin, atan, atan2, exp, pow, logn, log10, abs, mod, root, and sqrt became available starting with the INFORMIX-OnLine 6.0 engine. Root and pow work with fractional exponents and each take two arguments. You can try these functions on engine versions 5.0 or higher and they might work. Some features are often included in previous versions of Informix products prior to documentation and official release.

abs

The function abs returns the absolute value of the numeric argument.

```
abs ( <number> )
```

acos

The function `acos` returns the arc cosine of the numeric argument.

```
acos ( <number> )
```

asin

The function `asin` returns the arc sine of the numeric argument.

```
asin ( <number> )
```

atan

The function `atan` returns the arc tangent of the numeric argument.

```
atan ( <number> )
```

atan2

The function `atan2` returns the second arc tangent of the numeric argument.

```
atan2 ( <number> )
```

cos

The function `cos` returns the cosine of the numeric argument.

```
cos ( <number> )
```

current

The function `current` returns the current system date and time to the desired precision. If the precision is not specified, the default precision is `year to fraction (3)`.

```
current [ <larger datetime unit> to
   <smaller datetime unit> ]
```

The `datetime` units may be any of the following: `year`, `month`, `day`, `hour`, `minute`, `second`, and `fraction`. These are ordered here from larger units to smaller units.

date

The function `date` takes a `datetime` or a literal string argument and returns the equivalent date value. If the literal string cannot be interpreted as a date, the function will return an error.

```
date ( { <datetime> | <string> } )
```

day

The function `day` returns the day portion of a `date` or `datetime` argument. If "9/3/1997" is passed, the number 3 will be returned.

```
day ( { <date> | <datetime> } )
```

dbinfo

The `dbinfo` function is used to retrieve values from the `sqlca` record structure. Dbinfo can be used anywhere in SQL statements or stored procedures (although it is primarily intended for use with stored procedures—see Chapter 21). Dbinfo was unavailable when stored procedures were first intrduced into Informix products, but the functionality is available with more recent versions of the database engine.

```
dbinfo    ( { 'sqlca.sqlerrd1' |
            'sqlca.sqlerrd2' |
            'sessionid' |
            'DBSPACE', <table space number>
        }
    )
```

The `sqlca.sqlerrd1` option returns the value of the last serial number inserted into a table.

The `sqlca.sqlerrd2` code returns the number of rows processed by the most recent SQL statement (i.e., `select`, `insert`, `update`, `delete` and `execute procedure`).

In INFORMIX-OnLine, the `sessionid` option will return the ID of the current session.

In INFORMIX-OnLine, the `DBSPACE` option will return the name of the dbspace the indicated table is in.

dbservername

The function `dbservername` is an INFORMIX-OnLine function that returns the name of the current instance of INFORMIX-OnLine which you are running, as defined in the tbconfig file pointed to by the `TBCONFIG` environment variable. The function `sitename` is equivalent to `dbservername`.

```
dbservername
```

exp

The function `exp` returns the exponent of the numeric argument.

```
exp ( <number> )
```

extend

The function extend takes a date or a datetime value and returns a datetime value to the indicated precision. If no precision is indicated, the default precision is year to fraction (3).

```
extend ( { <date> | <datetime> }
        [,<larger datetime unit> to
           <smaller datetime unit>]
     )
```

hex

The function hex takes an integer argument and returns the hexadecimal equivalent.

```
hex ( <integer> )
```

length

The function length accepts a string argument and returns its length, not including trailing spaces.

```
length ( <string> )
```

log10

The function log10 returns the log base 10 of the numeric argument.

```
log10 ( <number> )
```

logn

The function `logn` returns the natural log of the numeric argument.

```
logn ( <number> )
```

mdy

The function `mdy` accepts three arguments: the numeric value of a month (1 through 12), the numeric value of the day of the month (1 through 31), and a numeric year. A value of type `date` is returned. If numbers are passed that do not comprise a valid date, an error is returned.

```
mdy ( <month number>, <day number>, <year number> )
```

month

The function `month` returns the month portion of a `date` or `datetime` argument. If "9/3/1997" is passed, the number 9 will be returned.

```
month ( { <date> | <datetime> } )
```

pow

The function `pow` returns the power x^y of the numeric arguments.

```
pow ( <number (base)>, <number (exponent)> )
```

root

The function `root` returns the yth root of x for the numeric arguments.

```
root ( <number>,
       <number (eg. 2 square root, 3 cube root)> )
```

The default of the second argument is 2, that is a square root of the first number is returned.

round

The function `round` accepts a numeric value and returns the number rounded to the indicated precision. The number of *digits of precision* specifies the number of digits to the right of the decimal point. If no precision is specified, the default precision is 0, and the number will be rounded to the nearest whole number. If a negative number is given for precision, this indicates the number of digits to the left of the decimal point.

```
round ( <number> [, <digits of precision> )
```

Some examples are:

Function	Returns
round (347.786)	348
round (347.786,2)	347.79
round (347.786,-2)	300

rowid

The `rowid` is a unique number stored for each row in your database. It should be remembered that if you plan to use `rowid`, that the `rowid`s will change and that this number should not be relied upon. The `rowid` represents the record number of a row. If one row is deleted and another added, these rows may have the same `rowid` number. If you change information in a row based on the `rowid` number, you may end up updating the wrong record. You should be warned that versions 6 and beyond of the engine handle `rowid` differently, and at some point it may be completely phased out. It is included here for completeness, but I do not recommend its use.

No arguments are passed to `rowid`:

```
rowid
```

sin

The function `sin` returns the sine of the numeric argument.

```
sin ( <number> )
```

sitename

The function `sitename` is an INFORMIX-OnLine function that returns the name of the current instance of INFORMIX-OnLine that you are running as defined in the tbconfig file pointed to by the `TBCONFIG` environment variable. The function `dbserver-name` is equivalent to `sitename`.

```
sitename
```

sqrt

The function `sqrt` returns the square root of the numeric argument.

```
sqrt ( <number> )
```

tan

The function `tan` returns the tangent of the numeric argument.

```
tan ( <number> )
```

today

The function `today` returns the current system date.

```
today
```

trunc

The function `trunc` accepts a numeric value and returns the number truncated to the indicated precision. The number of *digits of precision* specifies the number of digits to the right of the decimal point. If no precision is specified, the default precision is 0, and the number will be truncated to the nearest whole number. If a negative number is given for precision, this indicates the number of digits to the left of the decimal point.

```
trunc ( <number> [, <digits of precision> )
```

Some examples are:

Function	Returns
trunc (347.786)	347
trunc (347.786,2)	347.78
trunc (347.786,-2)	300

units

The function `units` allows you to specify units of time:

```
<number> units <datetime unit>
```

Any of the `datetime` units may be used: `year`, `month`, `day`, `hour`, `minute`, `second`, or `fraction`.

For example, the following expression specifies 10 days:

```
10 units day
```

user

The function `user` returns username of the user currently logged in.

```
user
```

weekday

The function `weekday` returns a number corresponding to the day of the week of a `date` or `datetime` argument.

```
weekday ( { <date> | <datetime> } )
```

The returned numbers listed below correspond to the listed day of the week:

Numeric Value	Day of Week
0	Sunday
1	Monday
2	Tuesday
3	Wednesday
4	Thursday
5	Friday
6	Saturday

year

The function `year` returns the year portion of a `date` or `date-time` argument. If "9/3/1997" is passed, the number 1997 will be returned.

```
year ( { <date> | <datetime> } )
```

Aggregates

An *aggregate* is a function that can be used in a `select` statement to retrieve information about groups of data. It is most frequently used with the `group by` clause and may also be used with the `having` clause, both described in the previous chapter.

Aggregates available for use with Informix's SQL are `avg`, `count`, `max`, `min`, and `sum`. Aggregates were discussed briefly in Chapter 6 under the discussion of the `group by` clause and the `having` clause.

The syntax for each aggregate function is described below. Following the syntax descriptions are notes and examples on how to use aggregate functions.

avg

Returns an average for the values in the indicated rows.

```
avg { ( { distinct | unique } <column name> |
        [ all ] { <column name> | <expression> }
      )
    }
```

count

Returns the number of items that meet a specified criterion.

```
count { (*) |
          count
               ( { distinct | unique } <column name> )
        }
```

max

Returns the largest value in the indicated rows.

```
max { ( { distinct | unique } <column name> |
          [ all ] { <column name> | <expression> }
        )
     }
```

min

Returns the smallest value in the indicated rows.

```
min { ( { distinct | unique } <column name> |
          [ all ] { <column name> | <expression> }
        )
     }
```

sum

Returns the total of the values in the indicated rows.

```
sum { ( { distinct | unique } <column name> |
          [ all ] { <column name> | <expression> }
        )
     }
```

Using Aggregate Functions

Aggregate functions may only be used in the `select` clause or in the `having` clause of the `select` statement. Whenever an aggregate function is used, all items in the `select` clause (except for any aggregates) must also be in the `group by` clause.

The `group by` clause in the `select` statement treats each complete set of information in the `group by` statement as a row of output. An aggregate will be related to the information in a row.

The `count (*)` notation counts the number of items that make up a row.

```
select store_name, count (*)
  from toy_order, toy_store
  where toy_order.store_number =
        toy_store.store_number
  group by store_name
  order by store_name
```

The `select` statement above will count the number of orders each store has placed with the toymaker and output this list alphabetically by store_name.

`Unique` and `distinct` are synonyms. You may use either word. When either of these keywords are used, the aggregate calculated is only for those values that are unique for that aggregate. Therefore, if the column my_numbers has the values 1, 3, 3, and 5 for a given aggregate, the only numbers used to calculate the aggregate will be 1, 3, and 5.

```
select description, sales_price,
        avg (distinct unit_price) average_price,
        min (distinct unit_price) minimum_price,
        max (distinct unit price) maximum_price
  from toy_order_item, toy
  where toy_order_item.toy_code = toy.toy_code
  group by description, sales_price
  order by description
```

The above `select` statement creates an alphabetical list of toys, the normal sales_price for each toy, and the average, minimum, and maximum of the prices each toy was sold for. This gives us a quick way of making certain reasonable prices are being charged for the toys.

Aggregates may be calculated for expressions and for individual columns.

```
select toy.description, count (*),
        sum (toy_order_item.quantity *
        toy_order_item.unit_price)
    from toy, outer toy_order_item
    where toy.toy_code = toy_order_item.toy_code
    group by toy.toy_code, description
    order by description
```

The above `select` statement will create a list of all toys listed alphabetically with the number sold and the sum of the gross revenue for each type of toy.

Subqueries

A *subquery* is a `select` statement that is executed as part of another SQL statement. Subqueries may be used with `select`, `insert`, `update`, and `delete` statements.

Using a subquery with a `select` statement allows you additional flexibility in performing queries.

There are several operators that can be used with subqueries. These include relational operators as well as `in`, `not in`, `exists`, and `not exists`, and relational operators used with `all`, `any`, and `some`.

Subqueries with Relational Operators

If a subquery returns a single row and a single value, you can use a relational operator to compare the value returned from the subquery as though it were an expression or column.

```
select *
    from toy_order_item
    where toy_code = (select toy_code from toy
                        where description = "JUMP ROPE")
```

This could also be expressed as:

```
select toy_order_item.*
   from toy_order_item, toy
   where toy.description = "JUMP ROPE" and
          toy_order_item.toy_code = toy.toy_code
```

When using a `select` statement you will frequently have the option of using a subquery or performing a join. For performance reasons you will usually want to use the join. However, there are many cases in which you will not have the option of a join, for instance, when using `insert`, `update`, and `delete` statements. The subquery becomes indispensable when working with these statements.

If a subquery returns a single value in one or more rows, you can use a relational operator to compare each value returned from the subquery.

```
select *, (quantity * unit_price) total_price
   from toy_order, toy_order_item
   where (quantity * unit_price) >
          (select avg (quantity * unit_price)
            from toy_order_item) and
         toy_order.order_number = toy_order_item.order_number
```

This `select` statement will return toy_order and toy_order_item information for every toy_order_item whose total price is greater than the average total price per line item.

in and not in

We have already used the `in` and `not in` keywords to find out whether a value is (or is not) contained in a set of values. We are doing exactly the same thing when using `in` and `not in` with a subquery, except that the set of information the value is compared with is the list of values returned by the subquery.

```
select * from toy
   where toy_code not in (select unique toy_code
                            from toy_order_item)
```

The above `select` statement will retrieve information about all toys for which there are no orders. Each toy in the toy table is checked against the values returned from the subquery. The subquery returns a list of toy_codes that have been ordered.

The subquery will be executed for each row in the toy table. It will often improve performance to run the subquery once, save it in a `temp` table, then use the `temp` table in your subquery. This is especially true if your subquery is long or complex.

```
select unique toy_code
   from toy_order_item
   into temp a1 with no log;

select * from toy
   where toy_code not in (select toy_code from a1);
```

In the above example, the elimination of duplicate items from the list of toy_codes will only need to be performed once with the use of the `temp` table, instead of for each comparison with the column toy_code.

exists **and** not exists

The `exists` and `not exists` operators are used exclusively with subqueries to determine whether any rows are returned from a subquery.

```
select order_number
   from toy_order
   where exists
         (select * from toy_store
            where toy_store.store_state = "NM" and
                  toy_store.store_number = toy_order.store_number)
```

The above `select` statement will return all order numbers that were ordered from stores located in New Mexico. Notice that the subquery uses a join with the table from the primary query.

Although most `select` *statements can use a join instead of a subquery, you will usually want to try running a subquery you plan to use in an* `insert`, `update`, *or* `delete` *statement with a* `select` *statement first to make certain your subquery returns the intended values.*

all, any, and some

The all, any, and some keywords are used with relational operators to determine if all values returned from a subquery meet a condition, or to determine if any or some values returned from a
subquery meet a condition. Any and some have the same meaning.

```
select *
  from toy_order_item
  where unit_price < any (select cost from toy
                              where sales_price < 10)
```

This select statement will select any toy_order_items whose
selling unit_price is less than the cost of the most expensive toy
which sells for less than $10.

```
select *
  from toy_order_item
  where unit_price < all (select cost from toy
                              where sales_price < 10)
```

Changing any to all brings back a list of toy_order_items
whose selling unit_price is less than the cost of all items whose
sales price is less than $10 (ie. whose unit_price is less than the
minimum cost toy).

When using any or some, if the subquery does not return any
values, the comparison condition result is false. When using all,
if the subquery does not return any values, the comparison condition result is true.

insert

Using a subquery with an insert statement allows you to select
values for insertion into a table.

```
insert into new_toy_table
  select * from toy
    where quantity > 100
```

This will select every row in the toy table where the quantity is
greater than 100 as with toys to be inserted into the
new_toy_table.

update

Using a subquery with an `update` statement allows you to update information in one table based upon information in another table. This can occur in the `set` clause or the `where` clause of the `update` statement:

```
update toy set sales_price =
    (select max (unit_price) from toy_order_item
        where toy_order_item.toy_code = toy.toy_code)

update toy set sales_price = 10
    where toy_code in (select unique toy_code from toy_order_item
                            where unit_price between 6 and 8)
```

The first `update` sets the sales_price equal to the maximum unit_price charged for a toy in the toy_order_item table. The second `update` sets the sales_price to $10 if any unit_price of a toy sold was between $6 and $8 dollars.

delete

Using a subquery with a `delete` statement allows you to delete information in one table based upon information in another table. This subquery would be issued as part of the `where` clause as in the `select` or the `update` statement.

```
delete from toy_order_item
    where unit_price <
(select cost from toy
        where toy.toy_code = toy_order_item.toy_code)
```

Self-Joins

A *self-join* allows you to compare values in different rows of the same table with each other. This is very simple once you realize that all you need to do is treat a single table as two different tables. You only need to list the table name twice in the `from` clause, and then use *display labels* to rename the tables for the duration of the `select` statement.

Suppose we wanted to go through the toy table to find out how many toy sales prices are not within $1 of each other. The following statement allows us to do this:

```
select a.description, a.sales_price, b.sales_price
  from toy a, toy b
  where a.sales_price not between (b.sales_price - 1) and
                                  (b.sales_price + 1)
  order by a.description
```

Query Optimization

Set explain on

The set explain statement may be turned on or off.

```
set explain { on | off }
```

When set explain is turned on, the file sqexplain.out is created (or appended to) in the current directory. For every statement executed, information will be written to this file that will help you determine how the engine is interpreting and running each statement.

You will be able to see which parts of the query are being run first, whether the indexes are being used to access information, and other similar information.

Temp Tables

The more tables involved in a single query, the longer the query will take to run. Temp tables are a good way of dividing queries into parts because they allow you to save the results in a table, then reuse them in another query.

A good rule of thumb when dividing a query is to run the parts of the query first that will most reduce the number of rows with which you are working. This will save you both temporary storage space and time. The fewer the number of rows, the more quickly they can be processed.

Also, don't forget to use the `with no log` clause when creating `temp` tables. This will save you additional time.

or **versus** union

Many queries that use an `or` condition (as opposed to an `and` condition) can be extremely inefficient in the Informix database engine. While future releases of the engine may change this, currently it is often much faster to write the query as two separate queries, then merge the result using a `union` of the two `select` statements.

Indexes

Remember that you can add a new index at any point where you find that you have a need for faster retrievals of information. The disadvantages of adding additional indexes is that `insert`, `update`, and `delete` statements will be slower and the index will use additional disk space.

The fewer duplicate values in the index, the more efficient it will be. You may find that an index you have created is on a very common value and this is making your database less efficient (in some cases the performance hit will be drastic). If this occurs, you can drop this index and create a *composite index* on your duplicate value and a unique value to improve database efficiency. Although you will use more disk space by making a larger index, the trade-off of improved performance should be worthwhile.

Forcing Use of Indexes

If you have an appropriate index for your search, have a look at the `set explain` output and make certain that your index is being used. If it isn't, there are a couple of things you can try.

First, try adjusting the optimization level.

```
set optimization [ high | low ]
```

The default optimization level is `high`. The high level examines more optimization options than the lower level of optimization, but you could find that for a particular situation, `low` will work better.

Adding to your `where` clause can also sometimes force an index to be used. For instance, suppose we have the query:

```
select *
  from toy_order, toy_store
  where toy_store.store_name = "DON'S TOY DUNGEON" and
        toy_order.store_number = toy_store.store_number
```

If this query were running slowly, we would turn `set explain` on and have a look at the output in the `sqexplain.out` file. If it turned out that the index on store_name wasn't being used, we might add the following to the `where` clause to try to force the use of the index:

```
select *
  from toy_order, toy_store
  where toy_store.store_name >= "A" and
        toy_store.store_name = "DON'S TOY DUNGEON" and
        toy_order.store_number = toy_store.store_number
```

The use of the greater than operator may force the use of the index. Trying various combinations of key fields and relational operators may help you find a solution to your problem.

Ultimately, you cannot force the optimizer to use an index, but these factors can help change if and which index is used.

Pattern Matching and Substrings

Using `like` and `matches` requires more overhead than using relational operators. If you have an option, use a substring or some other method of getting the same result.

```
select * from toy where store_name matches "DON*"

select * from toy where store_name [1,3] = "DON"
```

Of the two `select` statements above, the second one, using a substring instead of a `matches`, will be more efficient (at least under the current version of the optimizer).

If the store_name has an index on it, trying to use a substring that does not start at the beginning of the name is less efficient than using a substring that does start at the beginning of the string.

```
select * from toy where store_name [7,9] = "TOY"

select * from toy where store_name [1,3] = "DON" and
                        store_name [7,9] = "TOY"
```

That is not to say you should never use pattern matching capabilities because they can be extremely useful. However, if a more efficient solution exists, you should be aware of it.

Subqueries

Avoid the use of correlated subqueries when possible. A correlated subquery refers to values from the containing query inside of the subquery. A correlated subquery is evaluated for each comparison made. The performance cost of correlated subqueries can be very expensive.

You may be able to use a join instead of a subquery.

You may be able to reduce the overhead of the subquery by saving the results of a query in a temporary table, then using the temporary table in your subquery.

INFORMIX-OnLine Topics

This section discusses topics available to INFORMIX-OnLine users. These are:

- Accessing tables in other databases in the same INFORMIX-OnLine system, and
- Isolation levels

Accessing tables in other databases in different INFORMIX-OnLine systems is a networking topic, and is beyond the scope of this book.

Accessing Tables in Other Databases on the Same INFORMIX-OnLine System

To access a table in another database on the same INFORMIX-OnLine system, you will need to use the same level of logging in both databases. Once you are setup, the syntax is very simple:

```
<database name>:<table name>
```

If you are working in the widget database, and you want to access the toy table in the toymaker database, you could type:

```
select * from toymaker:toy
```

You can join this table with any table in the widget database and treat it like any other table.

You could also create a synonym for `toymaker:toy` in the widget database, as described earlier in this chapter.

Isolation levels

Isolation levels allow you to define how you want to handle information when two or more users are accessing it at the same time.

```
set isolation to { dirty read        |
                   committed read     |
                   cursor stability |
                   repeatable read
                 }
```

An `isolation level` is set for a single program. The four isolation levels are described briefly here. Going from `dirty read` to `repeatable read`, it becomes increasingly difficult to access and change data, however you do get better and better guarantees that the data you inspect will not change.

Isolation Levels

Isolation Level	Description
dirty read	This isolation level will allow access to any row at any time. This includes rows that have not yet been committed to the database and could later be rolled back. This is the isolation level used if you do not use transaction logging.
committed read	This isolation level will allow you to access only information which has been committed to the database and can no longer be rolled back. This level does not lock data, therefore data may be added, changed, or deleted by a user while another user is accessing the data. This is the default isolation level used for non-ANSI databases with logging.
cursor stability	This isolation level allows two users to view the same row of data; each user will have a shared lock on the data, but as long as more than one user is accessing the data, neither will be able to change or delete that row of data.
repeatable read	This isolation level creates shared locks for every row selected for the duration of a transaction. This allows other users to view this data, but not to change it. It is called repeatable read because if you reread the information within the same transaction, you will be reading the same data since no one else can modify it. This is the default isolation level in an ANSI database.

Updates and deletes always require an exclusive lock on data, regardless of the isolation level.

Summary

A `view` is a way of looking at all or part of the data in a single table or in a set of tables. A `view` is treated like a table in many of Informix's SQL statements.

```
create view <view name>
    [ ( <new column name> [, ...] ) ] as <select statement>
    [ with check option ]

drop view <view name>
```

A `synonym` is a name given to a table that may be used in place of the *table name* in many statements.

```
create [ public | private ]
    synonym [<owner name>.]<synonym name>
    for <table name>

drop synonym [<owner name>.<synonym name>]
```

Mathematical operators are: unary +, unary −, +, −, *, / .
Relational operators are: <, >, <=, >=, =, <>,!= .
Boolean operators are: not, and, or .
String operators are: ||, like, matches .
Set operators are in, not in, exists, not exists, all, any, some .
Null operators are is null, is not null .

To access a substring, use the syntax:

```
<column name> [ <first character position> ,
                    <last character position> ]
```

There are several functions which can be used in Informix's SQL. These are:

```
abs ( <number> )

acos ( <number> )

asin ( <number> )
```

```
atan ( <number> )

atan2 ( <number> )

cos ( <number> )

current [ <larger datetime unit> to <smaller datetime unit> ]

date ( { <datetime> | <string> } )

day ( { <date> | <datetime> } )

dbinfo ( { 'sqlca.sqlerrd1' |
            'sqlca.sqlerrd2' |
            'sessionid' |
            'DBSPACE', <table space number>
          }
        )

dbservername

exp ( <number> )

extend ( { <date> | <datetime> }
          [,<larger datetime unit> to <smaller datetime unit>]
        )

hex ( <integer> )

length ( <string> )

log10 ( <number> )

logn ( <number> )

mdy ( <month number>, <day number>, <year number> )

month ( { <date> | <datetime> } )

pow ( <number (base)>, <number (exponent)> )

root ( <number>,
        <number (eg. 2 square root, 3 cube root)> )
```

```
round ( <number> [, <digits of precision> )

rowid

sin ( <number> )

sitename

sqrt ( <number> )

tan ( <number> )

today

trunc ( <number> [, <digits of precision> )

<number> units <datetime unit>

user

weekday ( { <date> | <datetime> } )

year ( { <date> | <datetime> } )
```

An *aggregate* is a function that can be used in a `select` statement to retrieve information about groups of data. Aggregate functions available for use with Informix's SQL are:

```
avg { ( { distinct | unique } <column name> |
       [ all ] { <column name> | <expression> }
     )
   }

count { (*) |
       count ( { distinct | unique } <column name> )
     }

max { ( { distinct | unique } <column name> |
       [ all ] { <column name> | <expression> }
     )
   }
```

```
min { ( { distinct | unique } <column name> |
          [ all ] { <column name> | <expression> }
      )
    }

sum { ( { distinct | unique } <column name> |
          [ all ] { <column name> | <expression> }
      )
    }
```

A *subquery* is a `select` statement that is executed as part of another SQL statement. Subqueries may be used with `select`, `insert`, `update`, and `delete` statements. Relational operators may be used in addition to `in`, `not in`, `exists`, `not exists`, `all`, `any`, and `some`.

A *self-join* allows you to compare values in different rows of the same table with each other.

The statement `set explain`, when turned on, writes to the `sqexplain.out` file.

```
set explain { on | off }
```

The optimization level can be set with the `set optimization` statement:

```
set optimization [ high | low ]
```

To access a table in another database in the same INFORMIX-OnLine system, use the syntax:

```
<database name>:<table name>
```

Isolation levels allow you to define how to handle information if two or more users are accessing it at the same time.

```
set isolation to { dirty read       |
                   committed read   |
                   cursor stability |
                   repeatable read
                 }
```

Stored Procedures and Triggers

- *Stored procedures*
- *Triggers*
- *Summary*

Stored Procedures

Stored procedures allow you to create procedures that are written in a combination of Informix's SQL and SPL (Stored Procedure Language). Stored procedures are stored in a preprocessed and optimized format. SQL statements that you will create and run in DB-Access and INFORMIX-4GL are preprocessed and optimized at runtime. This means stored procedures should run more quickly than SQL statements, which must be optimized at runtime. Keep in mind that while the statements will not need to be optimized at runtime, the stored procedures are stored with the engine. This will cause your database engine to grow slightly as you add stored procedures to your database.

Stored procedures can help you solve database privilege problems. If you create a stored procedure using the keyword dba, this will allow users to execute the stored procedure as if they have dba privileges, as long as they have the necessary privileges to run the stored procedure. This can keep you from having to grant insert, update, and delete access to tables for all database users.

The syntax for creating a stored procedure is as follows:

```
create [ dba ] procedure <procedure name>
  ( [ <variable name>
     { <data type> [ <default value> ] |
       like <table name>.<column name>
                     [ <default value> ] |
       references { byte | text }
                     [ default null ]
     } [, ...]
   ]
  )
  [ returning <data type> [, ...] ; ]
  { <SQL statement> | <SPL statement> } [...]
end procedure
[ document <quoted string> [, ...] ]
[ with listing in
    "<pathname for compile time warnings>" ]
```

An example of a simple stored procedure that returns the user-name of the user currently logged on is:

```
create procedure Get_Username ()
   returning char (15);

   return user;
end procedure

document "This procedure returns the username of
      the current user."

with listing in ""get_username.warn";
```

To run this procedure from DB-Access type:

```
execute procedure Get_Username ();
```

Notice that since `user` is a defined function in SQL, we were able to use it within the stored procedure.

Each SQL statement within the body of a stored procedure needs to end with a semicolon. Some SPL statements are also required to end in a semicolon. For SPL statements that are not required to end in a semicolon, the semicolon may optionally be added.

The `document` clause allows you to document your procedures. The documentation is available in the Informix system table `sysprocbody`. The following query will list each procedure name along with any documentation you have specified:

```
select procname, data
   from sysprocbody, sysprocedures
   where datakey = "D" and
         sysprocbody.procid = sysprocedures.procid
```

The following `select` statement will list (albeit not very neatly) each procedure name and its contents:

```
select procname, data
   from sysprocbody, sysprocedures
   where datakey = "T" and
         sysprocbody.procid = sysprocedures.procid
```

The `with listing in` clause allows you to specify a file in which any compile-time warnings generated by a `create procedure` statement are stored. Any errors will cause the `create procedure` statement to fail, but it is generally worthwhile to have a glance at the warning messages as well.

You should note that the syntax for the `select` statement is extended slightly for stored procedures and for INFORMIX-4GL (for both ANSI and non-ANSI mode). You may use an `into` clause following your `select` clause to specify variables for the items listed in your `select` clause to be read into. The variables in the `into` clause should match the items in the `select` clause in order and in type. When you use a `select...into` statement, your `select` statement can only return a single row.

Example:

```
define p_last_name, p_first_name    char (25)
define owner_name                   char (50)

select    last_name,    first_name
   into p_last_name, p_first_name
   from account
   where account_number = 90887

let owner_name = p_first_name || p_last_name
```

The following is a list followed by an alphabetical summary of the stored procedure language statements that can be used within a stored procedure. Comments in a stored procedure are anything on a line following double dashes (e.g., `--` This is a comment).

begin	if	set debug file
call	let	system
define	on exception	trace
for	raise exception	while
foreach	return	

begin *<SQL and SPL statements>* end

Statements occurring within a `begin` and an `end` constitute a block of statements that are treated as a single statement in the same way as a call to a function is treated as a single statement. You may define variables within a `begin`...`end` block that are valid for only that block.

The syntax for a block is:

```
begin
  { <SQL statement> | <SPL statement> } [...]
end
```

Blocks may be nested within other blocks. A variable declared within a block may be accessed by that block or by any block nested within that block, as long as the same variable name is not also declared locally within a nested block.

Example:
```
begin
   define x, y integer

   let x, y = 1, 2
   begin
      define x char (10)

      let x = "New Value"   -- y still equals 2
   end

   -- x is now 1 again, and y is still 2
end
```

call

`Call` is one of the statements you can use to call a stored procedure from within another stored procedure. You may also use the `let` statement (described below), or you can use the SQL statement `execute procedure`. The syntax when using the `call` statement is:

```
call <procedure name>
( [ [ <parameter name in called procedure> = ]
    { <expression> | <select statement> }
  ] [, ...]
)
[ returning <variable name> [, ...] ]
;
```

Because variables in a called procedure are referenced by name or by position, all variables in a procedure call must be referenced by name or by position, but not by both.

Examples:

```
call Get_Username () returning p_username

call Insert_Name (account_number = 789877,
                  last_name = "Flint",
                  first_name = "Vena")

call Check_Inventory (quantity_ordered,
                        select quantity from toy
                           where toy_code = p_toy_code)
            returning enough
```

Stored procedures may be called recursively.

define

The define statement allows you to define variables for a stored procedure or within a begin...end block of a stored procedure. The define statement must be located at the beginning of a stored procedure or at the beginning of a begin...end block.

```
define { global <variable name> [, ...]
           { <data type> [ default <value> ] |
           references { byte | text }
                                  [ default null ]
       } |
     <variable name> [, ...]
      { <data type> |
        references { byte | text } |
        like <table name>.<column name> |
        procedure
      }
    } ;
```

You may use any of the data types used in SQL except for serial.

A global variable in a stored procedure may be accessed by any other stored procedure called in the same session within the same database. The variable may be declared as global by more than one procedure. Global variables may be assigned default values.

Local variables may only be accessed within the stored procedure or the begin...end block in which they are declared. A begin...end block may use variables declared in the stored procedure the block is contained in, or variables declared in other begin...end blocks in which the block is nested.

BLOB data types are passed by reference. Only the location of the BLOB is passed. Any changes to the BLOB will effect its contents. All other data types are passed by value.

You may use the like syntax to indicate that a variable has the same type as a particular column in a table.

If you have given your stored procedure the same name as an Informix's SQL function, you may declare a variable as type procedure to disable the Informix's SQL function. To avoid confusion, you should give your stored procedures unique names. But, if you do decide to use Informix's SQL function names, note that when specifying stored procedures with the same name as an

aggregate function or named extend, you must qualify the
procedure name with the owner name.

Examples:

```
define global g_order_number        integer;
define x, y                         integer;
define i, j                         smallint;
define last_name                    char (100);
define image                        references byte;
define order_number                 like toy_order.order_number;
define max                          procedure;
```

Note that in the last example, a stored procedure called max is
being defined as type procedure, so when max is used in that
stored procedure, the stored procedure will be called and not the
Informix built-in function.

for

The for statement allows you to include a for loop within a
stored procedure. The body of the for loop is executed once for
each value it processes. The syntax is:

```
for <variable name>
  { = <expression> to <expression>
               [ step <expression> ]          |
    in ( <expression> [ to <expression>
                    [ step <expression> ] ]
          [, ...]
        )
  }
  { <SQL statement> |
    <SPL statement> |
    continue for;   |
    exit for;
  } [...]
end for [ ; ]
```

When a continue for statement is executed, control is
returned to the top of the for loop. When an exit for

statement is executed, the next statement executed will be the statement following the `end for`.

Examples:

```
for counter = 1 to 100 step 2
 ...
end for;

for last_name in ("SMITH", "JONES")
 ...
end for;

for p_number in (1 to x, x + y to 1 step -1, p_num1, p_num2)
 ...
end for;
```

foreach

The `foreach` statement allows you to perform a loop for each value or set of values returned from a `select` statement or a stored procedure.

```
foreach
  { { [ with hold ] |
         <cursor name> [ with hold ] for
    }
    <select statement with into clause> |
    execute procedure <procedure name>
    ( [ <variable name> = ] <expression> [, ...] )
    [ into <variable name> [, ...]
  }
  { <SQL statement> |
    <SPL statement> |
    continue foreach; |
    exit foreach;
  } [...]
end foreach [ ; ]
```

When using a `foreach` loop, you are working with a cursor. The cursor points to the current row of data that has been fetched by the `foreach` statement. If you do not specify a cursor name, you are still working with a cursor, it just won't have a name you will be able to refer to later.

Using a `foreach` statement allows you to return multiple rows from a `select...into` statement or from a stored procedure. For each row returned, the statements within the `foreach` loop are executed. If you are using a `select` statement, the values are returned to the variables specified in the `into` clause of the `select` statement. If you are executing a procedure, any returned values are returned to the variables listed in the `into` clause following the `execute procedure` statement.

The `with hold` clause causes the cursor to remain open after a transaction is completed. This allows you to perform `insert`, `update`, and `delete` statements without closing the cursor. Once the cursor is closed, no more information will be retrieved into your `foreach` loop, and the `foreach` loop will be exited.

If you wish to `update` or `delete` the current row of the table pointed to by your cursor, you may substitute the `where` clause in your `update` or `delete` statement with:

```
where current of <cursor name>
```

When a `continue foreach` statement is executed, control is returned to the top of the `foreach` loop. When an `exit foreach` statement is executed, the next statement executed will be the statement following the `end foreach`.

Examples:

```
foreach select account_number
        into p_account_number
        from account
        where balance_due >= 100
   ...
end foreach;

foreach toy_cursor with hold for select order_number
                                into p_order_number
                                from toy_order
                                where shipping_datetime is null

   ...
```

```
      update toy_order set shipping_datetime = current year to minute
         where current of toy_cursor
   end foreach;

   foreach execute procedure List_Toys ()
         into p_toy_code, p_description
      ...
   end foreach;
```

if

The if statement allows you to execute statements conditionally within a stored procedure.

```
if <Boolean expression> then
  { <SQL statement> | <SPL statement> } [...]
[ elif <Boolean expression> then
  { <SQL statement> | <SPL statement> } [...]
] [...]
[ else
  { <SQL statement> | <SPL statement> } [...]
]
end if [ ; ]
```

The following SQL statements may not be used within an if statement: check table, close database, create database, create procedure, database, info, load, output, repair table, rollforward database, start database, unload. You may only use a select statement within an if clause if it includes an into clause.

Example:

```
if balance_due < 100 then
   ...
elif balance_due < 1000 then
   ...
else  -- balance_due >= 1000
   ...
end if;
```

let

The `let` statement allows you to assign values to variables. The values assigned may be from an expression, returned from a `select` statement, or returned from a stored procedure.

```
let <variable name> [, ...] =
  { <expression> |
    <procedure name>
      ( [ [ <parameter name in called procedure> = ]
            { <expression> | <select statement> }
        ] [, ...]
      )
  };
```

The `let` statement allows you to assign multiple values to multiple variables in a single statement. The rightmost value will be assigned to the righmost variable, and so on, from left to right.

Because variables in a called procedure are referenced by name or by position, all variables in a procedure call must be referenced by name or by position, but not by both.

Example:

```
let a, b, c = 1, 2, 3;
let d, e = a * b, b * c;
let username = user;
let last_name, first_name =
                (select last_name, first_name
                 from account
                 where account_number = p_acct_num);
let min_num, max_num = Get_Min_Max (a, b, c, d, e);
```

on exception

The on exception statement allows you to trap errors that may occur during the execution of a stored procedure. The on exception statement must be located immediately after any define statements in either the stored procedure or in a begin...end block.

The on exception statement is a type of declaration, and as such, is treated in the same way as a defined variable. An on exception statement is valid for the stored procedure, block, or nested block in which it occurs. An on exception statement in a nested block cannot be accessed from an outer block or from the main portion of the stored procedure.

```
on exception
  [ in ( <error number> [, ...] ) ]
  [ set <integer variable for SQL error>
    [ , <integer variable for ISAM error>
      [ , <char variable for error message> ]
    ]
  ]
  { <SQL statement> | <SPL statement> }
end exception [ with resume ] [ ; ]
```

The in clause allows you to specify an on exception statement for only certain error numbers. You may have several on exception statements in a procedure. If the on exception statement does not include an in clause, all errors will be trapped.

The set clause allows you to store the SQL error number, the ISAM error number, and the text of the error message in variables.

You may use the body of the on exception statement to take any desired actions to recover from the error.

The with resume clause will cause the execution of the stored procedure to continue after the statement that caused the error. This gives you the option of completing the stored procedure or of aborting it when an error occurs.

An error caused by statements within an on exception will not call the same on exception statement again.

Examples:

```
on exception in (-213)
   -- Take no action on this error
end exception with resume

on exception
   set error_num
   return error_num
end exception with resume
```

raise exception

The raise exception allows you to pretend that an error occurred during the execution of a stored procedure. With the raise exception statement, you can specify whatever Informix error number you like. You can also define your own error message, error message number -746 is specifically intended for this use.

```
raise exception
   <integer variable for SQL error>
   [ , <integer variable for ISAM error>
     [ , <char variable for error message> ]
   ];
```

Examples:

```
raise exception -746, 0, "You cannot update that value!";

raise exception -746, 0, "Cannot delete a shipped order.";
```

The on exception statement can determine how to handle the errors you generate.

return

The `return` statement allows you to exit a stored procedure and, optionally, to return values from the stored procedure.

```
return [ <expression> [, ...] [ with resume ] ] ;
```

The `return` statement by itself will cause you to exit from a stored procedure.

If your `create procedure` statement specifies a returning clause, you will need to return the indicated values from your stored procedure.

The `with resume` clause allows you to return several sets of returned values. After a set of values is returned and processed, another set of values is generated and returned by the called procedure. This continues until there are no rows left to retrieve. If you are returning information to a `foreach` loop within a stored procedure, each set of values returned will be processed by the `foreach` loop in the calling stored procedure. If you return more than one set of values from a stored procedure called by DB-Access, the information returned will be displayed to the screen.

Examples: `return;`

`return a, b, c;`

`return x, y, z with resume;`

set debug file

The `set debug file` statement is used in conjunction with the `trace` statement. The `trace` statement allows you to write text and program values to a file to help you debug your stored procedure. The `set debug` statement allows you to specify the file to which the `trace` statements are written.

```
set debug file
    { "<file name>"    |
      <variable name> |
      <expression>
    }
    [ with append ];
```

The `with append` clause allows you to append to the debug file if it already exists.

Examples:

```
set debug file "debug.trace";

set debug file p_filename with append;
```

system

The `system` statement allows you to run an operating system command.

```
system { "<character expression>" |
         <character variable name> } ;
```

Examples:

```
system "echo Append this character string " ||
       "expression to a file. >> message.file";

system unix_command;
```

trace

The `trace` statement allows you to write statements to a debug file that will help you debug your stored procedures. You must run the `set debug` statement to specify the file where the debug statements will be written.

```
trace { on | off | procedure | <expression> } ;
```

The `on` keyword will turn on the trace. This will automatically trace all procedure arguments, variables, SQL error codes, ISAM error codes, and return values.
The `off` keyword will turn all tracing off.
The `procedure` keyword will trace only values passed to and from the stored procedure.

You may use an expression to write character strings or values you specify to the debug file.

Examples:

```
trace on;
trace off;
trace procedure;
trace "At beginning of foreach loop.";
trace "x = ", x, "  y = ", y
```

while

The while statement allows you to perform conditional looping. The body of the while statement is run continuously until the Boolean expression evaluates to false.

```
while <Boolean expression>
  { <SQL statement> |
    <SPL statement> |
    continue while; |
    exit while;
  } [...]
end while [ ; ]
```

When a continue while statement is executed, control is returned to the top of the while loop. When an exit while statement is executed, the next statement executed will be the statement following the end while.

Example:

```
let x = 1;
let y = 1;
let p_test_number = 1;

while x = y
  let x, y = select x, y from test_table
                where test_number = p_test_number
  let p_test_number = p_test_number + 1
```

```
   if p_test_number > 1000 then
      exit while
   end if
end while
```

dbinfo

The dbinfo function is used to retrieve values from the sqlca record structure. Dbinfo can be used anywhere in SQL statements or stored procedures (although it is primarily intended for use with stored procedures). Dbinfo was unavailable when stored procedures were first intrduced into Informix products, but the functionality is available with more recent versions of the database engine.

```
dbinfo    (    'sqlca.sqlerrd1' |
               'sqlca.sqlerrd2' |
               'sessionid' |
               'DBSPACE', <table space number>
          )
```

The sqlca.sqlerrd1 option returns the value of the last serial number inserted into a table.

The sqlca.sqlerrd2 code returns the number of rows processed by the most recent SQL statement (ie. select, insert, update, delete and execute procedure).

In INFORMIX-OnLine, the sessionid option will return the ID of the current session.

In INFORMIX-OnLine, the DBSPACE option will return the name of the dbspace the indicated table is in.

Examples:

```
let serial _value   = dbinfo ('sqlca.sqlerrd1');
let rows_processed  = dbinfo ('sqlca.sqlerrd2');
let my_session      = ('sessionid');
let my_dbspace      = ('DBSPACE', 123456);
```

Sample Stored Procedures

Here are some samples of stored procedures. The first example updates the toy table.

```
create procedure Change_Toy (old_toy_code    like toy.toy_code,
                             p_toy_code      like toy.toy_code,
                             p_description   like toy.description,
                             p_quantity      like toy.quantity,
                             p_cost          like toy.cost,
                             p_sales_price   like toy.sales_price)
   returning integer;

   define p_count, error_code     integer;

   on exception set error_code
      return error_code;
   end exception;

   let error_code = 0;

   select count(*) into p_count
      from toy
      where toy_code = old_toy_code;

   if p_count = 0 then
      raise exception -746, 0, "No rows updated.";
   end if;

   update toy
      set (toy_code,    description,   quantity,   cost,
                                                   sales_price)
      = (p_toy_code, p_description, p_quantity, p_cost,
                                                   p_sales_price)
      where toy_code = old_toy_code;

   return error_code;

end procedure
```

```
document "Change the toy information in the toy table."
with listing in "change_toy.warn";

execute procedure Change_Toy (100, 101, "TEST TOY", 200, 4, 8);
```

The next example uses a `foreach` loop to return a list of all toys.

```
create procedure List_Toys ()
  returning smallint, like toy.description;

  foreach select    toy_code,    description
            into p_toy_code, p_description
            from toy
            order by description
    return p_toy_code, p_description with resume;
  end foreach;

  return p_toy_code, p_description;

end procedure

document "List toy codes and descriptions from the toy table."
with listing in "list_toy.warn";

execute procedure List_Toys ();
```

The next example shows how INFORMIX-4GL code could be used with the previous example:

```
define p_toy_code            like toy.toy_code
define p_description         like toy.description

prepare toy_stmt from "execute procedure list_toys ()"
declare toy_cursor for toy_stmt

foreach toy_cursor into p_toy_code, p_description
    <whatever you want to do with the data>
end foreach
```

Privileges

You may grant and revoke privileges to a stored procedure. If you create a procedure using the keyword dba, a user who executes the procedure will have dba privileges while he is executing the stored procedure. Only users with DBA privileges can create dba procedures.

The user must have execute privilege to execute a stored procedure. You can grant and revoke these privileges as follows:

```
grant execute on <procedure name>
  to { public | <user name>  [, ...] }
  [ with grant option ]
  [ as <user name> ]
```

See Chapter 3 for more detailed information on privileges. You can revoke execute privileges by:

```
revoke execute on <procedure name>
  from { public | <user name> [, ...] }
```

Example:
```
revoke execute on Get_Username from public
grant  execute on Get_Username to don
```

Changing and Deleting Existing Stored Procedures

The only way to change a stored procedure is to delete it and then recreate it. To delete a stored procedure, use the following syntax:

```
drop procedure <procedure name>
```

Example: drop procedure my_proc

Update Statistics

Make certain you run `update statistics` periodically. Because SQL statements in stored procedures are optimized at the time the stored procedure is created, `update statistics` becomes especially important. `Update statistics` will re-optimize the query paths used by your stored procedures. You may also update the statistics for a single stored procedure:

```
update statistics for procedure <procedure name>
```

Example: `update statistics for procedure my_proc`

Triggers

Triggers allow you to specify actions at the time an `insert`, `update`, or `delete` statement is run on a table.

Triggered actions do not occur until you actually perform the `insert`, `update`, or `delete` statement. This means that while triggers can be used for data validation, if you are using INFORMIX-4GL, you will still need to use 4GL code to let your users know they have entered invalid data onto the screen. We will discuss data entry in the chapters on INFORMIX-4GL.

A trigger may call a stored procedure. The opposite is also true, a stored procedure can cause a trigger to be executed.

Like stored procedures, triggers are stored with the database engine. This will cause your engine to grow slightly as you add triggers.

The syntax used to create a trigger is shown on page 476.

```
create trigger <trigger name>
  { insert on <table name>
     { referencing new [ as ]
                          <temporary table name>
        <trigger action with foreach> |
        <trigger action>
     } |
    delete on <table name>
     { referencing old [ as ]
                          <temporary table name>
       <trigger action with foreach> |
       <trigger action>
     } |
    update [ of <column name> [, ...] ]
                                  on <table name>
     { referencing { new [ as ]
                        <temporary table name> |
                      old [ as ]
                        <temporary table name>
                    } [...]
       <trigger action with foreach> |
       <trigger action>
     }
  }
```

A trigger is designed to automatically execute when an
insert, update, or delete statement is run. A create
trigger involves either an insert, update, or delete on a
single table.

If a trigger is on an update, you may optionally specify
columns that will trigger an action. If you specify columns, only
one trigger is allowed per column. Only one trigger can be called
directly when a column is updated.

The referencing keyword allows you to specify a temporary
table name to refer to the columns in the table before they have
been updated or deleted or after they have been updated or
inserted. If you are using the referencing keyword, you must
also use a for each row clause as one of your actions.

A trigger action is defined as follows:

```
{ before
    [ when ( <Boolean condition> ) ]
      ( { <insert statement> |
          <delete statement> |
          <update statement> |
          <execute procedure statement>
        } [, ...]
      )
    [, ...]                          |
      for each row
    [ when ( <Boolean condition> ) ]
      ( { <insert statement> |
          <delete statement> |
          <update statement> |
          <execute procedure statement>
        } [, ...]
      )
    [, ...]                          |
  after
    [ when ( <Boolean condition> ) ]
      ( { <insert statement> |
          <delete statement> |
          <update statement> |
          <execute procedure statement>
        } [, ...]
      )
    [, ...]
} [...]
```

While the above syntax does not indicate this, you may use only a single `before`, `for each row`, and `after` statement. You may use one of each, and they must be in that order.

The `before` clause performs the trigger action a single time before the triggering statement is executed.

The `for each row` clause performs the trigger action for each row processed after the triggering statement has executed.

The `after clause` performs the trigger action a single time after the triggering statement has finished executing.

The trigger action may be an `insert` statement, a `delete` statement, an `update` statement, an `execute procedure` statement, or any combination of these statements.

If you are using a `before` or `after` clause, you may not refer to the information in the triggering table. There is one exception to this: if the triggering statement is an `update` statement and the trigger action is an `update` statement and neither `update` statement uses the same columns.

Examples

The following are examples of triggers. The first example implements a cascading delete. This means that when a deletion is made from one table, any rows in tables that are dependent on the deleted record should also be deleted. In this case, whenever a toy_order is deleted, any items associated with that order should also be deleted.

```
-- This trigger deletes any toy_order_item rows
-- associated with each deleted toy_order.

create trigger Delete_Order
   delete on toy_order
   referencing old as old_order
   for each row
      (delete from toy_order_item
          where order_number = old_order.order_number)
```

This next trigger occurs whenever a new toy_store is added.

```
-- This trigger calls a stored procedure to generate a catalog
-- mailing to new client toy stores, whenever a toy_store is
-- added.

create trigger Add_Store
   insert on toy_order
   referencing new as new_store
   for each row
      (execute procedure Mail_Catalog (new_store.store_number))
```

The final trigger is an update trigger that uses both a `for each row` and an `after` trigger action.

```
— This trigger inserts information to a log table every time an
— order item is updated.  After all rows have been updated,
— a stored procedure is called.

create trigger Update_Order_Item
  update on toy_order_item
  referencing old as old_order_item
              new as new_order_item
     for each row
       (insert into order_item_log values
          (old_order_item.order_number, old_order_item.toy_code,
          new_order_item.toy_code,         new_order_item.quantity,
          new_order_item.unit_price))

    after
      (execute procedure Check_Log ())
```

Looking at Existing Triggers

The following SQL statement will allow you to view all triggers
you have entered in your database.

```
select trigname, seqno, data
  from systrigbody, systriggers
  where systrigbody.datakey = "D" and
        systrigbody.trigid  = systriggers.trigid
  order by trigname, seqno
```

Changing and Deleting Existing Stored Procedures

The only way to change a trigger is to delete it and then recreate
it. To delete a trigger, use the following syntax:

```
drop trigger <trigger name>
```

Example: drop trigger my_trigger

Summary

The syntax for creating a stored procedure is as follows:

```
create [ dba ] procedure <procedure name>
   ( [ <variable name>
        { <data type> [ <default value> ] |
           like <table name>.<column name> [ <default value> ] |
           references { byte | text } [ default null ]
        } [, ...]
     ]
   )
   [ returning <data type> [, ...] ; ]
   { <SQL statement> | <SPL statement> } [...]
end procedure
[ document <quoted string> [, ...] ]
[ with listing in "<pathname for compile time warnings>" ]
```

The following is a summary of the stored procedure language statements that can be used within a stored procedure. Comments in a stored procedure are anything on a line following double dashes (e.g., -- This is a comment).

```
begin
   { <SQL statement> | <SPL statement> } [...]
end

call <procedure name>
     ( [ [ <parameter name in called procedure> = ]
        { <expression> | <select statement> }
      ] [, ...]
     )
     [ returning <variable name> [, ...] ]
     ;

define { global <variable name> [, ...]
           { <data type> [ default <value> ] |
             references { byte | text } [ default null ]
           } |
             <variable name> [, ...]
             { <data type> |
```

```
                   references { byte | text } |
                   like <table name>.<column name> |
                   procedure
               }
    ;

for <variable name>
    { = <expression> to <expression> [ step <expression> ]      |
     in ( <expression> [ to <expression> [step <expression>] ]
          [, ...]
          )
    }
    { <SQL statement> |
      <SPL statement> |
      continue for; |
      exit for;
    }  [...]
end for;

foreach
    { { [ with hold ] | <cursor name> [ with hold ] for }
       <select statement with into clause> |
      execute procedure <procedure name>
        ( [ <variable name> = ] <expression> [, ...] )
        [ into <variable name> [, ...]
    }
    { <SQL statement> |
      <SPL statement> |
      continue foreach; |
      exit foreach;
    }  [...]
end foreach;

if <Boolean expression> then
    { <SQL statement> | <SPL statement> } [...]
[ elif <Boolean expression> then
    { <SQL statement> | <SPL statement> } [...]
]
[ else
    { <SQL statement> | <SPL statement> } [...]
]
end if;
```

```
let <variable name> [, ...] =
  { <expression> |
    <procedure name>
      ( [ [ <parameter name in called procedure> = ]
            { <expression> | <select statement> }
        ] [, ...]
      )
  };


on exception [ in ( <error number> [, ...] ) ]
  set <integer variable for SQL error>
    [ , <integer variable for ISAM error>
      [ , <char variable for error message> ]
    ]
  { <SQL statement> | <SPL statement> }
end exception [ with resume ] ;


raise exception <integer variable for SQL error>
              [ , <integer variable for ISAM error>
                [ , <char variable for error message> ]
              ];


return [ <expression> [, ...] [ with resume ] ] ;


set debug file
    { "<file name>" | <variable name> | <expression> }
    [ with append ];


system { "<character expression>" |
        <character variable name>
        };


trace { on | off | procedure | <expression> };


while <Boolean expression>
  { <SQL statement> |
    <SPL statement> |
    continue while; |
    exit while;
  } [...]
end while;
```

If you wish to update or delete the current row of the table pointed to by your cursor, you may substitute the `where` clause in your `update` or `delete` statement with:

```
where current of <cursor name>
```

The `dbinfo` function is used to retrieve values from the `sqlca` record structure. Dbinfo can be

```
dbinfo  (   'sqlca.sqlerrd1' |
            'sqlca.sqlerrd2' |
            'sessionid' |
            'DBSPACE', <table space number>
        )
```

The user must have execute privilege to execute a stored procedure.

```
grant execute on <procedure name>
   to { public | <user name>  [, ...] }
   [ with grant option ]
   [ as <user name> ]

revoke execute on <procedure name>
   from { public | <user name> [, ...] }
```

The only way to change a stored procedure is to delete it and then recreate it. To delete a stored procedure, use the following syntax:

```
drop procedure <procedure name>
```

Make certain you run update statistics periodically to re-optimize your stored procedures. You may also update the statistics on a single stored procedure:

```
update statistics for procedure <procedure name>
```

The syntax used to create a trigger is as follows:

```
create trigger <trigger name>
  { insert on <table name>
      { referencing new [ as ] <temporary table name>
        <trigger action with foreach> |
        <trigger action>
      } |
    delete on <table name>
     { referencing old [ as ] <temporary table name>
       <trigger action with foreach> |
       <trigger action>
     } |
    update [ of <column name> [, ...] ]
                                 on <table name>
      { referencing
        { new [ as ] <temporary table name> |
          old [ as ] <temporary table name>
        } [...]
      <trigger action with foreach> |
      <trigger action>
      }
  }
```

A trigger action is defined as follows:

```
{ before
    [ when ( <Boolean condition> ) ]
      ( { <insert statement> |
          <delete statement> |
          <update statement> |
          <execute procedure statement>
        } [, ...]
      )
    [, ...]  |
      for each row
    [ when ( <Boolean condition> ) ]
      ( { <insert statement> |
          <delete statement> |
          <update statement> |
          <execute procedure statement>
        } [, ...]
```

```
          )
     [, ...]          |
  after
     [ when ( <Boolean condition> ) ]
        ( { <insert statement> |
             <delete statement> |
             <update statement> |
             <execute procedure statement>
           } [, ...]
         )
     [, ...]
} [...]
```

While the above syntax does not indicate this, you may use only a single before, for each row, and after statement. You may use one of each, and they must be in that order.

The only way to change a trigger is to delete it and then recreate it. To delete a trigger, use the following syntax:

```
drop trigger <trigger name>
```

Chapter

22

User-Defined Searches

- *Overview*
- *From the user's perspective*
- *Constructing a* where *clause*
- construct *features*
- *Completing the* select *statement*
- *Sample function*
- *Summary*

Overview

Now that we know how to display forms, we can allow users to search for information by entering information in the fields of the form using the `construct` statement.

After a form is displayed, the user can enter search criteria in the fields of the form. The `construct` statement translates the search criteria into a `where` clause that can be combined with a `select` statement to retrieve the desired information from the database and display it on the form for the user. Chapter 19 discusses the use of SQL statements in 4GL, this chapter gives you the information that will allow you to create a user defined `select` statement to use with that chapter.

From the User's Perspective

First let's look at what the user will see and do when beginning a search.

A form will be displayed on the screen (see Figure 22-1), most likely with a set of menu options displayed above it. One of the options may be Find (or perhaps Search or Query).

When the user chooses the Find option, the cursor is placed in the first field of the form and the user is prompted to enter search criteria. If the user wants to search for all orders from Don's Toy

```
 Order Indormation Menu:   Find Exit
 Find the information for an order.
 ------------------------------------------Press F1 for Help------
   Order number: [             ]

   Store:        [           ]     [                              ]

   Date Ordered: [           ]      Date Shipped:  [              ]

   Sales Code:   [       ]
```

Figure 22-1   *Screen menu displayed at the start of a search.*

Dungeon since July 1, 1997, the screen might appear as shown in Figure 22-2.

```
Please enter your search criteria.

----------------------------------------Press F1 for Help------
   Order number: [                ]

   Store:          [           ]       [Don*                          ]

   Date Ordered: [>=7/1/1997]      Date Shipped:  [              ]

   Sales Code:   [        ]
```

Figure 22-2   *The user enters the search criteria.*

The user would then press the *accept* key to indicate that the search criteria have been entered. At this point, the program would search for the information the user requested. A message at the top of the screen lets the user know that the request is being processed (see Figure 22-3).

```
Searching . . .

----------------------------------------Press F1 for Help------
   Order number: [                ]

   Store:          [           ]       [Don*                          ]

   Date Ordered: [>=7/1/1997]      Date Shipped:  [              ]

   Sales Code:   [        ]
```

Figure 22-3   *Screen waiting for a search to be completed.*

At this point we complete the search and display the data on the form. This is the point at which users will be able to browse through the returned information.

It is helpful to provide users with a list of special characters that can be used with the `construct` statement. These special charactes are:

Symbol	Description	Example
=	equal to	=9/28/1998
>	greater than	>1000
<	less than	<1000
>=	greater than or equal to	>=1000
<=	less than or equal to	<=1000
<>	not equal to	<>1000
!=	not equal to	!=1000
:	between	5:50
	(except for datetimes or intervals)	
..	between datetimes or intervals	09:45..10:45
	(or any data type)	
*	matches zero or more of any character	SMI*
?	matches any single character	SM?TH
|	or	SMITH|JONES
[]	use with * and ? include a list	[a:zA:Z]
^	means not in list when used in brackets	[^0:9]

An equal sign (=) by itself in a field will create a search for a null value. When a caret (^) is used as a special character, it must be the first character after the open square bracket. The not equal to symbols (<> and !=), when used by themselves in a field, will return any non null AND non blank values.

Users may combine several symbols to perform a more complex search. They may not combine wildcard characters (? and *) in the same field with an `or` symbol (\|). This limitation may be removed in a future version of INFORMIX-4GL.

Users may specify a search within a field that is longer than the field. If they do, the bottom line of the window will open to display the rest of the search criteria for that field.

If users do not enter search criteria, all items from the select statement will be retrieved.

Constructing a where Clause

The `construct` statement builds a where clause for your select statement based on information the user provides. You are responsible for adding conditions to the where clause to join tables and for adding any additional conditions to the where clause.

The `construct` statement has the form:

```
construct
  { by name <type char variable>
      on <table name>.{<column name>|*} [, ...] |
    <type char variable>
      on <table name>.{<column name>|*} [, ...]
      from
        { <form field name> [, ...]                |
          <screen record name>["["<row number>"]"].*
        } [, ...]
  }
  [ attribute ( <construct attribute> [, ...] ) ]
  [ help <help number> ]
  [ { { before construct                             |
        after  construct                             |
        before field <form field name> [, ...] |
        after  field <form field name> [, ...] |
        on key ( <special key> [, ...] )
      } [...]
    { <any 4GL statement>                            |
      next field { next | previous                   |
                   <form field name> }      |
      continue construct                             |
      exit construct                                 |
    } [...]
  } [...]
  end construct
]
```

The square brackets enclosed inside of the double quotes are part of the syntax and do not represent an option.

The basic `construct` statement is discussed in this section. The optional parts of the `construct` statement are discussed in the next section. The `end construct` statement is only needed if any of the optional statements other than `attribute` or `help` are used.

Using the form from the previous section as an example, we will now build a construct statement. First, let's have a look at the form:

```
{************************************************************
   toy_order
   This screen allows you to display and maintain toy_order
   information.
   ***********************************************************}

database toymaker
screen size 24 by 80

{
--------------------------------------Press F1 for Help------
   Order number: [f000          ]

   Store:        [f001       ]      [f005                  ]

   Date Ordered: [f002      ]       Date Shipped:  [f003      ]

   Sales Code:   [f004  ]
}
end

tables toy_order toy_store

attributes
   f000 = toy_order.order_number;
   f001 = toy_order.store_number;
   f005 = toy_store.store_name;
   f002 = toy_order.order_date;
   f003 = toy_order.shipping_datetime;
   f004 = toy_order.sales_code;

instructions
   screen record s_toy_order
      (order_number, store_number,       store_name,
       order_date,      shipping_datetime, sales_code)
end
```

There are two ways to build a `construct` statement. The first is by name, that is, the names of the columns in your database tables match the names of the fields in your form.

```
define where_clause                     char (100)

construct by name where_clause
   on toy_order.order_number,           toy_order.store_number,
      toy_store.store_name,             toy_order.order_date,
      toy_order.shipping_datetime,      toy_order.sales_code
```

If the names in your database tables are different from those in your form, you must specify which table and column correspond to each form field you plan to use in your `construct` statement.

```
define where_clause                     char (100)

construct where_clause
   on toy_order.order_number,           toy_order.store_number,
      toy_store.store_name,             toy_order.order_date,
      toy_order.shipping_datetime,      toy_order.sales_code
   from s_toy_order.*
```

or

```
define where_clause                     char (100)

construct where_clause
   on toy_order.order_number,           toy_order.store_number,
      toy_store.store_name,             toy_order.order_date,
      toy_order.shipping_datetime,      toy_order.sales_code
   from order_number,                   store_number,
        store_name,                     order_date,
        shipping_datetime,              sales_code
```

You do not need to allow users to search by every field in the form. Only those fields you include in your `construct` statement may be searched on.

The where clause string built by the construct statement will be stored in a type char variable, in this example where_clause. You should make this variable large enough to hold the where clauses will can be generated by the construct statement.

If no search criteria are given, the default where clause, "1 = 1", is returned. Since one is always equal to itself, this statement will evaluate to true for every row of your where clause, and every row of your select statement will be returned.

Construct Features

The features described in this section are optional parts of the construct statement. You will need to use an end construct statement if you use any of these options other than attribute or help.

attribute (*<construct attribute>* [, ...])

The attribute clause allows you to associate any of the following attributes with the construct statement:

normal	reverse	white	cyan
bold	blink	yellow	green
dim	underline	magenta	blue
invisible	red	black	

help *<help number>*

The help clause allows you to associate a help message with the construct statement. A useful help statement is a description for the user of how to perform a user defined search and an explanation of the special characters that may be used as part of the search criteria.

before construct

The before construct clause allows you to specify statements that are issued before the user enters the construct statement. For example, you may wish to assign default search values to a field and display them for the user.

```
define where_clause                char (100)
define p_toy_order record
          order_number            like toy_order.order_number,
          store_number            like toy_order.store_number,
          store_name              like toy_store.store_name,
          order_date              like toy_order.order_date,
          shipping_datetime       like toy_order.shipping_datetime,
          sales_code              like toy_order.sales_code
    end record

construct by name where_clause
    on toy_order.order_number,         toy_order.store_number,
       toy_store.store_name,           toy_order.order_date,
       toy_order.shipping_datetime,    toy_order.sales_code

    before construct
       let p_toy_order.order_date = today
       display p_toy_order.order_date to s_toy_order.order_date
end construct
```

Within a before construct, you may use any 4GL statement, next field, continue construct, or exit construct defined in this section. You must use an end construct clause when using the before construct clause.

after construct

The after construct clause allows you to specify statements that are issued after the user exits the construct statement. For example, you may wish to make certain the user has entered values in certain fields, or you may wish to capture a particular value entered by a user.

```
define where_clause                char (100)
define char_order_number           char (50)
```

```
construct by name where_clause
   on toy_order.order_number,          toy_order.store_number,
      toy_store.store_name,            toy_order.order_date,
      toy_order.shipping_datetime,     toy_order.sales_code

   after construct
      let char_order_number = get_fldbuf (order_number)
end construct
```

Within an `after construct`, you may use any 4GL statement, `next field`, `continue construct`, or `exit construct` defined in this section. You must use an `end construct` clause when using the `after construct` clause.

before field *<form field name>* [, ...]

The `before field` clause allows you to specify statements that are issued each time before the user enters a field. For example, you may wish to assign a value to a field just before the user enters it.

```
define where_clause                   char (100)
define p_toy_order record
            order_number              like toy_order.order_number,
            store_number              like toy_order.store_number,
            store_name                like toy_store.store_name,
            order_date                like toy_order.order_date,
            shipping_datetime         like toy_order.shipping_datetime,
            sales_code                like toy_order.sales_code
   end record

construct by name where_clause
   on toy_order.order_number,          toy_order.store_number,
      toy_store.store_name,            toy_order.order_date,
      toy_order.shipping_datetime,     toy_order.sales_code

   before field order_date
      if get_fldbuf (order_date) is null or
         get_fldbuf (order_date) > today then
         let p_toy_order.order_date = today
         display p_toy_order.order_date to s_toy_order.order_date
      end if
end construct
```

Within a before field, you may use any 4GL statement, next field, continue construct, or exit construct defined in this section. You must use an end construct clause when using the before field clause.

after field <form field name> [, ...]

The after field clause allows you to specify statements that are issued each time the user leaves a field. The after field clause allows you to perform data checking to make certain valid information has been entered by the user.

```
define where_clause                 char (100)

construct by name where_clause
   on toy_order.order_number,        toy_order.store_number,
      toy_store.store_name,          toy_order.order_date,
      toy_order.shipping_datetime,   toy_order.sales_code

   after field order_date
      if get_fldbuf (order_date) > today then
         error "Order date must not be a future date."
         next field order_date
      end if
end construct
```

Within an after field, you may use any 4GL statement, next field, continue construct, or exit construct defined in this section. You must use an end construct clause when using the after field clause.

on key (*<special key>* [, ...])

The on key clause allows you to specify actions to be taken when the user presses a special key. Any of the following special keys may be used:

```
F1 through F64       Control-<letter -except a, d, h, l, r, or x>
accept               help              prevpage
delete·              insert            return
down                 interrupt         right
esc                  left              tab
escape               nextpage          up
```

You may wish to allow users to look up valid data values for a field when they press a key.

```
define where_clause              char (100)
define p_toy_order record
        order_number             like toy_order.order_number,
        store_number             like toy_order.store_number,
        store_name               like toy_store.store_name,
        order_date               like toy_order.order_date,
        shipping_datetime        like toy_order.shipping_datetime,
        sales_code               like toy_order.sales_code
    end record

construct by name where_clause
  on toy_order.order_number,        toy_order.store_number,
     toy_store.store_name,          toy_order.order_date,
     toy_order.shipping_datetime,   toy_order.sales_code

  on key (F3)   { Perform Lookup }
    if infield (store_number) or infield (store_name) then
      call Lookup_Store (p_toy_order.store_number,
                    p_toy_order.store_name)
            returning  p_toy_order.store_number,
                       p_toy_order.store_name

      display p_toy_order.store_number, p_toy_order.store_name
         to s_toy_order.store_number, s_toy_order.store_name
    end if
end construct
```

Within an on key, you may use any 4GL statement, next field, continue construct, or exit construct defined in this section. You must use an end construct clause when using the on key clause.

<any 4GL statement>

Specifies that you may use any 4GL statement from within a before construct, after construct, before field, after field, or on key clause.

next field { next | previous | <form field name> }

Next field specifies the form field in which the cursor should be positioned. Next specifies the next field on the form, previous specifies the previous field on the form, and a form field name specifies a field on the form. Next field can be issued from within a before construct, after construct, before field, after field, or on key clause. Statements following a next field are not executed.

continue construct

Continue construct switches program control back to the beginning of the construct statement and places the cursor in the form field it was last in. Continue construct can be issued from within a before construct, after construct, before field, after field, or on key clause.

exit construct

Exit construct simply switches program control to the statement after the construct statement. Exit construct can be issued from within a before construct, after construct, before field, after field, or on key clause.

Completing the select Statement

The `construct` statement merely provides a `where` clause for your `select` statement. You need to provide everything else, including the key word `where` and any table joins. Let's look briefly at how this works:

```
construct by name where_clause
   on toy_order.order_number,      toy_order.store_number,
      toy_store.store_name,        toy_order.order_date,
      toy_order.shipping_datetime, toy_order.sales_code

let sql_stmt =
   "select toy_order.order_number,      toy_order.store_number, ",
       "toy_store.store_name,           toy_order.order_date, ",
       "toy_order.shipping_datetime, toy_order.sales_code ",
     "from toy_order, toy_store ",
     "where ", where_clause clipped, " and ",
          "toy_order.store_number = toy_store.store_number ",
     "order by toy_order.order_number"
```

We concatenate the string segments using commas. Notice that the end of each string segment, except for the last string segment, has a space as the final character. Remember that you are responsible for the syntax of the `select` statement being valid. If you need a space in the result string, include one at the beginning or end of each string segment.

It is also a good idea to clip trailing spaces from the `where` clause. This will help to prevent the string containing your SQL statement from becoming too long to fit in the string variable holding your SQL statement.

You are responsible for specifying the syntax of the `select` statement, except for the part of the `where` clause that your `construct` statement will return.

You can use the `get_fldbuf` function to save the information entered by the user into variables. Then you can display these variables back in a `before` `construct` clause to allow the user to edit a query and then re-run it. This will not work with older versions of INFORMIX-4GL, but it is a really nice feature in the versions where it is available.

Sample Function

Now that we are familiar with the various parts of the `construct` statement, let's have a look at how they fit together:

```
database toymaker

main
  call Find_Toy_Order () { You will probably call your find
                           function from a menu, within another
                           function }
end main

function Find_Toy_Order ()
  define where_clause            char (100)
  define sql_stmt                char (300)
  define p_toy_order record
          order_number           like toy_order.order_number,
          store_number           like toy_order.store_number,
          store_name             like toy_store.store_name,
          order_date             like toy_order.order_date,
          shipping_datetime      like toy_order.shipping_datetime,
          sales_code             like toy_order.sales_code
        end record

  open window w_toy_order1 at 2,2 with form "toy_order1"
    attribute (border)

  display "Please enter your search criteria." at 1,1

  construct by name where_clause
    on toy_order.order_number,       toy_order.store_number,
       toy_store.store_name,         toy_order.order_date,
       toy_order.shipping_datetime,  toy_order.sales_code

  display "Searching..." at 1,1

  let sql_stmt =
    "select toy_order.order_number,      toy_order.store_number, ",
        "toy_store.store_name,       toy_order.order_date, ",
        "toy_order.shipping_datetime, toy_order.sales_code ",
```

```
        "from toy_order, toy_store ",
        "where ", where_clause clipped, " and ",
             "toy_order.store_number = toy_store.store_number ",
        "order by toy_order.order_number"

    { This is where you need to read Chapter 19 to find out what
      happens next. }

    close window w_toy_order1

end function  { Find_Toy_Order }
```

Summary

By using the `construct` statement, we can allow users to search for information by entering information into the fields of a form. The `construct` statement will return part of a `where` clause that can be put into an SQL statement and run.

Special characters that can be used to enter search criteria for a `construct` statement are:

Symbol	Description	Example
=	equal to	=9/28/1998
>	greater than	>1000
<	less than	<1000
>=	greater than or equal to	>=1000
<=	less than or equal to	<=1000
<>	not equal to	<>1000
!=	not equal to	!=1000
:	between (except for datetimes or intervals)	5:50
..	between datetimes or intervals (or any data type)	09:45..10:45
*	matches zero or more of any character	SMI*
?	matches any single character	SM?TH
|	or	SMITH|JONES
[]	use with * and ? include a list	[a:zA:Z]
^	means not in list when used in brackets	[^0:9]

The syntax for the construct statement is:

```
construct
   { by name <type char variable>
       on <table name>.{<column name>|*} [, ...] |
     <type char variable>
       on <table name>.{<column name>|*} [, ...]
       from
         { <form field name> [, ...]                |
           <screen record name>["["<row number>"]"].*
         } [, ...]
   }
   [ attribute ( <construct attribute> [, ...] ) ]
   [ help <help number> ]
   [ { { before construct                            |
         after   construct                           |
         before field <form field name> [, ...] |
         after   field <form field name> [, ...] |
         on key ( <special key> [, ...] )
       } [...]
     { <any 4GL statement>                      |
       next field { next | previous          |
                     <form field name> }  |
       continue construct                        |
       exit construct                            |
     } [...]
   } [...]
   end construct
]
```

The square brackets enclosed inside of the double quotes are part of the syntax and do not represent an optional part of the syntax.

The attribute clause allows you to associate any of the following attributes with the construct statement:

normal	reverse	white	cyan
bold	blink	yellow	green
dim	underline	magenta	blue
invisible	red	black	

The on key clause allows you to specify actions to be taken when the user presses a special key. Any of the following special keys may be used:

F1 through F64	Control-<letter -except a, d, h, l, r, or x>	
accept	help	prevpage
delete	insert	return
down	interrupt	right
esc	left	tab
escape	nextpage	up

The Input Array Statement

- *Input array overview*
- *4GL functions*
- *Editing the input*
- *Data validation*
- *Sample function*
- *Summary*

Input Array Overview

The `input array` statement allows you to view, insert, delete, and update rows in a multiple-line screen form.

Much of the `input array` statement is very similar to the `input` statement. The main differences arise from needing to be concerned about which row of the screen and which row of the array you are currently working with.

As with the `display array` statement, the `input array` statement gives the user the ability to scroll through the `input array` and view the information in the array. The user may decide to change the data, delete the data, insert new data, or let it remain unchanged.

The syntax for the `input array` statement is:

```
input array <program array name>
  [ without defaults ]
  from <screen record name>.*
  [ help <help number> ]
  [ attribute ( <input attribute> [, ...] ) ]
  [ { before { input | row | insert | delete }|
      before field <form field name> [, ...]    |
      after  field <form field name> [, ...]     |
      after  { input | row | insert | delete }|
      on key ( <special key> [, ...] )
    }
    { <any 4GL statement> }  |
      next field { <form field name> |
                    previous | next } |
      continue input          |
      exit input
    }
    end input
  ]
```

If your screen form defines a screen record with the name sa_my_record, then the following are examples of basic `input array` statements.

For adding new records (no existing rows are displayed):

```
define pa_my_record       array [100] of record like my_table.*
define counter            smallint

call set_count (0)

input array pa_my_record from sa_my_record.*
```

For displaying existing rows and performing adds, changes, and deletes:

```
define pa_my_record       array [100] of record like my_table.*
define num_filled_rows    smallint

{ Assign values to pa_my_record and num_filled_rows }

call set_count (num_filled_rows)

input array pa_my_record without defaults from sa_my_record.*
```

You may use any of the following attributes with the `input array` statement:

normal	reverse	white	cyan
bold	blink	yellow	green
dim	underline	magenta	blue
invisible	left	red	black

4GL Functions

The following functions are available for use with the `display array` statement.

arr_count

The function `arr_count` returns the number of rows stored in an input array.

```
arr_count ()
```

Example: define max_rows   smallint
           let max_rows = arr_count ()

arr_curr

The function arr_curr returns the record number within the
input array or display array statement of the current cursor
position.

```
arr_curr ()
```

Example: define array_position   smallint
           let array_position = arr_curr ()

infield

The function infield is passed the name of a screen form field,
and returns true if the cursor is currently positioned in that field,
and returns false otherwise. Infield may be used within input
and input array statements.

```
infield ( <screen form field name> )
```

Example:

```
define p_last_name                  char (30)

input p_last_name from last_name
  on key (F1)
    if infield (last_name) then
      call Lookup_Clients () returning p_last_name
    end if
end input
```

scr_line

The function `scr_line` returns the current row of the screen the
cursor is positioned on in an `input array` or `display array`
statement.

```
scr_line ()
```

Example:

```
define num_records                  smallint
define my_record record
        account_number              char (9),
        last_name                   char (30),
        first_name                  char (15)
    end record
define record_number                smallint

. . .

call set_count (num_records)
display array my_record to my_screen.*
  on key (F1)
    let record_number = scr_line ()
    call Bold_Screen_Line (record_number)
end display
```

set_count

The function `set_count` initializes the number of rows for an
`input array` or `display array`. This function should be called
before an `input array` or `display array` statement.

```
set_count ( <integer expression> )
```

Example:

```
define num_records              smallint
define my_record record
        account_number          char (9),
        last_name               char (30),
        first_name              char (15)
     end record


...


call set_count (num_records)
display array my_record to my_screen.*
```

Editing the Input

The editing keys available for use with the `input array` statement, generally have the same meanings as the editing keys available for use with the `input` statement. There is a difference in the use of the up arrow and down arrow keys. While adding and changing data in a form, you can use any of the following keys:

Key	Description
Control-a	Toggles between insert and typeover mode. Default is typeover mode.
Control-d	Deletes everything from the current position to the end of the field.
Control-h	Moves the cursor to the left.
Control-l	Moves the cursor to the right.
Control-r	Redraws the screen.
Control-x	Deletes the current character.
down arrow	Moves to the next field on the form or to the same field below the current row if you are in an `input array` statement. The action of the down arrow key may vary depending on whether the `options` statement has the field order set to `constrained` or `unconstrained`.

left arrow	If you are at the beginning of the field, moves to the previous field; otherwise, moves one space to the left.
right arrow	Moves one space to the right; if you are at the end of the field, moves to the next field.
up arrow	Moves to the previous field on the form or to the same field above the current row if you are in an `input array` statement. The action of the up arrow key may vary depending on whether the `options` statement has the field order set to `constrained` or `unconstrained`.

Unfortunately, short of remapping your keyboard, these keys cannot be redefined.

Data Validation

If you use any of the following statements in your `input array` statement, you will need to end the `input array` statement with an `end input` clause. Keep in mind that `before`, `after`, `on key`, `next field`, and `exit input` must be located within the `input array` statement. You can make calls to other functions, but the functions cannot contain any of these statements (unless they are contained within an `input array` statement located in that function).

The `before` and `after` clauses described below are executed in the following order:

```
before input
before insert or before delete
before row
before field
after field
after row
after insert or after delete
after input
```

before { input | row | insert | delete }

The `before input` clause allows you to execute statements before the user enters the `input` statement.

The `before row` clause allows you to execute statements before a row is entered.

The `before insert` statement allows you to execute statements before the user begins to input a new row.

The `before delete` statement allows you to execute statements after the user has pressed the *delete* key, but before the row has been deleted.

Example:

```
before input
   let my_record.username = p_username
   display by name my_record.username

before row
   let i = arr_curr ()
   let orig_my_record.* = pa_my_record[i].*
```

before field *<form field name>* [, ...]

The `before field` clause allows you to execute statements just before a user enters the specified field. For instance, you could assign a default value to a field and display it to the form before the user enters a field.

Example:

```
before field department
   if p_my_record.toy_code < 10 then
      let p_my_record.department = 1
   else
      let p_my_record.department = 2
   end if

   display by name p_my_record.department
```

after field <form field name> [, ...]

The after field clause allows you to execute statements immediately after the user exits the specified field. After field clauses are a great place for performing data validation.

Example:

```
after field account_number
  if p_my_record.account_name is null then
    next field account_number
  end if
```

after { input | row | insert | delete }

The after input clause allows you to execute statements after the input statements have all been executed, but before the input statement has actually been exited.

The after row clause allows you to execute statements before a row is entered.

The after insert statement allows you to execute statements after a user has input a new row.

The after delete statement allows you to execute statements after a row has been deleted.

Example:

```
after input
  if p_my_record.last_name is null and
     p_my_record.business_name is null then
    next field last_name
  end if

after row
  let i = arr_curr ()
  if data_changed then
    update my_table set
      (col1, col2, col3)
    = (pa_my_record[i].col1,
       pa_my_record[i].col2,
       pa_my_record[i].col3)
  end if
```

on key (*<special key>* [, ...])

The on key clause allows you to specify actions to be taken when the user presses a special key. Any of the following special keys may be used:

F1 through F64	Control-<letter -except a, d, h, l, r, or x>	
accept	help	prevpage
delete	insert	return
down	interrupt	right
esc	left	tab
escape	nextpage	up

Example:

```
on key (F1)
  if infield (toy_code) then
    call Lookup_Toys (toy_code)
          returning  p_toy_item.toy_code,
                     p_toy_item.description

      display by name p_toy_item.toy_code,
                      p_toy_item.description
    end if
```

<any 4GL statement>

Any 4GL statement can go inside of a before, after, or on key clause.

next field { *<form field name>* | previous | next }

The next field statement positions the cursor in the specified field. The keyword previous specifies that the cursor is to be positioned in the previous field of the form. The keyword next specifies that the cursor is to be positioned in the next field of the form. Make sure you give users a way out of the form or they may get stuck in an infinite loop.

Example: next field last_name

The 4GL functions `fgl_lastkey` and `fgl_keyval` can be useful in determining which key was last pressed. This information may be useful when determining which field you want to be positioned in next.

continue input

`Continue input` returns the program control to the top of the `input` statement. The cursor is returned to its most recent field position in the form.

exit input

`Exit input` exits the `input` statement. The `after input` clause, if one exists, will be executed before the `input` statement is exited.

Sample Function

The sample function listed below can easily be added to the `display array` module we created in Chapter 13. This module should be called from the `Find_Order_Item` function. The `input array` routine calls a `delete`, `add`, and `change` function which are listed, and some validity checking and lookup functions which are not listed.

The following sample function once again uses the ordered items multiple-line screen we used in Chapter 13. Notice that two of the fields have been given the attribute `noentry` so that they may not be entered by the user. The user should not enter the toy description field since this is merely a display field. The user should not enter the total price field since this is a calculated field.

This module retrieves all items associated with a particular purchase order and allows the user to make adjustments to each row. Notice that we do not allow the user to change the toy_code field since this is part of the key. The user may delete an existing row, enter a new row, or change the quantity or unit price.

F1 is used as the `insert` key if the user wishes to insert a row. F2 is used as the *delete* key if the user wishes to delete a row. These defaults may be changed by using the `options` statement.

Notice that when the user deletes a row, a menu pops up to ask if the user wants to delete the record. If the user answers no, the record will still disappear from the screen, but the data will remain in the database. If the user answers yes, the data will disappear from the screen and from the database.

The screen form code for the sample module is listed first, followed by the INFORMIX-4GL code which goes with it.

```
{ *****************************************************************
   toy_order_item
   This  screen  allows  you  to  display  and  maintain  toy_order_item
   information.
   *****************************************************************}


database toymaker
screen size 24 by 80


{
---------------------------------------Press F1 for Help------

  Toy Code/Description           Quantity  Unit Price  Total Price
[f011   |f014                  |f012    |f013       |f015      ]
[f011   |f014                  |f012    |f013       |f015      ]
[f011   |f014                  |f012    |f013       |f015      ]
[f011   |f014                  |f012    |f013       |f015      ]
[f011   |f014                  |f012    |f013       |f015      ]
[f011   |f014                  |f012    |f013       |f015      ]
[f011   |f014                  |f012    |f013       |f015      ]
[f011   |f014                  |f012    |f013       |f015      ]
}
end


tables toy_order_item toy
```

```
attributes
  f011 = toy_order_item.toy_code;
  f014 = toy.description,       noentry;
  f012 = toy_order_item.quantity;
  f013 = toy_order_item.unit_price;
  f015 = formonly.total_price, noentry;

instructions
  delimiters "||"

  screen record sa_order_item [8]
    (toy_code, description, quantity, unit_price, total_price)
end
```

The 4GL code for the sample function is listed here:

```
{ Global definitions for the module }
database toymaker

define pa_order_item            array [100] of record
        toy_code                like toy_order_item.toy_code,
        description             like toy.description,
        quantity                like toy_order_item.quantity,
        unit_price              like toy_order_item.unit_price,
        total_price             decimal (8,2)
      end record


{*****************************************************************
  Input_Order_Item
  This function displays the rows of data and allows the user to
look
  through them
*****************************************************************}
function Input_Order_Item (p_order_number, counter)
  define p_order_number         like toy_order.order_number
  define counter, i, j          smallint
  define is_valid               smallint
  define trans_type             char (1)
  define orig_order_item        record
              toy_code          like toy_order_item.toy_code,
              description        like toy.description,
```

```
            quantity            like toy_order_item.quantity,
            unit_price          like toy_order_item.unit_price,
            total_price         decimal (8,2)
        end record

whenever error stop

{ Display }
display "" at 1,1
display "" at 2,1
display "Use the arrow keys and the Page Up and Page Down keys"
                                                    at 1,1
display "to look through the items.      F1=Insert    F2=Delete"
                                                    at 2,1


call set_count (counter)

input array pa_order_item without defaults from sa_order_item.*
   help 19

    before insert
       let trans_type = "I"

    after insert
       let i = arr_curr ()

       if not int_flag and
          (pa_order_item[i].toy_code    is not null or
           pa_order_item[i].quantity    is not null or
           pa_order_item[i].unit_price is not null) then
          call Insert_Order_Item (p_order_number, i)
       else
          error "Entry not complete."
          initialize trans_type to null
       end if

    before delete
       let i = arr_curr ()
       call Delete_Order_Item (p_order_number, i)
                   returning  trans_type
       { Redisplay input message }
       display "" at 1,1
```

```
    display "" at 2,1
    display "Use the arrow keys and the Page Up and Page Down keys"
                                                         at 1,1
    display "to look through the items.   F1=Insert  F2=Delete"
                                                         at 2,1

before row
  let i = arr_curr ()
  let j = scr_line ()

  initialize trans_type to null
  let orig_order_item.* = pa_order_item[i].*

after row
  let i = arr_curr ()
  let j = scr_line ()

  if not int_flag and trans_type is null and
    (pa_order_item[i].toy_code <> orig_order_item.toy_code or
     pa_order_item[i].quantity <> orig_order_item.quantity or
     pa_order_item[i].unit_price <> orig_order_item.unit_price)
                                                         then

    call Change_Order_Item (p_order_number, i)
  end if

after field toy_code
 { Don't let toy_code change }
 if pa_order_item[i].toy_code <> orig_order_item.toy_code and
    trans_type is null then
   error "Cannot change toy_code code - delete and re-enter."
   let pa_order_item[i].toy_code = orig_order_item.toy_code
   display pa_order_item[i].toy_code
       to sa_order_item[j].toy_code
 else
   call Valid_Toy_Code (pa_order_item[i].toy_code)
           returning  is_valid
   if not is_valid then
     error "Invalid toy code - press F1 for choices."
     next field toy_code
   end if
```

```
            call Get_Toy_Unit_Price (pa_order_item[i].toy_code)
                    returning  pa_order_item[i].unit_price
          display pa_order_item[i].unit_price
              to sa_order_item[j].unit_price
        end if

    after field quantity, unit_price
      let pa_order_item[i].total_price =
      pa_order_item[i].quantity * pa_order_item[i].unit_price

      display pa_order_item[i].total_price
          to sa_order_item[i].total_price

    on key (F1)
      if infield (toy_code) then
        call Lookup_Toy_Code (pa_order_item[i].toy_code)
                    returning  pa_order_item[i].toy_code,
                               pa_order_item[i].description

        display pa_order_item[i].toy_code,
              pa_order_item[i].description
            to sa_order_item[i].toy_code,
              sa_order_item[i].description
      else
        error "Sorry, lookup of data unavailable in this field."
    end if
  end input

  let int_flag = false
end function  { Input_Order_Item }


{*******************************************************************
  Delete_Order_Item
  This function deletes a toy_order_item record.
  *****************************************************************}
function Delete_Order_Item (p_order_number, array_row)
  define p_order_number        like toy_order.order_number
  define array_row             smallint
  define trans_type            char (1)

  initialize trans_type to null
```

```
    menu "Delete? "
       command "No"                    "Do not delete this order item."
                help 20
                exit menu

       command "Yes"                   "Delete this order item."
                help 21

                whenever error continue

                { Delete this order item }
                delete from toy_order_item
                 where order_number = p_order_number and
                       toy_code      = pa_order_item[array_row].toy_code

                if sqlca.sqlcode = 0 then
                  message "Deleted."
                  let trans_type = "D"
                else
                  error "Error number ", sqlca.sqlcode,
                        " deleting order item."
                end if

                whenever error stop

                exit menu
    end menu

    return trans_type

end function   { Delete_Order_Item }


{*****************************************************************
   Insert_Order_Item
   This function inserts a row into the toy_order_item.
 *****************************************************************}
function Insert_Order_Item (p_order_number, array_row)
   define p_order_number          like toy_order.order_number
   define array_row               smallint

   whenever error continue
```

```
insert into toy_order_item
    (order_number, toy_code, quantity, unit_price)
  values
    (p_order_number,
     pa_order_item[array_row].toy_code,
     pa_order_item[array_row].quantity,
     pa_order_item[array_row].unit_price)

if sqlca.sqlcode <> 0 then
  error "Error number ", sqlca.sqlcode, " adding item."
end if

whenever error stop
end function  { Insert_Order_Item }


{********************************************************************
  Change_Order_Item
  This function updates the information in the toy_order_item
  table.
  *******************************************************************}
function Change_Order_Item (p_order_number, array_row)
  define p_order_number       like toy_order.order_number
  define array_row            smallint

  whenever error continue

  update toy_order_item set (quantity, unit_price)
    = (pa_order_item[array_row].quantity,
       pa_order_item[array_row].unit_price)
    where order_number = p_order_number and
          toy_code     = pa_order_item[array_row].toy_code

  if sqlca.sqlcode <> 0 then
    error "Error number ", sqlca.sqlcode, " changing item."
  end if

  whenever error stop
end function  { Change_Order_Item }
```

Summary

The `input array` statement allows you to view, insert, delete, and update rows in a multiple-line screen form.

```
input array <program array name>
   [ without defaults ]
   from <screen record name>.*
   [ help <help number> ]
   [ attribute ( <input attribute> [, ...] ) ]
   [ { before { input | row | insert | delete }  |
       before field <form field name> [, ...]  |
       after  field <form field name> [, ...]  |
       after  { input | row | insert | delete }  |
       on key ( <special key> [, ...] )
     }
     { <any 4GL statement> }              |
       next field { <form field name> |
                      previous | next } |
       continue input              |
       exit input
     }
     end input
   ]
```

You may use any of the following attributes with the `input array` statement:

normal	reverse	white	cyan
bold	blink	yellow	green
dim	underline	magenta	blue
invisible	left	red	black

The following functions are available for use with the `display array` statement:

```
arr_count ()
arr_curr ()
infield ( <screen form field name> )
scr_line ()
set_count ( <integer expression> )
```

While adding and changing data in a form using the `input array` statement, you can use any of the following keys:

Key	*Description*
`Control-a`	Toggles between insert and typeover mode. Default is typeover mode.
`Control-d`	Deletes everything from the current position to the end of the field.
`Control-h`	Moves the cursor to the left.
`Control-l`	Moves the cursor to the right.
`Control-r`	Redraws the screen.
`Control-x`	Deletes the current character.
`down arrow`	Moves to the next field on the form or to the same field below the current row if you are in an `input array` statement. The action of the down arrow key may vary depending on whether the `options` statement has the field order set to `constrained` or `unconstrained`.
`left arrow`	If you are at the beginning of the field, moves to the previous field; otherwise, moves one space to the left.
`right arrow`	Moves one space to the right; if you are at the end of the field, moves to the next field.
`up arrow`	Moves to the previous field on the form or to the same field above the current row if you are in an `input array` statement. The action of the up arrow key may vary depending on whether the `options` statement has the field order set to `constrained` or `unconstrained`.

The `on key` clause allows you to specify actions to be taken when the user presses one of the following special keys:

`F1 through F64`	`Control-<letter -except a, d, h, l, r, or x>`	
`accept`	`help`	`prevpage`
`delete`	`insert`	`return`
`down`	`interrupt`	`right`
`esc`	`left`	`tab`
`escape`	`nextpage`	`up`

Input of a One-to-Many Relationship

- *One-to-many input overview*
- *Sample module*
- *Summary*

One-to-Many Input Overview

Allowing a user to enter a one-to-many relationship onto a screen form is not difficult. You have already learned all the statements and functions you need, all you have to do now is decide how you want to handle the input.

Do you want to have separate menu options for the *one* part of the relationship and the *many* part of the relationship? Do you want to send the user through all of the fields in the one relationship before allowing him to access the many part of the relationship?

All you need to do is add options to your menu or call functions from wherever you decide an action should be performed and you're done.

Sample Module

The sample module and screen that follow incorporate what we have learned in previous chapters. This module allows you to view all of the information for a toy order, then add, delete, or change the toy orders or the toy order items.

```
{*****************************************************************
   input one-to-many relationship example
   This module allows you to view, add, change and delete informa-
tion
   in the toy_order and toy_order_item tables table.

   The following functions are in this module:
                    Toy_Order_Menu
                    Find_Toy_Order
                    Close_Toy_Order_Cursor
                    Next_Toy_Order
                    Previous_Toy_Order
                    Delete_Toy_Order
                    Add_Change_Toy_Order
                    Find_Order_Item
                    Display_Order_Item
                    Input_Order_Item
                    Delete_Order_Item
                    Insert_Order_Item
                    Change_Order_Item
 ****************************************************************}


database toymaker

{ Define variables global to this module }
define p_toy_order              record
          order_number          like toy_order.order_number,
          store_number          like toy_order.store_number,
          store_name            like toy_store.store_name,
          order_date            like toy_order.order_date,
          shipping_datetime     like toy_order.shipping_datetime,
          sales_code            like toy_order.sales_code
        end record

define pa_order_item            array [100] of record
          toy_code              like toy_order_item.toy_code,
          description           like toy.description,
          quantity              like toy_order_item.quantity,
          unit_price            like toy_order_item.unit_price,
          total_price           decimal (8,2)
        end record

define cursor_open              smallint
```

```
main
  defer interrupt
  defer quit
  options message line last
  call Toy_Order_Menu ()
end main


{*******************************************************************
  Toy_Order_Menu
  ******************************************************************}
function Toy_Order_Menu ()

  whenever error stop

  let cursor_open = false
  initialize p_toy_order.* to null

  open window w_toy_order at 2,2 with form "toy_order"
    attribute (border)

  menu "Toy Order Menu"

    command "Find"                   "Find toy orders."
            help 1
            call Find_Toy_Order ()

    command "Next"                   "View the next toy order."
            help 2
            call Next_Toy_Order ()

    command "Previous"               "View the previous toy order."
            help 3
            call Previous_Toy_Order ()

    command "Add"                    "Add this toy order."
            help 10
            call Add_Change_Toy_Order ("A")
            call Find_Order_Item (p_toy_order.order_number)
            next option "Find"

    command "Change"                 "Change this toy order."
            help 11
            call Add_Change_Toy_Order ("C")
            next option "Find"
```

```
    command "Delete"                   "Delete this toy order."
            help 6
            call Delete_Toy_Order ()
            next option "Find"

    command "Items"                    "View all toy order items."
            help 19
            call Find_Order_Item (p_toy_order.order_number)
            next option "Find"

    command key ("E","X") "Exit"    "Exit from this menu."
            help 9
            exit menu
  end menu

  call Close_Toy_Order_Cursor ()

  close window w_toy_order

end function  { Toy_Order_Menu }


{******************************************************************
  Find_Toy_Order
  Find the toy order for the user and display the first order.
 ******************************************************************}
function Find_Toy_Order ()
  define where_clause       char(300)
  define sql_statement      char(600)

  clear form
  let int_flag = false
  call Close_Toy_Order_Cursor ()
  initialize p_toy_order.* to null

  display "" at 1,1
  display "" at 2,1
  display "Please enter your search criteria." at 1, 1

  construct by name where_clause on
      toy_order.order_number,        toy_order.store_number,
      toy_store.store_name,          toy_order.order_date,
      toy_order.shipping_datetime,   toy_order.sales_code
    help 1

  { Allow user to press break during construct to cancel search }
```

```
if int_flag then
  message "Toy order search cancelled."
  let int_flag = false
  return
end if

display "" at 1,1
display "" at 2,1
display "Searching..." at 1, 1

let sql_statement =
  "select toy_order.order_number,      toy_order.store_number, ",
        "toy_store.store_name,         toy_order.order_date, ",
        "toy_order.shipping_datetime, toy_order.sales_code ",
    "from toy_order, toy_store ",
    "where ", where_clause clipped, " and ",
          "toy_order.store_number = toy_store.store_number ",
    "order by order_number"

whenever error continue
prepare statement1 from sql_statement
if sqlca.sqlcode < 0 then
  call Error_Recovery ()
  return
end if
declare toy_order_cursor scroll cursor with hold for statement1
if sqlca.sqlcode < 0 then
  call Error_Recovery ()
  return
end if
open toy_order_cursor
if sqlca.sqlcode < 0 then
  call Error_Recovery ()
  return
end if
let cursor_open = true

fetch first toy_order_cursor into p_toy_order.*
if sqlca.sqlcode <> 0 then
  if sqlca.sqlcode = notfound then
    message "No toy orders meet this criteria."
  else
    call Error_Recovery ()
    return
  end if
end if
```

```
  whenever error stop

  display p_toy_order.* to s_toy_order.*
  call Find_Order_Item (p_toy_order.order_number)

end function   { Find_Toy_Order }



{*****************************************************************
  Close_Toy_Order_Cursor
  Close and free the cursor.
  ***************************************************************}
function Close_Toy_Order_Cursor ()

  whenever error continue

  fetch first toy_order_cursor into p_toy_order.*
  if cursor_open then
    close toy_order_cursor
    if sqlca.sqlcode < 0 then
      call Error_Recovery ()
    end if
    free  toy_order_cursor
    if sqlca.sqlcode < 0 then
      call Error_Recovery ()
    end if
    let cursor_open = false
  end if

  whenever error stop

end function   { Close_Toy_Order_Cursor }



{*****************************************************************
  Next_Toy_Order
  This function fetches the previous row of information.
  ***************************************************************}
function Next_Toy_Order ()

  if p_toy_order.order_number is null then
    error "You must Find a toy order before you can see ",
          "the next toy order."
    return
  end if
```

```
whenever error continue
fetch next toy_order_cursor into p_toy_order.*
if sqlca.sqlcode <> 0 then
  if sqlca.sqlcode = notfound then
    message "You are at the end of the list."
            attribute (reverse)
  else
    call Error_Recovery ()
    return
  end if
end if
whenever error stop

message ""
display p_toy_order.* to s_toy_order.*
call Find_Order_Item (p_toy_order.order_number)

end function  { Next_Toy_Order }


{*******************************************************************
  Previous_Toy_Order
  This function fetches the previous row of information.
  ******************************************************************}
function Previous_Toy_Order ()

  if p_toy_order.order_number is null then
    error "You must Find a toy order before you can see ",
          "the previous toy order."
    return
  end if

  whenever error continue
  fetch previous toy_order_cursor into p_toy_order.*
  if sqlca.sqlcode <> 0 then
    if sqlca.sqlcode = notfound then
      message "You are at the beginning of the list."
              attribute (reverse)
    else
      call Error_Recovery ()
      return
    end if
  end if
  whenever error stop
```

```
  message ""
  display p_toy_order.* to s_toy_order.*
  call Find_Order_Item (p_toy_order.order_number)

end function  { Previous_Toy_Order }



{**************************************************************
  Delete_Toy_Order
  Delete the toy_order and any related toy_order_items.
**************************************************************}
function Delete_Toy_Order ()

  if p_toy_order.order_number is null then
    error "You must Find a toy order before you can delete it."
    return
  end if

  menu "Delete?"
    command "No" "Do not delete this toy order."
            help 20
            message "Deletion of toy order cancelled."
                    attribute (reverse)
            exit menu

    command "Yes " "Delete this toy order item."
            help 21

            { First delete any related toy_order_items }
            whenever error continue
            delete from toy_order_item
              where order_number = toy_order.order_number

            if sqlca.sqlcode = 0 or sqlca.sqlcode = notfound then
                delete from toy_order
                    where order_number = toy_order.order_number
            else
              call Error_Recovery ()
              exit menu
            end if
            whenever error stop

            { If you are using transactions, you would put a begin
              work in front of the first delete, then you could do
              either a commit work or rollback work after the
              second delete, depending on the error status }
```

```
                 if sqlca.sqlcode = 0 then
                    message "Toy order deleted."
                            attribute (reverse)
                 else
                   call Error_Recovery ()
                   exit menu
                 end if

                 clear form
                 exit menu
      end menu  { Delete? menu }

end function  { Delete_Toy_Order }


{******************************************************************
   Add_Change_Toy_Order
   This function allows the user to add or change a row in the
   toy_order table.
   *****************************************************************}
function Add_Change_Toy_Order (add_change)
   define add_change                char (1)
   define is_valid                  smallint
   define orig_toy_order record
             order_number       like toy_order.order_number,
             store_number       like toy_order.store_number,
             store_name         like toy_store.store_name,
             order_date         like toy_order.order_date,
             shipping_datetime  like toy_order.shipping_datetime,
             sales_code         like toy_order.sales_code
          end record

   if add_change = "C" and p_toy_order.order_number is null then
      error "You must Find a toy_order before you can change one."
      return
   end if

   clear form

   display "" at 1,1
   display "" at 2,1
   display "Press Accept when finished or Interrupt to cancel."
                                                          at 2,1

   if add_change = "A" then
      display "ADD a new toy order." at 1,1
```

```
      initialize orig_toy_order.* to null
   else
      display "CHANGE a toy order." at 1,1
      let orig_toy_order.* = p_toy_order.*
   end if

   input by name    p_toy_order.store_number thru
                    p_toy_order.sales_code    without defaults
      help 14

      before input
         if p_toy_order.order_date is null then
            let p_toy_order.order_date = today
            display by name p_toy_order.order_date
         end if

      after field order_date
         if p_toy_order.order_date > (today + 91) then
            error "Order date cannot be over 90 days from now."
            next field order_date
         end if

         after field store_number, store_name
         if not Valid_Store (p_toy_order.store_number,
                             p_toy_order.store_name) then
            error "Not a valid toy store.  Press F3 for choices."
            next field store_number
         end if

      after field sales_code
         call Valid_Sales_Code (p_toy_order.sales_code)
                   returning  is_valid

         if not is_valid then
            error "Not a valid sales_code.  Press F3 for choices."
            next field sales_code
         end if

      on key (F3)
         case
            when infield (store_number) or infield (store_name)
               call Lookup_Toy_Store (p_toy_order.store_number)
                      returning      p_toy_order.store_number,
                                     p_toy_order.store_name
```

```
            display by name p_toy_order.store_number,
                           p_toy_order.store_name

         when infield (sales_code) then
             call Lookup_Sales_Code (p_toy_order.sales_code)
                        returning  p_toy_order.sales_code

             display by name p_toy_order.sales_code

         otherwise
             error "Sorry, pop-up help is not available in this field."
      end case

   after input
      if int_flag = false then
         if date (p_toy_order.shipping_datetime) <
                              p_toy_order.order_date then
         error "The shipping date cannot be before the order date."
         next field order_date
         end if
      end if
end input

if not int_flag then
   if add_change = "A" then
     insert into toy_order
         (toy_order.order_number,  toy_order.store_number,
          toy_order.order_date,    toy_order.shipping_datetime,
          toy_order.sales_code)
       values
         (0,                        p_toy_order.store_number,
          p_toy_order.order_date,  p_toy_order.shipping_datetime,
          p_toy_order.sales_code)

     if sqlca.sqlcode <> 0 then
       error "Error ", sqlca.sqlcode, " inserting toy_order."
     end if
   else  { add_change = "C" }
       update toy_order set
              (toy_order.store_number,     toy_order.order_date,
            toy_order.shipping_datetime,  toy_order.sales_code)
         = (p_toy_order.store_number,     p_toy_order.order_date,
            p_toy_order.shipping_datetime, p_toy_order.sales_code)
         where order_number = p_toy_order.order_number
```

```
          if sqlca.sqlcode <> 0 then
            error "Error ", sqlca.sqlcode, " changing toy_order."
          end if
      end if  { add_change = "A" }
    else
      clear form
      let p_toy_order.* = orig_toy_order.*
      display by name p_toy_order.*
      let int_flag = false
      if add_change = "A" then
        message "User interrupt - row not added."
      else
        message "User interrupt - row not changed."
      end if
    end if
end function  { Add_Change_Toy_Order }


{ *****************************************************************
  Find_Order_Item
  Find order items for this order.
  *****************************************************************}
function Find_Order_Item (p_order_number)
  define p_order_number    like toy_order.order_number
  define sql_stmt          char (400)
  define counter           smallint

  if p_order_number is null then
    error "You must Find an order before you can view its items."
    return
  end if

  let int_flag = false

  let sql_stmt =
    "select toy_order_item.toy_code, toy.description, ",
          "toy_order_item.quantity, toy_order_item.unit_price, ",
          "(toy_order_item.quantity * ",
             "toy_order_item.unit_price) total_price ",
      "from toy_order_item, toy ",
      "where toy_order_item.order_number = ? and ",
           "toy_order_item.toy_code = toy.toy_code ",
      "order by toy.description"
```

```
whenever error continue
prepare statement2 from sql_stmt
if sqlca.sqlcode < 0 then
  call Error_Recovery ()
  return
end if
declare ord_item_cursor scroll cursor for statement2
if sqlca.sqlcode < 0 then
  call Error_Recovery ()
  return
end if
open ord_item_cursor using p_order_number
if sqlca.sqlcode < 0 then
  call Error_Recovery ()
  return
end if

let counter = 0
while counter < 100  { Maximum number of records to display }
  let counter = counter + 1
  initialize pa_order_item[counter].* to null
  fetch ord_item_cursor into pa_order_item[counter].*
  if sqlca.sqlcode <> 0 then
    if sqlca.sqlcode = notfound then
      let counter = counter - 1
      exit while
    else
      call Error_Recovery ()
      return
    end if
  end if
end while
whenever error stop

if counter = 0 then
  message "There are no items matching your search criteria."
          attribute (reverse)
else
  call Display_Order_Item ()
end if

whenever error continue
close ord_item_cursor
if sqlca.sqlcode < 0 then
  call Error_Recovery ()
end if
```

```
free  ord_item_cursor
if sqlca.sqlcode < 0 then
  call Error_Recovery ()
end if
whenever error stop

end function  { Find_Order_Item }


{*******************************************************************
  Display_Order_Item
  This function displays the rows first eight rows of order items.
 ******************************************************************}
function Display_Order_Item ()
  define counter              smallint

  display "" at 1,1
  display "" at 2,1
  display "Use the arrow keys and the Page Up and Page Down keys"
                                                       at 1,1
  display "to look through the items.  Press ESC to exit."  at 2,1

  for counter = 1 to 8
    display pa_order_item[counter].* to sa_order_item[counter].*
  end for

end function  { Display_Order_Item }


{*******************************************************************
  Input_Order_Item
  This function displays the rows of data and allows the user to
  look through them.
 ******************************************************************}
function Input_Order_Item (p_order_number, counter)
  define p_order_number        like toy_order.order_number
  define counter, i, j         smallint
  define is_valid              smallint
  define trans_type            char (1)
  define orig_order_item       record
         toy_code              like toy_order_item.toy_code,
         description           like toy.description,
         quantity              like toy_order_item.quantity,
         unit_price            like toy_order_item.unit_price,
         total_price           decimal (8,2)
       end record
```

```
{ Display }
display "" at 1,1
display "" at 2,1
display "Use the arrow keys and the Page Up and Page Down keys"
                                                       at 1,1
display "to look through the items.      F1=Insert   F2=Delete"
                                                       at 2,1


call set_count (counter)

input array pa_order_item without defaults from sa_order_item.*
  help 19

  before insert
    let trans_type = "I"

  after insert
    let i = arr_curr ()

    if not int_flag and
        (pa_order_item[i].toy_code    is not null or
         pa_order_item[i].quantity    is not null or
         pa_order_item[i].unit_price is not null) then
      call Insert_Order_Item (p_order_number, i)
    else
        error "Entry not complete."
        initialize trans_type to null
    end if

  before delete
    let i = arr_curr ()
    call Delete_Order_Item (p_order_number, i)
              returning  trans_type

    { Redisplay input message }
    display "" at 1,1
    display "" at 2,1
    display "Use arrow keys and the Page Up and Page Down keys"
                                                       at 1,1
      display "to look through the items.   F1=Insert   F2=Delete"
                                                       at 2,1

  before row
      let i = arr_curr ()
      let j = scr_line ()
```

```
         initialize trans_type to null
         let orig_order_item.* = pa_order_item[i].*

     after row
       let i = arr_curr ()
       let j = scr_line ()

       if not int_flag and trans_type is null and
         (pa_order_item[i].toy_code <> orig_order_item.toy_code or
          pa_order_item[i].quantity <> orig_order_item.quantity or
          pa_order_item[i].unit_price <> orig_order_item.unit_price)
                                                              then
         call Change_Order_Item (p_order_number, i)
       end if

     after field toy_code
       { Don't let toy_code change }
       if pa_order_item[i].toy_code <> orig_order_item.toy_code and
          trans_type is null then
          error "Cannot change toy_code code - delete and re-enter."
          let pa_order_item[i].toy_code = orig_order_item.toy_code
          display pa_order_item[i].toy_code
               to sa_order_item[j].toy_code
       else
          call Valid_Toy_Code (pa_order_item[i].toy_code)
                  returning  is_valid
          if not is_valid then
            error "Invalid toy code - press F1 for choices."
            next field toy_code
          end if

          call Get_Toy_Unit_Price (pa_order_item[i].toy_code)
                      returning  pa_order_item[i].unit_price
          display pa_order_item[i].unit_price
               to sa_order_item[j].unit_price
       end if

     after field quantity, unit_price
          let pa_order_item[i].total_price =
          pa_order_item[i].quantity * pa_order_item[i].unit_price

          display pa_order_item[i].total_price
               to sa_order_item[i].total_price

     on key (F1)
          if infield (toy_code) then
```

```
        call Lookup_Toy_Code (pa_order_item[i].toy_code)
                returning  pa_order_item[i].toy_code,
                           pa_order_item[i].description

        display pa_order_item[i].toy_code,
                pa_order_item[i].description
             to sa_order_item[i].toy_code,
                sa_order_item[i].description
      else
         error "Sorry, lookup of data unavailable in this field."
      end if
  end input

  let int_flag = false
end function  { Input_Order_Item }


{ * * * * * * * * * * * * * * * * * * * * * * * * * * * * * * * * * * * * * * * * * * * * * * * * * * * * * * * * * * * * * *
  Delete_Order_Item
  This function deletes a toy_order_item record.
  * * * * * * * * * * * * * * * * * * * * * * * * * * * * * * * * * * * * * * * * * * * * * * * * * * * * * * * * * * * * * * }
function Delete_Order_Item (p_order_number, array_row)
  define p_order_number    like toy_order.order_number
  define array_row         smallint
  define trans_type        char (1)

  initialize trans_type to null

  menu "Delete? "
    command "No"  "Do not delete this order item."
           help 20
           exit menu

    command "Yes" "Delete this order item."
           help 21

           whenever error continue

           { Delete this order item }
           delete from toy_order_item
             where order_number = p_order_number and
                   toy_code    = pa_order_item[array_row].toy_code

           if sqlca.sqlcode = 0 then
             message "Deleted."
             let trans_type = "D"
```

```
                else
                   error "Error number ", sqlca.sqlcode,
                          " deleting order item."
                end if

                whenever error stop

                exit menu
       end menu

       return trans_type

   end function  { Delete_Order_Item }


   {*****************************************************************
      Insert_Order_Item
      This function inserts a row into the toy_order_item.
   *****************************************************************}
   function Insert_Order_Item (p_order_number, array_row)
      define p_order_number      like toy_order.order_number
      define array_row           smallint

      whenever error continue

      insert into toy_order_item
          (order_number, toy_code, quantity, unit_price)
        values
          (p_order_number,
           pa_order_item[array_row].toy_code,
           pa_order_item[array_row].quantity,
           pa_order_item[array_row].unit_price)

      if sqlca.sqlcode <> 0 then
        error "Error number ", sqlca.sqlcode, " adding item."
      end if

      whenever error stop
   end function  { Insert_Order_Item }
```

```
{*********************************************************************
   Change_Order_Item
   This function updates the information in the toy_order_item
table.
*********************************************************************}
function Change_Order_Item (p_order_number, array_row)
   define p_order_number         like toy_order.order_number
   define array_row             smallint

   whenever error continue

   update toy_order_item set (quantity, unit_price)
      = (pa_order_item[array_row].quantity,
         pa_order_item[array_row].unit_price)
      where order_number = p_order_number and
            toy_code     = pa_order_item[array_row].toy_code

   if sqlca.sqlcode <> 0 then
      error "Error number ", sqlca.sqlcode, " changing item."
   end if

   whenever error stop
end function   { Change_Order_Item }
```

This sample module uses the following screen form.

```
{*********************************************************************
   toy_order
   This screen allows you to display and maintain toy_order and
   toy_order_item information.
*********************************************************************}

database toymaker
screen size 24 by 80

{
---------------------------------------Press F1 for Help------
   Order number: [f000        ]

   Store:        [f001        ]        [f005                            ]

   Date Ordered: [f002        ]        Date Shipped:  [f003            ]

   Sales Code:   [f004   ]
```

```
     Toy Code/Description            Quantity   Unit Price   Total Price
     [f011    |f014                   |f012      |f013        |f015       ]
     [f011    |f014                   |f012      |f013        |f015       ]
     [f011    |f014                   |f012      |f013        |f015       ]
     [f011    |f014                   |f012      |f013        |f015       ]
     [f011    |f014                   |f012      |f013        |f015       ]
     [f011    |f014                   |f012      |f013        |f015       ]
     [f011    |f014                   |f012      |f013        |f015       ]
     [f011    |f014                   |f012      |f013        |f015       ]
     }
     end

tables toy_order toy_store toy_order_item toy

attributes
    f000 = toy_order.order_number;
    f001 = toy_order.store_number;
    f005 = toy_store.store_name;
    f002 = toy_order.order_date;
    f003 = toy_order.shipping_datetime;
    f004 = toy_order.sales_code;

    f011 = toy_order_item.toy_code;
    f014 = toy.description;
    f012 = toy_order_item.quantity;
    f013 = toy_order_item.unit_price;
    f015 = formonly.total_price;

instructions
    delimiters "||"

    screen record s_toy_order
        (order_number, store_number,      store_name,
         order_date,    shipping_datetime, sales_code)

    screen record sa_order_item [8]
        (toy_code, description, quantity, unit_price, total_price)
end
```

Summary

Allowing a user to enter a one-to-many relationship onto a screen form is not difficult. All you must do is add options to your menu or call functions from wherever you decide an action should be performed, and you're done.

Chapter 25

Basic Report Writing

- *Report overview*
- *Getting the report data*
- *Formatting the report*
- output
- order by
- *Control blocks*
- on every row
- *Headers and footers*
- *Aggregates*
- *Grouping*
- *Final totals*
- *Sample report*
- *Summary*

Report Overview

All the work we've done up until now has been great. We can put data into a database, get it back out, change it—anything we want. Now we will tackle the task of transforming data into information that is useful to the user. We will now create reports.

A report gathers a set of data, formats it, and prints it out. Report writing in INFORMIX-4GL is extremely powerful, but without some imagination, it may initially seem somewhat limited. In this chapter we will discuss basic report writing. In the next chapter, we will learn some tricks, to take us beyond basic report writing.

The following is an outline of an INFORMIX-4GL report. There are two parts to every report. The first is the section the report is called from where data can be gathered and manipulated. The second section is the `report` section where the data is formatted and written to the report.

It is generally easier to store each report in a separate module. This makes future changes and modifications easier. Each module would include:

1. a `database` statement,
2. a section the report is called from, and
3. a `report` section.

```
database  <database name>

function New_Report ()
   define new_rec record(s)
        <Elements in record(s)>
     end record

   declare new_cursor cursor for
     <select statement>
   start report Format_New_Report
     foreach new_cursor into new_rec.*
       output to report
              Format_New_Report (new_rec.*)
     end foreach
   finish report Format_New_Report
end function   { New_Report }
```

```
report Format_New_Report (new_rec)
   define new_rec records
         <Same as new_rec record in the section
          the report is called from>
end record

   format
      every row

end report  { Format_New_Report }
```

The reporting statements used to call and handle report processing are:

```
start report <report name>
   output to report <report name>
                        ( <parameters passed> )
      terminate report <report name>
finish report <report name>
```

The `report` section contains many new statements that will be covered later in this chapter. Notice that this is a `report` instead of a `function`. The statements allowed within a `report` are different from those allowed in a regular `function`.

Getting the Report Data

The first step in creating a report is determining what information should go into it. This is the data gathering portion of the report. Let's start by going through the section the report is called from in the above report outline line by line.

```
function New_Report ()
```

The first step is a normal `function` statement.

```
define new_rec records
      <Elements in records>
      end record
```

This step is the same as defining a record for use in a screen. The elements defined in the record should be in the same order and of a compatible type as those used in the `select` statement.

Note that you can use a `construct`, command line arguments, or any other means you like to gather input from the user at this point.

```
declare new_cursor cursor for
    <select statement>
```

This step declares a `select` statement for use in a screen. You will probably want to take this opportunity to order your data. This is the easiest and fastest way to determine the order in which the information in your report will be printed.

```
start report Format_New_Report
```

This statement tells INFORMIX-4GL to start the report. You should only have one `start report` statement in a report. The `start report` statement has the syntax:

```
start report <report name>
    [ to {   "<file name>" |
             <variable containing file name> |
             printer |
             pipe [ in { line | form } mode ] "<program name>" |
             pipe [ in { line | form } mode ]
                            <variable containing program name>
         }
    ]
```

By default, the report is displayed to the screen. The `to` part of this statement allows you to specify a file name, printer, or program where the output of the report should go. The `report` section of the report has an `output` clause that will allow you to specify these options, but specifying them here gives you more flexibility since you can use variables for the file name and program name. In the `report` statement these values must be set to literal strings and cannot change.

The `to <file name>` clause will write to the current directory unless a pathname is specified. If the report name already exists, it will be overwritten. If you want to customize the name of the report (e.g., with a date and time stamp or an order number), put the name of the report into a variable, then use the syntax: to `<file name variable>`.

The `to printer` clause will default to `lp` or `lpr`. If you wish to print to a different printer, change the DBPRINT environment variable to an appropriate print string, or use the `to pipe <program name>` clause.

The `to pipe <program name>` clause pipes the report output to another program. For example, if a user wants to print to any of several printers, then setting the DBPRINT environment variable and using the printer clause won't be useful. But you can set a variable, user_printer, for instance, to a print string and then say: `to pipe user_printer`. You may also choose whether you are in `form` mode (ie. the screen is not cleared and redrawn) or line mode when the pipe is executed.

```
foreach new_cursor into new_rec.*
```

We have already used the `foreach` statement. Make certain that the record (or variables) you read into are in the same order and have compatible types to those in your `select` statement.

```
output to report Format_New_Report (new_rec.*)
```

This statement for reports is the equivalent of `call <function name>` for functions. The only information that will be written to the report is what is passed in by this statement. Records and other variables are passed the same way they are passed to and from functions. If you want to screen out some data retrieved by your `select` statement from the report, simply put an `if-then` statement around the `output` statement.

note

Keep in mind that if the `output to report` *statement is never called, no report will be produced. You can get around this by setting a report flag to false before the* `foreach` *statement, then setting it to true if the* `output to report` *statement is called. After the* `foreach`*, if the report flag is still false, then initialize the report data to null, and call the* `output to report` *section.*

```
end foreach
```

This statement completes the foreach loop.

```
finish report Format_New_Report
```

This statement lets INFORMIX-4GL know there are no more rows of data in the report. This is the point at which the report totals are printed and the report is completed. You should have only one finish report statement in any report.

The terminate report statement can be used to terminate report processing before the report has actually completed. If the report is incomplete, the terminate report statement should be used to avoid leaving the report processing in an ambiguous state.

```
end function   { New_Report }
```

This is a regular end function statement.

Don't limit yourself in this section. Any regular 4GL statements will work in sections of code that call reports. In addition to defining a record that is used to fetch information from the select statement, you can also define a record containing information that will be passed to the report instead of the original record.

Below is the code which calls the report for our toys database. This report will tell us which toy stores have ordered which toys and how many of each type of toy was ordered over a specified time period.

```
{****************************************************************
  Toy_Orders_Report
  This report lists toy stores and the toys they ordered for the
  specified time period.
****************************************************************}
function Toy_Orders_Report (start_date, end_date)
  define start_date, end_date   date

  define toy_order_rec record
         store_name              like toy_store.store_name,
         toy_description         like toy.description,
         quantity                like toy_order_item.quantity,
         profit                  money (16,2)
       end record
```

```
define reported                  smallint

declare toy_orders_cur cursor for
   select toy_store.store_name, toy.description,
          toy_order_item.quantity,
          ((toy_order_item.unit_price - toy.cost)
                      * toy_order_item.quantity)  { profit }
      from toy_order, toy_order_item, toy_store, toy
      where toy_order.order_date
                        between start_date and end_date    and
        toy_order.order_number  = toy_order_item.order_number and
        toy_order_item.toy_code = toy.toy_code                and
        toy_order.store_number  = toy_store.store_number
      order by toy_store.store_name, toy.description

start report Format_Toy_Orders_Report to "toy_orders.rpt"

   let reported = false
   foreach toy_orders_cur into toy_order_rec.*

   output to report Format_Toy_Orders_Report
                   (start_date, end_date, toy_order_rec.*)
   let reported = true

   end foreach

   if not reported then
      initialize toy_order_rec.* to null
      output to report Format_Toy_Orders_Report
                   (start_date, end_date, toy_order_rec.*)
   end if
  finish report Format_Toy_Orders_Report

   close toy_orders_cur
   free toy_orders_cur
end function  { Toy_Orders_Report }
```

From this section of code, we are retrieving four pieces of information from our database that will make a simple, but useful
report. Notice that if no information exists for the report, we still
call the report routine to produce an empty report.

Formatting the Report

The `report` section is where the formatting of the report is done. A sloppy looking report can distract from the quality of the information. People are more likely to trust your data if it is neatly organized into a nice looking report.

The `report` section has the form:

```
report <report name> ( <variable names> )

    <define any variables passed into or
    used in report section>

    output   <output statements>

    order { internal | external } by <variable name> [ asc | desc ]
                                                       [, ...]

    format   <format statements>

end report
```

Remember that report names are like function names. A report name must fit the same criteria as a function name, including having a unique name within a program. A `function` and a `report` cannot have the same name, just as two functions and two reports cannot have the same name.

Variables and records are passed to the `report` section the same way they are passed to other functions. Any variables passed into or used in the `report` section must be defined in the `report` section.

Defining variables in the `report` section is exactly the same as defining variables in the `function` section. One useful feature to keep in mind is that, while a report is being produced, each time you call the report section, the variables defined locally within the report will keep their value from the last time you were in that section.

The output, format and order by sections are discussed in detail in the following sections.

The shortest report format possible is simply: format every row. No other formatting statements can be used when this format is used. INFORMIX-4GL determines the best format (horizontal or vertical) to use and prints a default report. This is fine for checking data while writing and testing a report, but its appearance should be improved before you give it to users.

An end report statement (similar to an end function statement) is needed to complete the report section.

For the toy order report we began earlier, the shortest report we can write to use with the function we have already written is:

```
{ ********************************************************************
   Format_Toy_Orders_Report
 ******************************************************************* }
report Format_Toy_Orders_Report (start_date, end_date,
                                   toy_order_rec)
   define start_date, end_date   date
   define toy_order_rec record
              store_name          like toy_store.store_name,
              toy_description     like toy.description,
              quantity            like toy_order_item.quantity,
              profit              money (16,2)
          end record

   format every row

end report   { Format_Toy_Orders_Report }
```

Output

The `output` statement goes between the definitions and the `format` in the `report` section. This section is optional. If it is not included, the defaults will be used.

The `output` section allows you to define the size of your report page and where you would like the report to print. The `output` options are:

```
left margin      <number of spaces - default column 5>
right margin     <number of spaces - default column 132>
top margin       <number of lines  - default 3>
bottom margin    <number of lines  - default 3>
page length      <number of lines  - default 66>
report to        <where report should print - default screen>
```

The numbers and the `report to` information used here must be constants. You cannot use variables for these values.

```
output
    top     margin 2
    bottom  margin 2
```

The `page length` specifies the number of lines that will fit on a page, not the number of lines printed on each page. A standard page (11 inches) in length is usually 66 lines long.

The `report to` clause is similar to the `report to` clause in the `start report` statement. It has the form:

```
report to {  "<file name>"  |
             printer  |
             pipe "<program name>" }
```

This is discussed in the previous section, where the `start report` statement is described. Keep in mind that if you use a `report to` statement here, you will need to know what the report name (or output location) will be when you are writing your code. If you want your report name to change depending on variable values, then use the option in the `start report` statement instead.

Order by

The `order by` statement can be used to sort the rows within the report, or to let the report know the rows in the report are already in a particular order. The `order by` statement goes after the `output` section and before the `format` section of the report.

```
order [ internal | external ]
   by <variable name> [, ...]
```

The sorting performed by the `select` statement when the data is initially fetched for the report, will usually make this statement unnecessary. But you may be manipulating your data in such a way that an `order by` statement in your `select` statement is not sufficient. If you want your data to be sorted from within the report, an example would be:

```
order by date_var, last_name
```

If the data is already sorted coming into the report, you may still need to use an `order external by` statement to let the report know how the data is sorted. This is useful when you are using `before` and `after` groups (described below) on more than one variable, and the report does not understand the order in which the data should be processed.

```
order external by date_var, last_name
```

The above statement tells the report the data has been sorted in the specified order. The keyword `external` tells the report the data has already been sorted, so that it does not sort it again. If your data is already sorted, use the `external` clause. Without the use of this `external` clause, an additional pass will be done at report runtime to sort the data. This will cause your report to take more time to produce and as well as using additional system resources. For improved performance, sort data before the report section whenever possible. Older versions of INFORMIX-4GL limited you to 8 columns of sorting, newer versions have removed this limit.

Control Blocks

The format section of a report is made up of control blocks. The control blocks used in INFORMIX-4GL are:

```
format
    every row
    first page header
    page header
    before group of <variable>
    on every row
    after group of <variable>
    page trailer
    on last row
```

Every statement executed within the `format` section must be executed within a control block. This means that a control block cannot be executed conditionally, but the statements within a control block can be executed conditionally.

This doesn't work:
```
if p_check = "Y" then
    on every row
        print variable_name
end if
```

This works:
```
on every row
    if p_check = "Y" then
        print variable_name
    end if
```

The `format every row` statement as discussed above is a special instance of a control block. When `format every row` is used, no other control block or statements can be used within the `format` section for that report.

Most INFORMIX-4GL statements that can be used in an INFORMIX-4GL function can also be used in a control block—except for interactive statements such as `input`, `menu`, `prompt`, `display array`, `input array` and the `return` statement. `Return` can cause some fairly nasty things to happen to your report (including skipping an occasional data record), so using it should be avoided (and newer versions of INFORMIX-4GL won't even compile with `return`).

There are also some statements that can be executed *only* within the control blocks. These are the statements that allow you to print and format data in a report. The statements are listed in the order of how frequently they are generally used.

```
print [ <expression> [, ...] ] [ ; ]
skip { <number> line[s] | to top of page }
need <number> lines
pause [ "<string>" ]
print file "<file name>"
exit report
```

print [<expression> [, ...]] [;]

This statement prints the information in the expression(s) to the report. An expression may be a quoted string, a variable, a function with a returning value, etc.

The word `column` may be used as part of an expression.

A semicolon (`;`) prints the expression(s) without advancing to the next line.

Numbers and dates can be formatted with the `using` clause as described in Chapter 9.

Examples:

```
print column 10, "Total: ",
      column 20, p_total using "$$$$,$-&.&&"

print column 10, "Hello "; { ';' prevents new line }
print column 20, "World!"

print start_date, " to ", end_date
```

skip { <number> line[s] | to top of page }

This statement skips the indicated number of lines in the report or skips to the top of the next page. The number of lines to skip must be a numeric constant; it may not be a variable.

Examples: `skip 3 lines`

`skip to top of page`

need <number> lines

This statement keeps the next user-specified number of lines of the report on the same page. If the number of lines needed is greater than the number of lines required to print that number of lines on the same page, the report will print the lines at the top of the next page.

Example:
```
need 3 lines
print "Keep"
print "these lines"
print "together"
```

pause ["<string>"]

The `pause` statement can only be used when the output is being displayed to the screen. It pauses the report output until the user hits the *return* key. This could be used to implement paging through a report on a screen by a user.

Example: `pause "Please press return to continue"`

print file "*\<file name>*"

This statement inserts the contents of the specified file into the report. This might be used for customized fill-in-the-blank forms. You can customize the top of a report with a customer name, and have the customer fill in the blanks below.

Example: print first_name clipped, " ", last_name
            skip 2 lines

            print file "/path/to/file name/blank_form"

exit report

This statement is available in more recent versions of INFORMIX-4GL to allow you to terminate the report from within the report. The return statement is specifically not permitted in reports, so the exit report statement allows you a way to immediately exit from a report without leaving anything in an ambiguous state.

Example: exit report

Several built-in operators can also be used in report control blocks.

```
column <number>
lineno
pageno
<number> space[s]
<character string> wordwrap
   [ right margin <number> ]
```

column *\<number>*

Column is used in conjunction with the print statement to print information starting at the indicated column position.). You may use a numeric variable for the number.

Example:

print column 20, "printing starting at column 20"

lineno

This operator contains the current line number being printed. For instance, if you want to print starting on line 50 of the current page, you could do the following:

```
Example:   define p_skip_lines, counter smallint
           ...
           let p_skip_lines = 50 - lineno + 1

           skip p_skip_lines line
```

pageno

This operator tells you the number of the page currently being printed. This is useful for printing the page number at the top of each page.

Example:

```
print column 100, "Page: ", pageno using "<<<<<"
```

<number> space[s]

This operator prints the number of spaces specified (although it's usually easier to specify specific column positions with the column statement). You may use a numeric variable for the number.

Example:

```
print column 1, "|", 20 spaces, "|", 30 spaces, "|"
```

<character string> wordwrap
[right margin *<number>*]

This operator allows you to print a character string that will use several lines in a single print statement. The string will wrap automatically between words. New lines can be forced by printing ascii (10) (newline) or ascii (13) (return) where desired. A temporary right margin can be set while this statement is in use.

Example: `define paragraph char (800)`

         `...`

         `print paragraph wordwrap right margin 50`

Note that printing with `wordwrap` *will advance the line number in the report, so whatever is printed next will be printed after the entire* `wordwrap` *string has been printed. So if you have text you want to print to the right of a wordwrapped string, it will start on the line of the report the* `wordwrap` *finishes up on.*

On Every Row

`On every row` is an optional part of the `format` section of a report. This control block will be processed for each `output to report` call made.

From the example in the section of code the report is called from, we might format the report information as listed below.

Example:

```
format
on every row
   print column   5, toy_order_rec.store_name,
          column  40, toy_order_rec.toy_description,
          column  95, toy_order_rec.quantity,
          column 110, toy_order_rec.profit
```

Headers and Footers

Headers and footers are an optional part of the `format` section of a report. There are three control blocks we can use to dress up our reports so our data isn't floating around on a page all by itself. These statements are:

```
first page header
page header
page trailer
```

first page header

This control block will be executed only on the first page of a report. An elaborate heading may be appropriate on the first page, but not needed on successive pages.

In the following example, the first page header centers key report information on the first page. The column headings and line of dashes provide column headings for the data.

Example:

```
first page header
   print column  50, "Toy Store Order Report"
   print column  45, "For dates: ", start_date,
                     " to ", end_date
   print column  55, "Run date: ", today
   skip 2 lines

   print column   5, "Store",
         column  40, "Toy",
         column  95, "Quantity",
         column 110, "Profit"
   print column   1, "--------------------------",
                     "--------------------------",
                     "--------------------------",
                     "--------------------------",
                     "-----------",
```

You can also write some functions to perform common tasks such as figuring out where to start printing a string in order for it to be centered, or to return a string containing a specified number of dash marks.

page header

This control block will be executed at the top of every page of a report (except for the first page if there is a first page header control block).

The toy report might have the page header described below. It is often useful to print report information on each page of the report in case report pages get separated.

Example:

```
page header
   print column    1,  "Toy Store Order Report",
         column 110,  "Page: ", pageno using "<<<<<"
   print column    1,  "For dates: ", start_date, "
to ", end_date,
         column 110,  "Run date: ", today
   skip 2 lines

   print column    5,  "Store",
         column   40,  "Toy",
         column   95,  "Quantity",
         column 110,  "Profit"
   print column    1,  "----------------------------",
                       "----------------------------",
                       "----------------------------",
                       "----------------------------",
                       "------------",
```

page trailer

This control block will be executed at the bottom of every page of
a report. For instance, you might want to print page numbers at
the bottom center of every page.

Example:
```
page trailer
   print column 60, pageno using "<<<<<"
```

The page headers and page trailers must print the same number of lines each time they are executed.

This won't work:
```
page header
      if print_var = "Y" then
         print "Uneven heading"
      end if
```

This will work:
```
page header
    if print_var = "Y" then
       print "Uneven heading"
    else
       print " "
    end if
```

This feature can be very frustrating until you learn to work around it.

Aggregates

Aggregates are a way of grouping information within a report. They are generally used within grouping control blocks and at the end of a report (discussed later in this section). We have discussed the use of aggregates within `select` statements in earlier chapters. Using aggregates within reports is similar to using aggregates in the `select` statement.

The syntax for aggregates is:

```
[ group ]
{ count (*) | percent (*) |
   { sum | avg | min | max } ( <expression> )
}
[ where <where clause> ]
```

There will often be cases where you want to print subtotals and totals of information in a report. Sometimes you may want to print a report consisting only of totals, but you don't have a good way of doing this using aggregates within the `select` statement. Report aggregates will help you accomplish this.

The `group` should be used for aggregates within a `before group of` or `after group of` control block.

The report aggregates return the following information:

Report Aggregates	Description
count (*)	counts the number of rows
percent (*)	gives a percentage of count(*) to the total number of rows in the report
sum (<expression>)	returns the sum of values passed to the report
avg (<expression>)	returns the average of the values passed to the report
min (<expression>)	returns the minimum value passed to the report
max (<expression>)	returns the maximum value passed to the report

The where clause will allow you to calculate aggregates only on those values that meet the conditions in your where clause.

Grouping

Grouping control blocks are an optional part of the format section of a report. The grouping control blocks are:

```
before group of <variable>

after   group of <variable>
```

For each group of statement, you can only group on a single variable passed into the report. You cannot group by multiple variables on a single before group of or after group of statement.

You *can* use multiple before group of and after group of statements with different variables in the same report.

Using our on every row example we may want to format this information to make it look less cluttered.

Example:

```
format
  on every row
    print column    5, toy_order_rec.store_name,
           column   40, toy_order_rec.toy_description,
           column   95, toy_order_rec.quantity,
           column  110, toy_order_rec.profit
```

This format will print all information on every line of the report. It will look better if we only print a single stores' information on a separate page and only print out the store name when it changes. Let's also give a subtotal of the quantity and profit for each store.

Example:

```
format
  before group of toy_order_rec.store_name
    print column    5, toy_order_rec.store_name;

  on every row
    print column   40, toy_order_rec.toy_description,
          column   95, toy_order_rec.quantity
                                  using "###,##&",
          column  110, toy_order_rec.profit
                                  using "$$$$,$-&.&&"

  after group of toy_order_rec.store_name
    print column   95, "-------",
          column  110, "----------"
    print column   80, "Subtotals:",
          column   95, group sum (toy_order_rec.quantity)
                                  using "###,##&",
          column  110, group sum (toy_order_rec.profit)
                                  using "$$$$,$-&.&&"
    print column   95, "-------",
          column  110, "----------"
    skip to top of page
```

The data is already sorted by store name in the section of code the report is called from. The data used in the `before group of` and `after group of` statements should always be sorted in some way. If you are using multiple `before group of` and/or `after group of` statements and the report gets confused about the order in which these should be executed, use the `order external by` option in the `report` section to solve this problem.

Note that you could also define variables in the first page header block to avoid printing out format strings everywhere:

```
define money_format                    char (11)
define quantity format                 char (7)

format
   first page header
    let money_format = "$$$$,$-&.&&"
    let quantity_format = "###,##&"

   on every row
  print column   40,  toy_order_rec.toy_description,
         column   95,  toy_order_rec.quantity
                                 using quantity_format,
         column 110,  toy_order_rec.profit
                                 using money_format
```

Final Totals

Final totals are an optional part of the `format` section of a report. The control block is:

```
on last row
```

This control block is executed after the last row of the report is processed. This is where you can print report totals, end of report notes, and any other items.

In the group example in the previous section, we printed subtotals. Now let's print the final totals for this report:

Example:

```
on last row
    print column  95, "-------",
          column 110, "-----------"
    print column  80, "Grand Total:",
          column  95, sum (toy_order_rec.quantity)
                                using "###,##&",
          column 110, sum (toy_order_rec.profit)
                                using "$$$$,$-&.&&"
    print column  95, "=======",
          column 110, "==========="
```

Note that all we did was:

1. Change Subtotal to Grand Total
2. Change the `group sum` statements to `sum` statements, and
3. Change the single dashes to equal signs to indicate a final balance.

Sample Report

Now let's bring together all the pieces of the report to see what the complete report will look like:

```
{ * * * * * * * * * * * * * * * * * * * * * * * * * * * * * * * * * * * * * * * * * * * * * * * * * * * * * * * * * *
   Toy_Orders_Report
   This report lists toy stores and the toys they ordered for the
   specified time period.
* * * * * * * * * * * * * * * * * * * * * * * * * * * * * * * * * * * * * * * * * * * * * * * * * * * * * * * * * * * * * }
function Toy_Orders_Report (start_date, end_date)
   define start_date, end_date   date

   define toy_order_rec record
               store_name          like toy_store.store_name,
               toy_description     like toy.description,
               quantity            like toy_order_item.quantity,
               profit              money (16,2)
          end record
   define reported                 smallint

   declare toy_orders_cur cursor for
     select toy_store.store_name, toy.description,
            toy_order_item.quantity,
            ((toy_order_item.unit_price - toy.cost)
                       * toy_order_item.quantity)   { profit }
       from toy_order, toy_order_item, toy_store, toy
       where toy_order.order_date
                         between start_date and end_date    and
          toy_order.order_number = toy_order_item.order_number and
          toy_order_item.toy_code = toy.toy_code               and
          toy_order.store_number  = toy_store.store_number
       order by toy_store.store_name, toy.description

   start report Format_Toy_Orders_Report to "toy_orders.rpt"

     let reported = false
     foreach toy_orders_cur into toy_order_rec.*
```

```
        output to report Format_Toy_Orders_Report
                        (start_date, end_date, toy_order_rec.*)
      let reported = true

    end foreach

    if not reported then
    initialize toy_order_rec.* to null
      output to report Format_Toy_Orders_Report
                        (start_date, end_date, toy_order_rec.*)
    end if

  finish report Format_Toy_Orders_Report

  close toy_orders_cur
  free toy_orders_cur
end function  { Toy_Orders_Report }

{**********************************************************
    Format_Toy_Orders_Report
 **********************************************************}
report Format_Toy_Orders_Report (start_date, end_date,
  toy_order_rec)
  define start_date, end_date   date
  define toy_order_rec record
            store_name          like toy_store.store_name,
            toy_description      like toy.description,
            quantity            like toy_order_item.quantity,
            profit              money (16,2)
          end record

  output
    top      margin 2
    bottom margin 2

  format

    first page header
      print column  50, "Toy Store Order Report"
      print column  45, "For dates: ", start_date,
                        " to ", end_date
      print column  55, "Run date: ", today
```

```
        skip 2 lines
        print column    5,  "Store",
              column   40,  "Toy",
              column   95,  "Quantity",
              column  110,  "Profit"
        print column    1,  "---------------------------",
                            "---------------------------",
                            "---------------------------",
                            "---------------------------",
                            "-----------",

    page header
        print column    1,  "Toy Store Order Report",
              column  110,  "Page: ", pageno using "<<<<<"
        print column    1,  "For dates: ", start_date, " to ",
                                                        end_date,
              column  110,  "Run date: ", today
        skip 2 lines
        print column    5,  "Store",
              column   40,  "Toy",
              column   95,  "Quantity",
              column  110,  "Profit"
        print column    1,  "---------------------------",
                            "---------------------------",
                            "---------------------------",
                            "---------------------------",
                            "-----------",

    before group of toy_order_rec.store_name
        print column    5,  toy_order_rec.store_name;

    on every row
        print column   40,  toy_order_rec.toy_description,
              column   95,  toy_order_rec.quantity using "###,##&",
              column  110,  toy_order_rec.profit   using "$$$$,$-&.&&"

    after group of toy_order_rec.store_name
        print column   95,  "-------",
              column  110,  "-----------"
        print column   80,  "Subtotals:",
              column   95,  group sum (toy_order_rec.quantity)
                                                    using "###,##&",
```

```
             column 110, group sum (toy_order_rec.profit)
                                        using "$$$$,$-&.&&"
      print column  95, "-------",
             column 110, "-----------"
      skip to top of page


   on last row
      print column  95, "-------",
             column 110, "-----------"
      print column  80, "Grand Total:",
             column  95, sum (toy_order_rec.quantity)
                                        using "###,##&",
             column 110, sum (toy_order_rec.profit)
                                        using "$$$$,$-&.&&"
      print column  95, "=======",
             column 110, "==========="

end report  { Format_Toy_Orders_Report }
```

The output from this report would look something like
Figure 25-1 on page 574.

```
                        Toy Store Order Report
               For dates: 07/01/1997 to 07/31/1997
                      Run date: 08/01/1997

Store                        Toy              Quantity        Profit
---------------------------------------------------------------------
BUCKLEY'S BOOKS AND TOYS     COLORING BOOK         50       $  50.00
                             COLORING BOOK         20       $  20.00
                             CRAYONS               40       $  60.00
                             PUZZLE BOOK           10       $  30.00
                             PUZZLE BOOK           30       $  90.00
                                                 ------      ---------
                             Subtotals:           150       $ 250.00
                                                 ------      ---------


Toy Store Order Report                         Page: 2
For dates: 07/01/1997 to 07/31/1997            Run date: 08/01/1997

Store                        Toy              Quantity        Profit
---------------------------------------------------------------------
COOL TOYS FOR GIRLS AND BOY  BOOMERANG             30       $  75.00
                             FOOSBALL TABLE         3       $ 300.00
                             FOOSBALL TABLE         2       $ 200.00
                             MODEL AIRPLANE        20       $ 150.00
                             PAINT SET             30       $  60.00
                             PLAYING CARDS         80       $  80.00
                             PUZZLE BOOK           50       $ 150.00
                             YO-YO                 50       $  62.50
                                                 ------      ---------
                             Subtotals:           265       $ 1,077.50
                                                 ------      ---------
```

Figure 25-1 *Output of the toy order report.*

If we wanted to group each toy listing for each store instead of having each order listed separately, we could replace the on every row with:

```
after group of toy_order_rec.toy_description
   print column  40, toy_order_rec.toy_description,
      column  95, group sum (toy_order_rec.quantity)
                              using "###,##&",
      column 110, group sum (toy_order_rec.profit)
                              using "$$$$,$-&.&&"
```

This would give us the results seen in Figure 25-2.

```
                    Toy Store Order Report
            For dates: 07/01/1997 to 07/31/1997
                    Run date: 08/01/1997

Store                         Toy            Quantity        Profit
-----------------------------------------------------------------
BUCKLEY'S BOOKS AND TOYS      COLORING BOOK      70        $ 70.00
                              CRAYONS            40        $ 60.00
                              PUZZLE BOOK        40        $120.00
                                               ------      ---------
                              Subtotals:         150       $ 250.00
                                               ------      ---------


Toy Store Order Report                         Page: 2
For dates: 07/01/1997 to 07/31/1997            Run date: 08/01/1997

Store                         Toy            Quantity        Profit
-----------------------------------------------------------------
COOL TOYS FOR GIRLS AND BOY   BOOMERANG          30        $ 75.00
                              FOOSBALL TABLE      5        $ 500.00
                              MODEL AIRPLANE     20        $ 150.00
                              PAINT SET          30        $ 60.00
                              PLAYING CARDS      80        $ 80.00
                              PUZZLE BOOK        50        $ 150.00
                              YO-YO              50        $ 62.50
                                               ------      ---------
                              Subtotals:        265        $ 1,077.50
                                               ------      ---------
```

Figure 25-2   *Output of the modified toy orders report.*

Summary

There are two major parts of every report. The section of code the report is called from and the `report` section.

The report statements which can be used in the section of code the report is called from are:

```
start report <report name>
        [ to {   "<file name>" |
                <variable containing file name> |
                printer |
                pipe [ in { line | form } mode ] "<program name>" |
                pipe [ in { line | form } mode ]
                <variable containing program name>
            }
        ]

output to report <report name>

terminate report <report name>

finish report <report name>
```

The format of the `report` section is:

```
report <report name> ( <parameter> [, ...] )
  define <parameters and any other variables used>

  output
    left margin    <number of spaces - default column 5>
    right margin   <number of spaces - default column 132>
    top margin     <number of lines - default 3>
    bottom margin  <number of lines - default 3>
    page length    <number of lines - default 66>
    report to [ { <file name> | printer |
                  pipe <program name> } ]

  order [ internal | external ] by <variable name> [, ...]

  format
    every row { no other control blocks may be used }
```

```
      first page header
      page header
      before group of <variable>
      on every row
      after group of <variable>
      page trailer
      on last row
end report
```

Each control block within the `format` section must contain at least one `format` statement (e.g., `print`, `skip`). These sections may also contain any other statements that can be used in functions.

Statements that may be used only in report control blocks are:

```
print [ <expression> [, ...] ] [ ; ]
skip { <number> line[s] | to top of page }
need <number> lines
pause [ "<string>" ]
print file "<file name>"
exit report
```

Built-in operators that can be used in report control blocks:

```
column <number>
lineno
pageno
<number> space[s]
<character string> wordwrap
  [ right margin <number> ]
```

Aggregates have the syntax:

```
[ group ]
{ count(*) | percent(*) |
  { sum | avg | min | max } ( <expression> )
}
    [ where <where clause> ]
```

Complex Reports

- *Using temp tables, unions, and other SQL tricks*
- *Matrix reports*
- *Multi-part reports*
- *Summary*

Using Temp Tables, Unions, and Other SQL Tricks

After you have written a report, you may find that it does not run as quickly as you would like, or you may find that you are having trouble sorting it as you would like. This section serves as a review of some of the topics discussed in Chapter 20, *More Sophisticated SQL*.

It is important to optimize `select` statements when creating reports. It may be tempting to use a single `select` statement instead of taking the time to split a query into several `select` statements using `temp` tables. Queries will run more quickly when they involve fewer tables. When dividing a query into parts, start by running queries that will eliminate as much data as possible. Queries will run faster when they have less data to work with.

It is often useful to bring `select` statements into DB-Access to try them out and to fully optimize them. Use the optimization techniques discussed in Chapter 20 and make certain you run `update statistics` on a regular schedule.

If you are writing a report that reports only aggregate data, try to get your `select` statement to calculate the aggregates for you instead of calculating the aggregates within the report section.

If you found you needed an `order by` statement within your report section, see if you can replace it by doing an unusual sort using two (or more) `select` statements and a `union`. When using this method, you will add a constant value onto the `select` list of each `select` statement, then `order by` this constant in your final result. The discussion of the `union` clause in Chapter 6 contains an example of how this is done.

Matrix Reports

One type of report people often want to produce is a *matrix* report. This type of report lists one set of values across the top of the page and another set of values down the side of the page, then fills in a value for each row and column.

This report can be a little confusing to create using INFORMIX-4GL, but with some imagination, it can be done without too much difficulty. The key is to retrieve the data in your `select` statement ordered by first the column headings, then the row headings, and finally the table values.

The following report is an example of how to produce a matrix report. This report lists the toy codes across the top of the page and lists the toy stores down the left side of the page. For each toy and store combination, we list the number of each type of toy ordered by each store during the specified time period. Notice that we use temp tables to make the report as efficient as possible. If you use `temp` tables, don't forget to drop them when you are done with them so they won't continue to use up system resources.

```
{*******************************************************************
  Matrix Report
*******************************************************************}

database toymaker

main
  call Toys_by_Store_Report ("07/01/1997","07/31/1997")
end main

{*******************************************************************
  Toys_by_Store_Report
  This report lists the number of toys ordered by toy store
  for the specified time period.
*******************************************************************}
function Toys_by_Store_Report (start_date, end_date)
  define start_date, end_date  date
  define toy_by_store record
          store_number        like toy_order.store_number,
          store_name          like toy_store.store_name,
          toy_code            like toy.toy_code,
          quantity            like toy_order_item.quantity
        end record

  define reported              smallint

  { Note: This select has no where clause making it a cartesian
    join.  This means that every combination of toy_code and
    store_number will be retrieved whether or not the store carries
    a particular toy or not
  }
  select toy_code, store_number
    from toy, toy_store
    into temp a1 with no log;

  select toy_order.store_number, toy_order_item.toy_code,
         sum (toy_order_item.quantity) sum_quantity
    from toy_order, toy_order_item
    where toy_order.order_date between start_date and end_date and
          toy_order.order_number = toy_order_item.order_number
    group by toy_order.store_number, toy_order_item.toy_code
    into temp a2 with no log;
```

```
declare toy_by_store_cur cursor for
   select a1.store_number, toy_store.store_name,
         a1.toy_code, a2.sum_quantity
     from a1, outer a2, toy_store
     where a1.store_number = a2.store_number        and
           a1.toy_code     = a2.toy_code            and
           a1.store_number = toy_store.store_number
     order by toy_store.store_name, a1.toy_code

 start report Format_Toys_by_Store_Report to "toys_by_store.rpt"

   let reported = false
   foreach toy_by_store_cur into toy_by_store.*

      output to report Format_Toys_by_Store_Report
                     (start_date, end_date, toy_by_store.*)
      let reported = true

   end foreach

   if not reported then
      initialize toy_by_store.* to null
      output to report Format_Toys_by_Store_Report
                     (start_date, end_date, toy_by_store.*)
   end if

 finish report Format_Toys_by_Store_Report

 close toy_by_store_cur
 free toy_by_store_cur

 drop table a1
 drop table a2
end function  { Toys_by_Store_Report }
```

```
{****************************************************************
  Format_Toys_by_Store_Report
  ***************************************************************}
report Format_Toys_by_Store_Report (start_date, end_date,
                                     toy_by_store)
  define start_date, end_date  date

  define toy_by_store record
        store_number            like toy_order.store_number,
        store_name              like toy_store.store_name,
        toy_code                like toy.toy_code,
        quantity                like toy_order_item.quantity
      end record
  define toy_code_list          array [15]
  define quantity               like toy_order_item.quantity
  define column_no              smallint
  define counter                smallint

  output
    top      margin 2
    bottom   margin 2

  { add external order by - INFORMIX-4GL is usually right,
    but just in case }
  order external by toy_by_store.store_name, toy_by_store.toy_code

  format

    first page header
      { Need a list of first 15 toy codes for toy_code_list array }
      declare toy_cursor cursor for
        select toy_code from toy order by toy_code

      let counter = 1
      foreach toy_cursor into toy_code_list[counter]
        let counter = counter + 1
        if counter >= 16 then
          exit foreach
        end if
      end for
```

```
       print column    1, "Toy Store Order Report",
             column 110, "Page: ", pageno using "<<<<<"
       print column    1, "For dates: ", start_date, " to ", end_date,
             column 110, "Run date: ", today
       skip 2 lines
       print column    1, "Store",
             column  20, "Toys:";
       let column_no = 27
       for counter = 1 to 15
         print column column_no, toy_code_list[counter] using "#&";
         let column_no = column_no + 5
       end for
       print column 102, "Total"
       print column    1,   "----------------------------",
                            "----------------------------",
                            "----------------------------",
                            "----------------------------",
                            "------------"

   page header
     print column    1, "Toy Store Order Report",
           column 110, "Page: ", pageno using "<<<<<"
     print column    1, "For dates: ", start_date, " to ", end_date,
           column 110, "Run date: ", today
     skip 2 lines
     print column    1, "Store",
           column  20, "Toys:";
     let column_no = 27
     for counter = 1 to 15
       print column column_no, toy_code_list[counter] using "#&";
       let column_no = column_no + 5
     end for
     print column 103, "Total"
     print column    1,   "----------------------------",
                          "----------------------------",
                          "----------------------------",
                          "----------------------------",
                          "------------"


   before group of toy_by_store.store_number
     print column    1, toy_by_store.store_name[1,22];
     let column_no = 25
```

```
on every row
  print column column_no, toy_by_store.quantity using "###&";
  let column_no = column_no + 5

after group of toy_by_store.store_number
  { Print horizontal total }
  print column column_no,
    group sum (toy_by_store.quantity) using "####&"

on last row
  let column_no = 25
  for counter = 1 to 16
    print column column_no, "—";
    let column_no = column_no + 5
  end for
  print "-"

  print column 15, "Total: ";
  let column_no = 25
  for counter = 1 to 15
    print column column_no,
      sum (toy_by_store.quantity)
        where toy_by_store.toy_code = toy_code_list[counter]
        using "###&";
    let column_no = column_no + 5
  end for
  print column column_no, sum (toy_by_store.quantity)
                                        using "####&"

  let column_no = 25
  for counter = 1 to 16
    print column column_no, "====";
    let column_no = column_no + 5
  end for
  print "="

end report  { Format_Toys_by_Store_Report }
```

The output for this report will look something like Figure 26-1 on page 586 and 587.

```
Toy Store Order Report
For dates: 07/01/1997 to 07/31/1997


Store                   Toys:    1       2       3       4       5       6
-------------------------------------------------------------------------------
BUCKLEY'S BOOKS AND TO           0       0       0       0       0       0
COOL TOYS FOR GIRLS AN          80       0       0       0      30      30
DAISY'S DELIGHTFUL TOY           0      25     175      90       0      65
DON'S TOY DUNGEON                0       0       0       0      50       0
GAMES FOR GROWN-UPS            200       0       0       0       0       0
KEVER'S KIDDIE KORNER            0      80     125      50       0      50
PETE'S PLAYHOUSE                 0       0       0       0      50       0
TOY PALACE                       0      50       0       0       0      50
TOY TOWN                         0      40     200      50       0      50
WAYNE'S WORLD OF TOYS            0       0       0       0     100       0
                               ---     ---     ---     ---     ---     ---
                    Total:     280     195     500     190     230     245
                               ===     ===     ===     ===     ===     ===
```

Figure 26-1   *Output of the sample matrix report.*

Multi-Part Reports

Another report that can be somewhat frustrating to produce is
the multi-part report. These reports are usually require the inclusion of several one-to-many relationships in the same report.

Again, with a little imagination it is possible to figure out what
is not immediately obvious. The following steps will allow you to
create your multi-part report without too much difficulty:

1. Declare a cursor for a `select` statement that retrieves key
   information out of the table that is common to all of the information you need to print.
2. Start your report and create a `foreach` loop to process each
   row of data.
3. For each row returned by the original cursor, and for each type
   of information you want to print, declare a new cursor for each

7	8	9	10	11	12	13	14	15	Total
40	0	0	0	0	0	0	70	40	150
50	50	0	0	20	0	5	0	0	265
0	0	0	0	0	30	0	25	25	435
0	100	0	50	0	150	5	0	0	355
0	30	0	0	45	0	5	0	0	280
0	0	200	25	0	75	0	0	0	605
0	80	0	30	20	0	0	100	100	380
0	0	0	0	0	50	0	0	0	150
50	50	50	0	0	100	0	50	50	690
50	100	0	0	0	0	4	0	0	254
---	---	---	---	---	---	---	---	---	----
190	410	250	105	85	405	19	245	215	3564
===	===	===	===	===	===	===	===	===	====

`select` statement that returns information to be printed. Create a variable called `cursor_type` and assign it a different value for each cursor you declare.

4. Process each row of information for these other cursors, one cursor at a time. Part of the processing is making calls to the report. You will need to pass the cursor type and all variables or records to the report that are needed at any time by the report. Close and free the cursor each time you finish processing a set of data.

5. Put logic into your report to tell it which information to print, depending on the value of the `cursor_type` that is passed into the report.

6. When you have finished processing all of the data, finish your report, then close and free your main cursor.

The following report prints a list for each store, information about each order, and the total number of each type of toy ordered by that store.

```
{**************************************************************
  Multi-Part report.
  ************************************************************}

database toymaker

globals
  define reported                smallint
end globals

main
  call Multi_Part_Report ("07/01/1997","07/31/1997")
end main



{**************************************************************
  Multi_Part_Report
  This report lists several pieces of information for each toy
  order.
  ************************************************************}
function Multi_Part_Report (start_date, end_date)
  define start_date, end_date  date

  define store_rec record
          store_number               like toy_store.store_number,
          store_name                 like toy_store.store_name
        end record

  define toy_order_rec record
          order_number               like toy_order.order_number,
          order_date                 like toy_order.order_date,
          ship_date                  date,
          order_amount               decimal (8,2)
        end record

  define toy_item_rec record
          toy_code                   like toy_order_item.toy_code,
          description                like toy.description,
          quantity                   like toy_order_item.quantity,
          unit_price                 like toy_order_item.unit_price
        end record
```

```
define cursor_type              char (1)
define report_name              char (80)

let report_name = time
let report_name = "multipart.", today using "yyyymmdd",
          report_name[1,2], report_name[4,5], report_name[7,8]

declare store_cursor cursor for
  select unique toy_order.store_number, toy_store.store_name
    from toy_order, toy_store
    where toy_order.order_date between start_date and end_date
                                                            and
          toy_order.store_number = toy_store.store_number
    order by toy_store.store_name

start report Format_Multi_Part_Report to report_name

  let reported = false
  foreach store_cursor into store_rec.*

    call Print_All_Orders (start_date, end_date,
                           store_rec.*, toy_order_rec.*,
                           toy_item_rec.*)

    call Print_All_Toys (start_date, end_date,
                         store_rec.*, toy_order_rec.*,
                         toy_item_rec.*)
  end foreach

  if not reported then
    let cursor_type = "E"
    initialize store_rec.* to null
    initialize toy_order_rec.* to null
    initialize toy_item_rec.* to null
    output to report Format_Multi_Part_Report
                   (start_date, end_date,
                    store_rec.*,
                    toy_order_rec.*,
                    toy_item_rec.*,
                    cursor_type)
  end if
```

```
   finish report Format_Multi Part_Report

   close store_cursor
   free  store_cursor

end function  { Multi_Part_Report }

{***************************************************************
   Print_All_Orders
   This function will print all order information a store to the
   report.
   ***************************************************************}
function Print_All_Orders (start_date, end_date,
                           store_rec, toy_order_rec, toy_item_rec)

   define start_date, end_date  date

   define store_rec record
              store_number          like toy_store.store_number,
              store_name            like toy_store.store_name
           end record

   define toy_order_rec record
              order_number          like toy_order.order_number,
              order_date            like toy_order.order_date,
              ship_date             date,
              order_amount          decimal (8,2)
           end record

   define toy_item_rec record
              toy_code              like toy_order_item.toy_code,
              description           like toy.description,
              quantity              like toy_order_item.quantity,
              unit_price            like toy_order_item.unit_price
           end record

   define cursor_type              char (1)

   let cursor_type = "O"
```

```
declare order_cursor cursor for
  select toy_order.order_number, order_date,
         date (shipping_datetime),
         sum (toy_order_item.quantity * toy_order_item.unit_price)
    from toy_order, outer toy_order_item
    where toy_order.store_number = store_rec.store_number   and
          toy_order.order_date between start_date and end_date and
          toy_order.order_number = toy_order_item.order_number
    group by 1, 2, 3
    order by 2

initialize toy_item_rec.* to null
foreach order_cursor into toy_order_rec.*

    output to report Format_Multi_Part_Report
                            (start_date, end_date,
                             store_rec.*,
                             toy_order_rec.*,
                             toy_item_rec.*,
                             cursor_type)
    let reported = true
end foreach

close order_cursor
free   order_cursor

end function  { Print_All_Orders }


{*****************************************************************
  Print_All_Toys
  This function will print all toys ordered for by store to the
  report.
  *****************************************************************}
function Print_All_Toys (start_date, end_date,
                         store_rec, toy_order_rec, toy_item_rec)

  define start_date, end_date      date
  define store_rec record
             store_number          like toy_store.store_number,
             store_name            like toy_store.store_name
         end record
```

```
define toy_order_rec record
        order_number           like toy_order.order_number,
        order_date             like toy_order.order_date,
        ship_date              date,
        order_amount           decimal (8,2)
    end record

define toy_item_rec record
        toy_code               like toy_order_item.toy_code,
        description            like toy.description,
        quantity               like toy_order_item.quantity,
        unit_price             like toy_order_item.unit_price
    end record

define cursor_type            char (1)


let cursor_type = "I"

declare item_cursor cursor for
  select toy_order_item.toy_code, description,
        sum (toy_order_item.quantity), avg (unit_price)
    from toy_order_item, toy, toy_order
    where toy_order.store_number    = store_rec.store_number and
          toy_order.order_date between start_date and end_date and
          toy_order_item.toy_code    = toy.toy_code           and
          toy_order_item.order_number = toy_order.order_number
    group by toy_order_item.toy_code, description

initialize toy_order_rec.* to null
foreach item_cursor into toy_item_rec.*

    output to report Format_Multi_Part_Report
                       (start_date, end_date,
                        store_rec.*,
                        toy_order_rec.*,
                        toy_item_rec.*,
                        cursor_type)
    let reported = true
end foreach
```

```
    close item_cursor
    free  item_cursor


end function  { Print_All_Orders }



{ * * * * * * * * * * * * * * * * * * * * * * * * * * * * * * * * * * * * * * * * * * * * * * * * * * * * * * * * * * * * * * * *
    Format_Multi_Part_Report
  * * * * * * * * * * * * * * * * * * * * * * * * * * * * * * * * * * * * * * * * * * * * * * * * * * * * * * * * * * * * * * * * }
report Format_Multi_Part_Report (start_date, end_date, store_rec,
                                 toy_order_rec, toy_item_rec,
                                 cursor_type)
    define start_date, end_date    date
    define store_rec record
            store_number               like toy_store.store_number,
              store_name               like toy_store.store_name
          end record

    define toy_order_rec record
              order_number             like toy_order.order_number,
              order_date               like toy_order.order_date,
              ship_date                date,
              order_amount             decimal (8,2)
          end record

    define toy_item_rec record
              toy_code                 like toy_order_item.toy_code,
              description              like toy.description,
              quantity                 like toy_order_item.quantity,
              unit_price               like toy_order_item.unit_price
          end record

    define cursor_type               char (1)

    output
      left margin 0
      top margin 2
      bottom margin 2

    format
```

```
page header
  print column   1, "Multi-Part Report",
        column 110, "Page: ", pageno using "<<<<<"
  print column   1, "For dates: ", start_date, " to ", end_date,
        column 110, "Run date: ", today
        skip 2 lines

before group of store_rec.store_number
  print column   1, store_rec.store_number using "<<<&",
        column   5, store_rec.store_name

before group of cursor_type
  if cursor_type = "O" then
    print column  10, "Orders: ";
  else
    if cursor_type = "I" then
      print column  10, "Items: ";
    end if
  end if

on every row
  case cursor_type
  when "O"  print column 20, "Number: ",
                              toy_order_rec.order_number
                                        using "<<<<<&",
            column 35, "Ordered: ", toy_order_rec.order_date,
            column 60, "Shipped: ", toy_order_rec.ship_date,
            column 85, "Amount: ",  toy_order_rec.order_amount
                                        using "$$$$$,$-&.&&"

  when "I"  print column 20, toy_item_rec.toy_code
                                        using "<<<<<#",
            column 30, toy_item_rec.description[1,20],
            column 55, "Qty: ",
                       toy_item_rec.quantity using "#####&",
            column 70, "Avg Price: ",
                       toy_item_rec.unit_price
                                        using "$$$$$,$-&.&&"

  when "E"  print column  1, "No data exists for this report."
  end case
```

```
     after group of cursor_type
       skip 1 line

     after group of store_rec.store_number
       skip 2 lines
end report  { Format_Multi_Part_Report }
```

The output of this report would look something like Figure 26-2.

```
Multi-Part Report                                                Page: 1
For dates: 07/01/1997 to 07/31/1997              Run date: 04/21/1997


7   BUCKLEY'S BOOKS AND TOYS
        Orders: Number: 8    Ordered: 07/14/1997   Shipped: 07/18/1997   Amount:    $ 100.00
                Number: 14   Ordered: 07/20/1997   Shipped: 07/21/1997   Amount:    $ 400.00

        Items:    14        COLORING BOOK        Qty:    70   Avg Price:    $ 2.00
                  15        CRAYONS              Qty:    40   Avg Price:    $ 3.00
                  7         PUZZLE BOOK          Qty:    40   Avg Price:    $ 6.00


9   COOL TOYS FOR GIRLS AND BOYS
        Orders: Number: 5    Ordered: 07/12/1997   Shipped: 07/15/1997   Amount:  $ 1,455.00
                Number: 20   Ordered: 07/22/1997   Shipped: 07/25/1997   Amount:    $ 700.00

        Items:    5         BOOMERANG            Qty:    30   Avg Price:     $ 5.00
                  13        FOOSBALL TABLE       Qty:     5   Avg Price:   $ 200.00
                  11        MODEL AIRPLANE       Qty:    20   Avg Price:   $ 15.00
                  6         PAINT SET            Qty:    30   Avg Price:    $ 4.00
                  1         PLAYING CARDS        Qty:    80   Avg Price:    $ 2.00
                  7         PUZZLE BOOK          Qty:    50   Avg Price:    $ 6.00
                  8         YO-YO                Qty:    50   Avg Price:    $ 2.50

8   DAISY'S DELIGHTFUL TOYS
        Orders: Number: 1    Ordered: 07/08/1997   Shipped: 07/13/1997   Amount:    $ 692.50
                Number: 17   Ordered: 07/20/1997   Shipped: 07/22/1997   Amount:    $ 945.00

        Items:    14        COLORING BOOK        Qty:    25   Avg Price:    $ 2.00
                  15        CRAYONS              Qty:    25   Avg Price:    $ 3.00
                  2         DOLL                 Qty:    25   Avg Price:   $ 14.40
                                                                        Continued
```

Figure 26-2   *Output of the sample multi-part report.*

	3	JACKS	Qty:	175	Avg Price:	$ 1.50
	4	JUMP ROPE	Qty:	90	Avg Price:	$ 3.00
	6	PAINT SET	Qty:	65	Avg Price:	$ 4.00
	12	TEDDY BEAR	Qty:	30	Avg Price:	$ 12.00

1   DON'S TOY DUNGEON

Orders: Number: 4   Ordered: 07/12/1997   Shipped: 07/15/1997   Amount: $ 1,850.00
        Number: 9   Ordered: 07/15/1997   Shipped: 07/19/1997   Amount: $ 500.00
        Number: 18   Ordered: 07/21/1997   Shipped: 07/23/1997   Amount: $ 1,450.00

Items:	5	BOOMERANG	Qty:	50	Avg Price:	$ 5.00
	10	DUMP TRUCK	Qty:	50	Avg Price:	$ 10.00
	13	FOOSBALL TABLE	Qty:	5	Avg Price:	$ 200.00
	12	TEDDY BEAR	Qty:	150	Avg Price:	$ 12.00
	8	YO-YO	Qty:	100	Avg Price:	$ 2.50

3   GAMES FOR GROWN-UPS

Orders: Number: 7   Ordered: 07/12/1997   Shipped: 07/15/1997   Amount: $ 1,100.00
        Number: 13   Ordered: 07/19/1997   Shipped: 07/21/1997   Amount: $ 1,050.00

Items:	13	FOOSBALL TABLE	Qty:	5	Avg Price:	$ 200.00
	11	MODEL AIRPLANE	Qty:	45	Avg Price:	$ 15.00
	1	PLAYING CARDS	Qty:	200	Avg Price:	$ 2.00

| | 8 | YO-YO | Qty: | 30 | Avg Price: | $ 2.50 |

2   KEVER'S KIDDIE KORNER

Orders: Number: 2   Ordered: 07/11/1997   Shipped: 07/14/1997   Amount: $ 2,232.50
        Number: 16   Ordered: 07/20/1997   Shipped: 07/23/1997   Amount: $ 2,175.00

Items:	9	BLOCKS	Qty:	200	Avg Price:	$ 8.00
	2	DOLL	Qty:	80	Avg Price:	$ 14.00
	10	DUMP TRUCK	Qty:	25	Avg Price:	$ 10.00
	3	JACKS	Qty:	125	Avg Price:	$ 1.50
	4	JUMP ROPE	Qty:	50	Avg Price:	$ 3.00

Figure 26-2   *Output of the sample multi-part report, continued.*

	6	PAINT SET	Qty:	50	Avg Price:	$ 4.00
	12	TEDDY BEAR	Qty:	75	Avg Price:	$ 12.00
5	PETE'S PLAYHOUSE					

Orders: Number: 6   Ordered: 07/12/1997   Shipped: 07/14/1997   Amount: $ 850.00

Number: 19   Ordered: 07/22/1997   Shipped: 07/26/1997   Amount: $ 700.00

	Items:	5	BOOMERANG	Qty:	50	Avg Price:	$ 5.00
		14	COLORING BOOK	Qty:	100	Avg Price:	$ 2.00
		15	CRAYONS	Qty:	100	Avg Price:	$ 3.00
		10	DUMP TRUCK	Qty:	30	Avg Price:	$ 10.00
		11	MODEL AIRPLANE	Qty:	20	Avg Price:	$ 15.00
		8	YO-YO	Qty:	80	Avg Price:	$ 2.50

| 10 | TOY PALACE | | | | | | |

Orders: Number: 12   Ordered: 07/19/1997   Shipped: 07/21/1997   Amount: $ 1,500.00

	Items:	2	DOLL	Qty:	50	Avg Price:	$ 14.00
		6	PAINT SET	Qty:	50	Avg Price:	$ 4.00
		12	TEDDY BEAR	Qty:	50	Avg Price:	$ 12.00

| 4 | TOY TOWN | | | | | | |

Orders: Number: 3   Ordered: 07/11/1997   Shipped: 07/13/1997   Amount: $ 1,105.00

Number: 11   Ordered: 07/18/1997   Shipped: 07/21/1997   Amount: $ 1,280.00

Number: 15   Ordered: 07/20/1997   Shipped: 07/22/1997   Amount: $ 600.00

	Items:	9	BLOCKS	Qty:	50	Avg Price:	$ 8.00
		14	COLORING BOOK	Qty:	50	Avg Price:	$ 2.00
		15	CRAYONS	Qty:	50	Avg Price:	$ 3.00
		2	DOLL	Qty:	40	Avg Price:	$ 14.00
		3	JACKS	Qty:	200	Avg Price:	$ 1.50
		4	JUMP ROPE	Qty:	50	Avg Price:	$ 3.00
		6	PAINT SET	Qty:	50	Avg Price:	$ 4.00
		7	PUZZLE BOOK	Qty:	50	Avg Price:	$ 6.00
		12	TEDDY BEAR	Qty:	100	Avg Price:	$ 7.00
		8	YO-YO	Qty:	50	Avg Price:	$ 2.50

Continued

Figure 26-2   *Output of the sample multi-part report, continued.*

```
Multi-Part Report                                                          Page: 3
For dates: 07/01/1997 to 07/31/1997                          Run date: 04/21/1997


6    WAYNE'S WORLD OF TOYS
        Orders: Number: 10    Ordered: 07/15/1997    Shipped: 07/19/1997    Amount:    $ 1,850.00

        Items:    5          BOOMERANG            Qty:    100    Avg Price:      $ 5.00
                  13         FOOSBALL TABLE        Qty:      4    Avg Price:    $ 200.00
                  7          PUZZLE BOOK           Qty:     50    Avg Price:      $ 6.00
                  8          YO-YO                 Qty:    100    Avg Price:      $ 2.50
```

Figure 26-2 *Output of the sample multi-part report, continued.*

Summary

Remember to optimize your `select` statements when creating reports. It is often useful to bring your `select` statements into DB-Access to try them out and to fully optimize them. Use the optimization techniques discussed in Chapter 20 and make certain you run `update statistics` on a regular schedule. If you are writing a report that reports only aggregate data, try to get your `select` statement to calculate the aggregates for you instead of calculating the aggregates within the `report` section. Use the `union` statement to perform unusual sorts instead of ordering within the `report` section.

A matrix report lists one set of values across the top of the page and another set of values down the left side of the page, then fills in a value for each row and column. The key to producing a matrix report is to retrieve the data in your `select` statement ordered first by the column headings, then the row headings, and finally the table values.

Multi-part reports are usually the result of needing to include several one-to-many relationships in the same report. The key to producing multi-part reports is to have one main cursor that retrieves all of the common information, and additional cursors that are opened and perform the reporting for each set of data that needs to be printed. Assign a value to a cursor type variable for each cursor and use logic within the report to determine which information to print.

Chapter

27

The 4GL Debugger

- *Overview*
- *Get me started, quick!*
- *Environment*
- *Debugger commands*
- *Summary*

Overview

The Informix debugger can be a very helpful tool for debugging your INFORMIX-4GL code. The Informix debugger only works with r4gl, the rapid development system. It does not work with the compiled version of 4gl (c4gl). In order to run with the debugger, you simply need to use the debugger runner with your executable p-code.

Example:

```
fgldb my_program.4gi
```

This chapter provides an overview of the debugger tool and is designed to get you up and running the debugger quickly. If you would like more information on the debugger, see the Informix manual, *Guide to the INFORMIX-4GL Interactive Debugger*.

While the debugger can be a very useful tool, remember that it may not always be bug-for-bug compatible with the r4gl compiler. And if you are using it to debug code which will later be compiled with c4gl, keep in mind that (1) the debugger initializes your variables for you (as does r4gl) and c4gl does not, and (2) you are virtually guaranteed to have different bugs between c4gl and the debugger.

Get Me Started, Quick!

This section will present a few simple commands, which may be all you ever need to know to run the debugger. If you don't find it here, the rest of the chapter contains an overview of all debugger commands. So to start:

```
fgldb <program name>.4gi
```

Once you are in the debugger you will see that your screen is split in half, with the top portion containing the current line of program code and the bottom half containing your command area.

To pass command line arguments into the program, you need to enter the debugger, then pass the arguments from the run command. From within the command portion of the debugger, enter run, followed by the appropriate command line arguments:

```
run [ <arguments> ]
```

You can break out of the running program and go back into command mode by entering a control-c. If at any point you stop running the program by entering a control-c or by coming to a pre-defined break point, you can continue running from where you stopped with the command:

```
continue
```

If you were really trying to hit a program interrupt as part of your testing (as opposed to trying to break back into debugger command mode), simply reset the value of int_flag back to true before continuing:

```
let int_flag = true
continue
```

You can also continue running the program a single command at a time by typing:

```
step
```

or just:

```
s
```

You can continue running the program for any number of steps by typing:

```
s <any number>
```

A function call will normally be executed as a single step unless you specifically step into the function when you are positioned on the function call line:

```
step into
```

Before you start running the program or any time you are in the debugger command screen, you can set break points where the program will automatically return you to the debugger command screen. The easiest places to break are at a specific line number of the current module, or at the beginning of a function:

```
break 212

break my_function
```

To print values of variables, use the print command to print a single variable, an entire record, or all currently defined variables:

```
print var1
print record1.*
print all
```

When you're done using the debugger, simply exit to return to the command line:

```
exit
```

These simple commands will take you far. Read on for an overview of all debugger commands and their abbreviations to save you some typing.

Environment

This section describes information which will help you set up an optimal environment for running the debugger.

DBSRC

The DBSRC environment variable allows you to specify where the debugger will look for source code. By default, only the current directory is searched for source code, so if you have source code in multiple directories, you need to specify its location in order for the debugger to display it.

Example: `export DBSRC=/source/lib:/source/this_app`

You can also use the `fgldb -I` command line option to specify a search path.

Debugger Files (.4db)

You may create various debugger files to help you default your debugger working environment. These files may contain any debugger commands.

The file in `$INFORMIXDIR/etc/init.4db` initializes a working environment for all debugger users.

The file in your home directory called `init.4db` will be run every time you work in the debugger.

The file in the program directory called `<program name>.4db` will be run every time you run the program with that program name in the debugger. This initialization file can be overridden if you specify the `fgldb -f` option on the command line.

You can also use the read command from the command portion of the debugger to read in any `.4db` files you wish in addition to the command line option available with `fgldb`.

`fgldb` Command Line Options

The `fgldb` command has the following syntax:

```
fgldb [ -v |
        [ -I <pathname> [, ...] |
          -f <debugger initialization file (.4db)>
        ] <.4gi file with or without extension>
        ]
```

The `fgldb` command can be run with any of the following options:

-V   Version number of interactive debugger.
-I   Source code search directories.
-f   Name of debug file to initialize debugger with.

Examples:

```
fgldb my_prog.4gi
fgldb my_prog.4gi -I /source/lib,/source/this_app -
f my_prog.4db
```

Creating a Custom Debugger Runner

If you need to link C code into your debugger runner, you can create a custom debugger runner. The process for creating a custom debugger runner is almost the same as is used for creating a custom p-code runner. See chapter 28 for information on the *Linking Rapid Development System Code*, specifically on how to modify the fgiusr.c file. The cfgldb command is used to create the custom debugger runner in the same way the cfglgo command is used to create a custom p-code runner.

```
cfgldb
  { -V |
    fgiusr.c
       <C function file name>.{ c | o | ec } [...]
       [ -o <new fglgo name> ]
  }
```

The -V switch returns the version number.

You may specify either the source code or object code of your external C functions. If you don't specify a name for your 4GL runner, it will be called a.out.

Example:

```
cfgldb fgiusr.c round.c min.c max.c -o toy_fgldb
toy_fgldb toy_prog.4gi
```

Debugger Commands

The following is an overview of debugger commands followed by a description of how to use each command.

Command	Abbreviation	Brief Description
alias	al	Assign name or function key to a debugger command.
application device	ap	Redirect screen output to specified terminal device.
break	b	Set a break point.
call	ca	Execute the specified function and display returned values.
cleanup	cl	Reinitialize all variables, close windows, forms and database.
continue	co	Continue running program (or interrupt/quit program).
database	da	Select a database.
disable	di	Disable a breakpoint or tracepoint.
dump	du	Dump variables & values to the screen or a file.
enable	en	Activate a breakpoint or tracepoint.
_escape	!	Run an operating system command.
exit	ex	Exit the debugger.
functions	f	List programmer defined functions in current application.
grow	g	Grow (or shrink) command or source window.
help	h	Get help on any of these commands.
_interrupt	ctrl-c/del	Interrupt the program execution.
let	le	Assign a value to a program variable.
list	li	List current breakpoints, tracepoints, and display parameters.
nobreak	nob	Remove a breakpoint.
notrace	not	Remove a tracepoint.
print	p	Print variables/expressions to screen or a file.

read	re	Read commands from an operating system file.
_redraw	ctrl-r	Redraw the screen.
run	ru	Run the program from the beginning.
_screen	ctrl-p	Save the current screen to a file.
_search	/ or ?	Search for next or previous pattern.
step	s	Execute the current command or step into a function.
timedelay	ti	Control speed of display.
_toggle	ctrl-t	Toggle between debugger and application screens.
trace	tr	Trace a statement, function, or variable.
turn	tu	Control terminal display parameters.
use	u	Set or display the source code search path.
variable	va	Display variable declaration(s) to the screen or a file.
view	vi	View code from within the source window.
where	wh	Display functions and arguments used so far to screen or file.
write	wr	Write information to a file.

alias

Assign name or function key to a debugger command.

```
alias { * |
        <alias name> = <debugger command> |
        <alias_name> = "{" <debugger command> "}" [; ...] }
```

The curly braces in the quotation marks are meant to be typed. You can also include an alias in another alias.

To set function key 1 to help type:

```
alias f1 = help
```

To set x to exit type:

```
alias x = exit
```

To set z to print three variable values type:

```
alias z = { print var1; print var2; print var3; }
```

To view all of your current aliases type:

```
alias *
```

application device

Redirect screen output to specified terminal device.

```
application [ device ] <device name>
```

Example: `application device /dev/tty86`

break

Set a breakpoint. At a breakpoint, the execution of the program will be interrupted and control is returned to the command screen of the debugger.

```
break [ * ]
        [ ( <function name> ) ] * ]
        [ "<breakpoint name>" ]
        [ -<breakpoint count> ]
        { [ [ <module name>.]<line no> |
              <variable name> |
              <function name>
          ]
          [ if <condition> ]
        }
    [ "{" <list of debugger commands> "}" ]
```

An * indicates that the breakpoint is initially disabled. The function name in parenthesis indicates the scope of any variables referenced be in that function. A breakpoint count means that no break should occur until the breakpoint has been reached that number of times. A list of debugger commands can be automatically executed when a breakpoint is executed.

To break at line 20 of the current module, type:

```
break 20
```

To break at line 20 of the `calc.4gl` module, type:

```
break calc.4gl.20
```

To break at the function `get_value` if the value of x is greater than 10, type:

```
break get_value if x > 10
```

To break when the value of `p_toy_code` used in the `get_toy_code` function changes:

```
break (get_toy_code) p_toy_code
```

To create a breakpoint named break1 at line 5 which only breaks the second time the breakpoint is reached and have it initially disabled, type:

```
break * "break1" -2 5
```

To execute debugger commands when a breakpoint at line 20 is reached, type:

```
break  20 { print x }
```

call

Execute the specified function and display returned values.

```
call   <function name> ( [ <argument> [, ...] ] )
```

Example: `call enter_toys (toy_store)`

cleanup

Reinitialize all variables, close windows, forms and, optionally, close the database.

```
cleanup [ all ]
```

The `all` keyword specifies that the database should be closed.

Example: `cleanup all`

continue

Continue running program (or interrupt/quit program).

```
continue [ interrupt | quit ]
```

To continue running the program from where it was interrupted, type:

```
continue
```

To continue running the program and send it an interrupt signal:

```
continue interrupt
```

To continue running the program and send it a quit signal:

```
continue quit
```

database

Select a database.

```
database <database name>
```

Example: `database toys`

disable

Disable a breakpoint or tracepoint.

```
disable { <breakpoint name> |
          <tracepoint name> |
          <function name> |
          <reference number> |
          all }
```

Examples: disable calcbreak
           disable 5
           disable all

dump

Dump variables and values to the screen or a file.

```
dump [ globals | all ] [ >> <filename> ]
```

To dump all variables and their values in the current function, type:

```
dump
```

To dump all global variables and their values to the screen, type:

```
dump globals
```

To dump all local and global variables and their values to the file vars.out, type:

```
dump all >> vars.out
```

enable

Activate a breakpoint or tracepoint.

```
enable  { <breakpoint name> |
          <tracepoint name> |
          <function name> |
          <reference number> |
          all }
```

Examples: enable calcbreak
           enable 5
           enable all

_escape

Run an operating system command.

```
!
```

An exclamation point (!) from within the command window will allow you to perform a shell escape and enter an operating system command.

Example: !ls -l

exit

Exit the debugger.

```
exit
```

Example: exit

functions

List programmer defined functions in current application to the screen or to a file.

```
functions [ <pattern to match> ] [ >> <filename> ]
```

The pattern to match can use the following characters:

*   Match any string of zero or more non-blank characters.
?   Match any single non-blank character.
[x-y]   Match any of the specified characters in the ASCII collating sequence.

To list all programmer defined functions in the current application, type:

```
functions
```

To list all programmer defined functions starting with "ma" in the current application, type:

```
functions ma*
```

To list all programmer defined functions starting with "a", "b" or "c" in the current application, type:

```
functions [a-c]*
functions >> funclist.out
```

grow

Grow (or shrink) command or source window by the specified number of lines. A positive number grows the window and a negative number shrinks the window.

```
grow [ source | command ] <number of lines>
```

To shrink the command window by 2 lines and grow the source window by 2 lines, type:

```
grow command -2
grow source 2
```

help

Get help on any debugger commands.

```
help [ <debugger command> | all ]
```

Example: help
          help break
          help all

_interrupt

Interrupt the program execution. You can continue running the program with the continue command.

```
{ control-c | <delete key> }
```

let

Assign a value to a program variable.

```
let <variable name> = <value>
```

Example: `let int_flag = false`
           `continue`

list

List current breakpoints, tracepoints and display parameters.

```
list [ break ] [ trace ] [ display ]
```

Example: `list`
           `list break`

nobreak

Remove a breakpoint.

```
nobreak { <breakpoint name> |
         <function name> |
         <reference number> |
         all }
```

Examples: `nobreak calcbreak`
           `nobreak 5`
           `nobreak all`

notrace

Remove a tracepoint.

```
notrace { <tracepoint name> |
         <function name> |
         <reference number> |
         all }
```

Examples: `notrace nametrace`
           `notrace 5`
           `notrace all`

print

Print variables/expressions to screen or a file.

```
print { <variable including entire records and arrays> |
        <date or datetime function> |
        <arithmetic expression> |
        <quoted string> }
      [ >> <filename> ]
```

Examples:

```
print my_var
print my_record >> my_record.out
print p_days + today
```

read

Read and execute commands from an operating system debugger file. The file must have a .4db suffix.

```
read <filename>[.4db]
```

Examples: read my_file
            read my_file.4db

_redraw

Redraw the screen.

```
control-r
```

run

Run the program from the beginning. If your program requires command line arguments, they should be entered as part of the run command, not when invoking the debugger with the program name.

```
run <command line argument> [, ...]
```

Examples: run
            run 3 A "Jannine Mohr"

_screen

Save the current screen to a file. If the user is in the source window when `control-p` is pressed, the file is named `fgldbscr`, and if the user is in the application window when `control-p` is pressed, the file is named `fglapscr`. If the file already exists, it is appended.

```
control-p
```

_search

Search for next or previous pattern in either the source or the command window.

```
{ / | ? } [ <search pattern> ]
```

Use the following characters to search:

/   Search forwards.
?   Search backwards.

The pattern to match can use the following characters:

*   Match any string of zero or more non-blank characters.
?   Match any single non-blank character.
[x-y]   Match any of the specified characters in the ASCII collating sequence.

To search forwards for any string containing `toy` followed anywhere in the string by an s.

```
/toy*s
```

To search backwards for the words `var0` through `var9`:

```
?var[0-9]
```

step

Execute the current command or step into a function.

```
step [ <number of steps> ] [ into ] [ nobreak ]
```

To execute the next 5 instructions in the current module, type:

```
step 5
```

To enter a function while positioned on the function call, type:

```
step into
```

To execute the next 20 steps and ignore any breakpoints in those steps, type:

```
step 20 nobreak
```

To execute the next 10 steps, including steps within any functions, type:

```
step 10 into
```

timedelay

Controls speed of display. In the source window, there is a 1 second default delay after each line in the window is highlighted. In the command window, there is a default if no delay for each line of debugger output.

```
timedelay [ source | command ] <number of seconds>
```

To change the delay in the source window to 2 seconds and in the command window to 1 second, type:

```
timedelay source  2
timedelay command 1
```

_toggle

Toggle between debugger and application screens to allow the application screen to be viewed when desired.

```
control-t
```

trace

Trace a statement, function or variable. Show when a statement or function is reached or when the value of a variable changes.

```
trace [ * ]
        [ ( <function name> ) ]
        [ "<tracepoint name>" ]
        { [ <module name>.]<line no> |
            <variable name> |
            <function name> |
              functions
        }
        [ "{" <list of debugger commands> "}" ]
        [ >> <filename> ]
```

An * indicates that the tracepoint is initially disabled. The function name in parenthesis indicates the scope of any variables referenced in that function. The word `functions` means that all functions will be traced. A list of debugger commands can be automatically executed when a tracepoint is executed.

For a trace at line 20 of the current module, type:

```
trace 20
```

For a trace at line 20 of the `calc.4gl` module, type:

```
trace calc.4gl.20
```

For a trace of the function `get_value`:

```
trace get_value
```

For a trace of all functions and to write the information to the file `func.out`, type:

```
trace functions >> func.out
```

For a trace when the value of `p_toy_code` used in the `get_toy_code` function changes:

```
trace (get_toy_code) p_toy_code
```

To create a tracepoint named `trace1` at line 5 and have it initially disabled, type:

```
trace * "trace1" 5
```

To execute debugger commands when a tracepoint at line 20 is reached, type:

```
trace  20 { print x }
```

turn

Control terminal display parameters.

```
turn [ on | off ]
     { autotoggle |
       displaystops |
       exitsource |
       printdelay |
       sourcetrace
     } [...]
```

on and off enable and disable the display parameters.

autotoggle	On: application screen is displayed when program produces output.
displaystops	On: next source code line is displayed at program stops.
exitsource	Off: source window is exited only when an interrupt is typed.
printdelay	On: command window displays groups of lines instead of line by line.
sourcetrace	On: source window is displayed and highlights the current line.

Examples: turn on autotoggle
           turn off

use

Set or display the source code search path.

```
use [ [ = ] <pathname> [, ...]
```

An example of setting the source code search path is:

use = /source/lib:/source/this_app

Or:
use /source/lib:/source/this_app

To display the source code search path:

```
use
```

variable

Display variable declaration(s) to the screen or a file.

```
variable [ <variable name> | globals | all ] [ >> <filename> ]
```

To display the declaration of the variable x, type:

```
variable x
```

To display all local variables, type:

```
variable
```

To display all global variables, type:

```
variable global
```

To display all local and global variables to the file variable.list, type:

```
variable all >> variable.list
```

view

View code from within the source window.

```
view [ <module name> | <function name> ]
```

View by itself will move you into the current source window.

```
view
```

To view the module calc.4gl, type:

```
view calc.4gl
```

To view the function `calc_balance`, type:

```
view calc_balance
```

where

Display functions and arguments used so far to the screen or to a file.

```
where [ >> <filename> ]
```

Examples:

```
where
where >> debug.list
```

write

Write break, trace, display and/or alias information to a file.

```
write [ break ] [ trace ] [ display ] [ aliases ]
[ >> ] <filename>
```

Example: write break trace >> debug.info
            write aliases alias.out

Summary

The Informix debugger only works with `r4gl`, the rapid development system.

The `DBSRC` environment variable allows you to specify where the debugger will look for source code.

Example:

```
export DBSRC=/source/lib:/source/this_app
```

You can also use the `fgldb -I` command line option to specify a search path.

Debugger files (with a suffix of .4db) will help you default your debugger working environment.

The `fgldb` command has the following syntax:

```
fgldb [ -v |
         [ -I <pathname> [, ...] |
           -f <debugger initialization file (.4db)>
         ] <.4gi file with or without extension>
       ]
```

The `cfgldb` command is used to create a custom debugger runner:

```
cfgldb
  { -v |
    fgiusr.c
       <C function file name>.{ c | o | ec } [...]
       [ -o <new fglgo name> ]
  }
```

The following is a complete list of the syntax used for debugger commands:

```
alias { * |
        <alias name> = <debugger command> |
        <alias_name> = "{" <debugger command> "}" [; ...] }

application [ device ]   <device name>

break [ * ]
      [ ( <function name> ) ]
      [ "<breakpoint name>" ]
      [ -<breakpoint count> ]
      { [ [ <module name>.]<line no> |
            <variable name> |
            <function name>
        ]
        [ if <condition> ]
      }
      [ "{" <list of debugger commands> "}" ]
```

```
call   <function name> ( [ <argument> [, ...] ] )

cleanup [ all ]

continue [ interrupt | quit ]

database <database name>

disable { <breakpoint name> |
          <tracepoint name> |
          <function name> |
          <reference number> |
          all }

dump [ globals | all ] [ >> <filename> ]

enable  { <breakpoint name> |
          <tracepoint name> |
          <function name> |
          <reference number> |
          all }

!

exit

functions [ <pattern to match> ] [ >> <filename> ]

grow [ source | command ] <number of lines>

help [ <debugger command> | all ]

{ control-c | <delete key> }

let <variable name> = <value>

list [ break ] [ trace ] [ display ]

nobreak { <breakpoint name> |
          <function name> |
          <reference number> |
          all }
```

```
notrace { <tracepoint name> |
          <function name> |
          <reference number> |
          all }

print { <variable including entire records and arrays> |
        <date or datetime function> |
        <arithmetic expression> |
        <quoted string> }
      [ >> <filename> ]

read <filename>[.4db]

control-r

run <command line argument> [, ...]

control-p

{ / | ? } [ <search pattern> ]

step [ <number of steps> ] [ into ] [ nobreak ]

timedelay [ source | command ] <number of seconds>

control-t

trace [ * ]
      [ ( <function name> ) ]
      [ "<tracepoint name>" ]
      { [ <module name>.]<line no> |
        <variable name> |
        <function name> |
        functions
      }
      [ "{" <list of debugger commands> "}" ]
      [ >> <filename> ]

turn [ on | off ]
     { autotoggle |
       displaystops |
       exitsource |
```

```
      printdelay |
      sourcetrace
   } [...]
```

```
use [ [ = ] <pathname> [, ...]
```

```
variable [ <variable name> | globals | all ] [ >> <filename> ]
```

```
view [ <module name> | <function name> ]
```

```
where [ >> <filename> ]
```

```
write [ break ] [ trace ] [ display ] [ aliases ]
      [ >> ] <filename>
```

The pattern matching can use the following characters:

*	Match any string of zero or more non-blank characters.
?	Match any single non-blank character.
[x-y]	Match any of the specified characters in the ASCII collating sequence.

Mixing C and 4GL

- *Calling C functions from 4GL*
- *Calling 4GL functions from C*
- *Summary*

Calling C Functions from 4GL

When calling a C function from an INFORMIX-4GL program, use the same syntax you would use in calling a 4GL function. Use the name of the C function as the function name.

Examples:

```
call My_C_Function (param1, param2, param3)
        returning   result_var

let result_var = My_C_Function (param1, param2, param3)
```

Your C function will receive as its argument the number of parameters that have been passed to it. Any parameters passed to the C function are placed on the argument stack, from left to right. It is the responsibility of your C function to pop the number of parameters passed off of the argument stack and store them in C variables of an appropriate type.

Any values returned from the C function need to be placed on the argument stack by your C function, in the reverse order of the returning clause of your call statement.

The functions that are defined by INFORMIX-4GL for use in C are described in detail in Appendix A. While all of these functions are used from within your C code, the following functions are relevant to the topic at hand, calling C functions from 4GL. All other C functions are discussed in the section "Calling 4GL functions from C" later in this chapter.

decadd	decsub	popdate	retdate
deccmp	dectoasc	popdec	retdec
deccopy	dectodbl	popdtime	retdtime
deccvasc	dectoflt	popdub	retdub
deccvdbl	dectoint	popflo	retflo
deccvflt	dectolong	popint	retint
deccvint		popinv	retinv
deccvlong		poplocator	
decdiv		poplong	retlong
dececvt		popquote	retquote
decfcvt		popshort	retshort
decmul		popvchar	retvchar

The functions beginning with the letters dec are functions for handling the 4GL decimal type within C functions and programs.

Each pop function pops a value of the specified type off of the argument stack. The pop functions are used for parameters passed from your 4GL program to your C function.

Each return function pushes a value of the specified type off of the stack. The return functions are used to return values to a 4GL program. Remember to use the return functions in the opposite order as the variables are listed in your returning clause. It isn't necessary to return BLOB types since they are passed by reference to the C function.

Example:

```
{ Call to C function from 4gl file }
define x, e, exp_value          float

let x = 42.3
let e = 1.8

{ This calls the C function exp (defined below).  The value x
  is pushed onto the argument stack first, and the value e is
  pushed on to the stack next.  Since only the top value of the
  stack is accessible, the C function will pop the arguments off
  of the stack by retrieving e first, then x. }

call exp (x, e) returning exp_value
```

C function:

```
/************************************************************
   Function:      exp (C function called from INFORMIX-4GL)

   Input to C:    number of parameters passed onto arg stack
   Output from C: number of parameters passed out on arg stack

   Argument stack input:  x float variable from INFORMIX-4GL
                          e float variable from INFORMIX-4GL
   Argument stack output: result  (x to the e)

   Purpose:  This function returns the value x to the e power.
             (INFORMIX-4GL doesn't handle fractional exponents.)
 ************************************************************/

#include "/usr/include/math.h"

exp (num_args)   /* This number will be 2 since 2 arguments are
                    used in the call from the 4GL function */
   int   num_args;
{
   double x, e, result;

   /* pop passed arguments off of the stack for use -
      arguments are popped off in opposite order of the 4GL call */
   popdub (&e);
   popdub (&x);

   /* Calculate x to the e*/
     result = pow(x, e);

   /* put the result on the stack to be returned */
   retdub (&result);

   /* If more than one value is returned, remember that the return
      values need to be placed on the stack in the reverse of the
      order expected by the returning clause of the 4GL call */

   /* return a single argument */
   return (1);
}   /* exp */
```

Linking Compiled 4GL Code

It is very easy to include a C function in your c4gl executable code.

Since both 4GL and C compile to the same type of object code, just add your compiled C function to the list of modules needed for your executable code in your make file.

Linking Rapid Development System Code

In order to use a C function from within your r4gl code, you need to modify and compile the fgiusr.c file and link it to a new fglgo executable program.

The file fgiusr.c is stored in $INFORMIXDIR/etc. When using any of the C functions, you should copy this file to a different directory and modify the copy, not the original. Within this file you will need to add two lines for every C function you want to use.

Body of an empty fgiusr.c file:

```
#include "fgicfunc.h"

cfunc_t usrcfuncs[] =
    {
    0, 0, 0
    }
```

Syntax for adding a C function to the fgiusr.c file:

```
#include "fgicfunc.h"

int <C function name> ();

cfunc_t usrcfuncs[] =
    {
    "<C function name>", <C function name>,
                         [-] <number of arguments>,
    0, 0, 0
    }
```

Each function name must be defined in fgiusr.c in three places as follows: as an int, and on each row, first in quotes, then not in quotes. Finally, you need to pass in the number of arguments (a negative number indicates a variable number of arguments up to the maximum indicated by the number.

Given the C functions round, which accepts one argument; max, which accepts two arguments; and the function min, which accepts a variable number of arguments (up to 10); the new fgiusr.c file would look like this:

```
#include "fgicfunc.h"

int round ();
int max ();
int min ();

cfunc_t usrcfuncs[] =
    {
    "round",  round,  1,
    "max",    max,    2,
    "min",    min,    -10,
      0,        0,      0
    }
```

The function fgiusr.c can contain as many C functions as desired.

All you need to do at this point is to create a new runner. You have been using the standard runner file fglgo. If you wish to use C functions, you will need to create your own runner to execute your r4gl programs.

```
cfglgo
  { -V |
    -api [ -o <new fglgo name> ] |
    fgiusr.c
      <C function file name>.{ c | o | ec } [...]
      [ -o <new fglgo name> ]
  }
```

The -V switch returns the version number.

The -api switch must be used if you are calling a 4GL function from a C program.

You may specify either the source code or object code of your external C functions.

If you don't specify a name for your 4GL runner, it will be called `a.out`.

Example:

```
cfglgo fgiusr.c round.c min.c max.c -o toy_fglgo
toy_fglgo toy_prog.4gi
```

Calling 4GL Functions from C

The functions that are defined by INFORMIX-4GL for use in C are described in detail in Appendix A. A brief list of these functions (except for the return functions that are not used for calling 4GL functions) is listed here in alphabetical order:

decadd	decsub	popdate	pushdate
deccmp	dectoasc	popdec	pushdec
deccopy	dectodbl	popdtime	pushdtime
deccvasc	dectoflt	popdub	pushdub
deccvdbl	dectoint	popflo	pushflo
deccvflt	dectolong	popint	pushint
deccvint		popinv	pushinv
deccvlong		poplocator	pushlocator
decdiv	fgl_call	poplong	pushlong
dececvt	fgl_end	popquote	pushquote
decfcvt	fgl_exitfm	popshort	pushshort
decmul	fgl_start	popvchar	pushvchar

The functions beginning with the letters `dec` are functions for handling the 4GL `decimal` type within C functions and programs.

The functions beginning with `fgl` are used to set up the environment for a call to 4GL, to make the call to 4GL, then to reset the environment for use with your C code.

The `pop` functions are used to retrieve values of specified types returned from 4GL functions.

The `push` functions are used to pass values of specified types to 4GL functions.

You must include the file `fglapi.h` in your C program. The file is located in the directory `$INFORMIXDIR/incl`.

You will also need to use the following functions.

fgl_start

The function `fgl_start` is called by a C program to prepare everything that will allow you to call INFORMIX-4GL functions from your C program. If `fgl_start` fails, a negative error code is returned; otherwise 0 is returned.

```
fgl_start ()            /* for use with c4gl */


fgl_start            /* for use with r4gl */
( { <ptr to pathname of file containing compiled r4gl functions>,
    [ <num args on current command line including the C program>,
       <ptr to array containing char args to executing C program> ]
  }
)
```

The syntax includes no arguments if you are using compiled 4GL. If you are using the rapid development system, include the pathname to the file containing any compiled functions you wish to call. The `.4go` or `.4gi` suffix is optional.

If you pass the number of arguments and the array of actual arguments to the C program, these can be accessed by INFORMIX-4GL via the `arg_val` and `num_args` functions (see Chapter 17).

Examples:

```
fgl_start ();
fgl_start ("/path/to/file.4go");
fgl_start ("");

char              *pathname;
int               num_args;
char              *arg_array[];

/* Assign values to variables here */

fgl_start (pathname, num_args, arg_array);
```

fgl_call

The function `fgl_call` is called by a C program to execute an INFORMIX-4GL function.

```
fgl_call
  ( <C char - 4GL function name>,
    <C int - number of 4GL function parameters> )
```

The number of parameters being passed is passed to the 4GL function. Any parameters passed must be pushed onto the argument stack by the C program before the 4GL function is called by using the 4GL `push` functions.

fgl_exitfm

The function `fgl_exitfm` is called by a C program to reset the terminal to character mode if you have called an INFORMIX-4GL function that uses a form.

```
fgl_exitfm ()
```

fgl_end

The function `fgl_end` is called by a C program to free any system resources used by INFORMIX-4GL after calling an INFORMIX-4GL function.

```
fgl_end ()
```

Your C program code should be laid out as follows, although you can add C statements wherever you like.

```
#include <fglapi.h>

main ()
{
    fgl_start (pathname, num_args, arg_array)

    { Any push functions go here to pass parameters.
      Parameters should be pushed in the order specified by
      your 4GL function }

    fgl_call ( <C char - 4GL function name>,
               <C int - number of 4GL function parameters> )

    { Any pop functions go here to retrieve returned values.
      Parameters should be popped in the opposite order specified
      by your 4GL function }

    { Call if 4GL functions displays any forms }
    call fgl_exitfm ();

    fgl_end ();

}
```

Linking Compiled 4GL Code

The complete syntax of the c4gl command is described in
Chapter 7, but the following syntax describes how to compile and
link a C program that calls a 4GL function using compiled 4GL.

```
c4gl <C program file>.c <C function file>.c [...]
     <4GL function file>.4gl [...]
     -o <executable program file>
```

Example:

```
c4gl toy_prog.c toy_funct.4gl -o toys.exe

./toys.exe
```

Linking Rapid Development System Code

The following set of commands will compile, link, and run a C program that calls an INFORMIX-4GL function using the rapid development system.

```
fglpc <4GL function file>

cfglgo -api <C program file>.c
       <C function file>.c [...]
       -o <executable program file>

<executable program file> <4GL function file>
[...]
```

Example:

```
fglpc toy_funct.4gl

cfglgo -api toy_prog.c -o toys.exe

./toys.exe toy_funct
```

Summary

You can call C functions from 4GL and you can call 4GL functions from C.

When calling a C function from a 4GL program, use the same syntax you would use in calling a 4GL function. Use the name of the C function as the function name. Your C function will receive as its argument the number of parameters that have been passed to it.

The C functions listed below are relevant to calling C functions from 4GL and are discussed in detail in Appendix A.

decadd	decsub	popdate	retdate
deccmp	dectoasc	popdec	retdec
deccopy	dectodbl	popdtime	retdtime
deccvasc	dectoflt	popdub	retdub
deccvdbl	dectoint	popflo	retflo
deccvflt	dectolong	popint	retint
deccvint		popinv	retinv
deccvlong		poplocator	
decdiv		poplong	retlong
dececvt		popquote	retquote
decfcvt		popshort	retshort
decmul		popvchar	retvchar

To include a C function in your c4gl executable code, just add your compiled C function to the list of modules needed for the executable code in your make file.

In order to use a C function from within your r4gl code, you need to modify and compile the fgiusr.c file and link it into a new fglgo executable program.

```
#include "fgicfunc.h"

int <C function name> ();

cfunc_t usrcfuncs[] =
    {
    "<C function name>", <C function name>,
                         [-] <number of arguments>,
    0, 0, 0
    }
```

To create a new rapid development system runner:

```
cfglgo { -V |
          -api [ -o <new fglgo name> ] |
          fgiusr.c <C function file name>.{ c | o | ec } [...]
            [ -o <new fglgo name> ]
        }
```

Functions used when calling 4GL functions from a C program are defined in detail in Appendix A:

decadd	decsub	popdate	pushdate
deccmp	dectoasc	popdec	pushdec
deccopy	dectodbl	popdtime	pushdtime
deccvasc	dectoflt	popdub	pushdub
deccvdbl	dectoint	popflo	pushflo
deccvflt	dectolong	popint	pushint
deccvint		popinv	pushinv
deccvlong		poplocator	pushlocator
decdiv	fgl_call	poplong	pushlong
dececvt	fgl_end	popquote	pushquote
decfcvt	fgl_exitfm	popshort	pushshort
decmul	fgl_start	popvchar	pushvchar

You must include the file fglapi.h in your C program. The file is located in the directory $INFORMIXDIR/incl.

You will also need to use the following functions which were named above.

```
fgl_start ()                    /* for use with c4gl */


fgl_start                       /* for use with r4gl */
( { <ptr to pathname of file containing compiled r4gl functions>,
    [ <num of args on current command line including the C
                                                program>,
      <ptr to array containing char args to executing C
                                                program> ]
  }
)
```

```
fgl_call ( <C char - 4GL function name>,
           <C int - number of 4GL function parameters> )

fgl_exitfm ()

fgl_end ()
```

The complete syntax of the c4gl command is described in Chapter 7, but the following syntax describes how to compile and link a C program that calls a 4GL function using compiled 4GL.

```
c4gl <C program file>.c <C function file>.c [...]
     <4GL function file>.4gl [...]
     -o <executable program file>
```

The following set of commands will compile, link, and run a C program that calls a 4GL function using the rapid development system.

```
fglpc <4GL function file>
cfglgo -api <C program file>.c <C function file>.c [...]
       -o <executable program file>
<executable program file> <4GL function file> [...]
```

INFORMIX-4GL Functions Called from C

The use of C with INFORMIX-4GL is discussed in detail in Chapter 28. The functions that are defined in INFORMIX-4GL for use in C are described in the following list. They are listed in alphabetical order:

decadd	decsub	popdate	pushdate	retdate
deccmp	dectoasc	popdec	pushdec	retdec
deccopy	dectodbl	popdtime	pushdtime	retdtime
deccvasc	dectoflt	popdub	pushdub	retdub
deccvdbl	dectoint	popflo	pushflo	retflo
deccvflt	dectolong	popint	pushint	retint
deccvint		popinv	pushinv	retinv
deccvlong		poplocator	pushlocator	
decdiv	fgl_call	poplong	pushlong	retlong
dececvt	fgl_end	popquote	pushquote	retquote
decfcvt	fgl_exitfm	popshort	pushshort	retshort
decmul	fgl_start	popvchar	pushvchar	retvchar

The functions beginning with `dec` allow you to perform type conversions and arithmetic with decimal numbers from within C. If you do not use these functions to manipulate decimal data types from within C, your results may vary.

The functions beginning with `fgl_` allow you to call 4gl functions from C. These functions are demonstrated in Chapter 28.

The functions beginning with `pop` pop parameters off of the argument stack when they are passed from INFORMIX-4GL into C.

The functions beginning with `push` push parameters onto the argument stack for use in passing parameters into an INFORMIX-4GL function when called from C.

The functions beginning with `ret` are used when returning values to an INFORMIX-4GL function.

decadd

The function `decadd` allows you to add two `decimal` numbers from INFORMIX-4GL.

```
decadd      ( <decimal number>,
              <decimal number>,
              <decimal number result> )
```

Zero is returned if `decadd` is successful, -1200 if an overflow occurs, and -1201 if an underflow occurs.

All of these arguments are pointers to the `dec_t` structure. You must include the file `decimal.h` in your C code if you wish to use this function.

deccmp

The function `deccmp` compares two `decimal` numbers from INFORMIX-4GL to see of they are equal or if one is greater.

```
deccmp ( <decimal number>, <decimal number> )
```

Zero is returned if the numbers are equal, -1 if the first number is less than the second number, and 1 if the first number is greater than the second number.

Both of these arguments are pointers to the dec_t structure. You must include the file decimal.h in your C code if you wish to use this function.

deccopy

The function deccopy allows you to copy the structure that makes up the decimal number within your C program. This function dates back to the days when some C compiles did not allow structure assignment and is not needed these days.

```
deccopy   ( <original decimal number>,
            <new decimal number> )
```

Both of these arguments are pointers to the dec_t structure. You must include the file decimal.h in your C code if you wish to use this function.

deccvasc

Converts a C char value to a decimal number.

```
deccvasc  ( <original string>,
            <length of original string>,
            <result> )
```

Zero is returned if the function is successful, -1200 if an overflow occurs, -1201 if an underflow occurs, -1213 if the string contains non-numeric characters, and -1216 if the string has a bad exponent.

The original char string is a pointer to a char type. The length of original char string is an int type. The result is a pointer to the dec_t structure. You must include the file decimal.h in your C code if you wish to use this function.

deccvdbl

Converts a C double value to a decimal number.

```
deccvdbl  ( <C double precision floating point number>,
            <result> )
```

The result variable is a pointer to the dec_t structure. You must include the file decimal.h in your C code if you wish to use this function.

deccvflt

Converts a C float to a decimal number.

```
deccvflt  ( <C float number>,
            <result> )
```

The result variable is a pointer to the dec_t structure. You must include the file decimal.h in your C code if you wish to use this function.

deccvint

Converts a C int type to a decimal number.

```
deccvint  (<C integer number>,
           <result> )
```

The result variable is a pointer to the dec_t structure. You must include the file decimal.h in your C code if you wish to use this function.

deccvlong

Converts a C `long integer` to a `decimal` number.

```
deccvlong (<C long integer>,
           <result> )
```

The result variable is a pointer to the `dec_t` structure. You must include the file `decimal.h` in your C code if you wish to use this function.

decdiv

The function `decdiv` allows you to divide two `decimal` numbers from INFORMIX-4GL.

```
decdiv    (<decimal number>,
           <decimal number>,
           <decimal number result> )
```

Zero is returned if `decdiv` is successful, -1200 if an overflow occurs, -1201 if an underflow occurs, and -1202 if you try to divide by zero.

All of these arguments are pointers to the `dec_t` structure. You must include the file `decimal.h` in your C code if you wish to use this function.

dececvt

Converts the digits to the left of the decimal point in a `decimal` number to an ASCII string. The function returns a pointer to the string. You will normally want to use the function `dectoasc` for converting a decimal to a string since this function handles the conversion somewhat differently. The function returns a pointer to the string. The conversion of the string is for the number of significant digits of the number you specify, and the result is rounded. The result string does not contain a decimal point, but any digits specified to the right of the decimal point are zero filled. This is roughly equivalent to the UNIX function `ecvt (3)`.

```
dececvt    (<pointer to dec_t structure>,
            <length of ASCII string>,
            <C int - pointer to decimal place>,
            <C int - pointer to sign> )
```

The pointer to the decimal place is a number specifying the location of the decimal point in the string starting with the left-most significant digit in the string. The decimal point will not appear in the string, but any digits to the right of the decimal will be zero filled.

The integer that is the pointer to the sign is non-zero if the sign is negative; otherwise it is zero.

You must include the file `decimal.h` in your C code if you wish to use this function.

decfcvt

Converts the digits to the right of the decimal point in a `decimal` number to an ASCII string. The function returns a pointer to the string. You will normally want to use the function `dectoasc` for converting a decimal to a string since this function handles the conversion somewhat differently. The function returns a pointer to the string. The conversion of the string is for the number of significant digits of the number to the right of the decimal point, and the result is rounded. The result string does not contain a decimal point, but any digits specified to the right of the decimal are zero filled. Leading zeros are not considered significant and are not printed. This is roughly equivalent to the UNIX function `fcvt (3)`.

```
decfcvt    (<pointer to dec_t structure>,
            <number significant digits right of decimal>,
            <C int - pointer to decimal place>,
            <C int - pointer to sign> )
```

The pointer to the decimal place is a number specifying the location of the decimal point in the string starting with the left-most significant digit in the string. The decimal point will not appear in the string, but any digits to the right of the decimal will be zero filled.

The integer that is the pointer to the sign is non-zero if the sign is negative; otherwise it is zero.

You must include the file decimal.h in your C code if you wish to use this function.

decmul

The function decmul allows you to multiply two decimal numbers from INFORMIX-4GL.

```
decmul      (<decimal number>,
             <decimal number>,
             <decimal number result> )
```

Zero is returned if decmul is successful, -1200 if an overflow occurs, and -1201 if an underflow occurs.

All of these arguments are pointers to the dec_t structure. You must include the file decimal.h in your C code if you wish to use this function.

decsub

The function decsub allows you to subtract two INFORMIX-4GL decimal numbers.

```
decsub      (<decimal number>,
             <decimal number>,
             <decimal number result> )
```

Zero is returned if decsub is successful, -1200 if an overflow occurs, and -1201 if an underflow occurs.

All of these arguments are pointers to the dec_t structure. You must include the file decimal.h in your C code if you wish to use this function.

dectoasc

Converts a decimal number to a C char type.

```
dectoasc  (<pointer to dec_t structure>,
           <pointer to C char result string>,
           <length of original char string>,
           <number digits in result right of decimal> )
```

The number of digits to the right of the decimal is determined by the value of the decimal number if that argument is set to -1.

Zero is returned if the conversion occurs; -1 is returned otherwise.

You must include the file decimal.h in your C code if you wish to use this function.

dectodbl

Converts a decimal number to a C double type.

```
dectodbl
   (  <pointer to dec_t structure>,
      <pointer to double-precision floating point result> )
```

You must include the file decimal.h in your C code if you wish to use this function.

dectoflt

Converts a decimal number to a C float type.

```
dectoflt (  <pointer to dec_t number>,
            <pointer to floating point result> )
```

You must include the file decimal.h in your C code if you wish to use this function.

dectoint

Converts a `decimal` number to a C `int` type.

```
dectoint   (<pointer to dec_t number>,
            <pointer to int result> )
```

Zero is returned if the conversion occurs; -1 is returned otherwise.

You must include the file `decimal.h` in your C code if you wish to use this function.

dectolong

Converts a `decimal` number to a C `long` type.

```
dectolong (<pointer to dec_t number>,
           <pointer to long result> )
```

Zero is returned if the conversion occurs; -1200 is returned if an overflow occurs.

You must include the file `decimal.h` in your C code if you wish to use this function.

fgl_call

The function `fgl_call` is called by a C program to execute a 4GL function.

```
fgl_call  (<C char - 4GL function name>,
           <C int - number of 4GL function parameters> )
```

The number of parameters being passed is passed to the 4GL function. Any parameters passed must be pushed onto the argument stack by the C program before the 4GL function is called by using the 4GL push functions.

The `fgl_call` function is used with the `fgl_start`, `fgl_exitfm`, `fgl_end`, `push`, `pop` , and `return` functions. The use of these functions is discussed in more detail in Chapter 28.

fgl_end

The function `fgl_end` is called by a C program to free any system resources used by 4GL after calling a 4GL function.

```
fgl_end ()
```

The `fgl_end` function is used with the `fgl_start`, `fgl_call`, `fgl_exitfm`, push, pop, and return functions. The use of these functions is discussed in more detail in Chapter 28.

fgl_exitfm

The function `fgl_exitfm` is called by a C program to reset the terminal to character mode if you have called a 4GL function that uses a form.

```
fgl_exitfm ()
```

The `fgl_exitfm` function is used with the `fgl_start`, `fgl_call`, `fgl_end`, push, pop, and return functions. The use of these functions is discussed in more detail in Chapter 28.

fgl_start

The function `fgl_start` is called by a C program to prepare everything that will allow you to call INFORMIX-4GL functions from your C program. If `fgl_start` fails, a negative error code is returned; otherwise 0 is returned.

```
fgl_start ()                        /* for use with c4gl */

fgl_start  /* for use with r4gl */
 ({ <ptr to path of file containing compiled r4gl functions>,
    <num args on current command line including the C program>,
    <ptr to array containing char args to executing C program>
 }
)
```

The syntax includes no arguments if you are using compiled 4GL. If you are using the rapid development system, include the pathname to the file containing any compiled functions you wish to call. The .4go suffix is optional. The use of these functions is discussed in more detail in Chapter 28.

popdate

The function popdate is called by a C program or function to pop a date value off of the argument stack. The INFORMIX-4GL data type is date and the C data type is long.

```
popdate ( &<C date type variable> )
```

popdec

The function popdec is called by a C program or function to pop a decimal number off of the argument stack. The INFORMIX-4GL data type is decimal and the C data type is dec_t.

```
popdec ( &<C dec_t type variable> )
```

popdtime

The function popdtime is called by a C program or function to pop a datetime value off of the argument stack. The INFORMIX-4GL data type is datetime and the C data type is dtime_t.

```
popdtime
   ( &<C dtime_t type variable>,
    <C int binary representation ofdatetime qualifier> )
```

popdub

The function popdub is called by a C program or function to pop a float off of the argument stack. The INFORMIX-4GL data type is float and the C data type is double.

```
popdub ( &<C double type variable> )
```

popflo

The function popdtime is called by a C program or function to pop a smallfloat value off of the argument stack. The INFORMIX-4GL data type is smallfloat and the C data type is float.

```
popflo ( &<C float type variable> )
```

popint

The function popdtime is called by a C program or function to pop an integer value off of the argument stack. The INFORMIX-4GL data type is integer and the C data type is int.

```
popint ( &<C int type variable> )
```

popinv

The function popdtime is called by a C program or function to pop an interval value off of the argument stack. The INFORMIX-4GL data type is interval and the C data type is intrvl_t.

```
popinv
   ( &<C intrvl_t type variable>,
     <C int binary representation of datetime qualifier> )
```

poplocator

The function `poplocator` is called by a C program or function to pop a BLOB off of the argument stack. The INFORMIX-4GL data type is a `byte` or `text` BLOB and the C data type is `loc_t*`. BLOB values are passed by reference.

```
poplocator ( &<C loc_t pointer type variable> )
```

poplong

The function `poplong` is called by a C program or function to pop an `integer` value off of the argument stack. The INFORMIX-4GL data type is `integer` and the C data type is `long`.

```
poplong ( &<C long type variable> )
```

popquote

The function `popquote` is called by a C program or function to pop a character string off of the argument stack. The INFORMIX-4GL data type is `char` and the C data type is `char`.

```
popquote   (&<C char type variable>,
            <C int - length of character string + 1> )
```

popshort

The function `popshort` is called by a C program or function to pop a `smallint` value off of the argument stack. The INFORMIX-4GL data type is `smallint` and the C data type is `short`.

```
popshort ( &<C short type variable> )
```

popvchar

The function `popvchar` is called by a C program or function to pop a variable character string off of the argument stack. The INFORMIX-4GL data type is `varchar` and the C data type is `char`.

```
popvchar ( &<C char type variable>,
           <C int - length of character string + 1> )
```

pushdate

The function `pushdate` will push a `date` value onto the argument stack when calling an INFORMIX-4GL function from C. The C data type is `long` and the INFORMIX-4GL data type is `date`.

```
pushdate ( <C long type variable> )
```

pushdec

The function pushdec will push a decimal value onto the argument stack when calling an INFORMIX-4GL function from C. The C data type is dec_t and the INFORMIX-4GL data type is decimal.

```
pushdec ( <C dec_t type variable> )
```

pushdtime

The function `pushdtime` will push a `datetime` value onto the argument stack when calling an INFORMIX-4GL function from C. The C data type is `dtime_t` and the INFORMIX-4GL data type is `datetime`.

```
pushdtime ( <C dtime_t type variable> )
```

pushdub

The function pushdub will push a float value onto the argument stack when calling an INFORMIX-4GL function from C. The C data type is double and the INFORMIX-4GL data type is float.

```
pushdub ( <C double type variable> )
```

pushflo

The function pushflo will push a smallfloat value onto the argument stack when calling an INFORMIX-4GL function from C. The C data type is float and the INFORMIX-4GL data type is smallfloat.

```
pushflo ( <C float type variable> )
```

pushint

The function pushint will push an integer value onto the argument stack when calling an INFORMIX-4GL function from C. The C data type is int and the INFORMIX-4GL data type is integer.

```
pushint ( <C integer type variable> )
```

pushinv

The function pushinv will push an interval value onto the argument stack when calling an INFORMIX-4GL function from C. The C data type is intrvl_t and the INFORMIX-4GL data type is interval.

```
pushinv ( <C intrvl_t type variable> )
```

pushlocator

The function `pushlocator` will push the location of a BLOB value onto the argument stack when calling an INFORMIX-4GL function from C. The C data type is `loc_t` and the INFORMIX-4GL data type is a `byte` or `text` BLOB.

```
pushlocator ( <C loc_t type variable> )
```

pushlong

The function `pushlong` will push an `integer` value onto the argument stack when calling an INFORMIX-4GL function from C. The C data type is `long` and the INFORMIX-4GL data type is `integer`.

```
pushlong ( <C long type variable> )
```

pushquote

The function `pushquote` will push a character string value onto the argument stack when calling an INFORMIX-4GL function from C. The C data type is `char` and the INFORMIX-4GL data type is `char`.

```
pushquote (<C char type variable>,
           <length of string>  )
```

pushshort

The function `pushshort` will push a `smallint` value onto the argument stack when calling an INFORMIX-4GL function from C. The C data type is `short` and the INFORMIX-4GL data type is `smallint`.

```
pushshort ( <C short type variable> )
```

pushvchar

The function pushvchar will push a character string value onto the argument stack when calling an INFORMIX-4GL function from C. The C data type is char and the INFORMIX-4GL data type is varchar.

```
pushvchar (<C char type variable>,
           <length of string> )
```

retdate

The function retdate is called by a C program or function to return a date value to INFORMIX-4GL. The C data type is long and the INFORMIX-4GL data type is date.

```
retdate ( &<C long type variable> )
```

retdec

The function retdec is called by a C program or function to return a decimal value to INFORMIX-4GL. The C data type is dec_t and the INFORMIX-4GL data type is decimal.

```
retdec ( &<C dec_t type variable> )
```

retdtime

The function retdtime is called by a C program or function to return a datetime value to INFORMIX-4GL. The C data type is dtime_t and the INFORMIX-4GL data type is datetime.

```
retdtime ( &<C dtime_t type variable> )
```

retdub

The function `retdub` is called by a C program or function to return a float value to INFORMIX-4GL. The C data type is `double` and the INFORMIX-4GL data type is `float`.

```
retdub ( &<C double type variable> )
```

retflo

The function `retflo` is called by a C program or function to return a `smallfloat` value to INFORMIX-4GL. The C data type is `float` and the INFORMIX-4GL data type is `smallfloat`.

```
retflo ( &<C float type variable> )
```

retint

The function `retint` is called by a C program or function to return an `int` value to INFORMIX-4GL. The C data type is `int` and the INFORMIX-4GL data type is `integer`.

```
retint ( &<C int type variable> )
```

retinv

The function `retinv` is called by a C program or function to return an `interval` value to INFORMIX-4GL. The C data type is `intrvl_t` and the INFORMIX-4GL data type is `interval`.

```
retinv ( &<C intrvl_t type variable> )
```

retlong

The function `retlong` is called by a C program or function to return an `integer` value to INFORMIX-4GL. The C data type is `long` and the INFORMIX-4GL data type is `integer`.

```
retlong ( &<C long type variable> )
```

retquote

The function `retquote` is called by a C program or function to return a character string value to INFORMIX-4GL. The C data type is `char` and the INFORMIX-4GL data type is `char`.

```
retquote ( &<C char type variable> )
```

retshort

The function `retshort` is called by a C program or function to return a `smallint` value to INFORMIX-4GL. The C data type is `short` and the INFORMIX-4GL data type is `smallint`.

```
retshort ( &<C short type variable> )
```

retvchar

The function `retvchar` is called by a C program or function to return a character string value to INFORMIX-4GL. The C data type is `char` and the INFORMIX-4GL data type is `varchar`.

```
retvchar ( &<C char type variable> )
retquote ( &<C char type variable> )
```

Appendix B

CD Contents and Contributors

CD Contents

The CD includes most of the code used as examples throughout the book. Additionally, the following examples of code have been donated by various individuals and included on the CD.

This list contains the full names of the files. However, in order to conform to ISO 9660 8.3 naming conventions for the CD-ROM, some of the filenames have been truncated.

Some files in the *sh_arc.tar* archive are shell archives. They can be extracted by running the following command:

```
/bin/ar x filename
```

Shell archives in the ar_arc.tar should be extracted using the following command:

```
/bin/sha filename
```

4gltags_awk - generates vi tags file for 4GL source (AWK)
appstart - runs Informix applications setuid (C)
barcode - example of barcode entry code (4GL)
blackjack - the well-known casino game (4GL)

blob_char - converts a TEXT type to a CHAR type (C)

calc - 4GL calculator (4GL)

calx - pops up a calendar pick-list (4GL)

cfuncts - functions for use in 4GL, including a Soundex routine (C)

cgi_4gl - functions to help create WWW interface programs in 4GL (C)

check_ prt - examples of printing checks with dollar amounts as words (4GL)

cobawk - takes the cobawk3.dat data file as input to produce a master record file suitable for a GLOBALS record file

connect _4gl - 4GL callable ESQL/C code for handling CONNECT, etc. (4GL, ESQL/C)

constr_err - traps constraint error and tells which constraint failed (4GL)

cursor_name6 - prints strings that cause problems in 4GL 6.x cursor names (4GL)

cvtdatetime - functions to convert local datetime and Universal time (4GL)

datetime.4gl - a few sample date and datetime functions (4GL)

dbbeauty.sh - 4GL program beautifier

dbform.sh - generates default data entry forms

dbdiff2 - generates SQL that alters one database to be like another (4GL)

dbinfo.sh - prints the schema of a database table to stdout

dblist.sh - shell script to view database information

dbloader.sh - generates "load/unload" statements

dbref - analyzes referential integrity and builds (un)load scripts (C)

dbreorg.sh - generates SQL to reorg an Informix-OnLine database tab

dbrepair.sh - repair "dirpath" column in "systables" table

dbreserved.sh - scans Informix database tables for key words

dbrowlock.sh - set lock mode of a database table to row-level

dbsyntax.sh - checks the syntax of SQL statements

dbxref - cross-references 4GL variables, labels and functions (C)

db4glgen.sh - generates 4GL code for a basic data entry screen

easter - several methods of calculating Easter for a specified year

emacs_4gl - 4GL mode files for emacs

esql_proto2 - file describing ESQL/C function prototypes

esqlutil - generates C structs for database tables (ESQL/C)

faq - frequently asked questions file from the comp.databases.informix newsgroup (HTML)

fgl_crypt - several approaches to encrypting strings in a 4GL program (4GL, C)

fgl_run - runs commands without 4GL "run" statements (C)

flat_file - program to export data to spreadsheets (4GL)

gen_schm - build a readable datatype string representation

getpid -   shell scrip to get a process ID number

get_user - returns current login-ID to a 4GL program (C)

getopt - 4GL version of getopt (3) function

help_sys - generic help handling routines

hierarc_sql - handles hierarchical data like parts explosion
(SQL, ESQL/C, ACE)

idx_report - report of database indexes

iedit - simple text editor (4GL, C)

iid - Informix-4GL code beautifier (C)

inferr - scans.err files for for error messages (AWK)

infmx_tidy - Informix-4GL code beautifier (C)

inx20 - shows a listing of columns and what tables use each
column listed

inx30 - shows a listing of columns and what tables use each
column listed

kill_id -   program to kill Informix processes

loop_scr - generates multi-table SPERFORM screens (AWK, SH)

lu_cust - replaces DISPLAY/INPUT ARRAY for customer look-up/choosing
(4GL)

m4gl - m4 macro to provide define/include for 4GL

make_mks - a new twist on the make file

make_sccs - examples for using make and SCCS with 4GL

metaphone - several implementations of the Metaphone phonetic
algorithm (C)

msg_pmpt - displays message box and lets user choose option (4GL)

noncaseqry - converts WHERE clause for non-case sensitive query (4GL)

pop_ups - nifty dialogue box code for displaying information in pop-up
windows

privproc - reports privileges for Stored Procedures (ACE)

progtest - a test of twenty-five questions for 4GL programmers with answers

prt_decimal - methods of formatting decimal numbers for printing (4GL, C)

query_win - provides scrolling QBE pick-list in a pop-up window (4GL)

reccmp - compares data in two identically structured RECORDs in 4GL (C)

recursion - an example of recursion in 4GL (4GL, ESQL/C)

rpt_awk - functions to control AWK reports like 4GL or ACE (AWK)

rpt_blobs - prints BLOBs such as images and logos in 4GL reports (C, 4GL)

rpt_length - several approaches to having variable report lengths (4GL)

rpt_size - changes 4GL report dimensions at run-time (C)

setenv - an enhanced version of putenv(3) (C)

solitare - solitare game similar to the one on most Windows Pcs (4GL)

soundex - utilities for generating Soundex codes (4GL, C)

space_usage - reports table space usage in an OnLine database (4GL, C)

split_string -   functions for splitting/parsing 4GL strings (C)

sys_idx- builds a view of the sysindexes table

syst0609 - help pop-ups

syst rpt - systables report program

tcl4gl - functions for interfacing TCL with Informix-4GL (C)

test4glcomp - source code to test 4GL compiler

trofff - shows a listing of columns and what tables use each column to PERL

vertmenu - vertical pull-down menus for 4GL (C, 4GL)

vie.sh - views/corrects Informix-4GL error files
wordwrap - demonstrates using INPUT ARRAY and WORDWRAP (4GL)
work_days - methods for computing number of work days (4GL)
zipbundle - prints bundling instructions for bulk mailing by Zipcode (4GL)

Software Contributors

Clem Akins
Senior Consultant
International Support
Informix Software, Inc.
E-mail: clema@informix.com

Catalin Badea
Senior Technical Architect
Tecsys Inc.
E-mail: cat@tecsys.com
Web: www.tecsys.com

David Berg
Informix Software, Inc.
E-mail: dberg@informix.com

Snorri Bergmann
Strengur Consulting Engineers
Armuli 7
108 Reykjavik Iceland
E-mail: snorri@strengur.is
Web: www.strengur.is
Phone: +354 550 9000

Harry Bochner, Ph.D.
Software Engineer
Genome Therapeutics Corp.
E-mail:
bochner@deas.harvard.edu

Neil S. Briscoe
Network Security Consultant
FourthNet Limited
ICT at Work
E-mail: neil@fourthnet.co.uk
Phone: +44 (1252) 345441
Web: www.fourthnet.co.uk

Dr. Andrew Burt
President
Tech-Soft
E-mail: aburt@tech-soft.com

Steinar Overbeck Cook
Balder Dialog AS
E-mail: steinar@balder.no

Albert Dekker
Database Engineer
BVBA WeVeCos SPRL
Bergensesteenweg 1135
1070 BRUSSEL, Belgie
E-mail: taurus@glo.be

Mark Delaney (Dr. SPARC)
Software Engineer
Informix Software, Inc.
E-mail: mdelaney@informix.com

Scott Ellard
Ellard Consulting
E-mail: cse@wetware.com

Marco Greco
rem radioterapia srl
Via Salvatore Paola, 18
I95124 Catania
Italy
E-mail: marcog@ctonline.it
Web: www.ctonline.it/~marcog

Stu Heiss and Rick Mills
Jesus People USA
E-mail: stu@jpusa.chi.il.us
　　　　rick@jpusa.chi.il.us

Scott Holmes
E-mail: sholmes@pacificnet.net

Walt Hultgren
Emory University
954 Gatewood Road, NE
Atlanta, GA 30329
Phone: +1 404 727 0648
E-mail: walt@rmy.emory.edu

Paul Hutton
E-mail: huttonp@ozemail.com.au

Mark Jeske
Informix Software, Inc.
E-mail: markj@informix.com

Pavel Kazenin
INFORMIX DBA
St. Petersburg Clearing &
Settlement Org.
Russia
Phone: 7-812-294-3318
E-mail: pavel@cso.spb.su

Stuart Kemp
Computer Science Dept.
James Cook University
Townsville
Qld 4811, Australia
E-mail: stuart@cs.jcu.edu.au

Cathy Kipp
Principal Consultant
Database Strategies, Inc.
E-mail: ckipp@verinet.com

Lester Knutsen
Database Consultant, President
Advanced DataTools Corporation
4216 Evergreen Lane, Suite 136
Annandale, VA 22003
E-mail: lester@access.digex.net
Web: www.access.digex.net/~lester
Phone: 1-703-256-0267

Dave Kosenko
E-mail: davek@informix.com

Bradley M. Kuhn
Network and Unix Administrator
Independent Consultant
E-mail: bkuhn@acm.org

Michael J. Kuhn
Computer Systems Consultant
5916 Glenoak Ave.
Baltimore, MD 21214
Phone: 1-410-254-7060
E-mail: mkuhn@csd.clark.net
        csd@clark.net
        mkuhn@rhlab.com

Jonathan Leffler
Software Engineer, R&D Tools
Informix Software, Inc.
E-mail: johnl@informix.com or
        j.leffler@acm.org

Stuart Litel
E-mail: slitel@netcom.com

Darin Melin
E-mail:
rp29560@email.sps.mot.com

Christopher Moore
IT Manager
Sir John Fitzgerald, Ltd.
E-mail: chin@nihc.demon.co.uk

Joseph M. Morgan
TeamLeader/Senior
        Programmer Analyst
Hastings Books, Music & Video
Amarillo, TX
E-mail: morganj@hasting.com
        morganj@arn.net

Nils Myklebust
NM Data AS
P.O. Box 9090 Gronland
N-0133 Oslo
Norway
E-mail: Nils.Myklebust@idg.no

Jack Parker
E-mail: jparker@informix.com

Poul Pederson
Databaseadministrator
Kuwait Petroleum (Danmark) A/S
E-mail: pp@q8.dk

Dennis Pimple
Principal Consultant
Informix Software, Inc.
E-mail: dennisp@informix.com

R. Alan Popiel
Staff Database Administrator
Lockheed Martin Corporation
E-mail: alan@ast.lmco.com

Paul Redman
Software Consultant
E-mail:
pjredman@compuserve.com

Mike Reetz
E-mail: miker@iiug.org

Kerry Sainsbury
Quanta Systems
Auckland, New Zealand
E-mail: kerry@kcbbs.gen.nz

Tim Schaefer
E-mail: tschaefe@mindspring.com
Web: www.inxutil.com

Carlos Costa e Silva
Technical Director
Minimal Lda
Lisboa
Portugal
E-mail: ccs@minimal.pt
Phone: 351 1 7575772

Dave Snyder
Snide Computer Services
Folcroft, PA
E-mail: dave@snide.com
Web: www.ece.vill.edu/~dave/

Naomi Walker
Anasazi Inc.
Director of Systems Management
E-mail: naomi@anasazi.com

Bibliography and Other Informix Books from Prentice Hall PTR

Books on Informix

Leffler, Jonathan. 1991. *Using INFORMIX-SQL*, 2d ed. New York: Addison-Wesley. ISBN: 0-201-56509-9

Lumbley, Joe. 1995. *Informix Database Administrator's Survival Guide*. Englewood Cliffs, NJ: Prentice Hall PTR. ISBN: 0-13-124314-1

Mahler, Paul. 1995. *An INFORMIX-4GL Tutorial*. Englewood Cliffs, NJ: Prentice Hall PTR. ISBN: 0-13-464173-6

Suto, Liz. 1995. *INFORMIX-OnLine Performance Tuning*. Englewood Cliffs, NJ: Prentice Hall PTR. ISBN: 0-13-124322-5

Taylor, Art. 1995. *Advanced INFORMIX-4GL Programming*. Englewood Cliffs, NJ: Prentice Hall PTR. ISBN: 0-13-301318-9

Informix Manuals

Informix Press. 1995. *Informix Guide to SQL: Reference with Using Triggers*. Englewood Cliffs, NJ: Prentice Hall PTR. ISBN: 0-13-100363-1

Informix Press. 1995. *Informix Guide to SQL: Tutorial*. Englewood Cliffs, NJ: Prentice Hall PTR. ISBN: 0-13-100371-2

Informix Press. 1995. *INFORMIX-4GL by Example*. Englewood Cliffs, NJ: Prentice Hall PTR. ISBN: 0-13-100355-0

INFORMIX-4GL Reference Manual, Volume 1. Part number: 000-7044
INFORMIX-4GL Reference Manual, Volume 2. Part number: 000-7045
INFORMIX-4GL Supplement. Part number: 000-7023
INFORMIX-4GL User Guide. Part number: 000-7043
INFORMIX-OnLine Administrator's Guide. Part number: 000-7106
INFORMIX-SE Administrator's Guide. Part number: 000-7111
INFORMIX-SQL Quick Syntax Guide. Part number: 000-7119
INFORMIX-SQL User Guide. Part number: 000-7041
Informix Using Triggers. Part number: 000-7230

General Database

Brathwaite, Kenmore S. 1990. *The Data Base Environment: Concepts and Applications*. New York: Van Nostrand. ISBN: 0-442-00300-5

Date, C. J. 1987. *Introduction to Database Systems*, Vol. I. 4th ed. New York: Addison-Wesley. ISBN: 0-201-14201-5

Kozar, Kenneth A. 1989. *Humanized Information Systems Analysis and Design*. New York: McGraw-Hill Book Company. ISBN: 0-07-035600-9

Loomis, Mary E. S. 1987. *The Database Book*. New York: Macmillan. ISBN: 0-02-371760-2

Mattison, Robert M. 1993. *Understanding Database Management Systems*. New York: McGraw Hill Book Company. ISBN: 0-07-040973-0

Mortimer, Andrew J. 1993. *Information Structure Design for Databases*. Boston: Butterworth-Heinemann. ISBN: 0-7506-0683-5

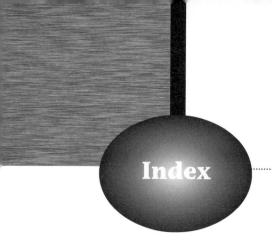

Index

A

Abs, 424
  Functions, 424
Absolute
  Fetch, 407, 414
Accept key
  Options, 322, 325, 330, 331
Accessing other databases
  Database, 446, 451
ACE, 28
Acos, 424, 425
  Functions, 424, 425
Add
  Alter table, 72, 94
  Input, 389
Add constraint
  Constraint, 72
After
  Triggers, 475, 483
After construct
  Construct, 488, 492, 500
After delete
  Data validation, 508
  Input array, 503, 508, 510, 520
After field
  Construct, 488, 494, 500
  Data validation, 508
  Input, 383, 387, 395
  Input array, 503, 508, 510, 520
After group of
  Control blocks, 555, 564, 575
  Grouping control blocks, 564
  Report, 555, 564, 575

After input
  Data validation, 508
  Input, 383, 387, 395
  Input array, 503, 508, 510, 520
After insert
  Data validation, 508
  Input array, 503, 508, 510, 520
After row
  Data validation, 508
  Input array, 503, 508, 510, 520
Aggregate, 434, 450
  Avg, 434, 450, 564, 576
  Count, 435, 450, 576
  Distinct, 436, 450
  Max, 435, 450, 564, 576
  Min, 435, 451, 564, 576
  Percent, 576
  Select statement, 162, 164
  Sum, 435, 451, 564, 576
  Unique, 436, 450
  Use of, 436
  Where, 564
Alias
  Debugger, 608, 609, 626
All, 422, 448
  Grant table, 77
  Revoke, table, 80
  Subquery, 440, 451
Alter index
  Index, 85
Alter table
  Add, 72, 94

Add constraint, 72
  Drop, 72
  Drop constraint, 72
  INFORMIX-OnLine, 94
  Lock mode, 73
  Modify, 72
  Modify next size, 73
  Revoke, table, 80
  Table, 72, 94
American National Standards
  Institute (ANSI), 27
And, 211, 219, 421, 448
  Expression, 157, 177
ANSI
  American National
    Standards Institute, 27
  c4gl, 185, 193
  Compliance, 27
  Cursor, 402
  DBANSIWARN, 32
  Form, 254
  Logging, 112
  r4gl, 184
  sqlca.sqlawarn, 376
  Start database, 54
Any, 422, 448
  Subquery, 440, 451
Any error
  Whenever, 341, 347
-anyerr
  c4gl, 342, 347
  fglgo, 342, 347
  fglpc, 342, 347
Application device
  Debugger, 608, 610, 626

Archives
    Level 0, 109
    Level 1, 109
    Level 2, 109
Argument stack
    C functions from 4GL, 630
Arg_val
    Command line argument
        value, 351
    Functions, etc 4GL, 350, 351,
        377
Array
    Data type, 207, 219
Arr_count
    Functions, etc 4GL, 350, 352,
        377
    Input array, 505, 520
Arr_curr
    Display array, 295, 320
    Functions, etc 4GL, 350, 352,
        377
    Input array, 505, 520
Ascii
    Functions, etc 4GL, 350, 352,
        377
Asin, 424, 425
    Functions, 424, 425
Assignment
    Let, 234, 247
Atan, 424, 425
    Functions, 424, 425
Atan2, 424, 425
    Functions, 424, 425
Attributes
    Construct, 488, 491, 500
    Display, 236, 247, 279, 281,
        284, 320, 322, 331
    Display array, 294, 320
    Display form, 319
    Error, 236, 247
    Form, 255, 262, 273, 279, 319
    Input, 322, 328, 330, 331,
        383, 384, 394, 395
    Input array, 503, 520
    Message, 237, 247
    Open window, 276, 318
    Options, 322, 327, 331
    Output, 235, 247
    Prompt, 238, 247
    upscol, 272
    Window, 276, 319

Audit trails, INFORMIX-SE, 121
    Create audit, 122, 125
    Drop audit, 122, 125
    Recover table, 122, 125
Autonext
    Form, 263, 273
Avg, 434, 450
    Aggregate, 434, 450, 564, 576
    Report, 564, 576

B

Backups, 107, 109, 124
    Critical dbspaces, 111
    INFORMIX-OnLine, 108, 124
    INFORMIX-SE, 108, 124
    Level 0 archive, 109
    Level 1 archive, 109
    Level 2 archive, 109
    Logging, INFORMIX-SE, 115
    Logical logs, 121
    onmonitor, 125
    Ontape, 109, 124, 125
    ontape -s, 110
    Recovery, 121
    tbmonitor, 110, 125
    Tbtape, 109, 124, 125
    tbtape -s, 110
    Warm restore, 111
bcheck
    Database integrity, 103, 123
    options, 104
Before
    Triggers, 475, 482
Before construct
    Construct, 488, 492, 500
Before delete
    Data validation, 508
    Input array, 503, 508, 509,
        520
Before field
    Construct, 488, 493, 500
    Data validation, 508
    Input, 383, 386, 395
    Input array, 503, 508, 509,
        520
Before group of
    Control blocks, 555, 564, 575
    Grouping control blocks, 564
    Report, 555, 564, 575

Before input
    Data validation, 508
    Input, 383, 386, 395
    Input array, 503, 508, 509,
        520
Before insert
    Data validation, 508
    Input array, 503, 508, 509,
        520
Before menu
    Menu, 223, 231, 232
Before row
    Data validation, 508
    Input array, 503, 509, 520
Begin
    Stored procedures, 456, 478
Begin work
    Logging, 112, 125
    Transaction, 112
Between, 421
    Expression, 157, 176
Binary Large Objects
    BLOB, 59
BLOB
    Binary Large Objects, 59
    Byte, 59
    Load, 137
    Stored procedures, 458
    Text, 59
Block
    Stored procedures, 456
Boolean operators, 211, 219,
    421, 448
Bottom margin
    Output, 553, 575
    Report, 553, 575
Bourne shell
    Environment variable, 29
Break
    Debugger, 605, 608, 610, 626
Buffered log
    Create database, 53, 91
By name
    Construct, 488, 500
    Display, 281, 319
    Input, 383, 394
Byte
    BLOB, 59
    Data type, 60, 207

C

C functions from 4GL, 630, 640
  Argument stack, 630
  cfgldb, 607, 626
  cfglgo, 634, 641
  Custom r4gl runner, 634, 641
  fgiusr.c, 607, 626, 633, 634,
    640, 641
  Linking, 633
C shell
  Environment variable, 29
c4gl, 180, 184, 185, 192
  ANSI, 185, 193
  -anyerr, 342, 347
  Functions called from C, 638,
    642
  INFORMIX-4GL, 180, 184,
    185, 192
  Options, 185
  Pros and cons, 180
Call
  Debugger, 608, 611, 627
  Functions, 200, 204
  Returning, 200, 204
  Stored procedures, 457, 478
  Whenever, 341
Cartesian product
  Join, 171
Cascading delete
  Triggers, 476
Case
  Conditionals, 241, 248
  Exit case, 241, 248
  Otherwise, 241, 248
  When, 241, 248
Century
  DBCENTURY, 32
cfgldb
  C functions from 4GL, 607,
    626
  Debugger, 607, 626
cfglgo
  C functions from 4GL, 634, 641
  Functions called from C, 634,
    639, 641
Char
  Data type, 55, 91

Character
  Conversions, 212
  Data type, 55, 91, 206
  Index, 22, 25
Check
  Constraint, 65, 92
Check table
  Database integrity, 102, 123
Cleanup
  Debugger, 608, 612, 627
Clear
  Form, 278, 319
  Screen, 278, 319
  Window, 278, 319
Clipped, 212, 219
  Functions, etc 4GL, 350, 353,
    377
Close, 412, 415
  Cursor, 411, 415
  SQL in 4GL, 411, 415
Close database
  Database, 54, 91
Close form
  Form, 280
Close window
  Window, 278, 319
Cluster
  Index, 22, 25
Cluster index
  Create index, 83
Color
  Form, 264, 273
Column
  Column name, 423
  Constraint, 65, 92
  Default, 92
  Definition, 4, 25
  Expression, 423
  Field, 4
  Functions, etc 4GL, 350, 353,
    377
  Report functions, 558, 575
Column table
  Table, 74
Combination
  Form, 261
Command
  Menu, 223, 232
Command key
  Menu, 225

Command line
  DB-Access, 43
  INFORMIX-4GL, 183
Command line argument value
  Arg_val, 351
Comment
  INFORMIX-4GL, 202
  Stored procedures, 455
Comment line
  Options, 322, 323, 331
  Window, 280
Comments
  Form, 264, 273
Commit work
  Logging, 112, 125
  Transaction, 112
Committed read
  Isolation levels, 446, 451
Compiled 4GL
  INFORMIX-4GL, 180
Complex reports
  Matrix, 578, 601
  Multi-part, 585, 601
  Query optimization, 601
  Report, 578
  Temp table, 578
  Unions, 578
Composite
  Index, 20, 25
Composite index, 443
  Constraint, 69
  Index, 443
Concatenation, 212, 219, 421,
  448
Conditional
  Expression, 157
Conditionals, 240
  Case, 241, 248
  If-then-else, 240, 248
Confidence
  Update statistics, 100, 101,
    123
Connect
  Revoke, 80
Constants
  False, 374, 380
  Notfound, 374, 380
  True, 374, 380
Constrained
  Field order, 322, 328, 330, 331

Constraint, 69
    Add constraint, 72
    Check, 65, 92
    Column, 65, 92
Constraint, *continued*
    Composite index, 69
    Create table, 65
    Drop constriant, 72
    Foreign key, 65, 66, 93
    Index, 66
    Not null, 65, 66, 92, 93
    Primary key, 65, 66, 92, 93
    References, 66, 92, 93
    Table, 65, 93
    Unique, 65, 66, 92, 93
Construct, 485, 488, 500
    After construct, 488, 492, 500
    After field, 488, 494, 500
    Attribute, 488, 491, 500
    Before construct, 488, 492, 500
    Before field, 488, 493, 500
    By name, 488, 500
    Continue construct, 488, 496, 500
    Default where clause, 491
    Exit construct, 488, 496, 500
    From, 488, 500
    Help, 488, 491, 500
    Next field, 488, 496, 500
    On, 488, 500
    On key, 495, 500
    Search characters, 487, 499
    Select, 497
    User search, 485
    Where, 488
Context sensitive
    Help, 334, 338
Continue
    Debugger, 604, 608, 612, 627
    Whenever, 341, 347
Continue construct
    Construct, 488, 496, 500
Continue for
    For, 243, 248
Continue foreach
    Foreach, 403, 413
Continue input
    Input, 383, 388, 395
    Input array, 503, 512, 520

Continue menu
    Menu, 223, 228, 232
Continue while
    While, 244, 248
Control blocks
    After group of, 555, 564, 575
    Before group of, 555, 564, 575
    First page header, 555, 560, 561, 575
    Format every row, 555, 575
    On every row, 555, 575
    On last row, 555, 567, 575
    Page header, 555, 560, 562, 575
    Page trailer, 555, 560, 563, 575
    Report, 556
Conversions
    Character, 212
    Data type, 61, 212
    Datetime, 214
    Interval, 214
    Numeric, 213
    String, 212
Cos, 424, 425
    Functions, 424, 425
Count, 435, 450
    Aggregate, 435, 450, 576
    Report, 576
Create
    Role, 81
Create audit
    Audit trails, INFORMIX-SE, 122, 125
Create database
    Buffered log, 53, 91
    Database, 52, 91
    Dbspace, 53
    In, 53
    INFORMIX-Online, 53, 91
    INFORMIX-SE, 52, 91
    Log mode ansi, 53
    Mode ansi, 52, 91
    Unbuffered log, 53, 91
    With log in, 52, 91
Create index
    Ascending, 84
    Cluster, 83
    Descending, 84
    Distinct, 84, 96

    Index, 83, 96
    Index name, 84
    Performance, 84
    Table name, 84
    Unique, 83
Create procedure
    Stored procedures, 453, 478
Create schema authorization, 82, 96
Create synonym
    Synonym, 448
Create table
    Constraint, 65
    Dbspace, 70
    Default, 63
    Extent size, 70
    In, 69
    INFORMIX-OnLine, 70, 93
    INFORMIX-SE, 69, 93
    Lock mode page, 71
    Lock mode row, 71
    Next size, 70
    Referential integrity, 65
    Table, 62, 92
Create temp table
    Table, 93
Create trigger
    Triggers, 474, 482
Create view
    View, 417, 448
Critical dbspaces
    Backups, 111
    Ontape, 111
Current, 424, 426, 449
    Datetime, 64
    Fetch, 407, 414
    Functions, 424, 426, 449
    Functions, etc 4GL, 350, 354, 377
Current window
    Window, 277, 318
Cursor
    ANSI, 402
    Close, 411, 415
    Declare, 401, 413, 414
    Fetch, 407, 414
    Flush, 411, 414
    Foreach, 403, 413
    Free, 412, 415
    Insert, 399, 402, 411, 412
    List, 401

Cursor, *continued*
    Open, 405, 414
    Put, 410, 414
    Select, 399, 402, 404, 411
    Stored procedures, 460
    Update, 402, 409
    Where current of, 409, 414
Cursor name
    Mangling, 354, 409, 414
Cursor stability
    Isolation levels, 446, 451
cursor_name
    Functions, etc 4GL, 350, 354,
        409, 414
Custom r4gl runner
    C functions from 4GL, 634,
        641

D

Data
    Report, 546
Data type, 54, 55, 91, 205
    Array, 207, 219
    Byte, 60, 207
    Char, 55, 91
    Character, 55, 91, 206
    Conversions, 61, 212
    Date format, 57, 207
    Datetime, 57, 207
    Dec, 91, 206
    Decimal, 55, 91, 206
    Double precision, 55, 91, 206
    Float, 55, 91, 206
    Int, 55, 91, 206
    Integer, 56, 91, 206
    Interval, 58, 207
    Like, 207, 219
    Money, 56, 91, 206
    Nchar, 56, 91
    Numeric, 56, 91, 206
    Nvarchar, 61
    Real, 56, 91, 206
    Record, 207, 219
    Serial, 56, 91, 206
    Small float, 57
    Smallfloat, 91, 206
    Smallint, 57, 91, 206
    Text, 60, 207
    Varchar, 60, 206

Data validation
    After field, 508
    After input, 508
    After insert, 508
    After row, 508
    Before delete, 508
    Before field, 508
    Before input, 508
    Before insert, 508
    Before row, 508
    upscol, 272
Database, 197, 203
    Accessing other databases,
        446, 451
    Close database, 54, 91
    Create database, 52, 91
    dbschema, 89, 97
    Debugger, 608, 612, 627
    Definition, 3
    Drop database, 53, 91
    Exclusive, 53, 91
    Form, 253, 272
    Info, 88, 97
    Locking, 131
    Privileges, 75
    Start database, 54, 91
Database administrator
    Dba, 49
Database exclusive
    Locking, 131, 148
Database integrity, 102, 123
    bcheck, 103, 123
    Check table, 102, 123
    INFORMIX-OnLine, 107
    INFORMIX-OnLine log file,
        105
    INFORMIX-SE, 102
    oncheck -cc, 107, 124
    oncheck -cD, 107
    oncheck cD, 124
    oncheck -ce, 107, 124
    oncheck -cI, 107, 124
    oncheck -cr, 107, 124
    Repair table, 104, 123
    tbcheck, 124
    tbcheck -cc, 107
    tbcheck -cD, 107
    tbcheck -ce, 107
    tbcheck -cI, 107
    tbcheck -cr, 107

Database maintenance, 101
    Update statistics, 99
Datatype
    Dec, 55
Date, 424, 426, 449
    DBCENTURY, 32
Date format
    Data type, 57, 207
    DBDATE, 33
    Format, 216
    Functions, 424, 426, 449
    Functions, etc 4GL, 355, 378
    Today, 64
Datetime
    Conversions, 214
    Current, 64
    Data type, 57, 207
    Format, 57, 217
Datetime unit
    Day, 58
    Fraction, 58
    Hour, 58
    Minute, 58
    Month, 58
    Second, 58
    Year, 58
Day, 424, 426, 449
    Datetime unit, 58
    Functions, 424, 426, 449
    Functions, etc 4GL, 350, 355,
        378
Day-time
    Interval class, 59
Dba
    Database administrator, 49
    Grant, database, 75
    Privileges, 76
    Revoke, database, 80
    Stored procedures, 453, 478
DB-Access, 45
    Command line, 43
    Definition, 27
    Menu structure, 40
    Ring menu access, 41
    Using, 39
DBANSIWARN
    ANSI, 32
    Environment variable, 32
DBCENTURY
    Environment variable, 32

DBDATE
  Date Format, 33
  Environment variable, 33
DBDELIMITER
  Environment variable, 34
  Load, 34, 136
  Unload, 34
DBEDIT
  Environment variable, 34
  Text editor, 34
dbexport, 144, 150
  Options, 145
DBFORMAT
  Environment variable, 34
  Format numeric data types, 34
dbimport, 144, 146, 150
  Options, 147
  Performance, 147
Dbinfo, 427, 449
  Functions, 427, 449
  Stored procedures, 469, 481
DBLANG
  Environment variable, 35
  Foreign language support, 35
  mkmessage, 36
dbload, 138, 149
  Command file, 138
  Fixed length records, 140
  Options, 139, 149
  Performance, 147
  Variable length records, 140
dbload command file, 149
  DELIMITER, 140, 149
  FILE, 140, 149
  INSERT, 141
  VALUES, 141
dblog
  Logging, 117, 125
DBMONEY
  Environment variable, 36
  Money, 36
DBPATH
  Environment variable, 37
  PATH, 37
DBPRINT
  Environment variable, 37
  Printer default, 37
  Report, 548
DBREMOTECMD
  Environment variable, 37

dbschema
  Database, 89, 97
Dbservername, 424, 427, 449
  Functions, 424, 427, 449
  Sitename, 64
Dbspace
  Create database, 53
  Create table, 70
  Definition, 70
  Root_dbspace, 70
DBSRC
  Debugger, 605, 625
  Environment variable, 605,
    625
DBTEMP
  Environment variable, 37
  Temporary files, 37
Debugger, 602
  Alias, 608, 609, 626
  Application device, 608, 610,
    626
  Break, 605, 608, 610, 626
  Call, 608, 611, 627
  cfgldb, 607, 626
  Cleanup, 608, 612, 627
  Continue, 604, 608, 612, 627
  Database, 608, 612, 627
  DBSRC, 605, 625
  Disable, 608, 613, 627
  Dump, 608, 613, 627
  Enable, 608, 614, 627
  Escape, 608, 614, 627
  Exit, 605, 608, 614, 627
  fgldb, 603, 606, 626
  Functions, 608, 615, 627
  Grow, 608, 616, 627
  Help, 608, 616, 627
  Initialization file, 606, 626
  Interrupt, 608, 616, 627
  Let, 604, 608, 616, 627
  List, 608, 617, 627
  Nobreak, 608, 617, 627
  Notrace, 608, 617, 628
  Pattern matching, 615, 619,
    629
  Print, 605, 608, 618, 628
  Read, 609, 618, 628
  Redraw, 609, 618, 628
  Run, 604, 609, 619, 628
  Screen, 609, 619, 628

  Search, 609, 619, 628
  Step, 604, 609, 620, 628
  Timedelay, 609, 621, 628
  Toggle, 609, 621, 628
  Trace, 609, 621, 628
  Turn, 609, 623, 628
  Use, 609, 623, 629
  Variable, 609, 624, 629
  View, 609, 624, 629
  Where, 609, 625, 629
  Write, 609, 625, 629
Dec
  Data type, 91, 206
  Datatype, 55
Decadd
  Functions called from C, 373,
    380, 630, 635, 640, 641,
    642, 643
Deccmp
  Functions called from C, 373,
    380, 630, 635, 640, 641,
    642, 644
Deccopy
  Functions called from C, 373,
    380, 630, 635, 640, 641,
    642, 644
Deccvasc
  Functions called from C, 373,
    380, 630, 635, 640, 641,
    642, 644
Deccvdbl
  Functions called from C, 373,
    380, 630, 635, 640, 641,
    642, 645
Deccvflt
  Functions called from C, 373,
    380, 630, 635, 640, 641,
    642, 645
Deccvint
  Functions called from C, 373,
    380, 630, 635, 640, 641,
    642, 645
Deccvlong
  Functions called from C, 373,
    380, 630, 635, 640, 641,
    642, 646
Decdiv
  Functions called from C, 373,
    380, 630, 635, 640, 641,
    642, 646

Dececvt
  Functions called from C, 373,
    380, 630, 635, 640, 641,
    642, 647
Decfcvt
  Functions called from C, 373,
    380, 630, 635, 640, 641,
    642, 648
Decimal
  Data type, 55, 91, 206
Declare, 403, 407, 413, 414
  Cursor, 401, 413, 414
  For, 401, 413, 414
  For update, 401, 413, 414
  Of, 401, 413, 414
  Scroll cursor, 402, 413, 414
  SQL in 4GL, 401, 413, 414
  With hold, 402, 413, 414
Decmul
  Functions called from C, 373,
    380, 630, 635, 640, 641,
    642, 648
Decsub
  Functions called from C, 373,
    380, 630, 635, 640, 641,
    642, 648
Dectoasc
  Functions called from C, 373,
    380, 630, 635, 640, 641,
    642, 649
Dectodbl
  Functions called from C, 373,
    380, 630, 635, 640, 641,
    642, 649
Dectoflt
  Functions called from C, 373,
    380, 630, 635, 640, 641,
    642, 649
Dectoint
  Functions called from C, 373,
    380, 630, 635, 640, 641,
    642, 650
Dectolong
  Functions called from C, 373,
    380, 630, 635, 640, 641,
    642, 650
Default
  Column, 92
  Create table, 63
  Form, 265, 274

Options, 331
Table, 92
Defer interrupt
  Interrupt key, 340, 346
Defer quit
  Quit key, 340, 346
Define, 208
  Report, 551, 575
  Scope, 210
  Stored procedures, 459, 478
  Variable, 208, 219
Delete, 130, 148
  Revoke, table, 80
  Subquery, 441, 451
  Triggers, 474, 482
Delete key
  Options, 322, 325, 330, 331
DELIMITER
  dbload command file, 140,
    149
Delimiters
  Form, 255, 273
Design
  Form, 251
Dirty read
  Isolation levels, 446, 451
Disable
  Debugger, 608, 613, 627
Display, 281, 319
  Attribute, 236, 247, 279, 281,
    284, 320, 322, 331
  By name, 281, 319
  Form mode, 236
  Line mode, 236
  One-to-many relationship, 305
  Output, 236, 247
  To, 281, 320
Display array, 294, 320
  Arr_curr, 295, 320
  Attribute, 294, 320
  Exit display, 294, 320
  On key, 294, 320
  Scr_line, 295, 320
  Set_count, 295, 320
  To, 294, 320
Display attribute
  Options, 327, 330
Display form
  Attribute, 319
  Form, 279, 319

Display label
  Order by, 166
  Select statement, 154, 166
Display like
  Form, 265, 274
Distinct
  Aggregate, 436, 450
  Create index, 84, 96
Distributions
  Update statistics, 100, 101,
    123
Document
  Stored procedures, 453, 454,
    478
Double precision
  Data type, 55, 91, 206
Downshift
  Form, 265, 274
  Functions, etc 4GL, 350, 356,
    378
Drop
  Role, 81
Drop audit
  Audit trails, INFORMIX-SE,
    122, 125
Drop constraint
  Constraint, 72
Drop database
  Database, 53, 91
Drop index
  Index, 85, 96
Drop procedure
  Stored procedures, 472, 481
Drop synonym
  Synonym, 420, 448
Drop table
  Table, 74, 94
Drop trigger
  Triggers, 477
Drop view
  View, 419, 448
Dump
  Debugger, 608, 613, 627
Duplicate
  Index, 21, 25

E

Editing
  Input array, 508, 521

Enable
  Debugger, 608, 614, 627
End
  Stored procedures, 456, 478
Environment variable
  Bourne shell, 29
  C shell, 29
  DBANSIWARN, 32
  DBCENTURY, 32
  DBDATE, 33
  DBDELIMITER, 34
  DBEDIT, 34
  DBFORMAT, 34
  DBLANG, 35
  DBMONEY, 36
  DBPATH, 37
  DBPRINT, 37
  DBREMOTECMD, 37
  DBSRC, 605, 625
  DBTEMP, 37
  Fgl_getenv, 359
  INFORMIXDIR, 30, 46
  INFORMIXSERVER, 31, 46
  INFORMIXTERM, 30, 46
  Needed, 30
  NOSORTINDEX, 38
  ONCONFIG, 31, 46
  OPTCOMPIND, 38
  Optional, 32
  PATH, 30, 46
  PDQPRIORITY, 38
  Setting, 28
  SQLEXEC, 39
  TBCONFIG, 31, 46
  TERM, 31, 46
  TERMCAP, 31, 46
  TERMINFO, 31, 46
Error
  Attribute, 236, 247
  Error_Recovery function, 346
  Output, 236, 247
  sqlca.sqlcode, 375
  Status, 344
  Whenever, 341, 347
Error line
  Options, 322, 324, 330, 331
Error log, 343
  Errorlog, 344, 347
  Err_get, 344, 348
  Err_print, 344, 348

Err_quit, 344
  fgl_errorlog, 344, 347
  fgl_startlog, 343, 347
  Startlog, 343, 347, 368
Error message
  finderr, 45
Errorlog
  Error log, 344, 347
  Functions, etc 4GL, 350, 357,
    378
Error_Recovery function
  Error, 346
Err_get
  Error log, 344, 348
  Functions, etc 4GL, 350, 356,
    378
Err_print
  Error log, 344, 348
  Functions, etc 4GL, 350, 356,
    378
Err_quit
  Error log, 344
  Functions, etc 4GL, 350, 357,
    378
Escape
  Debugger, 608, 614, 627
ESQL/C, 180
Exclusive
  Database, 53, 91
Execute, 401, 413
  SQL in 4GL, 400, 413
  Using, 400, 413
Exists, 422, 448
  Subquery, 439, 451
Exit
  Debugger, 605, 608, 614,
    627
Exit case
  Case, 241, 248
Exit construct
  Construct, 488, 496, 500
Exit display
  Display array, 294, 320
Exit for
  For, 243, 248
Exit foreach
  Foreach, 403, 413
Exit input
  Input, 383, 389, 395
  Input array, 503, 512, 520

Exit menu
  Menu, 223, 232
Exit program, 202, 204
Exit report
  Report, 556, 558, 575
Exit while
  While, 244, 248
Exp, 424, 427
  Functions, 424, 427
Exponentiation, 211
Expression, 420
  And, 157, 177
  Between, 157, 176
  Column, 423
  Conditional, 157
  Functions, 424
  In, 159, 176
  Is not null, 157, 158, 176
  Is null, 157, 158, 176
  Like, 157, 160, 177
  Literal constant, 423
  Matches, 157, 160, 177
  Not, 157, 176
  Operators, 421
  Or, 157, 158, 177
  Subquery, 157, 162, 177
  Update, 128
Extend, 424, 428, 449
  Functions, 424, 428, 449
  Functions, etc 4GL, 350, 358,
    378
Extent size
  Create table, 70
  Definition, 70

F

False, 240
  Constants, 374, 380
Fetch, 408, 414
  Absolute, 407, 414
  Current, 407, 414
  Cursor, 407, 414
  First, 407, 414
  Into, 407, 414
  Last, 407, 414
  Next, 407, 414
  Previous, 407, 414
  Prior, 407, 414
  Relative, 407, 414
  SQL in 4GL, 407, 414

fgiusr.c
    C functions from 4GL, 607, 626, 633, 634, 640, 641
fglapi.h
    Functions called from C, 636, 641
fgldb
    Debugger, 603, 606, 626
fglgo, 183, 193
    -anyerr, 342, 347
    r4gl, 183, 193
fglpc, 183, 184, 193
    -anyerr, 342, 347
    Functions called from C, 639, 642
    Options, 184
    r4gl, 183, 193
Fgl_call
    Functions called from C, 373, 380, 635, 637, 641, 642, 650
Fgl_drawbox
    Functions, etc 4GL, 350, 358, 378
Fgl_end
    Functions called from C, 373, 380, 635, 637, 641, 642, 651
fgl_errorlog
    Error log, 344, 347
    Functions, etc 4GL, 350, 359, 378
Fgl_exitfm
    Functions called from C, 373, 380, 635, 637, 641, 642, 651
Fgl_getenv
    Environment variable, 359
    Functions, etc 4GL, 350, 359, 378
Fgl_keyval
    Functions, etc 4GL, 350, 360, 378
Fgl_lastkey
    Functions, etc 4GL, 350, 360, 378
Fgl_start
    Functions called from C, 373, 380, 635, 636, 641, 642, 652

fgl_startlog
    Error log, 343, 347
    Functions, etc 4GL, 350, 361, 378
Field
    Column, 4
Field order
    Constrained, 322, 328, 330, 331
    Options, 322, 328, 331
    Unconstrained, 322, 328, 331
Field tag
    Form, 254
Field_touched
    Functions, etc 4GL, 350, 362, 378
FILE
    dbload command file, 140, 149
File suffixes
    INFORMIX-4GL, 181
finderr
    Error message, 45
Finish report
    Report, 546, 575
First, 323, 331
    Fetch, 407, 414
First normal form
    Normalization, 11, 25
First page header
    Control blocks, 555, 560, 561, 575
    Report, 555, 560, 561, 575
Fixed length records
    dbload, 140
Float
    Data type, 55, 91, 206
Flush, 411, 414
    Cursor, 411, 414
    Insert, 411
    SQL in 4GL, 411, 414
For
    Continue for, 243, 248
    Declare, 401, 413, 414
    Exit for, 243, 248
    Looping, 243, 248
    Step, 243, 248
    Stored procedures, 460, 479
For each row
    Triggers, 475, 482

For update
    Declare, 401, 413, 414
Foreach, 404, 413
    Continue foreach, 403, 413
    Cursor, 403, 413
    Exit foreach, 403, 413
    Into, 403, 413
    SQL in 4GL, 403, 413
    Stored procedures, 462, 479
    using, 403
Foreign key
    Constraint, 65, 66, 93
    Definition, 6, 25
    Referential integrity, 93
Foreign language support
    DBLANG, 35
Form, 250
    ANSI, 254
    Attribute, 255, 262, 273, 279, 319
    Autonext, 263, 273
    Clear, 278, 319
    Close form, 280
    Color, 264, 273
    Combination, 261
    Comments, 264, 273
    Database, 253, 272
    Default, 265, 274
    Delimiters, 255, 273
    Design, 251
    Display form, 279, 319
    Display like, 265, 274
    Downshift, 265, 274
    Field tag, 254
    form4gl -d, 256
    Format, 266, 274
    Generate, 257
    Graphics, 254
    Include, 267, 274
    Instructions, 255, 273
    Menu, 250
    Modified generated form, 258
    Multiple record, 260
    Noentry, 267, 274
    Open form, 279
    Picture, 268, 274
    Required, 269, 274
    Reverse, 269, 274
    Screen, 253, 272
    Screen record, 255, 256, 273

Form, *continued*
  Single record, 259
  Size, 254
  Tables, 254, 272
  Type, 269, 274
  upscol, 272, 274
  Upshift, 270, 274
  Validate like, 270, 274
  Verify, 270, 274
  Wordwrap, 271, 274
Form line
  Options, 322, 324, 330, 331
  Window, 280
Form mode
  Display, 236
  Options, 322, 329, 331
  Run, 246, 248
form4gl, 186, 194
  Forms, 186, 194
  Options, 186
form4gl -d
  Form, 256
Format
  Date format, 216
  Datetime, 57, 217
  Form, 266, 274
  Numeric, 217
  Report, 551
  Using, 216
Format every row
  Control blocks, 555, 575
  Report, 552, 555, 575
Format numeric data types
  DBFORMAT, 34
Forms
  form4gl, 186, 194
Fraction
  Datetime unit, 58
Free, 412, 415
  Cursor, 412, 415
  SQL in 4GL, 412, 415
From
  Construct, 488, 500
  Input, 383, 394
  Input array, 503, 520
  Prepare, 399, 413, 414
  Put, 410, 414
  Select statement, 155, 176

Functions, 197, 201, 204, 424
  Abs, 424
  Acos, 424, 425
  Asin, 424, 425
  Atan, 424, 425
  Atan2, 424, 425
  Call, 200, 204
  Cos, 424, 425
  Current, 424, 426, 449
  Date, 426, 449
  Date format, 424
  Day, 424, 426, 449
  Dbinfo, 427, 449
  Dbservername, 424, 427, 449
  Debugger, 608, 615, 627
  Exp, 424, 427
  Expression, 424
  Extend, 424, 428, 449
  Hex, 424, 428, 449
  Length, 424, 428, 449
  Log10, 424, 428
  Logn, 424, 429
  Mdy, 424, 429, 449
  Mod, 424
  Month, 424, 429, 449
  Pow, 424, 429
  Return, 201
  Root, 424, 430
  Round, 424, 430, 450
  Rowid, 424, 431, 450
  Sin, 424, 431
  Sitename, 424, 431, 450
  Sqrt, 424, 431
  Tan, 424, 432
  Today, 424, 432, 450
  Trunc, 424, 432, 450
  Units, 424, 432
  User, 424, 433, 450
  Weekday, 424, 433, 450
  Year, 424, 434, 450
Functions called from C, 635, 640
  c4gl, 638, 642
  cfglgo, 634, 639, 641
  Decadd, 373, 380, 630, 635,
    640, 641, 642, 643
  Deccmp, 373, 380, 630, 635,
    640, 641, 642, 644
  Deccopy, 373, 380, 630, 635,
    640, 641, 642, 644

  Deccvasc, 373, 380, 630, 635,
    640, 641, 642, 644
  Deccvdbl, 373, 380, 630, 635,
    640, 641, 642, 645
  Deccvflt, 373, 380, 630, 635,
    640, 641, 642, 645
  Deccvint, 373, 380, 630, 635,
    640, 641, 642, 645
  Deccvlong, 373, 380, 630,
    635, 640, 641, 642, 646
  Decdiv, 373, 380, 630, 635,
    640, 641, 642, 646
  Dececvt, 373, 380, 630, 635,
    640, 641, 642, 647
  Decfcvt, 373, 380, 630, 635,
    640, 641, 642, 648
  Decmul, 373, 380, 630, 635,
    640, 641, 642, 648
  Decsub, 373, 380, 630, 635,
    640, 641, 642, 648
  Dectoasc, 373, 380, 630, 635,
    640, 641, 642, 649
  Dectodbl, 373, 380, 630, 635,
    640, 641, 642, 649
  Dectoflt, 373, 380, 630, 635,
    640, 641, 642, 649
  Dectoint, 373, 380, 630, 635,
    640, 641, 642, 650
  Dectolong, 373, 380, 630,
    635, 640, 641, 642, 650
  fglapi.h, 636, 641
  fglpc, 639, 642
  Fgl_call, 373, 380, 635, 637,
    641, 642, 650
  Fgl_end, 373, 380, 635, 637,
    641, 642, 651
  Fgl_exitfm, 373, 380, 635,
    637, 641, 642, 651
  Fgl_start, 373, 380, 635, 636,
    641, 642, 652
  Linking, 638
  Popdate, 373, 380, 630, 635,
    640, 641, 642, 652
  Popdec, 373, 380, 630, 635,
    640, 641, 642, 652
  Popdtime, 373, 380, 630, 635,
    640, 641, 642, 652
  Popdub, 373, 380, 630, 635,
    640, 641, 642, 653

Popflo, 373, 380, 630, 635, 640, 641, 642, 653
Popint, 373, 380, 630, 635, 640, 641, 642, 653
Popinv, 373, 380, 630, 635, 640, 641, 642, 653
Poplocator, 373, 380, 630, 635, 640, 641, 642, 654
Poplong, 373, 380, 630, 635, 640, 641, 642, 654
Popquote, 373, 380, 630, 635, 640, 641, 642, 654
Popshort, 373, 380, 630, 635, 640, 641, 642, 654
Popvchar, 373, 380, 630, 635, 640, 641, 642, 655
Pushdate, 373, 380, 635, 641, 642, 655
Pushdec, 373, 380, 635, 641, 642, 655
Pushdtime, 373, 380, 635, 641, 642, 655
Pushdub, 373, 380, 635, 641, 642, 656
Pushflo, 373, 380, 635, 641, 642, 656
Pushint, 373, 380, 635, 641, 642, 656
Pushinv, 373, 380, 635, 641, 642, 656
Pushlocator, 373, 380, 635, 641, 642, 657
Pushlong, 373, 380, 635, 641, 642, 657
Pushquote, 373, 380, 635, 641, 642, 657
Pushshort, 373, 380, 635, 641, 642, 657
Pushvchar, 373, 380, 635, 641, 642, 658
Retdate, 373, 380, 630, 640, 642, 658
Retdec, 373, 380, 630, 640, 642, 658
Retdtime, 373, 380, 630, 640, 642, 658
Retdub, 373, 380, 630, 640, 642, 659
Retflo, 373, 380, 630, 640, 642, 659

Retint, 373, 380, 630, 640, 642, 659
Retinv, 373, 380, 630, 640, 642, 659
Retlong, 373, 380, 630, 640, 642, 660
Retquote, 373, 380, 630, 640, 642, 660
Retshort, 373, 380, 630, 640, 642, 661
Retvchar, 373, 380, 630, 640, 642, 661
Functions, etc 4GL
  Arg_val, 350, 351, 377
  Arr_count, 350, 352, 377
  Arr_curr, 350, 352, 377
  Ascii, 350, 352, 377
  Clipped, 350, 353, 377
  Column, 350, 353, 377
  Current, 350, 354, 377
  cursor_name, 350, 354, 409, 414
  Date, 355, 378
  Day, 350, 355, 378
  Downshift, 350, 356, 378
  Errorlog, 350, 357, 378
  Err_get, 350, 356, 378
  Err_print, 350, 356, 378
  Err_quit, 350, 357, 378
  Extend, 350, 358, 378
  Fgl_drawbox, 350, 358, 378
  Fgl_errorlog, 350, 359, 378
  Fgl_getenv, 350, 359, 378
  Fgl_keyval, 350, 360, 378
  Fgl_lastkey, 350, 360, 378
  Fgl_startlog, 350, 361, 378
  Field_touched, 350, 362, 378
  Get_fldbuf, 350, 362, 379
  Infield, 350, 363, 379
  Length, 350, 363, 379
  Lineno, 350, 364, 379
  Mdy, 350, 364, 379
  Month, 350, 364, 379
  Num_args, 350, 365, 379
  Pageno, 350, 365, 379
  Scr_line, 350, 366, 379
  Set_count, 350, 366, 379
  Showhelp, 350, 367, 379
  Space, 350, 367, 379
  Sqlexit, 350, 368, 379

  Startlog, 350, 368, 379
  Time, 350, 368, 379
  Today, 350, 369, 379
  Units, 350, 370, 379
  Upshift, 350, 370, 379
  Using, 350, 371, 379
  Weekday, 350, 371, 379
  Wordwrap, 350, 372, 380
  Year, 350, 372, 380

G

Generate
  Form, 257
Get_fldbuf
  Functions, etc 4GL, 350, 362, 379
Global variable
  Stored procedures, 458
Global variables, 374
  int_flag, 374, 380
  quit_flag, 374, 380
  sqlca record structure, 375, 380
  sqlca.sqlawarn [1], 376
  sqlca.sqlawarn [2], 376
  sqlca.sqlawarn [3], 376
  sqlca.sqlawarn [4], 376
  sqlca.sqlawarn [5], 377
  sqlca.sqlawarn [6], 377
  sqlca.sqlawarn [7], 377
  sqlca.sqlawarn [8], 377
  sqlca.sqlcode, 375
  sqlca.sqlerrd [1], 375
  sqlca.sqlerrd [2], 376
  sqlca.sqlerrd [3], 376
  sqlca.sqlerrd [4], 376
  sqlca.sqlerrd [5], 376
  sqlca.sqlerrd [6], 376
  sqlca.sqlerrm, 375
  sqlca.sqlerrp, 375
  status, 374, 375, 380
Globals, 197, 198, 203
Go to
  Whenever, 341, 347
Goto
  Whenever, 341, 347
Goto-label
  Label, 245, 248
  Looping, 245, 248

Grant
    Privileges, 95
Grant execute
    Stored procedures, 472
Grant execute on
    Stored procedures, 472, 481
Grant privileges
    Role, 81, 96
Grant table
    All, 77
Grant, database, 95
    Dba, 75
    Privileges, 75
    Resource, 75
Grant, table, 95
    Privileges, 77
    References, 78
Graphics
    Form, 254
Group
    Report, 563, 575
Group by
    Select statement, 162, 177
Grouping control blocks
    After group of, 564
    Before group of, 564
    Order external by, 566
    Report, 564
Grow
    Debugger, 608, 616, 627

H

Having
    Select statement, 164, 177
Help, 334
    Construct, 488, 491, 500
    Context sensitive, 338
    Debugger, 608, 616, 627
    File, 334, 338
    Help, 336, 338
    Input, 383, 395
    Input array, 503, 520
    Menu, 223, 226, 232
    Menu descriptions, 334
    mkmessage, 336, 338
    Prompt, 238, 247
    Screen comments, 334
    Shell script, 338

Showhelp, 337, 338, 367
    Using, 336
Help file
    Options, 322, 326, 330, 331
Help key
    Options, 322, 325, 330, 331
Hex, 424, 428, 449
    Functions, 424, 428, 449
Hidden options
    Menu, 228
Hide option
    Menu, 223, 229, 232
High
    Update statistics, 100, 123
Hour
    Datetime unit, 58

I

i4gl
    INFORMIX-4GL, 182, 192
If
    Stored procedures, 462, 479
If-then-else
    Conditionals, 240, 248
In, 422, 448
    Create database, 53
    Create table, 69
    Expression, 157, 159, 176
    Not in, 451
    On exception, 464
    Subquery, 438
Include
    Form, 267, 274
Index, 443
    Alter index, 85
    Character, 22, 25
    Cluster, 22, 25
    Composite, 20, 25
    Composite index, 443
    Create Index, 83, 96
    Definition, 19, 25
    Drop index, 85, 96
    Duplicate, 21, 25
    Numeric, 22, 25
    Performance, 20, 443
    Query optimization, 444
    Revoke, table, 80
    Short, 21, 25

Small table, 22, 25
Strategies, 19
Subquery, 437, 451
Unique, 21, 25
When to, 20
Indexes
    Constraint, 66
Infield
    Functions, etc 4GL, 350, 363, 379
    Input, 384, 395
    Input array, 505, 520
Info
    Database, 88, 97
INFORMIX-4GL
    c4gl, 180, 184, 185, 192
    Command line, 183
    Comment, 202
    Compiled 4GL, 180
    File suffixes, 181
    i4gl, 182, 192
    r4gl, 180, 182, 192
    Rapid development system, 180
    Suffixes, 192
INFORMIXDIR
    Environment variable, 30, 46
INFORMIX-ESQL/C, 180
INFORMIX-OnLine, 50
    Alter table, 94
    Backups, 108, 124
    Compared to INFORMIX-SE, 50
    Create database, 53, 91
    Create table, 70, 93
    Database integrity, 107
    Logging, 117
    SQLEXEC, 39
INFORMIX-OnLine log file
    Database integrity, 105
INFORMIX-SE, 50
    Audit trails, 121
    Backups, 108, 124
    Compared to INFORMIX-OnLine, 50
    Create database, 52, 91
    Create table, 69, 93
    Database integrity, 102
    Logging, 114
    SQLEXEC, 39

INFORMIXSERVER
  Environment variable, 31, 46
INFORMIX-SQL, 27
  Definition, 45
  Statement separator, 91
INFORMIXTERM
  Environment variable, 30, 46
Initialize
  Null, 210, 219
Input, 383, 394
  Add, 389
  After field, 383, 387, 395
  After input, 383, 387, 395
  Attribute, 322, 328, 330, 331,
    383, 384, 394, 395
  Before field, 383, 386, 395
  Before input, 383, 386, 395
  By name, 383, 394
  Continue input, 383, 388,
    395
  Exit input, 383, 389, 395
  From, 383, 394
  Help, 383, 395
  Infield, 384, 395
  Next field, 383, 388, 395
  On key, 383, 388, 395, 396
  One-to-many relationship,
    523, 543
  Without defaults, 383, 394
Input array, 503, 520, 521
  After delete, 503, 510, 520
  After field, 503, 508, 510, 520
  After input, 503, 508, 510,
    520
  After insert, 503, 508, 510,
    520
  After row, 503, 508, 510,
    520
  Arr_count, 505, 520
  Arr_curr, 505, 520
  Attribute, 503, 520
  Before delete, 503, 508, 509,
    520
  Before field, 503, 508, 509,
    520
  Before input, 503, 508, 509,
    520
  Before insert, 503, 508, 509,
    520

  Before row, 503, 508, 509,
    520
  Continue input, 503, 512,
    520
  Editing, 508, 521
  Exit input, 503, 512, 520
  From, 503, 520
  Help, 503, 520
  Infield, 505, 520
  Next field, 503, 511, 520
  On key, 503, 511, 520
  Scr_line, 506, 520
  Set_count, 507, 520
  Without defaults, 503, 520
Input attribute
  Options, 327, 330
Input wrap
  Options, 322, 328, 330, 331
Insert, 126, 148
  Cursor, 399, 402, 411, 412
  dbload command file, 141
  Flush, 411
  Revoke, table, 80
  Serial data type, 127
  Subquery, 440, 451
  Triggers, 474, 482
Insert key
  Options, 322, 325, 330, 331
Instructions
  Form, 255, 273
Int
  Data type, 55, 91, 206
Integer
  Data type, 56, 91, 206
Interrupt
  Debugger, 608, 616, 627
Interrupt key
  Defer interrupt, 340, 346
  int_flag, 340, 346
Interval
  Conversions, 214
  Data type, 58, 207
Interval class
  Day-time, 59
  Year-month, 59
Into
  Fetch, 407, 414
  Foreach, 403, 413

  Select, 397
  SQL in 4GL, 397
Into temp, 177
  Select statement, 177
  Temp table, 168
int_flag
  Global variables, 374, 380
  Interrupt key, 340, 346
Is not null, 211, 220, 422, 448
  Expression, 157, 158, 176
  Null, 157, 158, 176, 211
Is null, 211, 220, 422, 448
  Expression, 157, 158, 176
  Null, 157, 158, 176, 211
Isolation levels, 446, 451
  Committed read, 446, 451
  Cursor stability, 446, 451
  Dirty read, 446, 451
  Locking, 447, 451
  Repeatable read, 446, 451
  Set isolation level, 446

J

Join, 170, 178
  Cartesian product, 171
  Nested outer join, 172
  Outer join, 172, 178
  Select statement, 155
  Self-join, 441
  Simple outer join, 172

K

Key
  Menu, 223, 232

L

Label
  Goto-label, 245, 248
  Whenever, 341, 347
Label alias
  Select statement, 155
Last, 323, 331
  Fetch, 407, 414
Left margin
  Output, 553, 575
  Report, 553, 575

Length, 424, 428, 449
  Functions, 424, 428, 449
  Functions, etc 4GL, 350, 363, 379
Let
  Assignment, 234
  Debugger, 604, 608, 616, 627
  Null, 210
  Stored procedures, 463, 480
Level 0 archive
  Backups, 109
Level 1 archive
  Backups, 109
Level 2 archive
  Backups, 109
Like, 211, 219, 421, 444, 448
  Data type, 207, 219
  Expression, 157, 160, 177
  Query optimization, 444
Line mode
  Display, 236
  Options, 322, 329, 331
  Run, 246, 248
Lineno
  Functions, etc 4GL, 350, 364, 379
  Report functions, 559, 575
Linking
  C functions from 4GL, 633
  Functions called from C, 638
List
  Cursor, 401
  Debugger, 608, 617, 627
Literal constant
  Expression, 423
Literals, 423
Load, 135, 148
  BLOB, 137
  DBDELIMITER, 34, 136
  Delimiter, 135, 136, 148
  Performance, 147
  Special characters, 136
Lock mode
  Definition, 70
  Page-level locking, 71
  Row-level locking, 71
Lock mode page, 134, 148
  Create table, 71
Lock mode row, 134, 148
  Create table, 71

Lock table
  Locking, 132, 148
Locking, 131, 148
  Database, 131
  Database exclusive, 131
  Isolation levels, 447, 451
  Lock mode page, 134, 148
  Lock mode row, 134, 148
  Lock table, 132, 148
  Logging, 113
  Set lock mode, 133, 148
  Table, 132, 148
  Unlock table, 132, 148
Log mode ansi
  Create database, 53, 91
Log10, 424, 428
  Functions, 424, 428
Logging, 111
  ANSI, 112
  Backups, INFORMIX-SE, 115
  Begin work, 112, 125
  Commit work, 112, 125
  dblog, 117, 125
  INFORMIX-OnLine, 117
  INFORMIX-SE, 114
  Locking, 113
  onmonitor, 119, 125
  ontape, 119, 125
  ontape -a, 121, 125
  ontape -c, 121, 125
  Performance, 113
  Rollback work, 112, 125
  Rollforward database, 116, 125
  Set buffered log, 120, 125
  Set log (unbuffered), 120
  tbmonitor, 119, 125
  tbtape, 119, 125
  tbtape -a, 121, 125
  tbtape -c, 121, 125
  Turn off, 113
  Turn off, INFORMIX-SE, 114
  Turn on, INFORMIX-SE, 114, 125
Logical log backup, 121
  Automatic, 120, 125
  Continuous, 120, 125
  ontape -a, 121, 125
  ontape -c, 121, 125
  tbtape, 121
  tbtape -a, 121, 125
  tbtape -c, 125

Logn, 424, 429
  Functions, 424, 429
Looping, 242
  For, 243, 248
  Goto-label, 245, 248
  While, 244, 248
Low
  Update statistics, 100, 123

M

Main
  Program, 199, 203
Make utility, 187
  Make file, 187, 191
  Make rules file, 188
Mangling
  Cursor name, 354, 409, 414
Many-to-many
  Relationship, 9, 25
Many-to-one
  Relationship, 8, 25
Matches, 211, 219, 421, 444, 448
  Expression, 157, 160, 177
  Query optimization, 444
Mathematical operators, 211, 219, 421, 448
Matrix
  Complex reports, 578, 601
Max, 435, 450
  Aggregate, 435, 450, 564, 576
  Report, 564, 576
Mdy, 424, 429, 449
  Functions, 424, 429, 449
  Functions, etc 4GL, 350, 364, 379
Medium
  Update statistics, 100, 123
Menu, 222, 232
  Before menu, 223, 231, 232
  Command, 223
  Command key, 225
  Continue menu, 223, 228, 232
  Exit menu, 223, 232
  Form, 250
  Help, 223, 226, 232
  Hide option, 223, 229, 232
  Key, 223, 232
  Next option, 223, 226, 232
  Ring, 222
  Show option, 223, 230, 232

Menu line
    Options, 322, 324, 330, 331
Message
    Attribute, 237, 247
    Output, 237, 247
Message line
    Options, 322, 324, 330, 331
    Window, 280
Min, 435, 451
    Aggregate, 435, 451, 564, 576
    Report, 564, 576
Minute
    Datetime unit, 58
mkmessage
    DBLANG, 36
    Help, 336, 338
Mod, 424
    Functions, 424
Mode ansi
    Create database, 52, 91
Modified generated form
    Form, 258
Modify
    Alter table, 72
Module, 200
Modulus, 211
Money
    Data type, 56, 91, 206
    DBMONEY, 36
Month, 424, 429, 449
    Datetime unit, 58
    Functions, 424, 429, 449
    Functions, etc 4GL, 350, 364, 379
Multi-part
    Complex reports, 585, 601
Multiple record
    Form, 260

N

Nchar
    Data type, 56, 91
Need
    Report, 556, 557, 575
Nested outer join
    Join, 172

Next
    Fetch, 407, 414
Next field
    Construct, 488, 496, 500
    Input, 383, 388, 395
    Input array, 503, 511, 520
Next key
    Options, 322, 326, 330, 331
Next option
    Menu, 223, 226, 232
Next size
    Create table, 70
    Definition, 70
Nobreak
    Debugger, 608, 617, 627
Noentry
    Form, 267, 274
Normalization
    Definition, 10
    First normal form, 11, 25
    Formal, 10
    Intuitive, 15, 25
    Performance, 18
    Second normal form, 12, 25
    Third normal form, 13, 25
NOSORTINDEX
    Environment variable, 38
Not, 211, 219, 421, 448
    Expression, 157, 176
Not between, 421
Not exists, 422, 448
    Subquery, 439, 451
Not found
    Whenever, 341, 347
Not in, 422, 448
    In, 451
    Subquery, 438, 451
Not null
    Constraint, 65, 66, 92, 93
Notfound
    Constants, 374, 380
Notrace
    Debugger, 608, 617, 628
Null
    Initialize, 210, 219
    Is not null, 157, 158, 176, 211
    Is null, 157, 158, 176, 211
    Let, 210
    Null operators, 422, 448

Null operators, 211, 220
Numeric
    Conversions, 213
    Data type, 56, 91, 206
    Format, 217
    Index, 22, 25
Num_args
    Functions, etc 4GL, 350, 365, 379
Nvarchar
    Data type, 61

O

On
    Construct, 488, 500
On every row
    Control blocks, 555, 575
    Report, 555, 560, 575
On exception, 465
    In, 464
    Set, 464
    Stored procedures, 465, 480
On key
    Construct, 495, 500
    Display array, 294, 320
    Input, 383, 388, 395, 396
    Input array, 503, 511, 520
    Prompt, 238
On last row
    Control blocks, 555, 567, 575
    Report, 555, 567, 575
oncheck -cc
    Database integrity, 107, 124
oncheck -cD
    Database integrity, 124, 107
oncheck -ce
    Database integrity, 107, 124
oncheck -cI
    Database integrity, 107, 124
oncheck -cr
    Database integrity, 107, 124
ONCONFIG
    Environment variable, 31, 46
One-to-many
    Relationship, 8, 25
One-to-many relationship
    Display, 305
    Input, 523, 543

One-to-one or zero
Relationship, 25
onmonitor
Backups, 125
Logging, 119, 125
Ontape, 109, 124
Backups, 125
Critical dbspaces, 111
Logging, 119, 125
Warm restore, 111
ontape -a
Logging, 121, 125
Logical log backup, 121, 125
ontape -c
Logging, 121, 125
Logical log backup, 121, 125
ontape -r
Recovery, 111
ontape -s
Backups, 110
Open
Cursor, 405, 414
SQL in 4GL, 407, 414
Using, 405, 414
Open, 407, 414
Open form
Form, 279
Open window
Attribute, 276, 318
Window, 276, 318
With, 276, 318
With form, 276, 318
Operator precedence, 422
Operators, 211, 219, 421, 448
Boolean, 211, 219, 421
Expression, 421
Mathematical, 211, 219, 421
Null, 211, 220, 422
Relational, 211, 219, 421
Set, 422, 448
String, 211, 219, 421, 448
OPTCOMPIND
Environment variable, 38
Options, 322, 330, 331
Accept key, 322, 325, 330,
331
Attribute, 322, 331
Attributes, 327
c4gl, 185
Comment line, 322, 323, 331

Default, 331
Delete key, 322, 325, 330, 331
Display attribute, 327, 330
Error line, 322, 324, 330, 331
fglpc, 184
Field order, 322, 328, 331
Form line, 322, 324, 330, 331
Form mode, 322, 329, 331
form4gl, 186
Help file, 322, 326, 330, 331
Help key, 322, 325, 330, 331
Input attribute, 327, 330
Input wrap, 322, 328, 330, 331
Insert key, 322, 325, 330, 331
Line mode, 322, 329, 331
Menu line, 322, 324, 330, 331
Message line, 322, 324, 330,
331
Next key, 322, 326, 330, 331
Pipe, 322, 329, 331
Previous key, 322, 326, 330,
331
Prompt line, 322, 330, 331
Run, 322, 329, 331
Sql interrupt, 329, 330, 331
Window, 280
Or, 211, 219, 421, 448
Expression, 157, 158, 177
Query optimization, 443
Order by
Ascending, 166
Column number, 166
Descending, 166
Display label, 166
Report, 551, 554, 575
Select statement, 166, 177
Order external by
Grouping control blocks, 566
Report, 551, 554, 566, 575
Order internal by
Report, 551, 554, 575
Otherwise
Case, 241, 248
Outer
Select statement, 172
Outer join
Join, 172
Nested outer join, 172
Select statement, 156
Simple outer join, 172

Output, 234
Attribute, 235, 247
Bottom margin, 553, 575
Display, 236, 247
Error, 236, 247
Left margin, 553, 575
Message, 237, 247
Page length, 553, 575
Prompt, 238, 247
Report, 551, 553, 575
Report to, 553
Right margin, 553, 575
Sleep, 239, 247
Top margin, 553, 575
Output to
Select statement, 175, 178
Output to report
Report, 546, 575

P

Page header
Control blocks, 555, 560, 562,
575
Report, 555, 560, 562, 575
Page length
Output, 553, 575
Report, 553, 575
Page trailer
Control blocks, 555, 560, 563,
575
Report, 555, 560, 563, 575
Page-level locking
Lock mode, 71
Pageno
Functions, etc 4GL, 350, 365,
379
Report functions, 559, 575
PATH
DBPATH, 37
Environment variable, 30, 46
Pattern matching
Debugger, 615, 619, 629
Pause
Report, 556, 557, 575
p-code
r4gl, 180
PDQPRIORITY
Environment variable, 38

Percent
  Aggregate, 576
  Report, 576
Performance
  Create index, 84
  dbimport, 147
  dbload, 147
  Index, 20, 443
  Load, 147
  Logging, 113
  Query optimization, 442
  Subquery, 438
  Update statistics, 101
  View, 418
Picture
  Form, 268, 274
Pipe
  Options, 322, 329, 331
Popdate
  Functions called from C, 373,
    380, 630, 635, 640, 641,
    642, 652
Popdec
  Functions called from C, 373,
    380, 630, 635, 640, 641,
    642, 652
Popdtime
  Functions called from C, 373,
    380, 630, 635, 640, 641,
    642, 652
Popdub
  Functions called from C, 373,
    380, 630, 635, 640, 641,
    642, 653
Popflo
  Functions called from C, 373,
    380, 630, 635, 640, 641,
    642, 653
Popint
  Functions called from C, 373,
    380, 630, 635, 640, 641,
    642, 653
Popinv
  Functions called from C, 373,
    380, 630, 635, 640, 641,
    642, 653
Poplocator
  Functions called from C, 373,
    380, 630, 635, 640, 641,
    642, 654

Poplong
  Functions called from C, 373,
    380, 630, 635, 640, 641,
    642, 654
Popquote
  Functions called from C, 373,
    380, 630, 635, 640, 641,
    642, 654
Popshort
  Functions called from C, 373,
    380, 630, 635, 640, 641,
    642, 654
Popvchar
  Functions called from C, 373,
    380, 630, 635, 640, 641,
    642, 655
Pow, 424, 429
  Functions, 424, 429
Prepare, 399, 413, 414
  From, 399, 413, 414
  Question mark, 400
  SQL in 4GL, 400, 413, 414
Previous
  Fetch, 407, 414
Previous key
  Options, 322, 326, 330, 331
Primary key
  Constraint, 65, 66, 92, 93
  Definition, 5, 25
  Referential integrity, 92, 93
Print
  Debugger, 605, 608, 618,
    628
  Report, 556, 575
Print file
  Report, 556, 558, 575
Printer Default
  DBPRINT, 37
Prior
  Fetch, 407, 414
Private
  Synonym, 419, 448
Privileges, 75
  Database, 75
  Dba, 76
  Grant, database, 75
  Grant, table, 77
  Revoke, 80, 95
  Revoke, table, 80
  Stored procedures, 453, 472

  View, 417
Program
  Main, 199, 203
Prompt
  Attribute, 238, 247
  Help, 247
  On key, 238
  Output, 238, 247
Prompt line
  Options, 322, 324, 330, 331
  Window, 280
Prototyping, 192
Public
  Synonym, 419, 448
Pushdate
  Functions called from C, 373,
    380, 635, 641, 642, 655
Pushdec
  Functions called from C, 373,
    380, 635, 641, 642, 655
Pushdtime
  Functions called from C, 373,
    380, 635, 641, 642, 655
Pushdub
  Functions called from C, 373,
    380, 635, 641, 642, 656
Pushflo
  Functions called from C, 373,
    380, 635, 641, 642, 656
Pushint
  Functions called from C, 373,
    380, 635, 641, 642, 656
Pushinv
  Functions called from C, 373,
    380, 635, 641, 642, 656
Pushlocator
  Functions called from C, 373,
    380, 635, 641, 642, 657
Pushlong
  Functions called from C, 373,
    380, 635, 641, 642, 657
Pushquote
  Functions called from C, 373,
    380, 635, 641, 642, 657
Pushshort
  Functions called from C, 373,
    380, 635, 641, 642, 657
Pushvchar
  Functions called from C, 373,
    380, 635, 641, 642, 658

Put, 410, 414
  Cursor, 410, 414
  From, 410, 414
  SQL in 4GL, 410, 414

Q

Query optimization
  Complex reports, 601
  Index, 444
  Like, 444
  Matches, 444
  Or, 443
  Performance, 442
  Set explain on, 442, 451
  Set optimization, 443, 451
  Subquery, 445
  Temp table, 442
  Union, 443
Question mark
  Prepare, 400
Quit key
  Defer quit, 340, 346
  quit_flag, 340, 346
quit_flag
  Global variables, 374, 380
  Quit key, 340, 346

R

r4gl, 180, 192
  ANSI, 184
  fglgo, 183
  fglo, 193
  fglpc, 183, 193
  INFORMIX-4GL, 180, 182, 192
  p-code, 180
  Pros and cons, 180
Raise exception
  Stored procedures, 465, 480
Rapid development system
  INFORMIX-4GL, 180
  rds, 180
rds
  Rapid development system, 180
Read
  Debugger, 609, 618, 628

Real
  Data type, 56, 91, 206
Record
  Data type, 207, 219
  Row, 4
Recover table
  Audit trails, INFORMIX-SE, 122, 125
  Recovery, 122
Recovery, 116, 121
  Backups, 121
  ontape -r, 111
  Recover table, 122
  Rollforward database, 116, 125
  tbtape -r, 111
Recursive
  Stored procedures, 457
Redraw
  Debugger, 609, 618, 628
References
  Constraint, 66, 92, 93
  Grant, table, 78
  Referential integrity, 65
  Revoke, table, 80
Referencing
  Triggers, 474, 482
Referential integrity
  Create table, 65
  Foreign key, 93
  Primary key, 93
  References, 65
  Table, 93
Relational Database
  Definition, 3, 23
Relational operators, 211, 219, 421, 448
  Subquery, 437, 451
Relationship
  Many-to-many, 9, 25
  Many-to-one, 8, 25
  One-to-many, 8, 25
  One-to-one or zero, 7, 25
Relative
  Fetch, 407, 414
Rename Column
  Table, 74, 95
Rename table
  Table, 74, 95
Repair table
  Database integrity, 104, 123

Repairing
  Fix by hand, 105
Repeatable read
  Isolation levels, 446, 451
Report, 197, 203, 545, 551, 575
  After group of, 555, 564, 575
  Avg, 564, 576
  Before group of, 564, 575
  Bottom margin, 553, 575
  Complex reports, 578
  Control blocks, 556
  Count, 576
  Data, 546
  DBPRINT, 548
  Define, 551, 575
  Exit report, 556, 558, 575
  Finish report, 546, 575
  First page header, 555, 560, 561, 575
  Format, 551
  Format every row, 552, 555, 575
  Group, 563, 575
  Grouping control blocks, 564
  Left margin, 553, 575
  Max, 564, 576
  Min, 564, 576
  Need, 556, 557, 575
  On every row, 555, 560, 575
  On last row, 555, 567, 575
  Order by, 551, 554, 575
  Order external by, 554, 566, 575
  Order internal by, 554, 575
  Output, 551, 553, 575
  Output to report, 546, 575
  Page header, 555, 560, 562, 575
  Page length, 553, 575
  Page trailer, 555, 560, 563, 575
  Pause, 556, 557, 575
  Percent, 576
  Print, 556, 575
  Print file, 556, 558, 575
  Report name, 551, 575
  Report to, 553
  Right margin, 553, 575
  Skip, 556, 557, 575
  Start report, 546, 547, 575
  Sum, 564, 576

Report, *continued*
   Terminate report, 546, 575
   Top margin, 553, 575
   Variables, 551
   Where (for aggregates), 564
Report functions
   Column, 558, 575
   Lineno, 559, 575
   Pageno, 559
   Space[s], 558, 559, 575
   Wordwrap, 559, 575
Report funtions
   Pageno, 575
Report name
   Report, 551, 575
Report to
   File, 553, 575
   Output, 553
   Pipe, 553, 575
   Printer, 553, 575
   Report, 553
Required
   Form, 269, 274
Resolution
   Update statistics, 100, 101, 123
Resource
   Grant, database, 75
   Revoke, database, 78
Retdate
   Functions called from C, 373,
     380, 630, 640, 642, 658
Retdec
   Functions called from C, 373,
     380, 630, 640, 642, 658
Retdtime
   Functions called from C, 373,
     380, 630, 640, 642, 658
Retdub
   Functions called from C, 373,
     380, 630, 640, 642, 659
Retflo
   Functions called from C, 373,
     380, 630, 640, 642, 659
Retint
   Functions called from C, 373,
     380, 630, 640, 642, 659
Retinv
   Functions called from C, 373,
     380, 630, 640, 642, 659

Retlong
   Functions called from C, 373,
     380, 630, 640, 642, 660
Retquote
   Functions called from C, 373,
     380, 630, 640, 642, 660
Retshort
   Functions called from C, 373,
     380, 630, 640, 642, 661
Return
   Functions, 201
   Stored procedures, 466, 480
Returning
   Call, 200, 204
   Run, 246, 248
Retvchar
   Functions called from C, 373,
     380, 630, 640, 642, 661
Reverse
   Form, 269, 274
Revoke
   Connect, 80
   Privileges, 80, 95
Revoke execute
   Stored procedures, 472
Revoke execute on
   Stored procedures, 472, 481
Revoke, database, 95
   Dba, 80
   Resource, 78
Revoke, table, 95
   All, 80
   Alter table, 80
   Delete, 80
   Index, 80
   Insert, 80
   References, 80
   Select, 80
   Update, 80
Right margin
   Output, 553, 575
   Report, 553, 575
   Wordwrap, 559, 575
Ring
   Menu, 222
Ring menus
   List, 43
   Use of, 42

Role
   Create, 81, 96
   Drop, 81
   Grant privileges, 81, 96
   Set, 82, 96
Roles, 81
Rollback work
   Logging, 112, 125
   Transaction, 112
Rollforward database
   Logging, 116, 125
   Recovery, 125
Root, 424, 430
   Functions, 424, 430
Root_dbspace
   Dbspace, 70
   Definition, 70
Round, 424, 430, 450
   Functions, 424, 430, 450
Row
   Definition, 4, 25
   Record, 4
Rowid, 424, 431, 450
   Functions, 424, 431, 450
Row-level locking
   Lock mode, 71
Run
   Debugger, 604, 609, 619, 628
   Form mode, 246, 248
   Line mode, 246, 248
   Options, 322, 329, 331
   Returning, 246, 248
   UNIX, 246
   Without waiting, 246, 248

S

Sample database
   Creation, 86
   Description, 23
Scope
   Define, 210
   Variable, 210, 219
Screen
   Clear, 278, 319
   Debugger, 609, 619, 628
   Form, 253, 272
Screen form, 250

Screen record
　Form, 255, 256, 273
Scroll, 298
　By, 298
　Down, 298
　Up, 298
Scroll cursor
　Declare, 402, 413, 414
Scr_line
　Display array, 295, 320
　Functions, etc 4GL, 350, 366, 379
　Input array, 506, 520
Search
　Debugger, 609, 619, 628
Search characters
　Construct, 487, 499
Second
　Datetime unit, 58
Second normal form
　Normalization, 12, 25
Select
　Construct, 497
　Cursor, 399, 402, 404, 411
　Into, 397
　Revoke, table, 80
　Select statement, 176
　Subquery, 451
Select statement, 151, 176
　Aggregate, 162, 164
　Display label, 154, 166
　From, 155, 176
　Group by, 162, 177
　Having, 164, 177
　Into temp, 168, 177
　Join, 155
　Label alias, 155
　Order by, 166, 177
　Outer, 172
　Outer join, 156
　Output to, 175, 178
　Select, 153, 176
　Union, 169, 178
　Where, 157, 176
Self join, 451
Self-join
　Join, 441
Serial
　Data type, 56, 91, 206

Set
　On exception, 464
　Role, 82, 96
Set buffered log
　Logging, 120, 125
Set debug
　Stored procedures, 467, 480
Set debug file
　Stored procedures, 467, 480
Set explain on
　Query optimization, 442, 451
　sqexplain.out file, 442, 451
Set isolation level
　Isolation levels, 446
Set lock mode
　Locking, 133, 148
Set log (unbuffered)
　Logging, 120
Set operators, 422, 448
Set optimization
　Query optimization, 443, 451
Set_count
　Display array, 295, 320
　Functions, etc 4GL, 350, 366, 379
　Input array, 507, 520
Shell script
　Help, 338
Show option
　Menu, 223, 230, 232
Showhelp
　Functions, etc 4GL, 350, 367, 379
　Help, 337, 338, 367
Simple outer join
　Join, 172
Sin, 424, 431
　Functions, 424, 431
Single record
　Form, 259
Sitename, 424, 431, 450
　Dbservername, 64
　Functions, 424, 431, 450
Skip
　Report, 556, 557, 575
Sleep
　Output, 239, 247
Smallfloat
　Data type, 57, 91, 206

Smallint
　Data type, 57, 91, 206
Some, 422, 448
　Subquery, 440, 451
Space
　Functions, etc 4GL, 350, 367, 379
Space[s]
　Report functions, 558, 559, 575
SPL
　Stored Procedure Language, 453
sqexplain.out file
　Set explain on, 442, 451
SQL
　Structured Query Language, 27
SQL in 4GL
　Close, 411, 415
　Declare, 401, 413, 414
　Execute, 400, 413
　Fetch, 407, 414
　Flush, 411, 414
　Foreach, 403, 413
　Free, 412, 415
　Into, 397
　Open, 407, 414
　Prepare, 400, 413, 414
　Put, 410, 414
　Where current of, 409, 414
　Without cursors, 397, 413
Sql interrupt
　Options, 329, 330, 331
sqlca record structure
　Global variables, 375, 380
sqlca.sqlawarn
　ANSI, 376
sqlca.sqlawarn [1]
　Global variables, 376
sqlca.sqlawarn [2]
　Global variables, 376
sqlca.sqlawarn [3]
　Global variables, 376
sqlca.sqlawarn [4]
　Global variables, 376
sqlca.sqlawarn [5]
　Global variables, 377
sqlca.sqlawarn [6]
　Global variables, 377

sqlca.sqlawarn [7]
  Global variables, 377
sqlca.sqlawarn [8]
  Global variables, 377
sqlca.sqlcode
  Error, 375
  Global variables, 375
sqlca.sqlerrd [1]
  Global variables, 375
sqlca.sqlerrd [2]
  Global variables, 376
sqlca.sqlerrd [3]
  Global variables, 376
sqlca.sqlerrd [4]
  Global variables, 376
sqlca.sqlerrd [5]
  Global variables, 376
sqlca.sqlerrd [6]
  Global variables, 376
sqlca.sqlerrm
  Global variables, 375
sqlca.sqlerrp
  Global variables, 375
Sqlerror
  Whenever, 341, 347
SQLEXEC
  Environment variable, 39
  INFORMIX-OnLine, 39
  INFORMIX-SE, 39
Sqlexit
  Functions, etc 4GL, 350, 368,
    379
Sqlwarning
  Whenever, 341, 347
Sqrt, 424, 431
  Functions, 424, 431
Start database
  ANSI, 54
  Database, 54, 91
  With log in, 54
Start report, 546, 547, 575
  Report, 546, 547, 575
  To file, 547, 575
  To pipe, 547, 575
  To printer, 547, 575
Startlog
  Error log, 343, 347, 368
  Functions, etc 4GL, 350, 368,
    379
Statement separator
  INFORMIX-SQL, 91

Status
  Error, 344
  Global variables, 374, 375, 380
Step
  Debugger, 604, 609, 620, 628
  For, 243, 248
Stop
  Whenever, 341, 347
Stored Procedure Language
  SPL, 453
Stored procedures, 453
  Begin, 456, 478
  BLOB, 458
  Block, 456
  Call, 457, 478
  Comment, 455
  Create procedure, 453, 478
  Cursor, 460
  Dba, 453, 478
  Dbinfo, 469, 481
  Define, 459, 478
  Document, 453, 454, 478
  Drop procedure, 472, 481
  End, 456, 478
  For, 460, 479
  Foreach, 462, 479
  Global variable, 458
  Grant execute, 472
  Grant execute on, 472, 481
  If, 462, 479
  Let, 463, 480
  On exception, 465, 480
  Privileges, 453, 472
  Raise exception, 465, 480
  Recursive, 457
  Return, 466, 480
  Revoke execute, 472
  Revoke execute on, 472, 481
  Semicolon, use of, 454
  Set debug, 467, 480
  Set debug file, 467, 480
  System, 467, 480
  Trace, 468, 480
  Update statistics, 473, 481
  Where current of, 461, 481
  While, 469, 480
  With hold, 460
  With listing in, 453, 455, 478
  With resume, 466
String
  Conversions, 212

String operators, 211, 219, 421,
    448
Structured Query Language
  SQL, 27
Subquery, 437, 451
  All, 440, 451
  Any, 440, 451
  Delete, 441, 451
  Exists, 439, 451
  Expression, 157, 162, 177
  In, 438
  Index, 437, 451
  Insert, 440, 451
  Not exists, 439, 451
  Not in, 438, 451
  Performance, 438
  Query optimization, 445
  Relational operators, 437, 451
  Select, 451
  Some, 440, 451
  Update, 441, 451
Subscript, 423
Substring, 423
Suffixes
  INFORMIX-4GL, 192
Sum, 435, 451
  Aggregate, 435, 451, 564, 576
  Report, 564, 576
Synonym, 419
  Create synonym, 448
  Definition, 419
  Drop synonym, 420, 448
  Private, 419, 448
  Public, 419, 448
System
  Stored procedures, 467, 480

T

Table
  Alter table, 72, 94
  Column table, 74
  Constraint, 65, 93
  Create table, 62, 92
  Create temp table, 93
  Default, 92
  Definition, 4, 23
  Drop table, 74, 94
  Locking, 132, 148
  Referential integrity, 93
  Rename column, 74, 95

Table, *continued*
    Rename table, 74, 95
    Table name, 423
Tables
    Form, 254, 272
Tan, 424, 432
    Functions, 424, 432
tbcheck
    Database integrity, 124
tbcheck -cc
    Database integrity, 107
tbcheck -cD
    Database integrity, 107
tbcheck -ce
    Database integrity, 107
tbcheck -cI
    Database integrity, 107
tbcheck -cr
    Database integrity, 107
TBCONFIG
    Environment variable, 31, 46
tbmonitor
    Backups, 110, 125
    Logging, 119, 125
Tbtape, 109, 124
    Backups, 125
    Logging, 119, 125
tbtape -a
    Logging, 121, 125
    Logical log backup, 121, 125
tbtape -c
    Logging, 121, 125
    Logical log backup, 121, 125
tbtape -r
    Recovery, 111
tbtape -s
    Backups, 110
Temp table
    Complex reports, 578
    Into temp, 168
    Query optimization, 442
    Temporary table, 71
    With no log, 71, 168
Temporary files
    DBTEMP, 37
Temporary table
    Temp table, 71
TERM
    Environment variable, 31, 46

TERMCAP
    Environment variable, 31, 46
Terminate report
    Report, 546, 575
TERMINFO
    Environment variable, 31, 46
Text
    BLOB, 59
    Data type, 60, 207
Text editor
    DBEDIT, 34
Third normal form
    Normalization, 13, 25
Time
    Functions, etc 4GL, 350, 368,
        379
Timedelay
    Debugger, 609, 621, 628
To
    Display, 281, 320
    Display array, 294, 320
Today, 424, 432, 450
    Date, 64
    Date format, 64
    Functions, 424, 432, 450
    Functions, etc 4GL, 350, 369,
        379
Toggle
    Debugger, 609, 621, 628
Top margin
    Output, 553, 575
    Report, 553, 575
Trace
    Debugger, 609, 621, 628
    Stored procedures, 468, 480
Transaction, 112
    Begin work, 112
    Commit work, 112
    Definition, 111
    Rollback work, 112
Triggers, 473, 482
    After, 475, 483
    Before, 475, 482
    Cascading delete, 476
    Create trigger, 474, 482
    Delete, 474, 482
    Drop trigger, 477
    For each row, 475, 482
    Insert, 474, 482
    Referencing, 474, 482

Update, 474, 482
    When, 475, 482
True, 240
    Constants, 374, 380
Trunc, 424, 432, 450
    Functions, 424, 432, 450
Turn
    Debugger, 609, 623, 628
Turn off, INFORMIX-SE
    Logging, 114
Turn on, INFORMIX-SE
    Logging, 114, 125
Type
    Form, 269, 274

U

Unbuffered log
    Create database, 53, 91
Unconstrained
    Field order, 322, 328, 331
Union
    Query optimization, 443
    Select statement, 169, 178
Unions
    Complex reports, 578
Unique
    Aggregate, 436, 450
    Constraint, 65, 66, 92, 93
    Create index, 83
    Index, 21, 25
Units, 424, 432
    Functions, 424, 432
    Functions, etc 4GL, 350, 370,
        379
UNIX
    Run, 246
Unload, 135, 137, 148
    DBDELIMITER, 34
    Delimiter, 137, 148
Unlock table
    Locking, 132, 148
Update, 128, 148
    Cursor, 402, 409
    Expression, 128
    Revoke, table, 80
    Subquery, 441, 451
    Triggers, 474, 482
Update restrictions
    View, 419

Update statistics, 99
    Confidence, 100, 101, 123
    Database maintenance, 99
    Distributions, 100, 101, 123
    For procedure, 100, 123
    For table, 100, 123
    High, 100, 123
    Low, 100, 123
    Medium, 100, 123
    Performance, 101
    Resolution, 100, 101, 123
    Stored procedures, 473, 481
upscol
    Attribute, 272
    Data validation, 272
    Form, 272, 274
Upshift
    Form, 270, 274
    Functions, etc 4GL, 350, 370, 379
Use
    Debugger, 609, 623, 629
User, 424, 433, 450
    Functions, 424, 433, 450
    Username, 64
User search
    Construct, 485
Username
    User, 64
Using, 212, 219
    Execute, 400, 413
    foreach, 403
    Format, 216
    Functions, etc 4GL, 350, 371, 379
    Open, 405, 414

V

Validate like
    Form, 270, 274
VALUES
    dbload command file, 141
Varchar
    Data type, 60, 206
    Issues when using, 60
Variable
    Debugger, 609, 624, 629
    Define, 208, 219

Scope, 210, 219
Variables
    Report, 551
Verify
    Form, 270, 274
View, 417
    Create view, 417, 448
    Debugger, 609, 624, 629
    Drop view, 419, 448
    Performance, 418
    Privileges, 417
    Update restrictions, 419
    With check option, 418

W

Warm restore
    Backups, 111
    Ontape, 111
Warning
    Whenever, 341, 347
Weekday, 424, 433, 450
    Functions, 424, 433, 450
    Functions, etc 4GL, 350, 371, 379
When
    Case, 241, 248
    Triggers, 475, 482
Whenever, 341, 347
    Any error, 341, 347
    Call, 341, 347
    Compile time directive, 341
    Continue, 341, 347
    Error, 341, 347
    Go to, 341, 347
    Goto, 341, 347
    Label, 341, 347
    Not found, 341, 347
    Sqlerror, 341, 347
    Sqlwarning, 341, 347
    Stop, 341, 347
    Warning, 341, 347
Where, 128
    Aggregate, 564
    Construct, 488
    Debugger, 609, 625, 629
    Select statement, 157, 176
Where (for aggregates)
    Report, 564
Where current of, 409, 414

Cursor, 409, 414
    SQL in 4GL, 409, 414
    Stored procedures, 461, 481
While
    Continue while, 244, 248
    Exit while, 244, 248
    Looping, 244, 248
    Stored procedures, 469, 480
Window, 276
    Attribute, 276, 319
    Clear, 278, 319
    Close window, 278, 319
    Comment line, 280
    Current window, 277, 318
    Form line, 280
    Message line, 280
    Open window, 276, 318
    Options, 280
    Prompt line, 280
    Width, 279
With
    Open window, 276
With hold
    Declare, 402, 413, 414
    Stored procedures, 460
With listing in
    Stored procedures, 453, 455, 478
With resume
    Stored procedures, 466
Wordwrap
    Form, 271, 274
    Functions, etc 4GL, 350, 372, 380
    Report functions, 559, 575
    Right margin, 559, 575
Write
    Debugger, 609, 625, 629

Y

Year, 424, 434, 450
    Datetime unit, 58
    Functions, 424, 434, 450
    Functions, etc 4GL, 350, 372, 380
Year-month
    Interval class, 59

LICENSE AGREEMENT AND LIMITED WARRANTY

READ THE FOLLOWING TERMS AND CONDITIONS CAREFULLY BEFORE OPENING THIS CD PACKAGE. THIS LEGAL DOCUMENT IS AN AGREEMENT BETWEEN YOU AND PRENTICE-HALL, INC. (THE "COMPANY"). BY OPENING THIS SEALED CD PACKAGE, YOU ARE AGREEING TO BE BOUND BY THESE TERMS AND CONDITIONS. IF YOU DO NOT AGREE WITH THESE TERMS AND CONDITIONS, DO NOT OPEN THE CD PACKAGE. PROMPTLY RETURN THE UNOPENED CD PACKAGE AND ALL ACCOMPANYING ITEMS TO THE PLACE YOU OBTAINED THEM FOR A FULL REFUND OF ANY SUMS YOU HAVE PAID.

1. GRANT OF LICENSE: In consideration of your purchase of this book, and your agreement to abide by the terms and conditions of this Agreement, the Company grants to you a nonexclusive right to use and display the copy of the enclosed software program (hereinafter the "SOFTWARE") on a single computer (i.e., with a single CPU) at a single location so long as you comply with the terms of this Agreement. The Company reserves all rights not expressly granted to you under this Agreement.

2. OWNERSHIP OF SOFTWARE: You own only the magnetic or physical media (the enclosed CD) on which the SOFTWARE is recorded or fixed, but the Company and the software developers retain all the rights, title, and ownership to the SOFTWARE recorded on the original CD copy(ies) and all subsequent copies of the SOFTWARE, regardless of the form or media on which the original or other copies may exist. This license is not a sale of the original SOFTWARE or any copy to you.

3. COPY RESTRICTIONS: This SOFTWARE and the accompanying printed materials and user manual (the "Documentation") are the subject of copyright. The individual programs on the CD are copyrighted by the authors of each program. Some of the programs on the CD include separate licensing agreements. If you intend to use one of these programs, you must read and follow its accompanying license agreement. If you intend to use the trial version of Internet Chameleon, you must read and agree to the terms of the notice regarding fees on the back cover of this book. You may not copy the Documentation or the SOFTWARE, except that you may make a single copy of the SOFTWARE for backup or archival purposes only. You may be held legally responsible for any copying or copyright infringement which is caused or encouraged by your failure to abide by the terms of this restriction.

4. USE RESTRICTIONS: You may not network the SOFTWARE or otherwise use it on more than one computer or computer terminal at the same time. You may physically transfer the SOFTWARE from one computer to another provided that the SOFTWARE is used on only one computer at a time. You may not distribute copies of the SOFTWARE or Documentation to others. You may not

reverse engineer, disassemble, decompile, modify, adapt, translate, or create derivative works based on the SOFTWARE or the Documentation without the prior written consent of the Company.

5.   TRANSFER RESTRICTIONS: The enclosed SOFTWARE is licensed only to you and may not be transferred to any one else without the prior written consent of the Company. Any unauthorized transfer of the SOFTWARE shall result in the immediate termination of this Agreement.

6.   TERMINATION: This license is effective until terminated. This license will terminate automatically without notice from the Company and become null and void if you fail to comply with any provisions or limitations of this license. Upon termination, you shall destroy the Documentation and all copies of the SOFT-WARE. All provisions of this Agreement as to warranties, limitation of liability, remedies or damages, and our ownership rights shall survive termination.

7.   MISCELLANEOUS: This Agreement shall be construed in accordance with the laws of the United States of America and the State of New York and shall benefit the Company, its affiliates, and assignees.

8.   LIMITED WARRANTY AND DISCLAIMER OF WARRANTY: The Company warrants that the SOFTWARE, when properly used in accordance with the Documentation, will operate in substantial conformity with the description of the SOFTWARE set forth in the Documentation. The Company does not warrant that the SOFTWARE will meet your requirements or that the operation of the SOFTWARE will be uninterrupted or error-free. The Company warrants that the media on which the SOFTWARE is delivered shall be free from defects in materials and workmanship under normal use for a period of thirty (30) days from the date of your purchase. Your only remedy and the Company's only obligation under these limited warranties is, at the Company's option, return of the warranted item for a refund of any amounts paid by you or replacement of the item. Any replacement of SOFTWARE or media under the warranties shall not extend the original warranty period. The limited warranty set forth above shall not apply to any SOFTWARE which the Company determines in good faith has been subject to misuse, neglect, improper installation, repair, alteration, or damage by you. EXCEPT FOR THE EXPRESSED WARRANTIES SET FORTH ABOVE, THE COMPANY DISCLAIMS ALL WARRANTIES, EXPRESS OR IMPLIED, INCLUDING WITHOUT LIMITATION, THE IMPLIED WARRANTIES OF MERCHANTABILITY AND FITNESS FOR A PARTICULAR PURPOSE. EXCEPT FOR THE EXPRESS WARRANTY SET FORTH ABOVE, THE COMPANY DOES NOT WARRANT, GUARANTEE, OR MAKE ANY REPRESENTATION REGARDING THE USE OR THE RESULTS OF THE USE OF THE SOFTWARE IN TERMS OF ITS CORRECTNESS, ACCURACY, RELIABILITY, CURRENTNESS, OR OTHERWISE.

IN NO EVENT SHALL THE COMPANY OR ITS EMPLOYEES, AGENTS, SUPPLIERS, OR CONTRACTORS BE LIABLE FOR ANY INCIDENTAL, INDIRECT, SPECIAL, OR CONSEQUENTIAL DAMAGES ARISING OUT OF OR IN CONNECTION

WITH THE LICENSE GRANTED UNDER THIS AGREEMENT, OR FOR LOSS OF USE, LOSS OF DATA, LOSS OF INCOME OR PROFIT, OR OTHER LOSSES, SUSTAINED AS A RESULT OF INJURY TO ANY PERSON, OR LOSS OF OR DAMAGE TO PROPERTY, OR CLAIMS OF THIRD PARTIES, EVEN IF THE COMPANY OR AN AUTHORIZED REPRESENTATIVE OF THE COMPANY HAS BEEN ADVISED OF THE POSSIBILITY OF SUCH DAMAGES. IN NO EVENT SHALL LIABILITY OF THE COMPANY FOR DAMAGES WITH RESPECT TO THE SOFTWARE EXCEED THE AMOUNTS ACTUALLY PAID BY YOU, IF ANY, FOR THE SOFTWARE.

SOME JURISDICTIONS DO NOT ALLOW THE LIMITATION OF IMPLIED WARRANTIES OR LIABILITY FOR INCIDENTAL, INDIRECT, SPECIAL, OR CONSEQUENTIAL DAMAGES, SO THE ABOVE LIMITATIONS MAY NOT ALWAYS APPLY. THE WARRANTIES IN THIS AGREEMENT GIVE YOU SPECIFIC LEGAL RIGHTS AND YOU MAY ALSO HAVE OTHER RIGHTS WHICH VARY IN ACCORDANCE WITH LOCAL LAW.

ACKNOWLEDGMENT

YOU ACKNOWLEDGE THAT YOU HAVE READ THIS AGREEMENT, UNDERSTAND IT, AND AGREE TO BE BOUND BY ITS TERMS AND CONDITIONS. YOU ALSO AGREE THAT THIS AGREEMENT IS THE COMPLETE AND EXCLUSIVE STATEMENT OF THE AGREEMENT BETWEEN YOU AND THE COMPANY AND SUPERSEDES ALL PROPOSALS OR PRIOR AGREEMENTS, ORAL, OR WRITTEN, AND ANY OTHER COMMUNICATIONS BETWEEN YOU AND THE COMPANY OR ANY REPRESENTATIVE OF THE COMPANY RELATING TO THE SUBJECT MATTER OF THIS AGREEMENT.

Should you have any questions concerning this Agreement or if you wish to contact the Company for any reason, please contact in writing at the address below.

Robin Short
Prentice Hall PTR
One Lake Street
Upper Saddle River, New Jersey 07458

About the CD

This is an ISO 9660 CD and as such can be read on Windows 3.1, 95, NT, and most UNIX systems. The code samples will work on all platforms supported by Informix OnLine Dynamic Server.

For a complete list of CD contents and instructions on extracting the archives, see Appendix B.

Prentice Hall does not offer technical support for this software. However, if there is a problem with the media, you may obtain a replacement copy by emailing us with your problem at: discexchange@phptr.com